ULTIMATE
HAPPINESS

Chasing It, Finding It, Living It.

A Memoir

Peter Mellen

ISBN: 1461099226
ISBN-13: 9781461099222

ALSO BY THE SAME AUTHOR

The Group of Seven
Landmarks of Canadian Art
Jean Clouet: The Complete Edition

DEDICATION

For Linda

TABLE OF CONTENTS

INTRODUCTION

Our essential nature is happiness.
Ramana Maharshi

Ultimate Happiness is the story of my search for the true self, or what some call enlightenment. It is based on my own direct experience—down-to-earth, gritty, intimate, and real. I've been fortunate enough to live a rich and unusual life, finding success in the world as a documentary filmmaker, best-selling author, and nationally known art history professor. And I've been through difficult life challenges—from being diagnosed with cancer, not once, but four times, to financial crises, hurricanes, and floods. I wouldn't have missed any of it. My first wife Fran died from breast cancer; my second wife Linda struggled with chronic illness for fifteen years and died in 2010. I'm also someone who loves life passionately and believes that good food, good wine, and good sex are just as "spiritual" as a path of renunciation and asceticism.

In my thirties I had everything most people dream of—family, friends, fame, fortune. I recklessly sought out every pleasure I could find, but it still wasn't enough. In no time my marriage was in trouble and I was miserable. *Surely there must be something more to life than this?* I told myself. Something was drawing me within, and I had no idea what it was.

Then I stumbled into a yoga class and found a peace I had never known. Like a modern-day Don Quixote, I set out on a quest for spiritual enlightenment, which I imagined to be a state of unending bliss and joy. Before I knew it, I was standing on my head, meditating twice a day, purifying my body, improving myself, and healing myself. I was told that if I practiced, and practiced, and practiced some more, that someday (or some future lifetime) I'd have this orgasmic mystical experience and be in permanent bliss.

Twenty years later I was no closer to my goal than when I began. I wondered, "What if all the traditional paths to enlightenment have got it all wrong? Surely there must be a direct path to self-realization? And, surely there must be a way of finding lasting happiness without having to give up the pleasures of sex, wine and chocolate!"

It was then that I was introduced to the teachings of the great Indian sage Ramana Maharshi. I met young Western teachers—Eckhart Tolle, Byron Katie, Gangaji, Adyashanti—who were teaching in the ancient tradition of Advaita, or nonduality. They all shared a similar message: true happiness is not found somewhere off in the future. It is available right here, right now as present moment awareness. No effort is needed. There's nowhere to go and nothing to achieve, because you already are what you're looking for! The answer is so utterly simple.

This book is written in one hundred compelling stories that move chronologically back and forth in time. You can pick it up, read a few stories, and put it down again. The narrative starts in Virginia, where I'm living on a farm with my second wife Linda, two dogs, three goats, and a flock of sheep. As the story unfolds, I flashback to my early life and the trauma that launched me on an inner search. You'll laugh along with me as I dive into the exotic world of yoga, meditation, healing, and personal growth. You'll meet some remarkably wise spiritual teachers, as well as some nasty sleazeballs. You'll read touching stories about facing illness and the loss of a loved one. Most of all, you'll find a moving love story about the two women—Linda and Fran—who change my world. All the events in the book are real (or at least as real as my memory makes them). Almost all the dates are accurate to the day (thanks to my compulsive record keeping) and only a few names have been changed.

My hope is that you will come away not only thoroughly entertained, but having discovered a radically new way of seeing the world. I have a ridiculously ambitious wish—that in reading this book you will have a glimpse of the ultimate happiness that already lies within you.

PART I

CHASING IT

We have only to follow the thread of the hero path, and where we had thought to find an abomination, we shall find a God. And where we had thought to slay another, we shall slay ourselves. Where we had thought to travel outwards, we shall come to the center of our own existence. And where we had thought to be alone, we will be with all the world.

Joseph Campbell

CHAPTER 1

HUNGRY FOR HAPPINESS

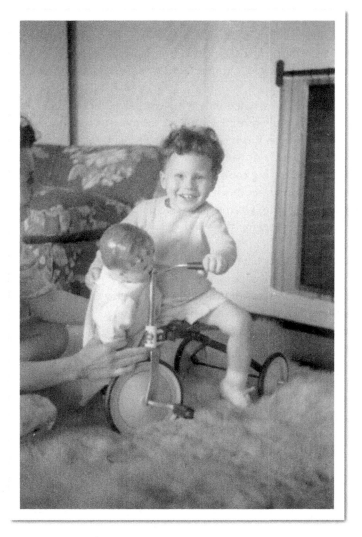

Peter on Tricycle

Is Anyone Truly Happy?
Mt Ayr Farm, Virginia, January 27, 2002

We all seek happiness and do not want suffering.
The Dalai Lama

I've just cracked open my new copy of the Dalai Lama's book *The Art of Happiness*, thrilled to read the first line: "I believe the very purpose of our life is to seek happiness." *Yes, he's so right,* I think, *and I'm having a delicious moment of happiness right now.*

I turn to look at my wife Linda lying in the bed next to me. She's snuggled under the duvet, happily reading a book. A warm fire is burning in the woodstove of our hundred-year-old Virginia farmhouse. Through the window I can see huge, fluffy snowflakes, gently drifting down, lit by a single floodlight. Our two Australian Shepherds are lying contentedly on their sheepskins enjoying the warmth. Such peace. Life doesn't get much better than this.

I go back to reading. On the next page he says, "I believe that happiness can be achieved through training the mind." *Damn, now he's going to tell me I have to do all these practices before I can be happy. Why does happiness have to be such hard work?* I flip through the next chapters, on subjects such as the benefits of compassion, finding meaning in pain and suffering, dealing with anger and hatred. Suddenly I find myself getting frustrated. I thump the book down on the bed.

"What's going on?" Linda asks.

"This book on happiness is making me miserable!"

"Huh?"

"I spent twenty years doing spiritual practices every day and it never brought me one step closer to true happiness. I stood on my head, I meditated twice a day, I practiced compassion, I ate vegetarian food, I cleaned out my nose with one of those stupid little cups—I even tried to be celibate . . . can you imagine? What a crock. All those practices have nothing to do with finding true happiness. It can be found just as easily through sex, wine, and chocolate!"

"Well, you're living proof of that," Linda quips.

"All it takes is for the mind to become still just for a moment and there is perfect peace. We don't have to *do* anything."

"You're right."

I look at Linda, seeing the love in her eyes. My frustration melts away instantly.

"Do you know anyone that is truly happy?" I ask.

"Yes, me . . ."

I didn't expect this response. "What do you mean?"

Somewhat reluctantly she puts her book down and gazes thoughtfully out the window at the softly falling snow.

After a moment, she turns to me, "I'm *so* happy," she sighs. "I'm so completely content. I'm married to you; I have those I love the most in the world right here in this room; and I know that when I die I'm going home. This 'Linda' is so happy!"

Wow! I think in surprise. *She really means it . . . and she has an auto-immune illness that leaves her in pain every day of her life. Most people in her situation would say that they had a wretched life.* I lean over and caress her hand, aware of the scars from where she burned her arm when she was nineteen.

"Before I got this disease my life was completely frantic—running here, running there," she continues. "I kept wishing I had more time to read. Well, now I have it."

Even in her early fifties, Linda looks young and beautiful, with her blond hair and glittering blue eyes. It must be those Nordic genes. No one would ever guess she was sick.

"What about you?" she asks. "Are you happy?"

"Not in this moment, but it doesn't really matter. The happiness I'm talking about includes both happiness *and* unhappiness. It doesn't take any effort—that happiness is right here," I say, placing my hand on my heart. A sensation of pure joy wells up from within.

"Now *you* look like the Dalai Lama."

"Yeah, he gets it," I smile. "And I know one other being that's happy . . ."

Our dog Luke is lying on his back, his soft white belly exposed and his legs sticking up in the air. I get out of bed and walk over to him. When he sees me approaching, he excitedly wiggles his entire body in anticipation and looks up at me with his big brown eyes. I kneel beside him and place my face on his pure white fur. It's warm and comforting and smells like a newborn baby. A deep sense of peace comes over me. My mind stops. It feels as if I am somehow merging with his consciousness. It lasts only a moment. *This is happiness, just this!*

Tears come to my eyes.

"Oh sweetheart," Linda says, once she sees how moved I am.

"There's such fullness right here, right now. I feel as if my whole body is expanding in love. There's no end to it."

"Yes, it's limitless," she nods, a knowing look on her face.

"I've chased after happiness so much of my life, trying to find it somewhere 'out there.' The harder I tried, the more it eluded me. Happiness was always somewhere off in the future . . . after I got enlightened, or had some great mystical experience."

Linda looks into my eyes with deep compassion.

"What a joke." I laugh. "All those years of effort and that happiness has been here all along—even when my life was a mess."

A memory floods in—of me in my twenties, living in Paris, depressed and suicidal. All I wanted to do was die. My God, what a journey it has been—from the self-torture and manic highs of my twenties, to the fleeting moments of success and fame in my thirties, to the years of chasing after enlightenment in my forties, then the dropping into the silence that came with living on the farm. All of it against the backdrop of being married to my first wife Fran for twenty-five years and raising our son Peter. And then, her terrible death from cancer, and the miracle of Linda entering my life in all her beauty. Now I feel I've come full circle back to the innocence and purity of when I was a child. Every step has brought me to this precious moment.

Feeling better, I go back to reading the Dalai Lama's words.

Longing for Love
Hotel de Bordeaux, Paris, September 1961

Life is full of misery, loneliness, and suffering—and it's all over much too soon.
Woody Allen

I had just turned twenty-two when I boarded a ship in Montreal and set sail for Europe. A few months earlier, I had graduated from McGill University, and now I was heading for Paris, where I planned to spend two years doing a masters degree in art history. I was staking everything on finding happiness in the City of Lights. Although my trip was ostensibly motivated by the noble goal of higher education, this was just a smokescreen. My fantasy was that I would have countless French women fall into my arms, all wanting to make passionate love with me. So far my relationships with women had been terrible to non-existent. I was sure that in the land of Brigitte Bardot, my craving for love would at last be fulfilled.

Having grown up in a puritanical upper middle class Montreal family and attended a private boy's school, I was totally naïve about what made women tick. I was one of those nice guys that girls like to have as friends, but not go to bed with—the kind of guy who always puts the toilet seat down after peeing. I had a couple of brief flings, but for the most part I fell madly in love with unattainable women who then proceeded to reject me. I cultivated the image of the tortured artist, indulging in mind-created misery. I must have reeked of neediness.

When I arrived in Paris on October 3, 1961, I stayed in a seedy hotel in the Latin Quarter called the Hotel de Bordeaux—a tiny room on the second floor with a shared bathroom two flights up, and a shower four flights up. There was a sink in the room, and another strange fixture that I peed in before I realized it was a bidet. I nearly fell through a hole in the floor and had to kill numerous bugs crawling on the wall, but it was home. Every night I washed my underwear in the sink and pressed my trousers by putting them under the mattress. No beautiful women flocked to my door, begging for me to make love to them – though one night I heard the girls from the third floor fooling with the guys next to me. I prayed they'd come to my door, but I was too shy to do anything but lie in bed with my heart beating in anticipation. I guess they weren't interested in the nice young Canadian boy in room #5.

With my limited French, I was too shy to strike up a conversation in the cafés and without familiar friends, the fun-loving image of a carefree extrovert collapsed like a house of cards. I ended up alone in my hotel room, spiraling deeper and deeper into depression. Like a dark poltergeist, it snuck up from behind and took over my mind. "You're worthless," it said. "You'll never find a woman to love you." At night I wandered the streets, venturing across the Seine to the Rue St. Denis, where hookers lined every doorway. I wrote tear-stained letters back home and came close to complete emotional breakdown. I felt completely alone in the world.

Once classes began at the University of Paris, I had no choice but to learn French, and to learn it fast, or flunk out. At least I had a new project to focus on other than my unhappiness. I made friends with other students, and before long I swung wildly over to the manic side, becoming more French than the French. I even had a Corsican girlfriend named Vanina. I knew that I'd finally made it when I was making love to her, and another girl was banging on the door to get in. I tore around Paris on my powder blue Vespa scooter and got to know every corner of the city. I became friends with native-born Parisians who saw me as "le gentil Canadien" (the nice Canadian). I skied in Gstaad in the winter and hung out with European princes and princesses; I visited French Canadian friends on the Cote d'Azur; I got invited to a friend's chateau in the French countryside. Two years later I completed a master's degree in art history, graduating at the top of my class. I was flying high.

In September 1963, after spending a summer in the Bavarian Alps learning German, I packed up my scooter with everything I owned, and headed for London. I had been accepted into the doctoral program at the Courtauld Institute of Art, and Sir Anthony Blunt had agreed to be my supervisor. I took the ferry across the Channel, passed through customs, and arrived in London dirty and gritty from being on the road. My new home was London House, a residence for graduate students from all over the world—many Aussies and Kiwis, and a few Canadians. I soon made new friends, and for a while it seemed that all was well.

But after numerous failed attempts at dating, I was once again attacked by a plague of loneliness that was terrifying and utterly complete. It wrapped itself around me like a cold, wet blanket, taking away all self-confidence and the will to live. I locked myself in my room for days and did nothing but fantasize about sex and throwing myself on the subway tracks ("underground tracks" doesn't have quite the same cachet). I desperately needed help. My family in Montreal picked up on the warning signals from my letters and came to the rescue (thank God for those who love us). They set me up to see a psychotherapist on world-renowned Harley Street, the home of many therapists and medical practitioners, including Anna Freud. There was still a huge taboo against psychotherapy; it was reserved for those with severe emotional problems. Sadly I realized that I was one of them. My father agreed to help out with the cost, which was about $10 per session. On January 29, 1964, I began classical Freudian therapy—five days a week, fifty weeks a year, lying on a couch and telling Dr. Hayley about my childhood, my dreams, my nightmares. It took over a year before I got up the courage to turn around and look at him.

The Red Chanel Suit
London House, London, January 29, 1964

Mamma always said life was like a box of chocolates.
You never know what you're gonna get.
Winston Groom, *Forrest Gump*

The day I had my first therapy session was the day I met Fran. Every so often London House hosted a cocktail party for the women's graduate residence across the square. Feeling apprehensive, I walked into a room of a hundred or so people sipping cocktails. I noticed an attractive woman with slim legs, full breasts, sensual lips, and her black hair pulled up into a bun. She was wearing horn-rimmed glasses and was talking to another woman. *Damn, she's beautiful. I can tell by her face that she's Jewish—I love Jewish women. I'm going to introduce myself. At least if I get rejected I can tell Dr. Hayley about it tomorrow.*

I screw up my courage and walk up to her, interrupting her conversation. At first she seems annoyed, flashing her brown eyes at me. She wants me to know that she is having an important "intellectual" conversation with her friend.

"Is that a Chanel suit you're wearing?" I ask in a somewhat supercilious tone.

"How did you know it was a Chanel?"

Oh boy, I can see that hooked her!

"Oh, I know about these things," I say with increased confidence (I don't tell her that my sister has one just like it).

We end up sitting next to each other at the dinner that follows.

"Would you like to come up and see my etchings?" I ask, after we've eaten.

"Do you think I'd really fall for that one?" Fran laughs.

"I really do have a signed Picasso in my room," I reply in all seriousness.

"I'll come, but on one condition—you have to bring a chaperone."

No problem. I get to choose the chaperone. I ask my friend Jose Luc d'Iberville Moreau to join us. He's a dissolute European aristocrat, who happens to love orgies. I don't tell Fran this. Thankfully, he performs his chaperone role impeccably.

After seeing that I do have a signed Picasso in my room (an etching I bought for $150), she becomes a little more trusting. I walk over to her and for some reason take off her glasses. She looks up at me with her big brown eyes, defenses gone, and a powerful spark of recognition passes between us.

I start taking Fran out, but am still so screwed up I can barely finish a sentence. By some miracle she sees something in me that I can't see myself. In no time we fall in love, and are soon spending every moment we can together. My crushed, insecure ego can barely believe it when she says "I shall say it a thousand times in a thousand different ways—you are everything to me; you are all men in one man." We excite each other to the heights of passion—physically, emotionally, spiritually. For the first time in my life, I find someone who is a match for my highly charged libido. We do it on the bed, on the floor, on the couch, against the wall, in the tub, upside down, and, like two lovers in a Chagall painting, we imagine doing it on the ceiling. My dreams have come true. I am filled with unspeakable happiness.

Buried Secrets
Harley Street, London, April 4, 1964

To know who you are without any delusions or sympathy is a moment of revelation that no one experiences unscathed. Some have been driven to madness by that stark reality. Most try to forget it.
Christopher Paolini, *Eragon*

Every day I show up at 2:30 for my appointment with Dr. Hayley and ring the buzzer next to the black door of his townhouse. He greets me at the door wearing a gray three-piece suit, and ushers me to his office down the hall. The room is dark and stuffy, with the curtains half–drawn, and smelling of old pipe tobacco. A large desk sits facing the door, bookcases line another wall, and against the back wall is the forbidding couch, with an armchair next to it. Dr. Hayley, who is in his fifties and a touch overweight, takes his seat, while I hesitantly lie on the couch, dressed in my Harris Tweed jacket and tie, corduroy trousers, and Wallabies.

I wait for him to say something. He remains silent. Minutes go by and I get more and more uncomfortable. *The bastard. Why doesn't he talk? I'm paying for this. Do I have to do all the work myself?* More silence. I can't stand it anymore, and blurt out. "I had this dream last night . . ."

From behind me I hear, "Uh-hmm."

"I'm being chased by two men. They have me in their headlights. One has a huge snake draped around his neck and is caressing it. He puts the snake's neck between his teeth and points towards me, saying, 'Go get him.' I'm in absolute terror. I can't move . . . I wake up terrified."

"What do you associate with the dream?" Dr. Hayley asks in a soothing voice.

"I think the man is my father."

"Go on."

"My father's a marshmallow," I say angrily, "and he's got a marshmallow penis. He's so weak. I can't stand him."

"And how does this relate to your life now?"

"All I think of is sex. My friends are calling me a sex maniac for talking about it so much. They say I'm nuts. Sometimes they're kidding, and sometimes they're not. Am I over the edge?"

Silence.

What does he want me to do—break down and cry in front of him? I can't. I won't. I feel rigid as a corpse lying on this damn couch.

"You said you were twelve when your mother died. Am I correct?" Dr. Hayley asks.

"Yeah, I think so." *I can't remember a damned thing.*

"Well, in your twelve-year-old mind it felt like you had killed her." He pauses to let that little piece of shocking news sink in. "You tell me that she had breast cancer and her breast had to be amputated. A part of you feels like you gave her the cancer that destroyed her. You never got to say goodbye to her. You shut her out of your mind forever."

"You mean deep down I think that I killed my mother?"

More silence.

"No wonder women run when they see me," I blurt out. "I'm sure they can sense the rage and despair beneath my 'nice guy' exterior."

I keep waiting for him to say something but he just sits there. Out of nowhere I'm suddenly paralyzed by fear. *Oh shit. Dr. Hayley's angry. He's going to seduce me. He's going to find out all those secrets I've buried so deep. Oh Christ, what a mess I'm in. Will I ever have a happy, normal life?"*

"Well, that's enough for today," he says softly.

The Edge of the Universe
Harley Street, London, June 4, 1964

So I invite you to look at the nightmares that you've suffered through and survived, and to see that freedom really is possible in your everyday life.
Byron Katie

My sessions with Dr. Hayley continue day after day, week after week. I go through every conceivable emotion in my limited repertoire of feelings (What anger? What grief?) as I grapple with my troubled past. It all goes back to my mother's death when I was twelve, and the fact that I pretty much shut out every memory of my childhood.

One session, after an interminable silence, I say to myself, *Screw him. I'm going to spend the whole time just lying here without saying anything. He's not going to get to me.*

Out of the blue he says, "Tell me what happened when your mother died."

Oh shit, he's nailing me. A flood of confusing images rush to mind, like a scratchy old Super 8 film. I shut my eyes, trying to remember. It's like pulling the tender thread of a dream from my subconscious.

"I was staying at the lake with my friend Donald. I'd just turned twelve. My father had sent me off to the country because my mother was sick and in the hospital. No one told me what she had, but I'd heard grown-ups talking about 'the Big C.' One evening Don and I were in his room telling jokes—probably fart jokes. It was way past our bedtime and we were laughing hysterically. His mom got really pissed and kept yelling at us to quiet down."

Another series of indistinct images come to mind. I squirm on the couch and wring my hands in discomfort as Dr. Hayley sits in silent witness. The memory of what happened next is indelibly printed on my mind.

"We both stopped talking and I lay in bed listening to the loon out on the lake. The house was unbelievably quiet. Don's parents were reading downstairs. Then the phone rang—a loud, jangling ring that made me jump. After a few rings I heard Don's dad answering. He always answered the phone saying, "Ici Southam," pretending he knew French. There was a long pause. Then I knew. In that moment I knew that my mother had died. I just knew it. I heard him say, 'Uh huh, uh huh. Yes, yes. We can do that.' Then he hung up. I lay there in the dark, listening to Don's parents talking quietly, thinking to myself, *Surely if my mom died, they would come and tell me? Maybe I'm wrong? Maybe she isn't dead?* But I knew she was."

"How did you know?" Dr. Hayley asks from his chair behind my head.

"I don't know. I just did." For a moment I try to recall how I knew. There is a glimmer of some deeper intuition, but I lose it.

"Go on."

"His parents came upstairs and went to bed. I wondered if they would come in and tell me then, but they didn't. The next day they told me I had to go to Montreal for a few days. I knew it was because my mom had died, but no one said anything and I didn't dare ask. Everyone was being extra nice. Mrs. Lawes, a neighbor, drove me to the city and dropped me off at our house. I walked up the steps and pushed open our big, front door. Everything was quiet inside. I could hear the gurgling of the huge aquarium that was set into the wall. I could see the fish darting around with unblinking eyes, unconcerned."

"No one was in the house?"

"My dad was there. He called out, 'Is that you, son?'"

"What was he doing?"

"He was in his chair reading a newspaper."

"And what did you do?"

"I ran over to him and threw myself on his lap, crumpling the newspaper. 'She's dead, isn't she?' I cried out."

"'Yes, she's gone,' my dad said."

"Then what happened?" Dr. Hayley quietly asks.

"In that moment something split off inside me. I was suddenly floating free in space—like a tiny speck in a huge, dark universe. There was nothing but blackness and stars all around me. There was no up or down, no beginning, no end. It felt as if I would drift through empty space forever, at the edge of the universe. It was both utterly terrifying and strangely comforting at the same time. Then I was back in his lap."

"I see," Dr. Hayley grunts. "Interesting."

"I sobbed tears on my father's big chest. I noticed he was crying too."

"And what are you feeling right now?" he asks.

"Right now I don't feel anything. It's like I'm reporting something that happened to someone else. Maybe I'm making it all up."

Dr. Hayley doesn't indulge my attempt at avoidance. "What happened after you cried?"

"That night I went upstairs to my room and went to bed alone. Before long I heard my sister go off to her room and my father to his. I heard their doors close. My little brother Richard was asleep in the room next to mine. He was six. He didn't even know that his mother has died."

Suddenly I start laughing on the couch, almost going into hysterics. "This is crazy," I laugh, "completely crazy! They didn't even tell my brother that his mom had died for over a year. They said she was on vacation! A year later a friend told him she was dead. Can you imagine?" *Why am I laughing so hard? This is such a horrible story.* Tears form at the edge of my eyes.

I hear Dr. Hayley shifting in his chair, but he doesn't say anything. *These damned Freudian therapists,* I think. *Can't he say something?* I smell the familiar odor of pipe tobacco. The room is warm and comfortable with a heavy silence hanging in the air. Eventually I give up waiting and go back to my story.

"So I went to bed and lay awake staring at the ceiling, feeling completely and utterly alone. The horrifying finality of my mom's death finally sank in. There was no bringing her back, no matter what I did. I was furious at God. 'How could you do this to me? How could you do this?' I silently cried out again and again."

"This was a very crushing experience for you," Dr. Hayley says.

"Yeah, No one in the family ever talked about my mom after that. It was as if she had never existed. Every possible memory of her was erased. Photos were taken down. Her dresses, shoes, and silk nightgowns were removed from her closet. The sweet smell of her perfume slowly faded away. She just disappeared off the face of the earth. No one shared memories of her around the dinner table. No one asked how I was doing or whether I missed my mom. I was left to manage on my own, coming home after school every day to an empty house and playing with my train set, or endlessly throwing a ball up against a wall and catching it."

I lie there on the couch, overwhelmed by the immensity of what happened. I was just a twelve-year old kid with no resources to cope. *No wonder I'm so screwed up. No wonder I fall into an abyss of loneliness and despair. Thank God I have Dr. Hayley to talk to. I couldn't do it without him. I probably would end up committing suicide.*

"Peter, you did very well today," Dr. Hayley says, interrupting my reverie.

Memories continue to flood in as I walk the two miles back to my room at London House.

When Having Everything is Not Enough
Toronto, September 15, 1966

I had every innocent source of joy the world offered. But I found myself thirsting for something more, much more, without knowing why.
Dante Alighieri, *The Divine Comedy*

Fran and I were married within a year. Fran grew up as an only child of an over-achieving Jewish family from Norfolk Virginia. Her father owned a small department store called Rice's and was prominent in the local temple, Ohef Sholom. Her mother was so furious when we announced our engagement that she flew all the way to London to try and break us up. But love prevailed, and she finally accepted the nice young *goyim* from Montreal. We were married by two rabbis in Norfolk on Jan 1st, 1965. After a two-day honeymoon in New York, we flew back to London, where I worked on my doctorate and Fran finished her Master's degree. This was London in the sixties. We waved at the Beatles from our scooter as they drove by in their limo; we saw Nureyev and Fontaine dance together in *Swan Lake*; we watched Sir Lawrence Olivier play Hamlet at the National Theatre. We even started our own art business, selling lithographs and prints by young English artists (much of it erotic art), and savored every moment of our newfound love.

In the summer we traveled around Europe, spending romantic times in castles and artists' lofts while I wrote my thesis, which was on an obscure French artist of the sixteenth century named Jean Clouet. My job was to attribute a body of work to Clouet that included over two hundred drawings and several paintings, including the famous portrait of Francis I in the Louvre. I delved into old manuscripts and drawings in the British Museum and the Bibliothèque Nationale in Paris; I visited Windsor Castle and various chateaux in France, where I had personal access to priceless drawings and paintings; I met with the head curator of the Louvre (shades of *The Da Vinci Code*), and in my research discovered that Clouet studied under Leonardo da Vinci when he was in France, and probably influenced Hans Holbein. Sir Anthony and I had long discussions about my thesis over the course of three years. Only later did I find out that he was the notorious spy called the "Fourth Man."

After completing my doctorate (and a year and a half of therapy), Fran and I come back to Canada, where I sign on to teach art history at the University of Toronto, at the staggering salary of $7,000 per year. I take up my new role as a professor with a good degree of terror—not only because I know nothing about the areas I am meant to teach, but because I've never stood in front of a class before. Add to that the fact that I've just turned twenty-seven, and look like I'm eighteen, and I had good reason to be petrified. But it doesn't take long for me to discover that there is a ham actor lurking just beneath the surface.

"In this painting, Tintoretto breaks all the rules," I say, strutting back and forth in front of a darkened room. "Notice how the use of perspective leads the eye further into the painting, giving it a three-dimensional quality." I use my long pointer to emphasize the diagonal line in the painting. "It's a virtuoso performance. That's what makes Tintoretto a great artist—he goes beyond convention to create something entirely new. Can we have the next slide please?"

A painting comes on the screen showing a nude woman sitting on a bed surrounded by cherubs. A child is sucking at her breast, sending stars shooting into the heavens.

"I think Tintoretto is trying to titillate us a little here . . ." I say, tongue in cheek. "This is called 'The Origin of the Milky Way' and was painted in 1570."

A ripple of laughter erupts from the 150 students seated before me in the darkened amphitheatre. It is Art History 101 and I'm the star of the show. I wink at the coeds, a big smile on my face. They adore me . . . and I adore them.

God, I've done it again, I think to myself. *I didn't know a thing about Tintoretto before I crammed down all that stuff last night.*

I jump into my new career as an art history professor feet first. I learn just enough about each artist before class so that I can pretend to know what I am talking about. During my first year of teaching I'm so nervous that I have the trots every day. But, whatever I'm doing, the students love it. I have my own set of groupies who show up after class. The other art history profs look down their noses at me, but I don't care. I'm on a roll.

In 1967, my thesis was published by the prestigious Phaidon Press in London as a big coffee table book called *Jean Clouet: The Complete Edition.* Before it came out I was on to my next project—a book about a group of artists who were active around the time of World War I. They went into the Canadian wilderness and painted it in a way it had never been painted before. One of them, Tom Thomson, a dark and handsome loner, mysteriously died in a canoe accident when he was forty. Another outfitted a boxcar with beds and a stove and had it taken by rail far into Northern Ontario so he and his friends could live in it while painting the fall colors. When they showed their paintings in Toronto, the critics were enraged at their use of bold, outrageous colors. The book was published as *The Group of Seven,* and much to my surprise, it soared to the top of the Canadian best seller list. It became one of the most successful art books ever published in Canada, selling over 40,000 copies. I became the darling of the Canadian art world, fawned over by

Toronto socialites, invited to give lectures across the country, appearing on talk shows, and hosting art conferences.

As a cocky thirty-year-old, I thought I had the world by the balls. I recklessly pursued happiness wherever I could find it—affairs, drugs, alcohol, and getting more stuff. My wife Fran and I split up for a year and I ran as fast as I could to keep from facing the pain. I was sure that if I could just keep surfing from one happiness to the next, I could keep the highs going forever. For awhile I succeeded. My publisher was after me to write more books. I wrote a book called *Landmarks of Canadian Art*, which gave a sweeping history of three thousand years of Canadian art. It was Gift Book of the Year and on the Book of the Month Club. The publisher printed a special signed edition that weighed twenty pounds and sold for $1,200. All it needed was legs.

Then, to everyone's surprise, I left the academic world and became a documentary filmmaker. I had found my true passion, diving into every aspect of filmmaking, from cinematography, to editing, and distribution. I produced several films on Canadian art that won awards. Fran also got bitten by the filmmaking bug. We got back together and became a husband and wife team, traveling the world together, making movies on art, solar energy, and nature. Our films were purchased by the National Film Board and Canadian television. We were in constant motion, making new film proposals or off on film shoots. Our next project was a trip to China to shoot a film on Paul Horn, the musician. It was a fast-paced, coffee-jagged, manic life, but we loved it.

When we weren't on the road, we lived in an old farmhouse next to a spectacular forty-foot waterfall in the Canadian backwoods. Our nearest neighbor was a mile away. This was the seventies, when it was chic to do the back-to-the-land thing. In winter we battled our way through five-foot snowdrifts to go on film shoots. Every morning we walked the half-mile-long driveway to put our son Peter on the school bus. In spring we made our own maple syrup, tapping our own trees; in summer we grew organic vegetables. We became friends with our farmer neighbors, as well as local potters, musicians, and other city transplants. We entertained, held outrageous parties, and lived a lifestyle everyone envied.

To the outside world it seemed that I had everything anyone could ever want—family, friends, fame, fortune. It was a life most people would kill for.

By all accounts I *should* have been very happy.

Yet I was miserable.

It was mid-winter, and I had just returned from a cross-country tour for my latest book. I had to leave for Toronto, a hundred miles away, to do more promotion on the book. The only way to get there was by car or by bus, and I hate the bus.

"Peter, you have to take the bus," Fran rails, when I tell her I'm leaving.

"Take the bus? I've got interviews and book signings. I have to meet with the publisher on the other side of town! I can't take the bus!"

"You're not getting the car. It's going to snow and I'm not going to be stranded out here all alone. That's final."

So much for being a best-selling author and minor celebrity in Canada.

Fran and I have been arguing a lot lately. She likes the quiet of the country; I like the excitement of the city. She likes to rage; I'm passive aggressive. We do therapy, we split up, we have affairs, we drink a lot, we experiment with drugs (Hey, this is the seventies). Now we're living in the middle of nowhere and working together 24/7, which makes for one long, hideous power struggle. With Fran, no matter what I do, it's never enough.

An hour later Fran and I are standing in the cold waiting for the bus in the dismal little town of Durham, Ontario. A bitter wind whips across the highway as the Greyhound bus comes down the hill, stirring up tornado-like eddies of snow behind it. As it pulls up in front of us I notice that the entire bus is splattered with dirty brown slush and salt. *God, how I hate these winters,* I think. The door opens and I'm about to climb up the steps when Fran turns to me and says, "Peter, I know you're angry at me. You have a real problem that you need to look at. Nothing is ever enough for you. It's as if you have this big hole inside that you'll never be able to fill up." I'm so shocked that I can't reply. I board the bus and the door hisses shut behind me.

Alone in my seat, I think about what Fran said. *Well, screw her. So what if I have a big hole that needs to be filled up? I think I've done a pretty good job of filling it. Look at all the stuff I've done . . . I even get teased about being "world famous in Canada!" Not bad for someone who was called "quarter wit" by his father and flunked a year of high school.*

I look out at the flat, barren snow-covered fields rushing by. They are the same dull grey as the sky. Patches of tan stubble show through where the wind has blown away the snow. Every so often a straight, narrow road leads off to a lonely farmhouse surrounded by a few trees. I haven't seen a human being for miles. What a depressing sight . . . a person could die out there.

Maybe Fran is right. I do feel empty inside. I've exhausted every avenue for finding happiness in the world outside me—and I haven't found what I'm looking for. Where do I go from here? My marriage is falling apart, my life is out of control, and I'm miserable. Change is pushing in on me and there is nothing I can do about it. I pull out my copy of *Autobiography of a Yogi* and start reading. A part of me is longing for something deeper, and I have no idea what it is.

I come to the place where Yogananda meets the wise yogi who is to become his teacher. The yogi recognizes him immediately:

"How many years I have waited for you!" the wise man says.

"Sir, I come for wisdom and God-realization," says Yogananda.

"I give you my unconditional love," responds the Master.

My heart opens in longing as I feel the limitless love coming through the enlightened Master. A part of me recognizes that this is what I have been looking for my entire life.

The First Taste
Toronto, January 28, 1974

So I took a deep breath like they keep saying on this meditation tape and tried to focus on being right in this room, right in this moment, and I actually felt better! It was amazing. I dragged that scared part of myself kicking and screaming into the present moment and it was so good to be there. I started grinning like an idiot.
Pearl Cleage, *What Looks Like Crazy on an Ordinary Day*

"Now raise zee legs," the teacher says in a strong German accent.

I'm lying face down on a dirty old carpet.

What the hell am I doing here? I ask myself.

It's a freezing cold winter night in Toronto. Fran is in the hospital overnight, recovering from having a benign cyst on her uterus removed. Feeling tired and stressed out, I decide to walk over to the community center, a few blocks away. A friend told me about a series of yoga classes that were beginning tonight, insisting that I go. "They're being led by Lila—she's a brilliant yoga teacher. You must try it!"

Sometimes an innocent step into the unknown is enough to change our entire life.

"Now zees posture is good for zee back," Lila says. "Stretch your arms out in front of you . . . goot!"

With the smell of musty carpet in my nose I stretch my arms towards the wall. This is my first yoga class, and I didn't know that I was supposed to bring a towel to lie on (There was no such thing as a yoga mat in those days). In 1974, the only people who did yoga were weirdoes in Birkenstocks. That was the year 300 typewritten copies of *Yoga Journal* were distributed—the very first issue; the only available book on yoga was B.K.S. Iyengar's *Light on Yoga*.

"Take a deep breath. Exhale!" Lila says as she walks amongst the prone bodies. Lila Ostermann is a petite German lady with short white hair and boundless energy. It's hard to believe she is sixty. I find out later that she was a nurse in Berlin at the end of World War II and witnessed terrible human suffering. In her forties, she had three vertebrae fused in her back and was told by her doctor that she might never walk again. Now she teaches yoga full time.

"Place zee forehead on zee floor. Slowly roll up zee forehead. Raise zee arms, now zee legs! Stretch out in front and in back. Hold . . . hold!" I glance around me. Compared to the others I'm hardly off the ground. This is much harder than it looks.

"Hold some more . . . very good! Now relax down and roll on zee back!"

Ahhhhh. That feels good. I've been out of touch with my body for so long.

I lie on the carpet in the corpse pose, my arms resting by my side, my legs slightly spread, my eyes closed. I realize that I haven't felt this relaxed since I was a kid of six or seven. Until now, the only paradigm I had was to push my body to the limit. Now someone's telling me to relax!

"Relax every muscle. Ya . . . don't do anything."

After a few minutes I start to drift out. What a delicious feeling. I let go, aware that for once I don't need to be in control. Something inside me shifts. I feel safe for the first time in a long time. A sense of inner peace emerges—familiar, but long forgotten.

After my first class I'm so high that I convince Fran to join the series of classes. In no time she is as passionate about yoga as I am, and we become friends with our instructor Lila.

"You are ready to go deeper," Lila tells us after a few months of practice. With a look that allows no refusal, she insists, "You *must* do meditation!"

One weekend the three of us drive out to the country and find a peaceful spot at the edge of a lake. "All right," Lila says. "Sit comfortably. Close zee eyes. Watch zee breath."

At first I feel awkward, sitting with my legs crossed. My knees start to hurt.

"Notice zee breath come in through the nostrils. Keep concentrating on zee breath. We do this for fifteen minutes."

After five minutes it seems like two hours have passed. I'm aware of the birds singing and the sound of water lapping on the shore. By ten minutes it seems like the meditation will never end. My mind is racing everywhere. Then, for a split second . . . I let go. I'm aware of a blue light somewhere in front of my forehead. A wave of bliss shoots through me. Wow! A few seconds later I hear Lila say from somewhere far off, "Now open zee eyes."

When I open them, everything is brighter and more colorful than ever before. The lake is a deeper blue. The leaves on the trees are dancing. The sky falls away into infinity. I turn to Lila and Fran, who are both looking at me with broad smiles on their faces.

I start to get up an hour earlier each morning to meditate. I do breathing exercises where I hold my breath and try to shoot energy up my spine. Then I sit until I'm not aware of my body at all. At other times I find myself getting a huge erection. *So this is it. It's happening. I'm going to have one of those great cosmic orgasms!* But nothing happens. What a let down. *If just a little bit of yoga and meditation makes me feel this great, why not more?*

The Spiritual Journey
Toronto, March, 1974

There's something that pulls a person toward this journey. Way away back deep inside is a memory . . . It's as if you have tasted something somewhere in your past that's been so high that nothing you can experience through any of your senses or your thoughts can be enough!
Ram Dass

Little did I know it, but I had become a spiritual seeker. It wasn't in my plans. All I knew is that I was being called on the journey.

I hadn't the slightest idea of what lay ahead; I just took the next step and the next step. Over the next few years my passion for yoga led me to join a spiritual community, where I swallowed an entire belief system about gurus, practices, and the 3000-year-old tradition of yoga, without questioning any of it. How could I go wrong, I thought, if my guru's lineage goes all the way back to the great Hindu god Shiva? Besides, it was all very exotic and exciting. I loved the incense, the robes, the shaved heads (or the very long hair), the rituals, the chanting, and the "cachet" of the path I had chosen.

Like everyone else joining a spiritual group, I was promised rewards along the way. I was told that if I practiced yoga, I'd reduce the stress in my life, be healthy, and have a supple spine that would keep me young forever—what's not to like? If I meditated I'd be able to calm my mind and experience inner peace—how nice! I was convinced that if I stuck with my practices and served the guru, someday (if I kept at it long enough), I might even reach the ultimate reward—spiritual enlightenment—the gold medal of the spiritual Olympics.

And who wouldn't want enlightenment, if it means finding true happiness and an end to suffering? Even better, if I become enlightened, I will no doubt acquire special *siddhis* or spiritual powers myself, and everyone will adore me. I'll be waited on hand and foot, just like all the other enlightened teachers I've read about. My worries will be over!

Like young Frodo in *Lord of the Rings*, I set out over hill and dale in search of self-realization. With pure heart and mind, bolstered up by high spiritual ideals, I began my journey. I didn't know it then, but there would be dangers to face, initiations to go through, stages to be reached, and miles and miles of endless road. I had no idea that it would be a journey where old friendships would fall away, where I'd encounter wise people, crazy people, bandits, and saints. There would be times when I wanted to give up in despair and times when I felt I could go on forever. There would be moments of incredible beauty, moments of sheer terror, and moments of opening to a love I never dreamed possible. With youthful naiveté, I declared, "I'm ready to die for this!"

I wasn't alone in my search. Many of us baby boomers went on spectacular adventures during the seventies and eighties in search of spiritual enlightenment. What we all dreamed of was a high that would never end—what we imagined to be ultimate happiness. What a time it was . . . treks through India, dysentery in Nepal, monasteries in Thailand, sex in Poona, psychedelics in the Himalayas, abuse by spiritual teachers, years of celibacy, swallowed up by cults. You name it and it was done. Did we ever find what we were looking for? Maybe not, but we came pretty close . . . and we had one hell of a time.

As Yogi Berra's friend Phil Rizzuto said to him once, "Hey yogi, I think we're lost!" Yogi Berra responded by saying, "Yeah, but we're making great time."

The one thing we never questioned is whether we needed to make the journey in the first place.

On another level, we had no choice.

CHAPTER 2

A HAPPY INNOCENCE

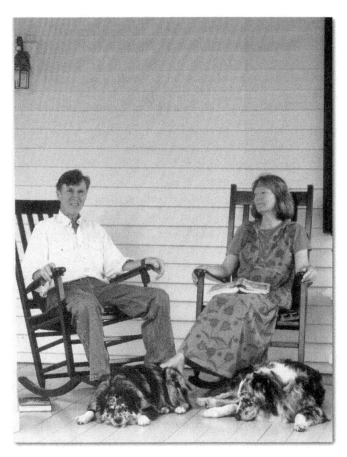

Peter & Linda at Mt Ayr Farm, Virginia

The Good Life
Mt. Ayr Farm, Virginia, September 1999

*Don't look here, there, anywhere. Peace is within you and within
the heart of all beings.*
H.W.L. Poonja (Papaji)

In 1996 Linda and I left New Mexico, our home for the past five years, and drove across the country in search of a new place to live. After enduring one of the worst droughts ever in the Southwest, we had put our retreat center up for sale, packed everything into a u-haul, and set out with our two dogs towards the rising sun. All we knew is that we wanted to be somewhere moist and green. As we drove across the country, we checked out towns such as Oxford, Mississippi, and Asheville, South Carolina, but none of them felt right for us. Just by chance we pulled off Highway 6 just south of Charlottesville, Virginia to take a stretch. It was a spring afternoon, when the wild roses were in bloom and the black locust trees gave off their fragrance. "I'm in heaven," Linda says, breathing in the perfumed air. "Let's stay here. This is our home."

Like many before us, we fell in love with this charming university town nestled close to the Blue Ridge Mountains. With its gracious southern spirit, liberal-minded residents, good restaurants, and breathtaking spring and fall weather, it was a perfect fit for Linda and me. We could sense the spirit of our hero Thomas Jefferson everywhere, from the University of Virginia, which he designed, to Monticello, his mountaintop home. We decided to settle here, and began looking for land. Over the course of a year we saw a gazillion properties, but none of them fit our long list of criteria. Discouraged, we gave up searching.

One day I noticed an ad for a farm auction in the paper and insisted that we go to it—something totally out of character for me—since I dislike auctions. Following the directions in the newspaper, I drove south on Highway 20 for fourteen miles, then headed east along narrow dirt roads. The dust swirled up behind us as we passed rich green hayfields and large horse estates with miles of white-board fences. I turned a corner and was stunned by the vista before me—a quaint red barn, gently rolling fields, and the Blue Ridge Mountains in the distance.

"I can't believe it," I say to Linda. "It looks just like the back roads of Vermont we love so much!"

"It's beautiful," Linda says excitedly. "This is just what we've been looking for!"

We know we're at the right place when we see a long line of pickups and cars parked alongside the road. After parking our Toyota 4Runner, Linda and I walk down the long drive towards the farmhouse, which sits on a knoll surrounded by magnificent old maple trees and the biggest holly tree I've ever seen. To my left, an auctioneer is standing in front of a large crowd rattling off bids on old farm equipment. Since I haven't the slightest interest in rusty plows and hay bines, I wander around the outbuildings—a barn, a long workshed, a garage, a chicken house, and even a blacksmith's shop. In the background I hear, "Gimme a four, gimme a four, gimme a five, right there a six . . ." The buildings are half falling down and filled waist deep in old junk. They give me the creeps. I take a quick peek inside each one, terrified I'll see a big black snake curled around a rafter. I've had a terror of snakes since I was eight—not just your everyday terror, but a full-blown phobia, with frequent nightmares and panic attacks.

Linda and I meet up at the old outdoor privy, where we notice a dignified lady standing next to the farmhouse, neatly dressed in a grey skirt and white blouse. Linda feels irresistibly drawn to talk to her. The lady introduces herself as Virginia Fulcher.

"My parents lived in this house for ninety years," she says in a soft Southern accent. "My daddy is ninety-six and mama is ninety–four. I just recently had to move them to a nursing home."

"I'm so sorry," I say. "That must be really hard for you."

"Yes, it is," Virginia says, tears welling up in the corner of her eyes.

"I used to own a farm in Oregon," Linda says. "I had a Jersey cow that I used to milk twice a day and a big vegetable garden. That was the happiest time of my life."

"She also had geese, turkeys, rabbits, chickens, and a pig," I add proudly, glad that one of us knows something about farms and livestock.

"Well, I declare. My father had cattle and some pigs too—and chickens of course. During the Depression he was the only one around here with food. People used to come all the way from town to buy food from him."

"Did you grow up on the farm?" I ask.

"Well, yes I did. I was born right in that front parlor sixty years ago. I went to school down in Scottsville, then to teacher's college in Farmville. I've been teaching mathematics at Charlottesville High School for thirty years. "

I shake my head in amazement. I later find out that Virginia has only been outside of the state a few times and has never flown in an airplane.

"We didn't have electricity or indoor plumbing until the 1950's," Virginia tells us.

"Really?" Linda says in surprise.

Finally it's time for my all-important question, "Do you have many snakes around here?"

"Well, there are quite a few, I reckon."

"Any poisonous ones?"

"Mama once stepped on a copperhead over by the door there, but it didn't bite her. You don't see them too often."

"That's good." *Or is it?* I think to myself.

We talk for another half-hour, as Virginia opens up her life to two complete strangers—not just any strangers—but Yankees from the North. We both feel a deep, unexplained connection with her, as if we've met a long-lost friend. All three of us are teary-eyed as we part.

Six months later Linda and I buy the 130 acres and crumbling farmhouse for $250,000—one of the last great buys in Albemarle County. What a shambles the house is. It was built a hundred years ago—a classic "two-over-two," with white clapboard siding, a black metal roof, and two brick chimneys on either end. Although it looks good from the outside, once we get inside, we see that the walls and first floor are so riddled with termites that it's a miracle it hasn't fallen down. We have to make a choice between bulldozing or just gutting it. We decide to renovate.

It takes a year of hard work to bring the farmhouse back to its pristine glory. Prior to starting the renovations, we live in the front parlor, propping up the corner of the bed with two phonebooks to make it level (and to my horror, watching a large black snake slither its way up the stairs into the attic). We use our own oak trees to make the flooring; we find old beams to replace the rotted ones; and we don't use one sheet of plywood in the entire house. It was later written up in *Natural Home* magazine for being such an environmentally "clean" house.

And yes, I did have to clean out all those outbuildings (my heart in my throat), loading up truckload after truckload of junk. And yes, there were snakes, but Virginia was right—no copperheads. Every time I saw one, I felt like the road runner in Looney Tunes, my feet just off the ground, frantically churning the air in terror. Determined to overcome my phobia, I gradually make friends with the snakes, giving them names and getting used to picking them up. I know I'm on my way to being cured when I walk into the living room one day with a four-foot black snake wrapped around my arm and say to Linda "Look what I found!"

Putting Up and Tearing Down
Mt. Ayr Farm, August, 2001

My life has no purpose, no direction, no aim, no meaning, and yet, I'm happy.
I can't figure it out. What am I doing right?
Charles Schultz, creator of Peanuts

Linda and I settle in to our new life on the farm. Each day flows into the next in a natural and effortless routine. Linda and I spend much of our time in silence, not because we're trying to, but because we enjoy the peace it brings. It's like being on a never-ending retreat. My mornings are spent working on my latest book. Afternoons (after the luxury of a nap) are spent outdoors—bush hogging the fields with the tractor, fixing fences, cutting trails, or tending to the sheep. Linda spends her days reading or doing crossword puzzles. We both go for long walks with the dogs on the trails that wind through our property.

Once or twice a week we go to Charlottesville to shop and have lunch with friends. Other days we drop by to visit neighbors or they come by to see us. One of our neighbors is Virginia, the lady at the auction, who becomes one of our dearest friends. Another is Kate, a colorful character who runs a little cafe in Scottsville. Then there is Laurie, an Englishwoman who raises sheep, and Woody, a wood-worker, who looks like Edge from U2 and plays bass guitar in a local band. We discover that we live in a wonderfully diverse neighborhood, from old Virginia gentry, to struggling farmers, millionaires, artists, and people who live below the poverty line.

Evenings are spent with a glass of wine, the nightly news, and a TV program or a movie. Then we curl up in bed with a good book and our dogs on the floor beside us.

Days and weeks go by in pure contentment—what I call radical happiness.

Reading this, you may well ask yourself, "That sounds great. I would be radically happy too if I could sit around all day and do whatever I wanted. By the way, where did you get the money to do all this? Are you one of the Pittsburgh Mellon's?"

The truth is that I have a secret hobby—secret because most people have no idea what I do for a living, and a hobby because I do it to please myself. So here it is: I'm a frustrated architect who loves to create beautiful places to live. I feel a little like Thomas Jefferson, who designed Monticello—his magnificent neo-classical home on a hilltop outside of Charlottesville, which I can see from my farm. Jefferson wanted to be remembered more for his distinction as an architect than his role as president. "Architecture is my delight," he said, "and putting up and tearing down one of my favorite amusements."

It took me a long time before I knew I had this passion. Every time I moved—and it was often—I looked at local real estate, scouring the countryside in search of property that everyone else had overlooked, but I could see vast potential in. I'd buy it for next to nothing, and turn it into a work of art. Sometimes I renovated an existing house; sometimes I designed a house and built it from scratch. Land and buildings became the blank canvas I painted on. After spending twenty-five years in the visual arts as an art historian and filmmaker, I had a pretty good eye.

It all started when I was in my twenties and bought a townhouse in Toronto with a $20,000 inheritance. Together with my first wife Fran, I stripped down the walls and renovated it. After developers tried to force us out by moving in drug dealers next door, I sold the house for twice what I paid for it. Most of the moves were because of major life events (and there were many—cancer, hurricanes, death, illness, financial distress). But sometimes we moved just on a whim! At one point I had a reading by a psychic. "Will this be our last house?" I asked. She laughed uproariously. "Oh, no! There will be many more houses—many more."

On and on it went, buying and selling properties, and to my surprise, making money each time I sold. Each house represented a vision of an ideal life. It was like making a wish on the astral plane and seeing it manifest in front of me. There was the dream of a quaint *On Golden Pond* cottage on a lake, which became a romantic summer cottage at the head of a nine-mile lake in Quebec; there was the desire to live an alternative lifestyle in the wilderness, which became an old caretaker's house next to a forty-foot waterfall in Ontario; there was everyone's fantasy of living in Hawaii, which turned out to be a spectacular Asian-Pacific house overlooking the Pacific Ocean. Another desire was to live in an Adirondack Lodge, which showed up as an enormous log home that I built in the woods outside of Lenox, Massachusetts. And who wouldn't want to experience living in an adobe house with a kiva fireplace, latillas, and vigas? This came into reality as an old hippie house on a mountainside outside of Taos, New Mexico. My most ambitious (and most devastating) dream was to own a retreat center. It manifested as a former Franciscan monastery on one hundred acres outside Albuquerque, New Mexico. And finally there was the daydream of living in an old farmhouse surrounded by woods, and streams, and a river. This is where I live now, grateful every day for my good fortune.

Even though it was incredibly hard work, and filled with huge financial risks and challenges, I loved doing it. It never felt like "work" because I was having so much fun expressing my creative vision. Meanwhile, I got to live in some of the most scenic spots in the world and to leave each place a little more beautiful than when I found it. I never expected to make money, but always came out ahead. It was like taking part in a huge banquet, tasting the many different pleasures of life. But it had its toll. As Linda said one day, "No wonder I'm so exhausted. I just figured out that we've moved fourteen time in six year."

The Tender Thread of Memory
Mt Ayr Farm, Virginia, April 10, 2002

I was deeply unhappy but I didn't know it because I was so happy all the time.
Steve Martin

One day I'm cleaning out the barn when I come across a box with the words
"PHOTOGRAPHS—FAMILY" written on the top. I pull back the sealing tape
and open the flaps, releasing the musty smell of old photographs. Inside the box
are three aging photo albums, all with worn black covers. I flip through the first
album, which has four or five small, now yellowing, black and white photographs
on each page. There are pictures taken by my father of seaplanes and ocean liners
from the 1930's, along with pictures of the 1939 New York World's Fair. Another
page has photos of him and his friends sitting in the back of a Cadillac convertible,
looking like they've stepped straight out of *The Great Gatsby*.

The second album contains pictures of my sister when she was six or seven
and some of me as a child. *Wow . . . that's me when I was two or three . . . there's my
mother!* I turn the page. *Are those my grandparents?* Excitedly, I close the box and
carry it to the farmhouse.

"Look at what I just found." I call out to Linda as I come rushing into the
living room. She's a little apprehensive, given the last time I made that announce-
ment I had a snake wrapped around my arm.

We spread the albums out on the table.

Linda turns to me and says, "Maybe they'll help you remember your childhood."

I flip through the pages, ignoring her comment. "Look," I say in surprise,
"there's one of me with a dog. I didn't even know I had a dog when I was that old."

Linda shakes her head in amazement. "You don't even remember having a
dog? I can list the names of every pet I ever had. You really *don't* remember anything!"

"Well," I laugh, "at least I now know that I had a dog."

I pull out a small black and white photo taken of me when I was about three.
I'm sitting on a tricycle, wearing shorts, a knit sweater, and little booties.

Leaning closer to get a better look, she says, "You're so cute—look at the curly
hair and freckles!"

"Hmmmm. I always thought I was a shy, sensitive kid. But there's an expression of pure joy on my face—it's that beautiful, happy innocence of childhood."

Linda points to an arm intruding in from the side of the picture, "There's your mom reaching out to keep you from falling."

I hadn't even noticed her at first. Her face is in profile and is partially cut off by the frame. I peer at her face. She appears to be smiling as she tries to steady me, looking at me with what is undeniably an expression of immense love.

"It's strange. I have no idea who she is. I can't even remember what her voice sounded like. I have no recollection of her holding me, reading to me, or tucking me in at night. I don't have a single memory of her laughing, being upset, or getting angry. It's all a blank."

"That's so sad," Linda says. "I can remember my mom as if she were here with me today. She's absolutely real."

"Maybe I have a memory problem because I used to break those old mercury thermometers in half and roll the mercury around on my desk."

"You did?"

"Yeah, no one knew about the dangers of mercury then."

Linda rolls her eyes.

"Or it could have happened when I ran head first into a brick wall."

"You what?"

Starting to laugh, I tell Linda about my dad giving me a World War II helmet. Thinking I was invincible, I put it on and ran headfirst into a brick wall, showing off to my friends.

"That sounds like something you would do. You've always been a daredevil."

"And a little nuts," I smile.

I hold up a color picture of me bundled in a heavy coat, red mittens, and a red hat. "Gee, I *am* kind of cute," I say. My cheeks are rosy from the cold and I have a big grin on my face, showing my buck teeth. I'm squinting in the bright sunlight while sitting on top of an eight-foot high snowbank, about to slide down. My mother is also in the picture, wearing a fur coat and boots, her head cut off by the frame.

"Why does your dad always cut your mother out of the picture? Did he and your mom have problems? She's never in the picture."

"No, no, no. I think you're reading into it. The truth is that I don't remember what their relationship was like."

I pick up another photo of me when I'm six, sitting in a rowboat wearing my bathrobe and slippers, my little hands gripping the huge oars. "Wow, look at that face. I'm totally in the moment. There's not a trace of worry or fear."

"That won't last long," Linda says, shaking her head sadly. She knows what lies ahead for me.

I've spent all my adult life trying to reconstruct these early years. I've done Freudian therapy, gestalt therapy, psychodrama, hypnosis, talking to relatives, combing old letters, and watching family films in search of clues. I even put together a leather-covered binder in which I've pieced together what happened to me every month of my life—from the time I was in my mother's womb right up to the present—using journals, day-timers, newspaper clippings, photos, and guesswork—hoping to unlock the secret recesses of memory.

Every so often I have a flashback to a childhood memory, but they are few and far between. One day I was stroking our neighbor's horse when the sweet smell of its coat brought back a long-forgotten memory. I must have been six or seven at the time. During the cold Canadian winter my family often drove from Montreal to the Laurentians to spend the weekend at our cottage on the lake. Because the road to the cottage was closed in winter, we had to take a sleigh across the now frozen lake to get there.

I remember how it was always dark and freezing by the time we got to the village of Ste. Agathe, where we picked up the sleigh. My dad, my mom, my sister and I crammed into the smoke-filled office of Reid's Taxi, while Reid called over to the barn to have a sleigh prepared. A few minutes later I'd hear the jingle of sleigh bells, announcing that the horses were coming out from the stable. Looking out the frost-covered window, I could see the sleigh and driver pull up under a single lamp outside the barn. We stepped out into the crisp night air and climbed into the sleigh with the help of the driver, a French Canadian bundled up in a big raccoon coat, his breath smelling of rum and tobacco. I can remember him throwing heavy buffalo robes over us to keep us warm and tucking us in. "Ca va?" he'd ask in French. "Vous êtes confortable?"

"Bien oui," my father said, which was about all the French he knew.

My young eyes watch in fascination as everything is loaded into the sleigh and the horses paw the frozen ground in anticipation. But most of all it is the smells—the damp scent of their coats as the steam rises off them after coming out of the warm stable, and the pungent odor of horse manure as they poop before heading out. It is these rich aromas that let me trace the tender thread of memory back to its source.

Climbing up front, the driver shouts "Hut, hut" to the horses and cracks the reins. The sleigh lurches forward and bounces down the rutted track to the lake, almost tipping over. At the bottom of the hill the curved runners splash across the slushy shoreline onto the solid surface of the lake. Once on the foot-thick ice, the horses trot rhythmically on, sleigh bells jingling, the runners squeaking over the frozen snow.

As we move further away from shore, the star-filled sky opens above us like a huge dome filled with a billion stars. With the moonlight reflecting on the snow-covered lake, it is almost as bright as daylight. Only a few lonely electric lights are visible, coming from the cottages scattered around the lake. The rest is nothing but the enormous vastness of sky and frozen silver lake stretching out in all directions. My mind is filled with wonder.

"Look," my sister says, "over there!"

Just above the northern horizon a magical display of phosphorescent blue and green lights dances in the sky.

"The Northern Lights!"

We silently watch the shimmering colors shoot high in the night sky as the sleigh glides over the lake, with us tucked under the musty smelling buffalo robes, lulled by the sound of horse's hooves and bells.

If there is a perfect moment in a perfect world, this must be it.

I carefully add this precious memory to my list—one that has taken over fifty years to recall.

Not all memories are quite that happy. I have no doubt that my dad loved me. He took me on trips, bought me just about everything I could ever want, and tried to be a good father. But like many fathers in the late forties, he was determined that I be a "real man." He had the handsome good looks of an Ernest Hemingway (even down to the barrel chest), and prided himself on being tough. I still have pictures of him in a bathing suit, flexing his muscles for the camera.

"Come on, son," he announces one day when I'm five or six. "I'm going to teach you to box,"

"I don't want to," I say.

"Wilson, don't make him do this if he doesn't want to," my mom says, interrupting her reading.

"Son, this is for your own good." He gets down on his knees so he'll be the same height as me. Grabbing my wrists, he pulls me over in front of him. "Now, hold up your fists like this and try to block me."

"Don't you dare hurt him," mom says uncomfortably.

"Now, when I hit you . . . you hit me back."

Suddenly he gives a slap to my face with the flat of his hand, stunning me.

Wild with rage, I try to hit him back, battering against his huge chest with both hands. It's like going up against a mountain. I feel totally powerless.

He jabs back at me. "You've got to keep your fists up."

"I don't want to do this anymore," I cry out.

"Stop that Wilson!" shouts my mom.

"Don't be such a sissy," he says, getting up from the floor with an air of disgust.

I run over to my mother and throw myself on her lap.

To his credit, after I was beaten up by a neighborhood bully a few years later, my father gave me more boxing lessons. I went up to the kid in a park and beat the crap out of him.

Much later I found out that my mom was the one who always protected me from my father. When I look at photographs of my mother I shake my head in bewilderment. Who was she? What was she thinking when these pictures were taken? Was she happy? Was she sad? I study the photographs like an art historian, noticing her sensitive face and gentle smile. She has the thin, wispy figure of a Kathryn Hepburn, with beautiful pin-curled auburn hair. People often tell me how kind she was, but I have no recollection. They say she was very artistic and used to draw and paint. All I can remember is a few small landscapes she painted in oil, and furniture she hand-painted with beautiful flowers and designs. My strongest memory—and for a long time my only memory—is of her coming downstairs in the morning and kissing me on the cheek while I ate my breakfast, leaving the faint smell of rouge behind.

Free from the Past
Mt Ayr Farm, Virginia, May 7, 2002

If there is a single definition of healing it is to enter with mercy and awareness those pains, mental and physical, from which we have withdrawn in judgment and dismay.
Stephen Levine

"Ow, ow, ow!" I cry out, easing myself into the 106 degree water of our spa. When we renovated the farm, we added a spa, partly so that Linda can ease the joint pain from her illness, but mainly because I love to soak in hot water (the life of a gentleman farmer is ever so hard).

Linda is already immersed in the tub, waiting for me to join her. She smiles as I slip naked into the water. "Pain is so very close to pleasure, isn't it?"

"Oh my God, that feels good," I groan, feeling the heat penetrate to my very bones.

"Tell me about your session with Bev."

I'd called Linda on my way home from Charlottesville to let her know that my session with my therapist, Bev Supler, had been a real breakthrough. Bev and I have been doing a series of sessions to help uncover my ongoing issues around abandonment. The Freudian therapy in London with Dr. Hayley saved my life many years earlier, but there is still more to uncover. Bev is a brilliant therapist, drawing from her extensive knowledge of traditional therapy, the Enneagram, and EMDR, a therapy often used with victims of trauma. EMDR (Eye Movement Desensitization and Reprocessing) can accomplish in a few sessions what traditional therapies take years to get to. No more lying on a couch with a psychiatrist sitting in silence behind me. Bev sits right in front of me and slowly moves her upright forefinger from side to side, about a foot from my face, as I follow the finger with my eyes. Somehow it "unhooks" the subconscious, making it safe to return to traumatic events.

"It was amazing," I say. "I finally touched on what I've been avoiding all these years."

"What was that?" she asks, looking at me through the clouds of steam. The refraction of light in the water makes her head seem disconnected from her body. Her voice seems to be coming from some far off place.

"Today I remembered what happened after the funeral. My God, that was fifty years ago!"

Linda reaches out through the water and finds my hand. "Oh yeah, that was horrible. You told me what your family said to you before the funeral, 'Peter, you're a big boy now and you mustn't cry.' My God, you were only twelve!"

"Until today I could only recall the funeral itself—I remember being dressed in my blue blazer and tie, sitting up front in the church with all those grown-ups behind me. I was trying to be a big boy and not cry, yet there was this huge casket in the aisle with roses on the top. I kept looking over at it thinking, *"My mom is in there and I'll never see her again."*

"You never got to say goodbye to her, did you?"

I shake my head. "No, that was hard . . . and I've really worked on that one. What I found out today was something I didn't even know had happened. I had this memory of being in a black limousine as it followed the hearse to the cemetery. There was a whole procession behind us. My sister and I were on the jump seats, and my father and grandmother were sitting opposite us, not saying a word. I hated it when we went through red lights and all the people on the sidewalk tried to stare in through the windows at us. I think I told you—this was the third funeral I had been to in six months. My grandpa Bill died, and then my Nana died. She was my mom's mother."

Linda shakes her head in amazement.

"It was a hot, steamy summer day in the city, and we turned into the cemetery and pulled up in front of this little chapel. No one told me why we were there. We all got out and went inside. A few minutes later these somber guys in black suits rolled the casket in and placed it in front of two big doors."

"I thought funeral processions always went to the grave site," Linda says, splashing water on her face.

"I did too. Then it dawned on me when I saw the doors. This is a crematorium."

"In a cemetery?"

"I don't know. I'm pretty sure it was in the cemetery. Then this priest got up and said a few words. As he talked, my twelve-year-old imagination ran wild. I knew that once we left the chapel, those huge doors would open and the casket would be rolled into a furnace room. I could imagine the casket—with my mom in it—being consumed by flames. The idea of her being burned up was so utterly terrifying that I tried not to feel anything—and I'm still doing that."

"No you aren't. You're open and loving," she says, looking at me with compassion, her blue eyes lit up in the mist.

The water suddenly gets too hot to bear and I start to feel suffocated. I sit up on the bench so that my torso is out of the water.

"In the session I got to be that little boy again. With the help of the EMDR I saw that a part of me was burned up in those flames along with the person I loved more than anyone else in the world. For the first time I experienced the tremendous rage I felt when my mother died. Oh God I was angry—angry at her for leaving me! I've never felt this before. I didn't even know I had that much anger inside me."

"I'm so proud of you. You've been running from this for so long."

"Actually, it was quite fun to get angry," I laugh. "You know me—I never get angry!"

"What did you do with Bev? Did you express the anger?"

"I didn't have to. I just felt it inside—my belly felt like it was on fire. And then I felt this sadness. You know that I never cried after the funeral. I didn't cry the night my mom died. I didn't cry the night after that. It was years before I cried. It was bottled up inside—the grief, the anger. I felt like a frozen kewpie doll. Now I'm finally free of it—at least for the time being. What a relief."

"I can't believe that you went off alone to your room every night and that no one held you or cuddled you." Linda says, incredulous. "I can see why you felt that God had betrayed you."

Cooled off by the brisk October air, I sink back into the hot water, relaxing into its soothing embrace.

"It's so sad," Linda says, gently rubbing my feet while sitting in the tub opposite me. "No one helped you understand what happened. Imagine how different it would have been if we had the understanding of death we have now? You'd know that there is no birth, and there is no death. All there is is consciousness. You'd know that her spirit is still alive."

"That's exactly what I came to in the session," I say. "For the first time ever I saw that her spirit did not die with her . . . her love is alive within me. And it will be the same when you and I die. Our bodies will go, but who we truly are never dies. It's eternal."

"You know that my love will always be with you too," Linda says.

I reach over and take her hand. "And mine with you . . ."

"You went through a lot today."

"I feel as if I've let go of a huge weight that I've carried around for years."

"We have such a screwed up perception of death," Linda smiles. "I love that quote: 'When we come into the world, we are crying and everyone is laughing. When we die, we are the ones who are laughing and everyone is crying.'"

"That's so true. It's nice to think my mom was laughing on the day she died and that we'll be laughing too on the day we die."

"You know," Linda says. "If people knew that we talked about this kind of stuff in a hot tub, they'd think we were nuts."

"Well, we are!" I laugh.

We both fall into the comfortable silence that comes from two lovers knowing each other so well.

I look out at the rolling farmland lit up by the late afternoon sun. At the edge of the field, the old oak trees are lit up in a brilliant tapestry of color. Steam swirls around me, sparkling in tiny rainbows. *How interesting.* I think. *Steam is nothing more than tiny water droplets in the process of turning to gas. Eventually they will turn back to water again . . . the unending process of creation and destruction. The droplets are indescribably beautiful, the essence of life itself.* I close my eyes. Then there is no thought at all . . . just the sensation of Linda gently touching my foot, the sound of a bird's wings as it flies overhead, the smell of wood smoke in the crisp fall air. Eyes open and register the reflections of the water dancing on the wall behind the spa. Eyes close. Everything rises into form and dissolves into the formless—I am so happy.

CHAPTER 3

THE ROAD LESS TAKEN

Yogi Amrit Desai

Angel Breath
Mt Ayr Farm, Virginia, November 20, 2003

Keep quiet. Stay wherever you are. Don't reject your worldly activities. Simply keep quiet for a single second and see what happens.
H.W.L. Poonja (Papaji)

I take up my new role as gentleman farmer with enthusiasm. Having grown up a city boy, at first I can barely tell one end of an animal from another. I feel just like Snoopy in my favorite *Peanuts* cartoon. Snoopy is out in the desert, leaning on a boulder with his fedora on, writing a letter: *Gentlemen. I have decided to become a shepherd. Please send me a dozen sheep and a book of directions.*

So I acquire a dozen sheep, two goats, two cows, and some chickens—a few more and I would have had enough for an ark. Before long I'm knee deep in the nitty-gritty of farming, giving the sheep their shots, trimming their hooves, docking their tails, castrating the males, mucking out the barn. If, at the end of each day, I haven't gotten blood, poop, or urine on my hands, I feel disappointed (the blood is usually my own). After a few months I've helped in the birthing of a dozen lambs and a baby goat. I become more adept at "throwing" sheep, a basic move which allows the shepherd to do everything from shearing, to giving shots, to trimming hooves. It involves twisting the sheep's head way back to one side, then lifting and pulling on their rear ends in the opposite direction so they flip over onto their backs. One day I walk up to a big ewe named Emma, who weighs in at over 180 pounds. I can see in her eyes that she knows exactly what I have in mind (talk about smart!) Somehow I end up riding on her back facing towards her rear as she races around the barnyard. Once I get over the shock, I start laughing hysterically, before she dumps me into a pile of manure.

To my surprise, working with the animals opens up a deep sense of joy and fulfillment. There is something primal about it—connecting me with traditions that go back thousands and thousands of years. I find out that the sheep are a lot smarter than some people. A mother sheep can pick out her lamb from among hundreds of other lambs. They stick together in a group, not because they're dumb, but for safety, just like most humans do. Within a year my dozen sheep have become two dozen. I get to know their individual personalities and habits, even giving them names (which shows how far I have to go before calling myself a farmer).

My favorite time of day is when I ring a cowbell, calling the sheep for their evening feed. They all come galloping across the field, with the goats leading the way at a gallop. They wolf down their food (no pun intended), then head out to pasture in single file. Creatures of habit, they follow a well-worn path that takes them to the upper pasture. One evening, with the sun just setting behind the Blue Ridge Mountains and the sky a luminous pink and gray, I take a deep breath in, smelling the first signs of spring—the pungent smell of old leaves and damp, moist earth. Mmmm, what a smell! After spreading out fresh bedding for the animals and filling their water buckets, I head out into the field to join the animals.

About a dozen sheep are grazing with their new-born lambs close by their side. The lambs are frisking and darting around, a sight I never tire of. As I approach the flock, they look up at me, then go back to their grazing. One lamb gets too far from its mother and lets out a frightened *baaaaa*. The mother responds with a loud bleat and the lamb darts back to her side.

I sit on the sweet-smelling grass a few yards away and remain still. The animals check me out once more to make sure I don't have any ulterior motives, such as rounding one of them up to check their teats, and seem satisfied that I am just there to enjoy their company. A few minutes later, my favorite ewe Isabel comes over and stands directly in front of me, her face in front of mine. I stroke the soft fur on her nose and under her chin while speaking to her softly, "Isabel, you're so beautiful . . . you're such a good mama . . . I'm so proud of you." Last year her lambs were stillborn and she was the only ewe who didn't have babies. This year she had twins. She remains perfectly still and looks at me with her big brown eyes, offering a transmission of pure love . . . a love that is beyond words. Then, without any fanfare, she turns and rejoins the other sheep. *This is what real love is,* I think in wonder, *it's purely impersonal. It's being totally present to what is.*

The three goats have been watching us. Even though they are a few years old, they are my "babies." I helped bring them into the world and once milked the two females, enjoying fresh goat's milk until it became too much of a chore to do it every day. Now they don't serve any useful function other than eating weeds and being mascots. When they see that I'm available for petting, two of them saunter over, eager to get in on the action. One of them, Princess, a brown and black Nubian, circles around to my right and comes up close so I can caress the underside of her long neck. Her coat is smooth and soft here, compared to the coarse fur on her sides. She stretches her head up and back like a deer, in a graceful movement that has me spellbound. Her eyes, with their horizontal pupils, look off into some unknown place. I am drenched in the sensuality of it all.

The other goat, Angel, a white Saanen, comes up behind me, out of my line of vision. I can sense her coming closer and closer as I continue to stroke Princess. Suddenly I'm aware of her breath on the back of my head, then I can feel the warmth of it touching my ear. Her breath is so gentle, even as she brings her soft lips right up against my ear. All my senses are heightened. I can smell the fresh chives on her breath as she breathes into my ear—whoosh, whoosh, whoosh.

I remain still, knowing that if she chose to, she could rip my ear off in a split second, like a leaf from a branch. She keeps on breathing, and her breath penetrates to the very core of my being. She knows exactly what she is doing. It feels like she is speaking to me in her own language, saying, "You are safe, you are safe, you are love." Something stirs within me. Suddenly there is just breath, nothing but breath—a holy communion of breath.

For a moment my mind stops. This is it. This is all there is . . . Angel breath.

The moment passes. Just as suddenly, both goats lose interest and start trotting back to the flock, which has moved a hundred yards away. I watch in dumbfounded silence as they suddenly stop and rear up on their hind legs, butting each other's heads. Again and again they rise up, their forelegs tucked back, heads butting, then dropping back down, as if in some primitive ritual out of time. No wonder the ancients worshipped the god Pan! Then, as quickly as they started, they stop and continue on their way.

Alone now, I am enveloped in peace, totally content.

Growing Up WASP
Mt. Ayr Farm, Virginia, January 25, 1998

I hope life isn't a big joke, because I don't get it.
Jack Handey

My sister Beverly visits from Montreal, and in true Mellen tradition, we have smoked salmon appetizers and a glass (or two) of wine before dinner. She has been staying with us for the last few weeks while she tries to figure out what to do with her marriage. We've become very close. "Do you remember anything about dad and mom's relationship?" I ask, glancing up from my book. Beverly is in her sixties, seven years older than me. She has the classic look of the French movie star Catherine Deneuve, but her smile has a warmth and innocence that is more Canadian than French. Like Catherine Deneuve, Beverly is always perfectly dressed for every occasion, in this case jeans, a beige turtleneck, and a delicate gold necklace.

"Oh God, I don't know," she says, putting her wine glass on the table. I notice that there are greasy fingerprints on it, something she manages to do every time she drinks wine, which puzzles me no end. She's so fastidious in every other way.

"But you must remember something!" I say, with a hint of desperation. Beverly is the only one of our family left who was around during my growing up years. She's the one person who can give me a clue as to what went on.

I pour us each another glass of wine, hoping it will loosen her up.

"Well, we were just a typical Montreal WASP family. What can I say?" Her voice has become loud and the slightest bit slurred after a few drinks.

"Yeah. I've been trying to escape from that all my life."

"Why? There's nothing wrong with being a WASP."

"For me it was an emotional wasteland. I'm still struggling to get past it."

"Well yes . . . we were a little uptight," she admits. "I remember grandmother Frances used to say to mother, 'Don't show the children too much affection. It will spoil them.'"

"Frances was amazing," I say. "I can see her sitting there with her long cigarette lighter and haughty attitude. She had two Welsh corgis didn't she?"

"They weren't corgis. They were West Highland whites." So much for my memory.

"We'd have to get dressed up when she'd visit on Sunday and have tea and crumpets with her. Wasn't one of her family a Lady in Waiting to Queen Victoria?"

47

"Yeah, it was her grandmother."

"Really? I didn't know that."

"Her grandfather was Sir Sidney Wishart, the mayor of London or something. I don't remember." She daintily picks up a smoked salmon appetizer and slips it in her mouth.

"Are you sure you can't remember?"

As she finishes chewing, she says, "Oh, Peter, what does any of this matter? It's all bullshit you know, this looking at the past. Why don't you just get on with living your life?"

I smile. "Maybe you're right!" I decide I'm not going to get any further in my family research tonight. "Have you heard my favorite WASP joke?" I ask.

"I didn't think you knew any jokes."

"How many WASPS does it take to screw in a light bulb?"

Beverly shakes her head.

I start laughing hysterically even before I give the punch line: "Three . . . two to stir the martinis and one to call the electrician."

"That's funny. Our father and mother sure liked their martinis. Do you remember how daddy used to drive off the road into a ditch coming home from those parties up at the lake?"

"Yeah, we had to call a tow truck every other weekend," I laugh. "One time he fell in a closet after getting home. It terrified me. But after falling into closets a few times myself, I have a little more compassion."

"Mother was so drunk once, she crawled into the house on her hands and knees."

"No, you're kidding! I never knew that. I remember her sitting in her chair with an Old Fashioned and a Philip Morris cigarette, but I had no idea she got drunk."

"Oh, they all did. At the sailing parties they drank like fishes."

Our family had a cottage on Lac des Sables in an exclusive area called "The Point." The small golf course nearby had a discreet RESTRICTED sign at the entrance to keep away Jews (It was in the bylaws that no "Hebrew" could own land on "The Point"). Every Sunday morning the summer residents held a sailing race, where eager young sailors like myself competed for sailing trophies. After the races, each neighbor took turns hosting a party. While the kids my age hung around an ice-filled bucket filled with cold soft drinks and ate potato chips, the grown-ups got down to serious drinking.

"What a scene that was," I say, taking a slug of wine. "They used to stand around the drink table in their Bermuda shorts and polo shirts."

"They're wearing the same thing now."

"I can't believe that the offspring of those families are still around, and that you know them all! My God, you even belong to the same clubs—the Racquet Club, the Hillside Club, Indoor Tennis Club!"

Beverly takes a sip of wine and smiles."Oh yeah, nothing ever changes."

"Do you remember the tour boat that took tourists around the lake?"

"Oh yes . . . the Alouette. It's still going."

"I got such a kick out of it. As the boat went by each house they'd announce who owned it over a loudspeaker: 'This is the home of Mr. Geoffrey Notman, president of Canadair; the house you see now is owned by Mr. George McCullagh, founder of The Globe & Mail; the home on the right belongs to Mr. Wilson Mellen, president of J.F. Hayden & Co . . .'"

Beverly laughs, "And dad had a little office with one secretary."

"Yes, but he loved being part of the Montreal elite. Remember when people used to ask him, 'Are you one of *the* Mellons?' referring to the billionaire Pittsburgh Mellons, and he'd answer, 'No we're the *Montreal* Mellens'? He was so proud of that."

At the time I had only a vague idea of what my father did for a living. I knew that he owned a small insurance company that insured American banks through Lloyds of London. The business had been set up by his father, an American entrepreneur who was known to write up insurance policies on the cuff of his dress shirt while traveling by ship to Africa in search of gold mines. My father inherited a passion for geology from his father, and every summer he took a train out West to the Canadian Rockies, hired a bunch of Swedes as laborers, then headed into the wilderness on horseback. His goal was to develop lead silver mines and make his fortune. It was untamed backcountry. He and his crew built their own roads and bridges with nothing more than a jeep, a few axes, and a lot of muscle. One of his men was attacked by a grizzly bear and my dad had to drive him sixty miles down the rutted road at night to the nearest doctor. At the end of the summer he returned home with slides of his adventures and more Native American artifacts to add to his collection.

We lived in a big, three-story home that my parents had built in Hampstead, a quiet Montreal suburb of tree-lined streets and friendly neighbors. It was a contemporary art-deco style house with a white stucco exterior and a graceful curving wall on one side. The interior was written up in magazines for its bold design, no doubt a result of my mother's artistic touch. It had warm oriental carpets over a shiny black floor, something ahead of its time.

On the third floor my father kept his collection of Native American Indian art—museum quality tomahawks, peace pipes, feathered headdresses, and an old skull in a glass case. Hanging from the rafters was an oar from when he was on the Cambridge rowing team. It was here that I set up my huge train set, made my model airplanes, and secretly climbed out the dormer window onto the metal roof, where there was a thirty-foot drop straight down. Like Superman in the comics, I had a deep inner certainty that if I threw myself off, I could really fly.

I went to a boy's private school in Montreal straight out of the movie *Dead Poets Society*—the school tie, the blue blazer, the grey flannels, teaching by rote, sports, caning for those who misbehaved. I wasn't the brightest of students, and by today's standards would be considered ADHD.

For all I knew, I would one day become a businessman, marry a beautiful debutante from Westmount, and take my place in Montreal society. I'd join the Hillside Tennis Club and the Racquet Club, and the University Club. I'd have a cottage on the lake, where my children would sail in summer regattas, and presumably, I would get drunk and fall drunk in the closet afterwards.

But life had other plans.

Rebel without a Cause
Montreal, Quebec, 1953 to 1956

From this point forth, we shall be leaving the murky marshes of memory into thickets of wildest guesswork.
J.K. Rowling

A year after my mother's death I turned thirteen. By then, thanks to the atmosphere of denial in the family, I had forgotten that she ever existed. I did what most teenagers do—I blew things up, got into trouble, rebelled, tried to look tough, and played sports. The day finally arrived when I discovered that great balm of teenagehood—masturbation, which went hand in glove with being in a boy's private school. I closely identify with the comedian Robin Williams when he describes his childhood: "I was alone a lot, except for Petey. Every so often he would wake up and then I'd have to wrestle with him." I remember one bizarre activity that I found highly erotic. I would make up a loincloth out of a towel, like the Indians wore, and go into my bathroom where I would do handstands up against the door for what seemed like hours on end. Was this some strange recall of a past-life as a yogi?

My two best friends were Don and "Fats" Roberts. We called ourselves "The Big Three," not because we were big, but because we thought we were so cool. We shot off my father's 30.06 hunting rifle in the country, smashing up patio furniture and a few windows, drove my father's car at 50 miles per hour on the frozen ice in the winter while towing my friends on skis behind it, and waterskied nude at night in the summer. During the school year we joined the Boy Scout troop and listened wide-eyed as our scout master Roy Williams told us about the orgies he had been to. If we scratched his back (quite literally), we could earn an extra badge. After a lot of scratching, I had enough badges to become a "Queen Scout," the equivalent of an Eagle Scout in America.

One day, when I was fourteen, Don accidentally threw hair tonic in my eye, burning off the skin of my cornea. I had to stay in bed for a month, with patches over both eyes. Don and "Fats" sometimes visited me in the afternoon after school, but most of my days were spent at home alone. Our housekeeper, Mrs. Clark, would bring me lunch, but otherwise there was no one around. When the phone rang I'd rush blindly to answer it in my father's room, my hands out in front of me, trying not to slam into an open door (which happened more than once).

When the accident happened there were two feet of snow on the ground; when the patches came off, spring had come and the flowers had bloomed.

The way I make it up in my mind, home was not a happy place. No music was ever played in the house; no one ever sang; my father never invited people over; discussion at the dinner table revolved around, "How was school today?" Any expression of emotion or affection was frowned upon. I spent most of my time in our third floor attic room, where I built model airplanes (never quite understanding why I loved the smell of airplane glue), and created an elaborate model train set. I lived in a fantasy world of World War II fighter pilots and Dave Dawson mystery books.

Soon after my mother died, my dad was out most nights, coming home drunk at 3:00 in the morning. My sister started dating at about the same time, and was gone just about every night of the week. I stayed at home with my brother and a housekeeper named Mrs. Clark, who lived on the third floor of our house. I kept a list of how many nights my dad and sister were out next to a list of how many times I masturbated. Guess who won? I often cuddled in bed with my little brother, who was eight, trying to give him—and myself—some love and affection, until the night my father saw us in bed together and shouted, "Cut that out, son. What are you, queer or something?" I kept secret girlie magazines in a folder behind my headboard. Some of them were in 3D (way ahead of their time) and came with free 3D glasses. The girls were always in bikinis, but their sultry, come hither looks excited my wildest fantasies.

I bumped along at the bottom of my class with no one questioning why I went from an A student to a D student. I spent most of my time staring out the window, my legs bouncing up and down uncontrollably under my desk, unable to concentrate. I even achieved the dubious distinction of falling asleep while in a one-on-one math tutorial. My tutor was Mr. Lane. He sat at his desk correcting papers while I sat opposite him doing equations. I had my elbow on the desk and my head on my hand—asleep. Eventually I flunked my graduation year and had to repeat it. My father jokingly called me a "quarter wit," thinking he was being clever. Even *my* math was good enough to know that a quarter wit was half a half-wit.

As if to prove his point, I started hanging out in Montreal's famous jazz and strip clubs at seventeen, barely missing my father as I snuck back in through an upstairs window at 4:00 AM. To keep me happy, my father gave me a powder blue Austin Healey sports car to drive around in. I imagined myself a budding race car driver and came close to killing myself on numerous occasions. I still have pictures of me flying off bumps in the Healey with all four wheels in the air. By this time I had started drinking. It never occurred to me *not* to drink and drive. If I hadn't had six beers, it was hardly worth getting in the car. I was on a reckless path toward self-destruction.

I became addicted to speed. It became my way of feeling alive. When I wasn't trying to kill myself on the highway, I hurtled down mountainsides at 50 miles per hour in downhill ski races. I became a competitive skier and won races. By the time I was nineteen I was considered a prospect for the Canadian Olympic ski team. In 1958 I sailed by boat to New Zealand so I could teach skiing during the New Zealand winter. For added fun I took up ski jumping—flinging myself off huge jumps and sailing 150 feet through the air. No one taught me how to do it; I just kept going off larger and larger jumps, until I suddenly was flying . . . floating effortlessly through the air.

Skiing gave me much-needed self-confidence, but I still had terrible self-esteem and was desperately insecure about my looks—red hair, freckles all over my body, ugly braces on my teeth, and what I imagined to be a weak chin and a small penis. Years of dentistry helped fix the teeth, jutting my jaw out helped fix the chin, and a few more years of growing helped fix the penis, but in my mind's eye I was still the shy, freckle-faced little kid—even though I had grown into quite a stud. There was a sad and lonely boy inside who craved to be seen and accepted.

Salvation came in the form of a charismatic red-haired Russian Jewish man who also happened to be my sister's boyfriend. His name was Bill Sofin, and he owned a hip pharmacy in downtown Montreal, called The Medical Arts Pharmacy. It wasn't just a pharmacy, but a restaurant and meeting place for Montreal's creative elite. Everyone used to come into the pharmacy, and Bill knew them all—artists, musicians, socialites, doctors, nurses, and the Mafioso. This was the time when Montreal was buzzing with creative activity—Leonard Cohen was writing his best poetry, William Shatner was a young Shakespearean actor, and Zubin Mehta was director of the Montreal Symphony. They all knew and loved Bill, whereas WASPs, like my father, couldn't stand him because he was Jewish. Bill was the opposite of everything my father and WASP culture stood for.

"Peter, Peter!" Bill would call out when he saw me walking into the pharmacy after school. The place was usually packed with customers. My heart would swell with pride when he came out from behind the counter and gave me a big hug.

"Hey, Bill." I'd say, a little self-conscious in my school blazer and tie. Bill was in his early thirties, impeccably turned out in a three piece suit and smelling of Caron after shave lotion. With his wavy red hair and aura of self-confidence, he was unlike anyone I had ever met. Bill was no ordinary pharmacist. He grew up in a poor Jewish family in the East end of Montreal, and through boldness and brashness had become a huge success.

"Peter, how are you? Are you happy?"

"Yeah, Bill. Things are good."

"Come and get something to eat!" He put his arm around my shoulder and escorted me to the back of the restaurant, adjoining the pharmacy.

"Marie," he called to the waitress. "We've got to get this boy something to eat. Give him a club sandwich!"

Bill sat opposite me and gave me his full attention as he asked me about my life, my girlfriends, my studies, and my spiritual life. I felt seen for the first time ever.

"Look I've got this book for you. It's called Siddhartha. You've got to read it. I want you to tell me about it when you do."

I soaked up his attention like a dry sponge. He taught me to respect learning; he listened to my problems; he took me to concerts and French restaurants; he didn't make fun of me when I fell for a Christian evangelist and gave my life to Christ (for a few days, anyway). I could tell him anything, including my worries about getting gonorrhea if I slept with someone (just make sure to pee afterwards, and you'll be OK). Through Bill I fell in love with French food, French music, French literature, French films, and French cafes. I went to hear Edith Piaf sing when she came to Montreal to give a concert. It became my dream to live in Paris.

Several years later, just after I turned seventeen, my dad became engaged to Nancy, a woman he had met at the Hillside Tennis Club. Nancy was thin and athletic, and had permed brown hair and a narrow face that always seemed furrowed in tension. My sister, brother, and I thought she was cold and uncaring, but he married her anyway. She tried hard to gain our acceptance, but didn't stand a chance. No one could replace our mom. Once she moved in—along with her teen-age son—she began to take over and assert her own taste. The rich oriental rugs were replaced with beige wall-to-wall carpet. The soft blue walls were painted a bland white; the curved couches and cozy conversation area gave way to uncomfortable chairs. The fireplace was blocked off permanently because it was too messy.

Night after night I sat in my room at the head of the stairs raging at my dad and stepmother as they argued downstairs in the living room. Unable to concentrate on my homework, I spent most of my time eating chocolate cake (which I kept in a drawer in my desk) or staring out at my neighbor Betty's house, hoping to see her undress in front of her window (which unfortunately never happened).

I could hear the drone of Nancy's tense, nasal voice drifting upstairs. "Wilson, that was a really stupid thing to do."

"Well I tried," he replied in a defeated, monotone voice.

"Well the next time he calls, you stand up for yourself, dammit."

"Yes, dear. I'll tell him."

"No you won't."

"All right, whatever you say dear."

This would be followed by silence, except for the sound of ice clinking in glasses.

Unable to stand listening to them argue night after night, I call my friend Don. "Nancy is driving me crazy. Every night they both get drunk and she nags away at my dad. It's like Chinese water torture. God, how I hate her. I'd like to fucking kill her."

I hear the click of the receiver as the extension is lowered on the other end. With a shock I realize Nancy had been listening to the entire conversation. It took an apology and many years of rebuilding trust before we came to appreciate and love each other.

A few months after dad and Nancy got married, our cottage on the lake caught fire and burned to the ground. All that was left standing was the chimney. Everything was burned to a charred pile of rubble—the colorful hooked rug that my mom had made by hand, the cabinets she had decorated, the antique pine furniture she and my father collected, our skis, our clothes, and our games. All of it was burned to a crisp—along with the happy innocence of childhood.

Much of my life has been played out against these psychic wounds of abandonment and loss. For years I tried to fill myself up in any way I could, seeking happiness everywhere I could grab it. God, how I tried . . . and almost succeeded! I got quite good at it, surfing from one happiness to the next, doing everything I could to avoid facing the underlying pain.

It wasn't until yoga and meditation came into my life, when I was in my thirties, that the only way *out* is *in*. I read the few spiritual books that were available at the time, such as *Autobiography of a Yogi*. All of them said that I needed a teacher to guide me along the way. Again and again I heard the adage, "When the student is ready, the teacher will appear." With starry-eyed idealism, I longed for a guru to lead the way.

All I could do was pray that he would someday appear.

Another old adage is, "Be careful what you wish for."

Meeting the Teacher
Toronto, March 24, 1979

I have not come to teach you, but to love you.
Yogi Amrit Desai

After I begin a disciplined routine of spiritual practices, Lila and my new yoga friends keep dropping hints about their teacher, an Indian guru called Yogi Amrit Desai, who has a small ashram in Pennsylvania. They speak of him with a sense of hushed awe. "You must meet him," Lila asserts. "It's time. You *must* have a teacher to show you the way. You can't do it alone." It just so happens that Yogi Desai is coming to Toronto for a seminar. Lila threatens dire consequences if Fran and I don't attend.

We resist going until the last minute, arriving late for the session. We take our seats in the back of the room, making sure we have an escape route. I glance around in shock. There are about three hundred people in the hall, all dressed in white and facing the front, where a strikingly handsome Indian man, with long black hair down to his shoulders, is sitting on a throne-like chair in meditation. He's wearing an immaculate white robe with gold embroidery around the collar and cuffs. His bare feet are resting on a small pillow. I get the sense of an effortless grace about him, an almost regal presence. He sits in silence, like a statue. Behind him there is a huge photograph of another Indian man, with elaborate flower arrangements on either side. Next to Yogi Desai's chair is a small table with a water glass covered by a neatly folded white handkerchief. There's a hint of incense in the air. It's all very exotic, and at the same time very comforting. I immediately begin to feel more peaceful inside.

After a time he slowly opens his eyes as if awakening from a deep sleep. He appears to be staring off into the distance, his eyes unblinking. Finally his eyes close again and he brings his hands together in prayer position, bowing his head forward in the traditional Indian gesture of greeting. Without thinking, I bring my palms together and bow my head too. He then opens his eyes and begins looking from person to person, stopping to give each one a penetrating stare. I've never experienced this kind of intensity before. Something else is happening here—and it's not just another lecture.

A woman wearing a white sari comes up with a microphone and sits on the edge of the podium. She welcomes everyone and introduces Amrit Desai, referring to him as Gurudev, meaning "beloved teacher". "Gurudev is so happy to be here," she says in a soothing voice. "He would come through rain or sleet or snow to be with you—which often happens in Canada." A ripple of child-like laughter goes through the audience. Gurudev smiles at her and then asks us to close our eyes. Everyone sits in silence while two people bring up a harmonium and place it on a table before him. A few moments later I hear the hypnotic drone of the instrument and Gurudev's voice rising up over it as he chants a long OM. The OM seems to go on forever. I can feel the reverberations of the chant move through me as the sound goes from low to high and back down again. The OMs then transform into sounds I have never heard before. It feels as if a drill is piercing my head. Out of nowhere I hear someone moan, then from another part of the room a piercing scream.

"Keep your eyes closed," Gurudev orders. "Pay attention to your own experience and don't worry about anyone else. Open yourself to the divine energy of Mother Shakti." The OMs continue to rise and fall. It feels as if the vibrations are buzzing through my body. I hear the sound of someone breathing heavily close by, as if they are panting. Another person starts sobbing. Before long there are three hundred people screaming, sobbing and whooping. It's total pandemonium. I try to focus on my experience, but keep getting distracted—especially when one person starts making barking noises.

Gradually the chanting subsides and the noise dies down. There are a few isolated sighs followed by a long silence. I open my eyes and see Gurudev sitting perfectly still, his eyes still closed. Every so often his body jerks involuntarily. *Wow. This is it. This is what I've been longing for!* I feel an overwhelming peace come over me. It's as if I've just made love. I look around the room. Everyone else seems to be in a similar place of peaceful bliss. I turn to Fran who is sitting beside me. "Are you OK?" I whisper.

"I feel a bit shaky and frightened. That energy went through me like a tornado. It felt like every cell was exploding."

I look back towards Gurudev. He is just opening his eyes, looking as if he is having to will himself back into his body. He begins speaking in a slow, deeply relaxed voice. "This is the divine energy of Kundalini Mother Shakti. Every one of us has this evolutionary energy lying dormant at the base of our spine. With the help of the teacher, this energy can be awakened, freeing us from the darkness of ignorance and ego."

People come up to share their experience. "I started crying," one person says, "and my feet started shaking uncontrollably. A rush of power threw me down on the floor. It was like a tremendous electrical force so great my body couldn't contain it. When the shaking finally stopped my whole body was different. Every nerve end seemed to have been stretched and a whole network inside of me was radiating light. Am I losing my mind?"

"No, you're not losing your mind," says Gurudev with a loving smile, "That is the shakti energy manifesting itself in your body. It is a healing energy that purifies your body in mysterious ways. Just allow it to do what it needs to do. It has its own wisdom. Just let it move through you. Don't resist it." Others share similar experiences. One person describes how their whole being was flooded with indescribable bliss. Another says that they saw a brilliant light emanating from Gurudev's face and thought it must be the sun shining on his face through the window. Only then did they realize that there was no window.

Fran and I leave before the session ends, feeling a bit stunned. As we walk back to our hotel I say to her, "That was really something. I feel frustrated though. Nothing much happened to me. I really wanted to be blasted off my feet and knocked unconscious."

"I don't know if you want it," she says. "It scared me half to death."

"I didn't plan to tell you this, but I saw a huge aura around his head."

"So did I!" she exclaims.

That night I wake up at 3:00 am and see what appears to be a life-sized holographic image of Gurudev at the foot of my bed. He is wearing a long purple robe and stands perfectly still. The expression on his face is neutral—neither benevolent nor malevolent. I shift my head to make sure I'm not seeing some kind of shadow, but the figure doesn't move. I blink my eyes and look again. Suddenly it dissolves and is gone. For some reason I'm not surprised to see him there. Finally I go back to sleep again.

Does this mean I have found my teacher? Is this the person who is going to show me the way to the divine bliss that I am longing for?

The Cosmic Orgasm
Toronto, April 5, 1979

Many mistake the intoxicating power of otherworldly charisma for enlightenment.
Adyashanti

Following my meeting with Amrit Desai, I try to get perspective on what I had experienced. Eastern religion is a totally foreign land and I have no reference points. I ask my old friend Jovan to have coffee with me. He's a championship pool player and has earned the nickname "the cosmic snooker" because of his prominent nose and his remarkable prowess with women. He had been to India in his early twenties and is soon regaling me with stories.

"I met this old yogi," Jovan says, taking a bite out of his sandwich. "He took me to a dingy little basement restaurant in Bombay and started to order all these dishes with meat in them. 'Eat!' he said. 'Eat! You'll never get to God through your stomach!'"

"I love it!" I say enthusiastically.

"Yeah," Jovan says. "I was shocked. I had been on a vegetarian diet for years. I was so proud of how pure I was. The yogi started shaking his finger in my face. 'Drop all these concepts around food,' he said. 'They're a hindrance. Drop all concepts around everything! Live your life!'"

"What did you do?"

"Ate meat."

"What happened then?" I ask.

"I went into the jungle and meditated for six weeks. One day I was meditating, when suddenly it felt as if a tree trunk crashed into my head, splitting it wide open. My whole being became flooded in light. I could barely move for days. It was like having a thousand orgasms all at once."

"A thousand orgasms? You're kidding!"

"No, I'm not."

"My God," I say. "This is what I want!"

I am high as a kite, and not just on the espresso. This whole realm of spiritual experiences has my eyes popping. There are so few people to talk to about it.

What about this yogi I just met? I ask. "He had three hundred people in the room all screaming and wailing."

"He's probably practicing a type of yoga called kundalini yoga," Jovan says. "There are masters of kundalini yoga who can transmit shakti with just a touch.

Others do it through mantras, some through a glance. I know of people who have been flattened for hours after being touched by their teacher. There's one guru I met in India who just looked at me and I almost passed out."

"Wow!" I say, taking another sip of espresso, getting higher each moment.

"You have this divine energy. I have it. Everyone has it. It's like a coiled serpent at the base of the spine. When awakened, it moves up the spine and brings higher states of consciousness. If your body isn't pure it can blow out your circuits . . . it can literally fry your brain."

"I don't care. I want it."

I was hungry for spiritual experiences and was certain that this was what enlightenment was all about. If seeing God was like having a thousand orgasms at once, I wanted enlightenment more than ever— even if it meant dying in the attempt.

CHAPTER 4

THE SIREN'S CALL

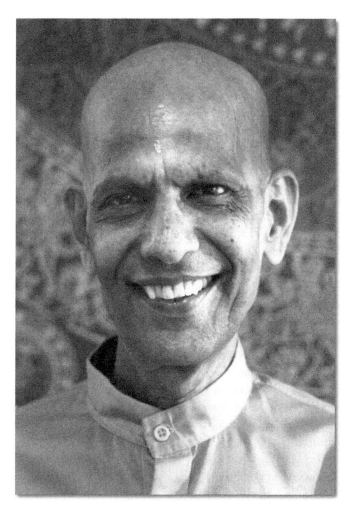

Swami Kripalu (Bapuji)

Why Would Anyone Want This?
Thai Garden Café, Charlottesville, April 19, 2000

Whether you are interested in enlightenment, freedom, you name it, you are interested in happiness without one moment of unhappiness, pleasure without pain—it is the same thing.
U.G. Krishnamurti

It's spring in Charlottesville, Virginia, that magical time of year when a dizzying array of trees and flowers explode in a spectacular display of color—yellow daffodils, pink and white dogwood trees, and shocking purple-pink redbuds. The downtown pedestrian mall is vibrating with life, as locals, tourists, hippies, and students from the University of Virginia shed winter coats and hats to enjoy the warmth and sunshine. Linda and I cross the mall and walk down First Street to the Monsoon Restaurant, where we plan to meet our friends Cynthia and Sarah for lunch. They're already waiting for us at an outdoor table under a huge oak tree. We greet each other with hugs, eager to share our latest adventures on the spiritual journey.

The past twelve months, which brought in the year 2000, have been a wild and rocky ride for all of us. Tumultuous shifts in awareness seem to happen overnight. Our recent discovery of the radical teachings of nonduality has had a profound effect on us. All our traditional views about spirituality have been turned upside down, as we discover the teachings of Eckhart Tolle, Gangaji, Robert Adams, and other teachers of non-duality. We all have the same goal, even though we have different ways of getting there—and that is to awaken from the dream of illusion —permanently, irrevocably, and in this lifetime.

"I must be crazy to want this," Cynthia says after we sit down. Cynthia is a yoga teacher with a dancer's body, a Greta Garbo face and long blond hair. She has a short summer dress on, which barely covers her crossed legs. "Ever since I started to get into these nondual teachings, all the things I used to care about no longer have any meaning."

"I went through the same thing," Linda says. "Nothing seems interesting anymore." Linda is the mystic among us, and has had some extraordinary spiritual experiences. With her blond hair, and slim, runner's body, she and Cynthia could almost pass for twins.

"It's a scary place. There's nowhere to land," muses Cynthia. "I loved to travel, but now I don't care if I go anywhere; I enjoyed great food, but now it doesn't matter what I eat. I was crazy about yoga and now I can take it or leave it—and I'm a yoga teacher!"

"I hope you don't feel that way about sex," I say, looking up from the menu.

Linda jabs me with her elbow. "Peter, we know that all you ever think about is sex. But eventually that will go too."

"Oh no," I cry in mock horror. "Maybe I don't want enlightenment."

Sarah, a psyche nurse with a bubbly personality, jumps in: "There's an old saying that you must want enlightenment as much as a drowning person craves air."

"I'm okay with that," I say, "as long as I don't have to give up sex."

"I always thought awakening would bring me happiness," Cynthia says. "Why else would anyone want it?"

"Well, I've experienced the bliss of being on the other side," Linda says. "After that, being in this world pales by comparison, sex included." Linda is wearing one of her long dresses and is sitting cross-legged on her chair with her shoes off.

Trying to regain my cred, I say, "The problem is that we think of happiness as a way of avoiding pain and finding pleasure. That has nothing to do with the happiness that comes with awakening. That happiness includes both happiness and unhappiness. I remember this beautiful Jesuit priest named Anthony de Mello who said, 'Before enlightenment I used to be depressed: after enlightenment, I continue to be depressed. But there's a difference: I don't care anymore.'"

"That's good," Cynthia laughs, impulsively reaching out to touch my hand with her long, slender fingers. "Now I can feel okay about being miserable."

"Maybe that means all my psych patients are enlightened," Sarah adds, almost ready to jump out of her seat with excitement. "They're all depressed!" Sarah is wearing jeans and a T-shirt. With her petite 4 foot 8 inch figure and pixie haircut, she looks younger than her two teenage sons. She and I were both disciples of Yogi Amrit Desai, and share a similar spiritual background.

"This is crazy," I say. "We've all been at this for twenty years at least. That makes 120 years between us, and not one of us has woken up. There's something wrong with this picture."

"Speak for yourself," Linda laughs. "The problem is that no 'one' can ever get enlightened. The ego can never wake up."

"I don't like that," Cynthia says. "That means I won't be there to enjoy it if I do wake up."

"That's right," Linda says.

"But what if we were to find out that we were awakened right here in this moment?" I ask. "What if sitting around this table—right here, right now—was all there is? Just This!"

"You mean even these smelly buses?" Sarah asks, as a bus roars by belching diesel.

"Yes. That's just what awakening looks like!" Linda says. "Don't you see? There's nothing special about it. Everything is absolutely perfect here in this moment—even the smelly bus."

"Yes, it includes *everything*," I add excitedly. ". . . the bus, the spring flowers, the homeless person on the corner, the dog poop on the sidewalk. It's what is!"

"That's why you have to be crazy to want this," Cynthia laughs, her eyes lighting up.

"Well, I don't care—I'll do whatever it takes." I laugh.

"That's just what's holding you back," Linda says. "*You* can't become enlightened. Enlightenment happens. There's nothing you can do to get there."

I shake my head. "Damn it. That drives me nuts. I'm so used to thinking 'I' can do anything. But 'I' can't awaken! That's frustrating!"

"I still believe you have to have a teacher who can take you there," Sarah says. "You need someone with a higher vibration to push you through. There must be a teacher somewhere that can . . ."

Another bus roars by, spewing fumes and drowning out the conversation.

"Say that again?" Linda asks.

"I said that I'm still looking for someone who can help me awaken. I want to be in bliss." Sarah is what I call a "shakti bunny," craving the high she once experienced during shakti sessions at Kripalu where she would jump up and down shouting, "Yip! Yip! Yip!"

"But what if I told you that you were already awake, right here in this moment?"

"I wouldn't believe you."

"But what if you knew that it was true?"

"Then I'd have to feel OK about smelly buses, wouldn't I?"

"Yes, you've got it!"

The bus smell is suddenly replaced by the delicious smell of Thai food. "I'm starving. Let's get something from the buffet."

"All you think about is food," enjoins Linda.

"And sex."

"Peter, you're such an old horndog," Cynthia laughs.

Some things never change.

In Search of Miracles
Interstate 91, Pennsylvania, July 28, 1979

There are no accidents in this business at all. To the ego, it looks like it's miracles and accidents. There are no miracles, no accidents.
Ram Dass

A few months after meeting Yogi Amrit Desai, Fran and I decide to bite the bullet and make the 550-mile-drive to the Kripalu Yoga Ashram near Reading, Pennsylvania. This is where Yogi Amrit Desai lives when he isn't traveling and giving seminars.

"I don't know why, but I'm high as a kite," I say.

Fran is driving, and I have my bare feet on the dashboard as we cruise down Interstate 81 in our red Jeep Wagoneer. Outside the car window the barren, scarred landscape of central Pennsylvania slowly drifts by. Even a sunny summer morning can't improve its appearance.

"I have a feeling this trip is going to change us forever," Fran says.

"It already has." I resisted all the way. I'd far prefer to spend my time staying at some luxurious country inn, with five course dinners, a bottle of wine, and making love every night.

"You and I have so much to give," she says. "We need to be less selfish. All we do is think of ourselves."

Oh shit, Fran is into her Mother Theresa thing again.

"Maybe you're right." I say.

Fran gives me a meaningful look. "It's no accident that the ashram's motto is 'Love, Service, and Surrender.'"

"Surrender! I can't stand that word! The last thing I want to do is give up my freedom."

"You'll get used to it."

"Let's hear some more Ram Dass," I suggest, trying to change the subject. I insert the cassette from *Be Here Now* where Ram Dass tells the captivating story of meeting his guru, Neem Karoli Baba, who on first meeting appears to be little more than a fat old man wrapped in a plaid blanket. But then he tells Ram Dass things about his mother that no one else knew. It blows Ram Dass's mind.

"I went through every super-CIA-paranoia I've ever had," he says over the car speakers. "My mind just gave up. It burned out its circuitry. There just wasn't a place I could hide in my head about this . . . I started to cry, and I cried, and I cried, and I cried. And I wasn't happy and I wasn't sad. The only thing I could say was it felt like I was home. Like the journey was over."

I'm entranced. Surely Gurudev must know on some level that I'm coming, just as Neem Karoli Baba knew about Ram Dass. Will I end up falling at his feet and crying? Will he greet me by saying, "I've been waiting for you such a long time?" A deep longing wells up in me. I so want this.

At that moment a car drives by with the license plate "OMM 1."

"Did you see that?" I call out to Fran in amazement. "It's a sign!"

I'm in search of miracles.

I also have to pee. The tape ends as we pull off the interstate and stop in front of a dingy restaurant with a neon beer sign in the window. I go inside, cringing at the smell of stale beer and cigarette smoke. *What a dismal place. These people are so unconscious—and I'm so spiritual.* I turn on the light in the bathroom, expecting it to be filthy. To my surprise, it's spotlessly clean. On the wall behind the toilet is a framed photograph of a reclining Buddha in all its glory. This must be another sign!

"Why don't you drive now?" Fran says when I return to the car. I get behind the wheel and pull across the road to a decrepit gas station. It's one of those old stations with a decaying Coca-Cola sign on the wall and a shed roof over the ancient pumps to provide protection from the weather. A guy in bib overalls comes out to pump gas. While the tank is filling he comes up to my window and leans over with a big smile. "You're Peter Mellen from Markdale, Ontario, aren't you?"

My mouth drops open. *What's happening here? How does he know my name?* Startled, I say, "Yes, that's me."

He looks at me and winks . . . then points to a sticker on the windshield with my name and address on it. "Beautiful day, beautiful day," he says.

"Yes, I say," still stunned.

"Every day's a beautiful day. Good to be alive, isn't it?"

My head is swimming as I pull out on the highway for the final leg of our journey. All we did was stop for gas.

"I can't believe it!" I say to Fran, incredulous. We're both laughing hysterically.

"This is even better than Ram Dass!" she laughs.

"Miracles are happening every moment and we don't even know it."

Shangri-La
Summit Station, PA, July 29, 1979

Be here now. Be someplace else later. Is that so complicated?
Jewish Buddhism

After passing through the old steel town of Pottsville, Pennsylvania, we take narrow country roads through green fields until we see a sign saying: KRIPALU YOGA ASHRAM. Underneath are the three words: LOVE, SERVICE, SURRENDER. *Oh no, there's that word 'surrender' again.* I take a deep breath. As Fran and I drive down the lane to the main buildings, several people along the road smile and wave to us. *Uh oh . . . what does this mean? Is this one of those "love-bomb" cults?* We pass by a number of rustic structures, an Olympic size swimming pool that has seen its better days, and a large pond. It looks like an old summer camp, which it probably was. Small signs identify the buildings: *Shanti Bhavan, Muhktidam, Sadhana Mandir.* They must be in Sanskrit. Something tells me this is not your usual summer camp.

We park the car and walk towards the main building, which is a two-story structure with arched entryways. I see a petite woman with white hair walking in our direction.

"Look, it's Lila!"

"Oh mein Got!" she exclaims as she sees us and rushes over.

"Lila—this is a miracle . . ."

"I can't believe that you're the first person we meet!" Fran says excitedly, giving her a hug. "We just drove in."

"How *vun*derful you're here," Lila says in her German accent, "Jai Bhagwan!"

"Jai . . . what?" I say.

"Jai Bhag*wan*," she repeats. "It means I honor the divine within you. That's the way everyone greets each other here. It's like *namaste*."

"Oh."

"Come. Come. I vill take you to the desk."

At the reception desk she introduces us to some of the residents. They all have Sanskrit names and the names go in one ear and out the other. The men are dressed in white trousers and white shirts, and the women are wearing white saris.

"Jai Bhagwan," they say with bright smiles and shiny eyes, as they bring their hands into prayer position.

"Jai Bhagwan," Fran and I repeat, as we awkwardly imitate them. *Have we landed on some other planet?*

We quickly discover that the women are called "sisters," and the men "brothers." They all look very holy. In contrast, I feel like an unwashed street bum after drinking half a bottle of wine with last night's steak dinner. Surely they can sense my dense vibrations—I feel like the bottom of a dirty ashtray.

"Hi, my name is Taponidhi," one of the brothers says with a warm smile. "I'll show you around." He is a good-looking man in his twenties with warm, kind eyes.

"Tapon . . .?" I ask, bewildered.

"You can call me Tap," he says, putting me at ease. "It can be a bit confusing here at first. You'll get used to it."

We walk past the small lake to the newly opened Health Center, located in an old farmhouse. Our Spartan room is on the second floor, with brown paneling on the wall, an overhead light on the ceiling, and two narrow beds with thin white towels and washcloths neatly folded on the skimpy comforters. The bathroom is down the hall.

"At least we don't have to sleep in a dormitory," I whisper to Fran.

Later we discover that we've been given the most palatial quarters in the place, and that most people sleep in the barn or tiny, cramped partitioned areas that serve as offices during the daytime. Tap tells us the day's schedule and asks us to dress modestly, especially around the pool. "The residents live a celibate lifestyle and it would be distracting for them to see someone in a bikini."

But I like bikinis!

On our way back to the main building we pass by a modest little cottage. "This is where Gurudev stays when he's here," Tap says.

"Is he here?" Fran asks expectantly.

"No, he just left for Toronto."

"But we just came from Toronto!" I say, trying to hide my disappointment. "Do you know when he'll be back?"

"No . . . it could be a week."

I'm crushed. After my lofty expectation of Gurudev waiting to greet me personally upon arrival, I may not see him at all.

That evening we attend our first satsang in the meditation hall. As we enter the dimly lit hall, I can scarcely believe my eyes. It is pandemonium—a sea of people, all dressed in white, are standing up facing the front of the room. They have their eyes closed and are chanting, some making strange movements with their hands and others swaying back and forth. The women are on one side and the men on the other. At the front of the room is a dais with a throne-like chair on it. Instead of a person in the chair, there is a huge picture of Gurudev. He appears to be looking straight at me.

PA BAMM, PA BAMM, PA BAMM, comes the sound of the drums—so loud I can actually feel the vibration in my belly.

Hare Ram, Hare Ram, Hare Ram someone chants into a microphone.

Hare Ram, Hare Ram, Hare Ram, everyone responds in unison.

The rhythm builds up faster and faster and soon everyone is jumping up and down clapping their hands together overhead.

"Jai Gurudev!" someone shouts out over the sound of the chanting.

Someone starts shrieking.

Oh my God, where am I? Is this some kind of a cult? What's going on here? Is it all because they can't have sex? I try to join in, closing my eyes and clapping my hands to the rhythm. Being musically challenged, I miss the beat, as usual.

Just when I think the chant will never end, it slowly winds down. I can hear heavy breathing and many sighs as everyone sits back down on the floor.

A woman in a sari comes up and sits on the edge of the dais, taking up the microphone. After a few moments of silence she says, "I'd like you to stand up and form two separate circles, one for the brothers, one for the sisters."

Oh no! I have to get up and participate! I find my place in a circle of brothers.

"Now turn to a partner and look into their eyes."

I look at the person next to me, a tall, good-looking man with red hair and blue eyes. He gazes directly into my eyes without blinking. I want to turn away in embarrassment. *Oh God. Maybe he'll think I'm gay!*

Someone with a guitar starts singing the words of a Sufi song:

You are the light,

Shining out in the world.

Open your heart and receive who I am . . .

As I turn from partner to partner, looking into each person's eyes, I feel my heart opening up. It feels like a heavy armor, which has been there for years and years, is falling away.

At the end of satsang, everyone bows down before the picture of Gurudev. *I'm not ready for that,* I tell myself, noticing that I'm the only one not bowing. Yet, I feel a deep sense of peace that is totally unfamiliar.

Five days later I've transformed from an exhausted and stressed out workaholic into a loose and relaxed yogi. I've gotten up at 4:30 each morning to jog before the sun comes up. Competitive as ever, I join the fastest group, and soon regret it. I puff and pant, struggling to keep up with the lean, young residents. Inspiring us onward, the leader calls out, "Visualize the prana flowing through your body. Look at the beauty of the sky! Imagine Gurudev jogging beside you!" *What is this, some kind of foreign legion?* Before breakfast I've not only stretched and run, but also done an hour of yoga and a swim. I feel great!

Mornings are spent in workshops, afternoons resting or having a massage. I learn about diet and nutrition, try biofeedback, and attend a massage workshop. Instead of my usual steak dinners, I have some rice and salad. Wednesday is dessert night, and the residents act like excited kids at a birthday party. I feel like

I've shed not only pounds, but also years of anxiety and stress. I try to think back to when I last felt this way. It was when I was ten years old! My eyes are clear, my face is soft and relaxed, and my body feels like rubber. Am I the same person who walked in here just a week ago? Soon I find myself talking about the "outside world" as if it were some far-off place. I watch the new arrivals, their faces worried and anxious. *Boy, do they look stressed out*, I think, with more than a touch of superiority.

I spend time with the residents, mostly young people in their twenties. It's a totally new experience for me to be with men and women who do not see everything in terms of sex and status. It really does feel like I'm with "brothers" and "sisters," sharing my feelings with no other agenda than being present and open. They appear to be truly living a life of "love, service, and surrender," not as serious and solemn monks, but with a sense of joy and laughter. They possess a childlike innocence that I have never seen before.

The word is out that Gurudev and his teacher Bapuji will be arriving tomorrow. I sit on a bench by the small lake as the sun goes down, reflecting on how much I have opened up over the past few days. People are quietly walking by on their way to satsang. They smile and acknowledge me as they pass, without any need for small talk. By now I recognize most of them; they already feel closer than my own family. I see that I wasn't ready to meet Gurudev five days ago. First I had to clean up my toxic body and empty my mind of all its garbage. I was so closed down emotionally I would not have recognized a spiritual teacher if I saw one.

For some reason I think of the 1939 film *Lost Horizon*, where the American diplomat Conway and several others stumble into a hidden valley in the Himalayan Mountains after their plane crashes. It is weeks before Conway is ready to meet the mysterious sage who is spiritual head of the community. During that time he discovers a world where people live happily, free from quarreling and anger. As I look around me it feels as if I've stumbled into a very similar kind of paradise, where everyone is young and healthy, living in peace and love. Taking a last look at the peaceful pond with the ducks swimming by, I stand up and walk over for evening satsang.

A Great Indian Saint
Summit Station, PA, August 2, 1979

The key to your own heart is locked in the heart of others.
Swami Kripalu (Bapuji)

Today is the day Gurudev and Bapuji return from Toronto. Fran and I are ripe. Boy, are we ripe. We even smell ripe, having doused ourselves with patchouli, the scent that Yogi Desai uses. Of course, we now refer to him as "Gurudev."

We're sitting on a bench overlooking the lake when Lila rushes up saying, "Come! Come! You must meet Bapuji." We hurriedly walk over to a crowd of people gathered in front of one of the buildings. "They say an enlightened master like him comes along only once every five hundred years!" Lila says as we stride along. "Zees is such a blessing. You can't imagine."

"Lila, I don't even feel worthy to be in his presence!" Fran says.

"Posh," replies Lila. "You wouldn't be here if you weren't ready to meet him. Do you know he spent twenty years in silence?"

"Twenty years?" I ask incredulously. I can barely stay in silence for five minutes.

"Ya, in India he has tens of thousands of followers. It's a miracle to have him here in America."

"Tens of thousands?" I ask, totally impressed.

"He is one of India's greatest saints."

"This is amazing," Fran says. "I can't believe I'll get to see him."

Lila nods her head. "Ya, it's a miracle."

Fran and I find out that Bapuji is a common term of affection meaning "beloved father." Bapuji's more formal name is Swami Kripalu—meaning "the compassionate one." Both the ashram and Kripalu Yoga are named after him. Lila tells us that Bapuji came to America four years ago at the invitation of Yogi Desai.

I discover from a little booklet put out by Kripalu that Bapuji had a mysterious guru named Dadaji, meaning "dear grandfather." One day, when Bapuji was nineteen, he felt such intense separation from God that he was considering suicide. While praying in a temple, a man came up to him and said, "Do not despair. I am here to help you." It turns out that the man was Dadaji, a guru who had an ashram in Mumbai. He invited Bapuji to visit his ashram, and later to become his student.

My heart skips a beat when I read how Dadaji had yogic powers or *siddhis*. There were stories of his bilocating—being in two places at the same time. Apparently Bapuji was walking with Dadaji one night, when on the very same evening others insisted that Dadaji had never left his meditation room. *This is just like the stories in Yogananda's book*, I think. *I'm finally getting my miracles!* Bapuji was with Dadaji for fifteen months, when he mysteriously disappeared.

Ten years later Bapuji was invited to see a huge stone column of black meteoric rock that some farmers had dug up from a field. It was over five feet tall and had the figure of a yogi sitting in meditation carved into it. When Bapuji saw the statue he was overwhelmed. The face carved in the statue was none other than the face of Dadaji, his guru! According to legend, the statue was an image of Lord Lakulish, an incarnation of Lord Shiva himself.

Suddenly there is a powerful blast of the conch horn, heralding the arrival of Gurudev and Bapuji. A maroon Buick turns into the drive, and moves in slow procession past all the waving residents and disciples. As it pulls up before the small house, the sounds of *Jaya Jaya Bapuji, Jaya Jaya Bapuji* reach a crescendo. Everyone is clapping their hands in rhythm (except me, of course). The drums are pounding out *PA-BAHM, PA-BAHM, PA-BAHM* in a fierce tempo.

Gurudev gets out, followed by two Indian swamis. With great deference he opens the passenger door and helps Bapuji out of the car. A slight figure dressed in the ochre robes of a swami emerges. Bapuji clasps his hands together in prayer position and walks slowly down the petal-strewn path with Gurudev and the other swamis following behind. He smiles and nods at each person as he delicately takes the flowers offered to him. He lightly taps one or two devotees on the head in blessing, his brown eyes twinkling. He wears an ochre knitted hat over his shaved head, even though it is a hot summer day. Although he's very frail, there is a force that emanates from him that I have never experienced before.

Lila grabs us both by the arm and pushes us up to the front of the crowd just as Bapuji sits down. A chair has been placed outside the entrance to the house and everyone gathers round. He remains silent, seemingly off in some other world. There is more chanting as the senior residents come forward to put garlands over his head. Bapuji then writes on a slate indicating that he wants Gurudev to tell a story. It's a story about a guru, a disciple and a hundred-foot-long sword. As Gurudev translates, Bapuji silently mimics the main points of the story. Everyone bursts into hysterical laughter at his playful expressions. There is a transparency and innocence about him that has me totally mesmerized.

I close my eyes, trying to sense what it means to be in the presence of this holy man. The only way I can describe it is like falling into a void of silence. It is as if time has stopped and I am wrapped in a cocoon, with the rest of the world far, far away. I open my eyes and feel my heart opening up to a love that I have never known. Tears stream down my cheeks. I feel as if I've come home.

The Die is Cast
Summit Station, PA, October 16, 1980

A courageous disciple, armored with the determination never to displease his teacher even at the cost of his life, so stable-minded that he is never shaken by immediate circumstances, who serves his teacher without caring for his own health or survival and obeys his every command without sparing himself at all—such a person will be liberated simply through his devotion.
Patrul Rinpoche

"I have not come to teach you," Gurudev says, "but to help you forget; to help you experience the universal language of love. It's the love that has the power to transform you. Love makes you fearless. Let that fearlessness work through you."

There are twenty of us squeezed into a small room, sitting on the floor around Gurudev. Fran and I have been invited to attend a darshan for his close disciples. This is considered a great honor—*darshan* means "to see" or to be in the presence of a holy person. It's unbearably hot and my knees are aching, but I'm taking in every word as if it is coming from the mouth of God. The truth of what he is saying resonates through my entire being. *The disciples sitting around Christ must have felt like this!*

"Usually when we speak of love, we are speaking of nothing more than attachment," Gurudev continues, looking directly at me, "but the love for the guru is a love that goes beyond attachment. The guru needs nothing from you. When you become totally absorbed in the guru, you become one with him, and this activates your own inner guru. Then you recognize that love is within you. When this happens all attachment dissolves and you enter into the realm of pure and non-attached love."

My eyes open wide in astonishment. *These words are the Truth!* Everyone around me is nodding and smiling as he talks. I glance over at Fran. She has a look of fierce concentration. Our comfortable little world is being turned upside down.

Over the next year we make numerous trips to the ashram. Gurudev asks us to make a documentary film on Bapuji, which we take as a great privilege (even though it costs us $20,000 of our own money to make it). But how often do you get to film a saint that comes along every five hundred years? During the filming we are the first people ever to be with Bapuji when he does his meditation practices. Normally he lives in complete seclusion. We also spend hours with Gurudev and his family, gaining insights into his daily life that few people get to see. As we become more involved with the community we keep double-checking with each other to make sure we are not joining some cult. We use all our powers of discernment—after all, we both have Ph.D.'s—and have seen a lot of the world. We are going in with eyes wide open.

By now the ashram feels like the home—and the ideal family—we never had. Every time we visit, the residents greet us warmly. We find that our room has been lovingly prepared with an anonymous love-note on our dresser. When we leave to drive back to Canada, we discover that someone has left flowers on the dashboard of our car. Again and again we are touched by their kindness and sincerity, which appear to be totally genuine. We never have experienced love in this way—we didn't know it existed on the planet! It finally comes to a point where we want to give up our film business and move in as residents. The more we get to know the community in depth, the more impressed we are by its ethical values. What else could we ever do in our life that could possibly have more meaning? What else could we do that would bring more happiness to our lives?

After the screening of the *Path of Love*—our half hour documentary on Bapuji—Fran and I are told that Gurudev has invited us to a private darshan. We are ushered into an immaculate room that is almost devoid of furniture, except for a few pillows and a low table. It serves as a meeting room during the day and Gurudev's bedroom at night. We find him seated on a cushion on the floor, wearing a white robe that has just been freshly pressed. He looks like he has just come out of a two-hour massage (which he probably has). There is a palpable silence in the room. The air is filled with the comforting smell of incense. Sitting to Gurudev's right is Uma, the main administrator of the ashram, wearing a traditional Indian sari.

As Fran and I sit cross–legged before him, Gurudev envelopes us in a warm smile. "I'm so happy to see you both," he says. "I've heard so much about you."

"This has become our home," I say. "We were considering taking a sabbatical to see other teachers, but now I'm not so sure."

"If you want to find water," Gurudev says in a soft, purring voice, "you don't dig a lot of small holes everywhere; you dig one hole and you dig it deep. You must stay single-minded on the path and not be distracted by other teachings."

"Ramakrishna, the spiritual energy is awakening in you," Uma says. "You need to be close to the guru." (I am no longer referred to as Peter; Fran and I were both initiated a few months ago. Fran's spiritual name is Ramadevi, meaning "servant of Rama"; mine is Ramakrishna, the name of one of India's most beloved saints.) "You must ease into it," she says. "You're so fervent I know you would crucify yourself for Gurudev if you could."

"Gurudev didn't call you Ramakrishna for nothing," Ramadevi adds proudly.

"Yes," Gurudev says. "You should come and live at the ashram. Find a house close by, something simple."

It becomes apparent the darshan is over.

Uma signals us to come forward and bow at Gurudev's feet. Our hearts open wide as we bow down before him. "You are both so beautiful," he says, as he pats us on the head like two puppy dogs. "I love you so much."

When we step outside from the meeting, our heads are spinning. "What have we done?" Fran asks. "I don't know if I can do this." She starts crying.

"I don't know if I can either. Damn it, I don't want to eat off lime green plastic trays for the rest of my life. I don't want to get up at 4:30 every morning. I don't want to live in a tiny room and have to walk fifty yards to a smelly bathroom!" I feel like I've been kicked in the stomach. A huge part of me knows that I want to move into the ashram, but another part of me is horrified. Somehow I know that I have no choice in all this. The die has been cast and there is no turning back.

A few months later, we are loading the moving van for our move to the United States. One night I have a dream where I enter a room shaped like a small rotunda. I hear Gurudev saying, "This is your home now. Go wherever you want!" Standing on the other side of the room is Gurudev's teacher Bapuji. I bring my hands to prayer position and say "Jai Bhagwan." Bapuji returns the greeting, and there is a sudden moment of recognition. He comes up to me with a look of total love in his eyes and hugs me. He seems so light, as if there is no one there. A gut-wrenching cry wells up from some place deep inside me. Tears pour down my face and I notice that he is crying too.

We drive up the long laneway, leaving the waterfall for the last time.

CHAPTER 5

TAKING THE LEAP

Peter, Yogi Desai & Fran

Down and Dirty
Mt. Ayr Farm, November 1, 2003

I'm at Two with Nature
Woody Allen

Before long the animals have become an integral part of my life. I come to appreciate how nearly every human on the planet had an intimate link with animals and nature for thousands of years. Today, most of us have never seen or touched a goat, a chicken, or a cow, unless it's in a petting zoo. We prefer our nature safely contained in Saran Wrap.

I still have a lot to learn. My newest challenge is that our heifer Jenna is about to give birth to her first calf. Exactly two hundred and eighty-three days ago Jenna was artificially impregnated by the local vet. Jenna is a black and white heifer who weighs about 1200 pounds (by now I've learned that a heifer is young female cow who has not yet had a calf). If my timing is right, Jenna is due today or tomorrow. In preparation, I've herded her into the barn with the help of my two Australian Shepherds (who more often than not, herd her in the wrong direction). Now all I need do is wait. The first birth is always the most difficult. Both the heifer and her newborn can easily die if the calf gets stuck coming out.

Every few hours I go down to the barn to check on her. Nothing yet. As the afternoon wears on, our friend Judy unexpectedly drops by for a visit. Together with Linda, we sit in the great room of the farmhouse having tea. Linda is lying on the couch feeling lousy, but to me she still looks beautiful, with her sweet smile, intelligent blue eyes, and blond hair smoothed out over the arm of the couch.

"Your cow is going to have a baby?" Judy asks in alarm, once I tell her what is going on. "Can I stay and watch?

"Of course," I say with a smile, noticing her shiny leather boots, designer jeans, and new LL Bean jacket. "I may really need your help . . . so far I haven't been able to get hold of the vets."

"But I don't know anything. I've never seen an animal give birth—I grew up in an apartment in New York!" Judy has become a close friend over the past months. She and her husband Jack, also a New Yorker, live in a stunning geodesic dome about thirty miles away.

"If it's any consolation, I've never seen a cow give birth either!"

"I wish I could be there too," Linda moans. "I pulled three calves from my Jersey cow when I had my farm. Now I have this damned illness. I'm so nauseated right now I can't even stand up." For years Linda used to teach all day, milk her cow morning and night, then run five miles to relax. Now she has to spend most of her time lying flat on her back.

"Don't worry," I say. "You can coach us from up here at the house."

The next time I check on Jenna, she's in full labor. Her vulva is dilated and she is pacing anxiously around her stall. I call the vet, and to my dismay, find out that he is off in another part of the county. I try another vet. It's Sunday afternoon and she is gone for the day. *Oh no. I'm going to have to do this myself! What if she dies?* With Judy's help, I collect together a few buckets of warm water and the old tool kit which has all my birthing supplies in it. It's already pitch dark and about 40 degrees when we take them down to the barn. The interior of the barn is dimly lit by a few bare bulbs. Judy stays safely on the other side of the strong walls of the pen while I step through the gate. I'm greeted by the strong smell of cow urine, manure, and straw. Jenna is lying on her side, breathing heavily.

"Oh my God, there's a big balloon coming out of her behind!" Judy cries out.

"Look, there are its feet in the sack—it's all happening so quickly!"

Judy and I watch Jenna panting and struggling to push her calf out. I softly give her words of encouragement, "Good girl, Jenna. You're doing fine. Keep pushing. That's it."

"Is there something wrong?" Judy asks. "Why doesn't she push harder?"

"I don't know." Fear rises up as I realize that I've been overconfident in thinking I could breeze through this myself. My arrogance could cause this beautiful animal to die.

We wait as the minutes slowly tick by and become an hour. After two hours she is still pushing. Her whole body arches up with the effort. It's horribly painful to watch. The hooves have not moved.

I become even more alarmed when I read the section on birthing in my how-to book: *If nothing happens in two hours, you need to intervene or the calf may suffocate.*

Finally I say to Judy, "I'm going to have to try and help her. Bring me the obstetrical chains. They're in the kit. Don't forget to sterilize them."

"How do I do that?"

"Dip them in hydrogen peroxide. The bottle and an empty bucket are right next to you."

I strip off my jacket and feel the cold night air on my skin. I slip on long latex surgical gloves that come up to my shoulders, then wash Jenna's vulva with warm, soapy water. Taking the scalpel, I cut into the sac, which makes a swoosh as the watery liquid pours out. Judy hands me the chains. They are lightweight and strong, less than half an inch in diameter—but strong enough to hook to a tractor during a really tough birth. I wrap them around the two protruding hooves. But as I pull on the chains, they slip off. *Damn. I need to get them further down the calf's forelegs. I'm going to have to go in.* I slide my gloved hands along the forelegs until they are deep inside her vagina; the pressure on my arms is astonishing. I feel around for the calf's head and can make out the snout. Thank God it's presenting correctly. I attach the chains to the legs and they hold. Sitting on the ground, I start to pull on the chains. Jenna—all 1200 pounds of her—starts thrashing up and down in pain.

"C'mon sweetheart. You can do it!"

I pull even harder, bracing my feet against her hips for leverage. I try to time my pulling with Jenna's breathing. From the other side of the gate, Judy cheers me on saying over and over, "Oh my God. I've never seen anything like this!"

Jenna pulls me forward on my behind into a pile of manure and urine. I can feel it oozing through my jeans. *What am I doing here? A former academic, city boy, and peace-loving yogi up to his ass in shit, trying to birth a calf? Not only that, I'm being helped by a New Yorker who knows even less than I do? This is crazy!*

"Push!" I yell. "C'mon Jenna, push!"

Suddenly the calf's forelegs start to slide out of Jenna's vulva, and then the head appears. With all my might I pull back on the chains. In one momentous pull, the head, then the shoulders, and the rest of the body, slides out. It lies on its side, all wet and slippery, with its grey tongue hanging out. "We did it, Jenna. What a girl you are! I'm so proud of you!"

"I don't believe this!" cries Judy in amazement.

I see that it's a big black bull calf and that it's breathing. It must weigh over one hundred pounds. But it's exhausted and needs help getting to the teat. Jenna lies there ignoring her baby. She seems to have no idea what to do. After a few minutes she struggles to get to her feet, her huge bulk filling the stall. She starts pacing around in distress, wanting nothing to do with this strange thing that has come out of her. *This is bloody dangerous. She could crush me against the wall!* Using all my strength, I press Jenna against the wall to keep her still, and pull the calf over to her. Warm milk starts squirts out all over me as I try to get the nipple into its mouth. After a few frustrating attempts, it takes the teat. Jenna lets out a loud "moo" and starts licking her newborn with her rough tongue. What a relief.

Late into the night, Judy and I walk back up to the farmhouse under a starlit sky. I feel exhilarated. How extraordinary to be able to help bring this new life into the world.

"We did it! She had her calf!" I cry out to Linda as we step back into the warmth of the great room. The dogs rush up excitedly, smelling my clothes with great interest.

"It was amazing!" Judy exclaims. "I've never seen anything like it. Peter pulled out this huge calf."

I lean over to the couch and give Linda a kiss.

"I'm so proud of you," Linda says with a big smile. "You're a real farmer now."

The Path of Love
Kripalu Yoga Ashram, Sumneytown, Pennsylvania, January 1981

Look at every path closely and deliberately. Try it as many times as you think
necessary. Then ask yourself and yourself alone one question . . . does this path have
a heart? If it does, the path is good. If it doesn't, it is of no use.
Carlos Casteneda

It seems like a lifetime ago, when on a cold, gray January morning in 1981, my wife Fran, our 13-year-old son Peter, and I crossed the slush-covered Rainbow Bridge over the Niagara River to US customs. We had just sold our film business, taken Peter out of school, and left behind our magical home next to a forty-foot waterfall in order to move to the United States. I'm nervous, anxious, and exhausted as we pull up to the line of booths marking U.S. Customs. I'm about to leave the country I grew up in and become a resident alien in the U.S.—that is, if they let me in.

I certainly feel like an "alien" as the customs officer directs us over to the foreboding inspection area. Two polite officials inspect our papers and look in (and under) our car. Our thirteen-year-old son Peter is in the back, along with two cats, several houseplants, our films, suitcases, and several ounces of gold (which we're smuggling in). He jokingly whispers that he's going to tell the customs officers about the gold, almost giving us a heart attack. After a cursory look, the inspectors determine we're not kidnapping our son, and wave us on. We've done it! We're in!

We get on I 90 East, heading for the original Kripalu ashram, which is located in Sumneytown, a small town located northwest of Philadelphia. Four hundred miles later we pull up to our destination, where we're greeted by a small oval sign with blue letters on a white background: "Kripalu Yoga Ashram: Love, Service, Surrender." It's a sobering reminder of why we're turning our backs on our home, our friends, and life as we knew it. We are at the peak of our careers—I am forty-one; Fran is thirty-eight.

There are about sixty residents living at the ashram, tucked into four or five buildings on a wooded, hillside property. The two buildings nearest the road are old Pennsylvania stone farmhouses, where the "sisters" live. Further up the hill there is a dorm building, built in seventies-style architecture, which houses the "brothers." Gurudev and his family live in a modest house hidden in the woods. Near the top of the hill there is a small cottage where Bapuji lives in seclusion. The residents live a strictly celibate lifestyle. Many of them work in the community and pay a monthly rent to live in the ashram. Others are on full-time staff and are paid $1 per month, which they usually spend on chocolate. Every month they go before Ashvin, the accountant, and ask (or plead) for bare necessities, such as toothpaste or a new pair of underwear. Their life is devoted to serving the guru and to their own inner spiritual transformation. This is where Fran and I—jet setting filmmakers, authors, and former professors—are choosing to live.

Once we arrive, followed by a huge Allied moving van, we unload all our belongings— furniture, clothing, books, and stereos, computers—into a rustic, poorly heated log cabin next to the ashram. I'm horribly embarrassed to see all the stuff we've brought with us, knowing how little the residents have. The reason Fran and I can make the move is that she has a modest income from a trust that allows us to live independently. We dedicate our services for free to the community. Our quaint little cabin is luxurious compared to the miniscule rooms the residents live in—a small living room with a loft upstairs (where Peter sleeps), and a bedroom off to the side (where Fran and I sleep on the floor). Out front there is a small pond and woods on three sides. The fact that the cabin is freezing in winter lets me at least feel that I'm experiencing some hardship. I'm desperate to be accepted by the residents as an equal. After taking a day or two to settle in, we meet with our coordinator Jyoti, and symbolically turn our lives over to the guru, requesting that we be treated like any other ashram resident.

Once the glamour and excitement of moving in wears off, I feel like I've jumped from the lifestyles of the rich and famous into a Trappist monastery. My past ceases to exist. No one knows or cares about my accomplishments. All the possessions and status symbols I've accumulated over the years mean nothing. As a freelance writer and filmmaker, I've had the luxury of choosing how I spend my time. Now I'm required to keep a time chart of how I spend every fifteen minutes of my day (so that I can serve the Guru more effectively). Every week I meet with Jyoti, my coordinator, to go over the time sheets and discuss how to deepen my commitment to Gurudev and my practices even more. Most of my time is spent working as a flunky for the senior administrator, Pat Sarley (Dinabandhu), helping to set up a fund-raising plan for expansion. Fran and I are appointed "coordinators" for the campaign because they want symbolic figureheads who have status in the "outside world." There are rumors afoot that the ashram may be putting in an offer on an old Jesuit Seminary near Lenox, Massachusetts. My job is to research the possibility of getting grants and to find out how other non-profits go about fundraising.

The first few months are unbearably hard. I feel like I'm being put through a washing machine. Previously when we came to visit, everyone stopped what they were doing and greeted us with open arms. Now I feel like I'm wallpaper. To the administrators, I'm a raw "newbie," and am only being tolerated because I offer credibility for potential donors (and they need to find something useful for me to do). I go through days of feeling lonely, dejected, and self-blaming. To top it all off, Gurudev is in India, Bapuji is in seclusion, and I can't find inspiration from their physical presence. When Fran and I made our film on Bapuji, called *The Path of Love*, we had ready access to both of them. We were the "chosen" ones. Now we're at the bottom of the totem pole.

Days begin at 4:30 AM, when I get up to do yoga and meditation—that's after a run in the dark with twenty other "brothers" beforehand. This is followed by a bare bones breakfast eaten in silence while sitting on the floor of the old farmhouse. Starting promptly at 7:15am, I begin my daily "seva," or selfless service, which goes until 4:45 PM, with a break for lunch. Six nights a week I attend satsang with the other residents.

Even though Fran and I are married, we are "encouraged" to refrain from sex.

"I can't stand this brahmacharya thing," I complain to Fran, as I lie in bed staring at the ceiling. "I'm going crazy not having sex—and I can't even hug people. This is nuts."

"Well, Gurudev says that this is the only way to advance on the path," Fran says, her back to me. "You have to channel the sexual energy up through the spine."

"Oh, that's just something someone made up."

"What's more important to you—having sex or getting enlightened?"

"Having sex."

"You have to give it a chance."

"But it's been weeks!" I sigh in exasperation. "I feel like I have a fire in my groin."

"Good. That's the tapas—the spiritual fire that burns away impurities, Fran says with the conviction of a convert. "You have to stick with it. Why else did we move down here?"

"I don't know if I can," I groan. Finally exhaustion overwhelms me and I fall asleep.

The next day I make a promise not to masturbate for the next month, which is like losing my best friend. What do I do with all this energy? Channel it? Sublimate it? Repress it? I've been at the mercy of it for thirty years. If I can just channel the energy up through my body, perhaps I can blast through and have that mystical experience I long for.

Some people take to this yogic lifestyle like a duck to water.

I don't.

I go into a desperate spin of craving for sex, food, chocolate, a new car, a more comfortable house—you name it. All my hang-ups come flying up to the surface—my need for approval, my ambitions, my compulsions. The "touch fast" between brothers and sisters drives me crazy. I can't even get a good hug without feeling guilty. Maybe I should have gone to Rajneesh's ashram in India, where I could be having orgies every day. Fran is so busy being a "good disciple" that we might as well be brother and sister. On top of it, our son Peter is having a terrible time adjusting to a new school, new friends (or no friends), and a life where we are away most of the time doing "seva." He starts to have difficulty with his grades. We're always on his case about homework. His only sense of normalcy is when we take him to the mall once a week for dinner out and a movie.

The schedule is relentless. Before long I'm so exhausted I can barely get through the day. I try to remember what Gurudev says, "Don't push yourself in life. Let your life be effortless. Don't try to change things overnight."

I'm a slow learner.

You may well ask (as some people did, including my worried family), "What sort of nut are you, giving up a comfortable life, a successful career—and sex—to get up at 4:30 AM, work all day, then scrub pots and pans at night? And please don't say that you're doing all this without getting paid for it?" It's true. I don't even get the $1 per month that permanent residents get. What I am getting is the chance to live close to the guru, do spiritual practices, practice loving service, and surrender to God—all in the hope of finding the true happiness that comes with enlightenment. When I see the pure love and bliss that emanates from Bapuji, I know that is what my heart wants more than anything else.

The months go by and I begin to let up on myself a bit. Fran eases up on herself too, and even agrees to make love a few times each month (now I can live again—but it did feel great to have that tingly feeling all over my body twenty-four hours a day). We get into the routines, and feel as if we're making a contribution. Gurudev comes back from India, and we once again spend time with Bapuji.

According to Bapuji the very heart of our practice is love and compassion. This love, in its purest expression, is a non-attached love without judgment, without expectations, without boundaries. It expresses itself as a natural overflow of an open heart. Each member of the Kripalu community attempts to live by this spiritual value, showing their love for each other and the world-family through compassionate action. As Bapuji says, "The key to your own heart is locked in the heart of others." I'm deeply touched to see how the residents express this love towards us every day—whether it's Nerendra coming by to help cut firewood, Devananda helping Peter with his homework, or Sukanya sharing her friendship as we work together on a book about Gurudev.

The more I drop my fears and open to love in my own life, the more the love comes back—especially to the one person I'm most judgmental about: myself. I begin to experience a level of self-acceptance I've never known before. It feels like I'm being held in the arms of the Mother. I've longed to be in the presence of this love my entire life but never dreamed it possible—it feels like heaven on earth. As time goes on, even our son Peter begins to flourish with all the attention given to him by the Kripalu family. He loves all the celebrations the residents manage to cook up, whether it's volleyball on the front lawn, an impressive fireworks display on July 4th, or a Halloween extravaganza. Much to my relief, he finally sees why we chose to move here. If there is a path with heart, this is it. How could anyone *not* want to devote their life to it?

The culmination of this extraordinary expression of love takes place every Sunday when Bapuji comes out of seclusion to bless the entire family. Dressed in our best whites, we gather in the small chapel and prepare ourselves for his arrival by chanting songs of devotion. At exactly 2:00 PM (Bapuji is always punctual) Gurudev drives Bapuji down from his cottage on the hill to the chapel. He is helped up the steps by the two swamis who take care of him, and makes his way slowly down the aisle, receiving flowers from devotees as he passes. Remaining in silence, he takes his seat and signals for the chanting to continue. As he sits absorbed in meditation, we come before him one by one for his blessing, bringing an offering of fruit, flowers, or a note. When we bow down at his feet, sometimes he has his eyes closed and doesn't show any response. At other times he may simply raise a hand in blessing. Or he might playfully tap one of us on the head with a wink and a smile. What astonishes me is the immense aura of silence that envelopes him. It is as if there is no one there—only love.

When the darshan is over, I stand outside the chapel in the warm sunlight, tears of gratitude pouring down my face. I didn't know such joy existed.

The Naked Monk and the Path of Austerity
Mt. Pavagadh, Gujurat Province, India, February 9, 1983

Spiritual people can be some of the most violent people you will ever meet. Mostly they are violent to themselves.
Adyashanti

Eager to find out more about the ancient traditions of yoga and to see where Bapuji and Gurudev were born, Fran and I go on a whirlwind trip to India with Gurudev and a group of devotees in 1986. There are about thirty of us traveling together. We visit the beautiful temple of Kayavarohan in Gujurat Province that Bapuji built through incredible surrender and faith. We see the dirt-floor hut where Gurudev was born. Every place we stop, we meet with extraordinary spiritual teachers, from a blind ninety-year-old swami who can recite the Vedas by heart, to a genteel Indian lady who claims to have seen her guru walk on water, to the stunningly attractive Gurumayi, who has just succeeded Swami Muktananda as spiritual head of the Siddha Yoga path.

One of the highlights of our trip is a visit to a Jain monastery. We are thrilled to hear that we can have an audience with one of the monks, because they rarely speak to foreigners. Before long we are all gathered around the monk, who is sitting cross-legged under a tree—totally naked.

We all listen intently as a bald, overweight Indian interpreter dressed in white describes the swami's life in heavily accented English: "The swami has no possessions. He has no home. He wanders barefoot from place to place except in the rainy season. He can only eat one meal a day. He can only eat while standing up and cannot eat more than can be held in his two cupped hands."

The swami sits peacefully in front of us while the interpreter speaks about the ten virtues that Jain monks live by. He holds what looks like a feather duster in his right hand, and every so often brushes the ground around him—not so ants and flies won't crawl over his body, but because he doesn't want to kill them accidentally. "He has taken a vow never to wear clothing, never to ride in a vehicle, and never to kill anything—even a fly."

I listen in amazement. *Here is a man who fears nothing! He has given it all up for God and has been given everything in return. Look at his face—it exudes extraordinary happiness!* Slightly embarrassed, I glance down at his body, which is strong and exquisitely proportioned. His head is shaved, his skin is dark, rich, and lustrous, and his eyes are sparkling with light. He is totally unselfconscious about sitting in front of us naked. I'm astonished to see that he is not all skin and bones after eating one meal a day. He looks healthier than all of us. *Maybe we should make this the new American diet?*

Gurudev has been watching all of this in delight and is clearly inspired by the swami's example. "Look at this!" he says. "I'm going to take you through this. If you only do ten percent of what this swami does, your life will be transformed. You'll see! I'm going to take you there!" Everyone nods enthusiastically.

After the talk, a few of us go up to the swami for a blessing. He taps everyone gently on the head with his feather duster. I bow down before him and look into his eyes with my heart wide open in love. He gives a merry laugh and then whacks me twice over the head with the duster. A jolt of energy, like an electric shock, goes through me. I can barely stand up. *What's happening? I've been zapped! This is just what I prayed for!*

Feeling lightheaded, I walk back through the Jain temple to the bus, thinking of what Gurudev just said. If I could just do ten percent of all the spiritual practices the Jain monk does, perhaps I could someday experience the same extraordinary peace I see in him. I realize that austerity for this monk is not austerity at all. From his point of view, we are the ones practicing austerity by missing out on the bliss that he experiences every moment!

When I return home I try my own version of austerities. At mealtime I limit myself to the food that I can pile on one plate (imagining the plate as my two palms). Unlike the swami I eat three meals a day, and don't eat standing up . . . no need to go quite that far. Every morning I rise at 4:30 AM and practice yoga and meditation, but unlike the swami I do wear clothes, because it is 35 degrees outside. Once a week I fast and give up ice cream, and for one long month I try abstaining from sex (now *that* was hard!) I jog half-naked in the winter snow and cleanse my nasal passages with a little "neti" bowl. I practice these austerities for weeks—and nothing happens. I try even harder for more long weeks—and still nothing happens.

From everything I've heard, spiritual austerities are one of the most direct routes to enlightenment—if you're into that sort of thing. There are stories of yogis doing what appears to be every bizarre form of self-abuse imaginable—not eating for years, standing twenty-four hours a day year in and year out, burying themselves underground for weeks. Do any of them find true happiness or enlightenment? I guess you'll have to dig them up to find out.

The Buddhists seem to have a penchant for extreme spiritual practices too. My favorite story is that of Tenzin Palmo, an Englishwoman who became a Tibetan Buddhist nun. She spent twelve years meditating in a cave in the Himalayas at an elevation of 13,200 feet. The cave was only five feet by seven, barely large enough to stand up in. Tenzin slept in a meditation box—a three-foot by three-foot wooden box— sitting upright—every night for twelve years. *And I sometimes complain about my king-size bed!* During the freezing Himalayan winters her only companions were wolves, snow leopards, and rodents. In the first year she nearly starved to death; in the next year she was nearly buried alive in a snowstorm. She survived for months on tea and turnips. Her only human contact was with a few visitors every year. Why would anyone want to go through this? Tenzin says she was following the instructions of her teacher, and her goal was to become the first Buddhist woman to become enlightened, which brought up the question for me, "Why aren't more Buddhist women enlightened?" Did she reach her goal? According to Tenzin Palmo, she still has a long way to go.

I've always admired those who take this particular path. There are some, though, who take up austerities for all the wrong reasons. Adyashanti—a Zen meditator for fifteen years—points out, "They violently try to control their minds, their emotions, and their bodies. No one ever became free through such violence."

After a few pathetic attempts I decide that austerity is not my path. I realize that I am more aligned with the comedian W.C. Fields, who once complained that, "While exploring the wilds of Borneo we lost our corkscrew, and were forced to survive on food and water for days!"

I had to find some other way of reaching the peace I had seen in the naked Jain monk.

The Making of a Guru
Summit Station, Pennsylvania, August, 1982

To project our dreams into the future or to make them come true is not the secret of life. The secret is our ability to attend to the experience of now.
Yogi Amrit Desai

One of the first projects Fran and I were given was to help our friend Sukanya work on a book called *Gurudev: The Life of Yogi Amrit Desai.* As I began my research, looking through boxes of old newspaper articles and photographs, I realized I had stumbled onto an amazing story.

Amrit Desai was born in a little town in Gujarat province that made its meager income by selling clay pots. The village had no running water, no electricity, and one well to serve the entire town. Each family had its own little one-room thatched hut. While on our trip to India, Amrit took us on a tour of the town. I remember how happy he was as he showed us the hut he was born in. It had a dirt floor, a little kitchen area in the back, and a swing with blankets piled up on it. The blankets were used for sleeping at night. Nearby was a dusty little one-room store that his father ran when he was alive. It had all the basic necessities, such as bidis (cigarettes), flour, cooking oil, and kerosene. Very humble beginnings— almost Christ-like—I thought, in my starry-eyed-worship of Gurudev.

When Amrit was ten, his family moved to the town of Halol, which had a population of 17,000 at the time. Amrit proudly led our little group—all dressed in whites—down the street where he lived, showing us his house—a narrow townhouse painted turquoise on the front. It consisted of two long rooms, one over the other. A white Brahmin cow lay on the street in front of the house, and the smell of sewage and a dead dog added to the local flavor. But hey, this is India. Our group spent several days in Halol seeing the sights. Fran and I stayed with Amrit's boyhood friend Niranjan and his family, who treated us like royalty. I found out from Niranjan how, after finishing high school and serving in the Indian Air Force, Amrit became a high school art teacher, earning $30 per month. Unlike Amrit's other friends, who were content with their lives in Halol, Amrit made the bold decision to go to America, and attend the Philadelphia College of Art.

Through magazine clippings and interviews with Amrit, I find out the rest of his story. He sold his watch, his bicycle, and saved up $600 for a plane ticket. Leaving his young wife Mataji and newborn son behind, he boarded a plane for America, arriving in Philadelphia in February, 1960. He arrived just after a snowstorm and had only a thin raincoat and no hat or winter shoes. With only a few hundred dollars in his pocket, he found a place to live and a job at a paper and bag company for $1.50 an hour. Frugal as always, he saved enough money for art school and to bring Mataji and his son to America a year later. While studying (and working full-time) he taught yoga classes on the side. The classes became so successful that by the mid-sixties he was head of The Yoga Society of Pennsylvania, which offered more than one hundred and fifty classes a week; he taught twenty-three of them. In 1961 he did a yoga presentation before 2,000 people at the International House—five years before the first pair of Birkenstocks made their way from Germany to the United States!

In 1970 he purchased the property in Sumneytown and founded the Kripalu Yoga Ashram. He named it after his teacher, Bapuji. At the time there was just a stone farmhouse and a few other structures on the property. On weekends his yoga students came out from Philadelphia to help renovate the buildings and hang out with him. Wearing jeans and a T-shirt, he joined in on the work, laying carpets and painting the walls. Gradually a small community formed around him.

Amrit made several trips to India to visit his teacher Bapuji, who was then living in silence. On one of these trips, he brought some of his students with him. After meeting Bapuji and seeing how gurus were revered in India, they began calling Amrit "Gurudev" (beloved teacher), and started to bow down before him as a sign of respect. The small community adopted other Eastern practices, including wearing saris, practicing Brahmacharya (celibacy), and living a life of renunciation and service. It wasn't long before they were asking for Sanskrit names and to be initiated as disciples. What surprised me was to see how organically the community took shape, stemming from Amrit's desire to have a place where he could retreat and do spiritual practices.

In 1970 Gurudev had a transcendent experience that transformed his life. While practicing yoga one day with friends, his body began to spontaneously move from one posture to the next in a meditative flow. "Suddenly, as if bursting upon me like an unexpected spring downpour," he said, "I was flooded with bliss throughout my entire being."

This meditative posture flow became the foundation of Kripalu Yoga. At seminars, Amrit repeated the same flow in front of large audiences. Some found themselves going into deep meditation, experiencing a similar kind of bliss; many felt shakti move through their bodies and started weeping. It was catching—everyone wanted more. When I first saw him do a posture flow, I was amazed to see his body move into incredible yoga poses. It was as if "he" wasn't doing them, and some force was moving through him. My eyes closed and I went into meditation, feeling waves of energy move through my chest. My breathing became fast and heavy; my arms tingled as electrical energy seemed to shoot out my fingers. *This is it—this is what I've craved all these years!*

Gurudev began giving seminars around the country and the community started to grow exponentially. Soon the small ashram was bursting at the seams. In 1982, the year Fran and I moved to Pennsylvania, Gurudev and the directors began looking for larger quarters. After a search that took them from Georgia, to the Catskills and California, they settled on an old Jesuit seminary in Lenox, Massachusetts. The only problem was that the fledgling Kripalu community had no money to buy it. In a huge leap of faith, we all set out to raise a million dollars and buy the building.

CHAPTER 6

CRAZY FOR YOGA

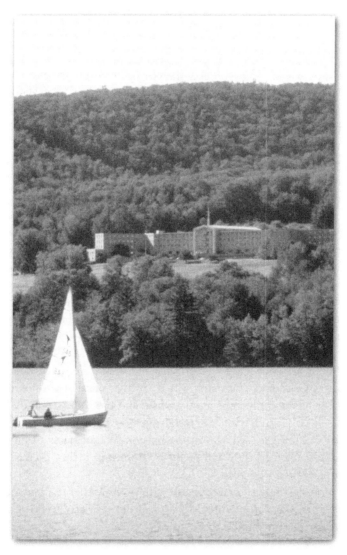

Kripalu Center for Yoga and Health, Lenox, Massachusetts

The Golden Years
Kripalu Center for Yoga and Health, Lenox, MA, September 1983

*Do everything with so much love in your heart that you would never want to do
it any other way.*
Yogi Amrit Desai

The grass clippings fly high into the air behind me as I ride the big John Deere tractor and its ten-gang mower across the stately lawns of the estate called Shadowbrook. Just down the hill is the glittering blue water of Lake Mahkeenac, and beyond that, a panoramic view of the Berkshire Mountains. I shift into low gear and turn the tractor up the hill, towards the huge four-story brick building, which was once a Jesuit seminary. The warm sun is beating on my back and the smell of fresh-cut grass fills the air. I'm having the time of my life, serving God, Guru, and community—and I couldn't be happier. It's 1983, and the tiny Kripalu Yoga Ashram has somehow managed to acquire this imposing 360-acre property, just outside of the fashionable town of Lenox, MA. The building had been deserted for years and was in a desperate state of disrepair. The old septic system was useless, the wiring out of date, the roof leaked, the ship-size boilers were broken, and the walls were a bilious green. With over an acre of floor space on each floor, it was a daunting task.

Within a year the building is transformed into a sparkling clean, freshly painted, newly-carpeted yoga and health center. The main chapel still has a gigantic 30-foot mosaic of St. Ignatius behind the altar, but now includes a portrait of Bapuji hanging under the Christian saint—a perfect blend of East and West. The traditional pews are gone and the enormous floor space is covered in a plush rose-colored carpet. Gurudev's chair sits in front of the mosaic on a raised dais. It is handmade out of smoothly polished dark oak, and has rich burgundy bolsters on three sides so that Gurudev can sit cross-legged on it. When he is not using it, a large picture of him is leaned against the bolster. No one dares sit on the "guru's chair," no doubt terrified they will be hit by lightning if they do so. It would be highly disrespectful of the guru.

I remember setting up for a program with several other residents. Apart from the five of us, the chapel is empty. Instead of deferentially walking around the chair, I take the picture off and sit down.

"My dear disciples," I say in jest, imitating Gurudev. "You must do yoga every day if you wish to become enlightened!" Miraculously, no lightning comes down from above.

"Ramakrishna, what are you doing?" Balaram says in shock.

Then everyone cracks up.

"Can I try next?" Rajen asks.

The rebellious teenager inside me is delighted at having challenged the sacred authority of the guru. *Everyday Gurudev tells us, "We are all one. You and I are no different,"* I think. *Why is his "one" any better than our "one"?* But there is no way I would ever tell him that in person—obedient disciple that I am.

Renovating the building is a perfect job for budding young karma yogis. The small Kripalu community puts their hearts and souls into this enormous task, doing almost all the work. The paint crew chants endless rounds of mantra as they paint acres of walls. After I boast of my painting skills, they put me to work in the large dining hall. But while on a ladder I spill a gallon of paint onto the linoleum floor—and get moved to the cleaning crew. I am told to think of Gandhi as I scrub the filthy toilets, and to remember that Gandhi cleaned toilets when others were too lazy to do so. All the different crews—construction, painting, household, maintenance, administration, get together in small groups before the start of the work day, and chant a long "Om" before beginning their jobs. Every day Gurudev walks the halls, encouraging the residents by his presence. After he passes by, they exchange starry-eyed glances, especially if he acknowledges them with a smile or a few words of praise. We all feel as if we have a purpose and a mission. We are serving God and guru; we are acting from our hearts, giving our all.

The newly renovated Kripalu Center for Yoga and Health opens in 1984. It rides a tidal wave of popularity as yoga enters the mainstream. Before long over 20,000 visitors a year are coming for a wide array of programs on yoga, holistic health, and self-discovery. In a few years Kripalu goes from a small community of sixty to over 350 full-time residents. Its reputation grows exponentially, with people coming from all over the world to attend programs. Celebrities such as Isabella Rossellini and Andie MacDowell show up, along with young professionals from New York and Boston. As head of the Rest and Relaxation Program, I am the one that gets to make sure all their needs are met.

These are the golden years. It is a heady experience to be part of this dynamic explosion of creative energy (and to have breakfast with Isabella Rossellini). I am a little older than most of the residents and have some experience in the "outside world." I am amazed that a group of young people in their twenties, with no business experience whatsoever, earning $35 per month (it had gone up from $1.00 per month), manage to turn a small ashram into a multi-million dollar business. Even more astonishing is that we are able to maintain our integrity and spiritual focus. It is a rare combination of charismatic leadership, a clear vision, and youthful energy where everything seems possible.

Gurudev rides this wave of success with grace and aplomb. He continues to live in a tiny gatehouse that has been renovated for him and his family. It seems that the success of Kripalu has little effect on him—his one big splurge is upgrading his car from an aging Chrysler to a Cadillac. He is awarded a variety of titles, from Yogi, to Doctor of Yoga Science, Yogacharya, and Maharishi (Great Sage), for his humanitarian work. Everyone is duly impressed when he remains unaffected by these awards. The residents are given more and more responsibilities and a conscious effort is made to hand over the running of the center to the administrators. Consultants are invited in to give management trainings and everyone works sixty-hour work weeks. We are convinced that we are doing something positive that will help transform the world.

Although the motto of "Love, Service, Surrender" has long disappeared from the sign at the gate and been replaced by a more corporate image (The Kripalu Center for Yoga and Health), it is still at the heart of the Kripalu lifestyle. Newer residents at Kripalu are often put in jobs intended to wear down the ego. An emergency room surgeon is assigned kitchen prep and peels vegetables all day long. Well-known artists are relegated to housekeeping duties. A corporate trainer is sent to accounting. As a former academic, I am put on the maintenance crew, where, after digging ditches, I graduate to mowing the lawns.

One day I am called off my tractor to a meeting with Dinabandhu (Patton Sarley), a senior administrator, who asks me to become the head of the Development Department—a role that involves being in charge of all fundraising for what is now a large organization. Overnight I am flung into the so-called fast lane, attending special meetings with Gurudev and the other administrators, commandeering an office overlooking the lake, and supervising a small staff. It is an exciting and demanding role and I love it. I am a combination camp counselor, big shot businessman, spiritual seeker, entrepreneur, and yogi, all rolled into one.

I am sure that I am on the path to God. After all, I am living a life of service. I am super-healthy, eating right, and doing yoga and meditation every day. I am working out, windsurfing on the lake during lunch break, hanging out with the brothers. My relationship with Fran is better than ever. We have learned how to communicate with respect and love and are grateful for every moment we have together. Our son Peter is doing well in high school. Our lives are on track. I am surrounded by a warm and caring "family," and have so many friends I can barely keep up with them. There is an endless stream of activities, from healing circles, to special yoga trainings, management trainings, meetings with visiting teachers, and programs to lead. Every few weeks there are celebrations for a variety of holidays, everything from Sivaratri, Guru Purnima, and the Guru's birthday, to

Christmas, Hanukkah, and Easter. With residents and guests coming from many different spiritual traditions, there is something for everyone.

Things can't get much better than this, I think. I'm living in a big house with three hundred best friends; everyone around me is loving, caring, and grounded at the same time; I have a spiritual teacher whom I love and admire and who promises to take me "all the way to God." There's even a distant hope that I might someday become enlightened— if I continue to do my practices and surrender my life to God. At least I know that I'm on the right train. Maybe I can at last put down my suitcase and enjoy the ride!

For the first time in my life I could say I was truly happy.

The Yoga of Devotion
Kripalu Center for Yoga and Health, Lenox, MA, 1984-1988

Give me your whole heart,
Love and adore me,
Worship me always,
Bow to me only,
And you shall find me:
This is my promise
Who love you dearly.
The Bhagavad Gita

At the heart of Kripalu is the tradition of Bhakti Yoga, the yoga of devotion. There is nothing quite so inspiring as the ancient path of coming to God through devotion. The Bhakti path is about falling in love, losing oneself in a love so powerful that it is beyond anything we can imagine love to be. It is about being consumed in the fire of love, so that our false identification with ego drops away and all that remains is the divine. It is about losing our mind to love. It is about being so in love that there is no sense of a separate self. Devotion can take any number of forms, from seeing everything in the universe as pervaded by God, to worshipping the guru as a divine being, to adoring some object as a representation of God.

I considered myself to be a real "Bhakta" (a follower of Bhakti Yoga). At Kripalu, this had little to do with the deeper states referred to in the Indian scriptures. In my case, it was closer to being a starry eyed "bliss bunny." I chanted all night long praying that God would appear; I cried for God with all my heart; I bowed before my guru; I bowed before his guru, Bapuji; I bowed before Bapuji's guru Dadaji; I bowed before Shiva and Krishna. I had pictures of my guru on my desk, on my wall, in my car, in my wallet, by my bed. From waking to sleeping, nearly every thought revolved around serving God and Guru—except my many fantasies about sex and ice cream (ashram life will do that to you). I fervently held on to the belief that a fully realized guru could ignite the smoldering fire of the disciple who sincerely longs for God. I suspected that my guru, Amrit Desai, wasn't fully realized, but it seemed like his teacher Bapuji was. So I covered my bases and prayed to both of them. And since the lineage of our path went all the way back to Lord Shiva, I prayed to him too.

The immense joke, which took me a long time to get, was that I was trying to satisfy my longing for the Divine by looking everywhere except where I would find it.

I was like the little man who went from door to door, looking for God. He knocked on every door, desperate to find God.

"Does God live here?" he cried out.

His knock went unanswered. He went to another door and asked, "Is God in here?"

"Go away," came the answer.

At the next door someone yelled, "You're crazy!"

But he kept on knocking and knocking until finally he was so exhausted he was ready to give up his search.

He knocked on one more door. "Does God live here?" he asked timidly.

A deep, booming voice said, "Yes, I am God, what can I do for you, my son?"

"Oh," the man replied. "I must have the wrong address!"

Turning around, he walked on to the next house, crying, "Where is God? Where is God?"

The path of devotion, at least as I was practicing it, had a fail-safe system to make sure I never found God in the one place God was hiding—my own heart. When I prayed to Gurudev he passed on my devotion on to his teacher, Bapuji (or professed to). Bapuji then passed it on to his teacher, and eventually it got all the way to God (a little like the Catholic Church). The beauty of this system is that Gurudev became the focal point for everyone to pour their love into, and for the most part, that love was pure and selfless. When it became channeled through chanting and meditation, as it often was, it created a powerful energetic field that was sacred—the holiest of holies.

But implicit in this belief system was the idea that the disciple could never surpass the person further up the ladder. Although Gurudev was very clear in saying that God was also in me, in actual practice there was an unspoken assumption that none of us would ever come to a place where we had the same sacred empowerment he had. If that happened, who would be there to serve the guru? Because my devotion was directed towards someone "out there," who I believed to be separate from me, wiser than me, holier than me, I was destined to spend the rest of my life going from door to door, crying out, "Where is God?"

What I failed to see for a long, long time was the possibility for my entire life to become devotion—not just to an external guru, not just to a set of practices—but to *all that is*. As the Indian sage H.W.L. Poonja (Papaji) said, "Devotion does not mean that you start loving anyone else. What about your own Self? This is the only devotion: that you must be dedicated and devoted to your own Self. Having done this, you have given love to everybody."

Wow! What a radical idea—the thought that true devotion, or true Bhakti, means losing your mind in love and merging into the Beloved. And even more surprising, is to realize that it doesn't come from effort, it comes from a natural overflowing of our being, like the beautiful scent of a flower. We've all experienced this love—it may have been when we're holding a small child in our arms or petting a dog or a cat. Imagine what joy it would be to have this devotion our moment to moment experience in life!

Who Is There to Serve?
Kripalu Center for Yoga and Health, Lenox, MA, 1984-1988

*I am not here to do service. There is no one to give service to. I wouldn't have the
arrogance to think that there was anything to serve you with. You are the divine
expression. How can I give you anything when you are that already?*
Tony Parsons

The other yogic path practiced at the Kripalu ashram was Karma Yoga. The goal
was for everyone in the community to selflessly consecrate their actions to God
and guru without needing anything in return, without taking credit for them,
and without being attached to the results. This ancient and lofty practice has been
honored for thousands of years as a path towards spiritual awakening. *The Bhagavad Gita*, written 2,500 years ago, clearly points the way: "In this world, aspirants
may find enlightenment by two different paths. For the contemplative is the path
of knowledge; for the active is the path of selfless action."

With over three hundred sexually charged celibate men and women in their
twenties and thirties, there was no way Kripalu was going to follow a contemplative path. So karma yoga (what we called *seva*) became the basis for daily practice
at Kripalu—a perfect way to channel all that energy. Kripalu was a workaholic
ashram—a constant grind of *seva*, practices, meetings, and special events that
could consume eighteen hours a day. In the remaining six hours, irrepressible
twenty-year olds still found ways to get into trouble, including indulging in such
forbidden pleasures as a movie or ice cream. The residents who worked the hard-
est got the most praise—not just from their peers—but from the guru himself.
Gurudev taught again and again on the importance of selfless service saying, "As
you dwell upon the guru in each daily activity, your life is transformed into one of
continuous meditation."

Gurudev's own life was a constant inspiration to stretch and give more. He
seemed indefatigable—leading meditation before dawn, holding meetings all day,
counseling disciples, teaching again at night. What's more, he seemed relaxed,
happy, and radiant—the perfect example of a yogi who had mastered "the art of
living." On the positive side, extraordinary things were accomplished when all
this energy was channeled into service. Visitors who came were touched by the
love they received from the residents, and the care that went into every detail of
their stay. When the work was a true expression of selfless service, the love burst
forth like brilliant rays of sunshine. On the flip side, many residents lost touch

with the true meaning of selfless service, and pushed themselves so hard that they often burned out in the process.

After years of serving at Kripalu, I assumed that my every breath was devoted to Karma yoga. I got up at 4:30 in the morning to lead yoga for the guests. I spent the day teaching programs and counseling people. I showed up at night to give introductory talks to the new arrivals. I worked six-and-a-half days a week with an afternoon off on Sunday—and I did all this for no remuneration whatsoever, except free meals (I hope you're impressed by my selflessness). I was sure that I was serving God and Guru—never mind that I was exhausted all the time. I was trying to live up to a spiritual ideal that I didn't fully understand. The change was subtle. I started to believe that "I" was the one "doing" karma yoga and prided myself on being one of the "best karma yogis" around. Along with that came the belief that I was "more spiritual" than those around me, especially those that didn't do "seva." What a slippery slope.

I now see that much of what passed for "selfless service" in our community was little more than "selfish service"—*hey, look at me, look at how I'm helping the world, look how hard I'm working!* True Karma yoga, I was later to discover, is when there is no doer. When there is no doer, there is no attachment to results. It is effortless action, given over to God.

The Direct Path
Kripalu Center for Yoga and Health, Lenox, MA, 1987

Unwavering in devotion, always united with me, the man or woman of wisdom surpasses all the others. To them I am the dearest beloved, and they are very dear to me.
Bhagavad Gita

There is another path to enlightenment, which was seldom, if ever, mentioned during my years at Kripalu. It is called Jnana Yoga, the path of wisdom or knowledge. First of all, how do you follow a path whose name you can't even pronounce? (Try *dyn-ah'-nuh*. Good luck!). From what I'd heard this path is reserved for a few select sages—certainly not for ordinary mortals like me—so why bother? It sounded like a graduate course in philosophy and about as interesting as a trip to the dentist (although I must say that I love going to the dentist). It seemed like a mental exercise. Where's the passion? Where's the excitement?

Little did I realize, but this is probably the most fascinating and juicy of all the paths that can lead to self-realization! It's as much about ecstatic love for God as the path of devotion; it's as much about a life consecrated to God as the path of Karma Yoga. In fact, there's no difference between them. Of all the paths, Jnana Yoga is viewed as the direct path—the "straight but steep course" that can lead directly to God, Source, or Self (more accurately, it doesn't lead you anywhere; it's the stripping away of illusion to realize that you *already* are the Self).

What shocked me is that Jnana Yoga aims at the destruction of the mind. What? Destroy the mind? Why? Because the ego—our sense of personal identity (which creates all our suffering)—is nothing more than the mind. Kill the ego— or the mind—and there is eternal bliss. As Ramana Maharshi said, "You do not acquire happiness: your very nature is happiness. Bliss is not newly earned. All that is done is to remove unhappiness." An easier way of describing it is that we no longer *identify* with the mind. The mind still goes on and is useful, but we no longer believe our thoughts to be real. If we're lucky, we discover that the mind doesn't even exist!

Contrary to what I imagined, the knowledge referred to in Jnana Yoga has nothing to do with book knowledge; it has nothing to do with acquiring *more* knowledge. It is the wisdom that comes from *direct* knowledge of God. This knowledge lies beyond the mind and is a result of direct seeing—recognizing the supreme reality that lies behind all things. It is arrived at by using the mind to go

103

beyond the mind. The purpose is to discover the nature of the Self through asking the question "Who am I"? No one demonstrates this process of self-inquiry more clearly than the Indian sage Ramana Maharshi.

Self-inquiry has its source in the ancient wisdom teachings of Advaita Vedanta. These are the teachings found in the Vedas, the oldest scriptures known to man. Advaita literally means "not two," implying that there is no separation between subject and object. Our individual self, and God, or Spirit, or the big Self, are one. We are not separate from Spirit, because we already *are* Spirit. Any movement in any direction is a step away from who we truly are. In the West, these teachings are referred to as nondualism.

The open secret is that this awareness is available to everyone. If it sounds intimidating and out of reach of folks like you and me, I assure you that it's not. All it takes is a simple shift in everyday perception to realize our true nature. It's an invitation to recognize that there is nothing but Consciousness and that you *are* that Consciousness! With this recognition you discover that your very nature is true and lasting happiness. The search is over.

But I'm giving away the punch line.

I had no idea that many years later this pathless path would be the gateway to open my heart.

Hopped Up on Yoga
Kripalu Center for Yoga and Health, Lenox, MA, February 1984

As one opens the door with a key, so the yogi should open the gate to liberation with Kundalini. He who knows Kundalini knows yoga.
Hatha Yoga Pradipika, 15th Century CE

It's 4:30 in the morning and pitch dark outside as fifteen of us stand in a circle around Gurudev in the auditorium. "This practice will make you spiritual warriors," he says with enthusiasm. As the top yoga teachers at Kripalu, we've been selected for a special training to be given by the guru himself. Gurudev strips off his shirt, so that he is naked from the waste up. For someone over fifty, he looks in better shape than most twenty-year-olds. I look at his lithe, thin, body, surprised to see that his breasts are more developed than most men. With his long black hair, he looks almost hermaphrodite.

"The exercise I'm going to demonstrate develops your *hara*, the power center in your belly," he informs us. *Hara* is a Japanese martial art term referring to the physical center of gravity in our bodies, located three inches below the navel.

He takes a deep breath, exhales the air with tremendous force, and bends forward, with his back arched up and his hands on his knees. With all the air expelled, he sucks his belly up towards his spine. Then he pumps it up and down like a bellows, still with his breath expelled. There are gasps from the onlookers as his whole stomach seems to disappear into his back. After completing several rounds, he stands up, his body glowing and flushed with new energy.

"Now this will make you strong," he says with one of his broad smiles. "You'll have no fear." Everyone stares at him, their mouths open in awe. "As you teach this to your students, you will help awaken their prana, or inner life force, which accelerates healing, and purification of body, mind and emotions."

So this is what happens when you practice yoga for years. I think. *You become fearless and look young forever!*

Like everyone else in the community, I'd been taught that yoga is a 3000-year-old science, not just the latest fitness fad. Now I'm being shown advanced practices by a master yogi—exercises that help bring the energy up the spine and lead to a kundalini awakening. In this esoteric yoga tradition, kundalini is described as a hidden, dormant force that resides within each one of us like a coiled serpent at the base of the spine. When this energy awakens, it rises up through subtle channels in the spine, opening the way to different levels of mystical experience.

Although it took a leap of faith to believe that there is a "hollow channel" running up my spinal cord, I had seen some impressive physical manifestations of what happens when kundalini awakens. A few years earlier I had made a film on Gurudev's teacher Bapuji—a master of kundalini yoga—and seen extraordinary photographs of Bapuji with his tongue rolled back into the roof of his mouth. Others showed his body in impossibly complex yoga postures. While filming him, I was the first Westerner to see his body move through a series of mudras, or gestures, activated by an inner meditative state. These were not his doing. They were the result of the energy moving his body without his volition. Gurudev tells us that with a purified body and a lifetime of dedication, these yoga practices can lead to spiritual enlightenment.

As a yogi-to-be, I was sure that I could eventually be one of those rare few who went all the way to enlightenment. I had had tiny glimmers of what it might be like—involuntary jerking, sensations of heat in my body, spontaneous movements, and intense feelings of pleasure. Oh, how I craved a double whammy! I was told terrifying stories of what can happen if the body isn't prepared for this energy. According to some, the awakening of Kundalini is like receiving a 20,000-volt shock—one where the body will self-destruct if it's not purified and ready for it. What an image—ZAAAAP—then smoke pouring out of my ears! This was obviously not something to be done at yoga classes given at the local Y. I bought the whole package, including the belief that you couldn't awaken *unless* you had a 20,000-volt experience of union with God.

For years I clung on to the belief that this was the *only* way to awaken. I was sure that enlightenment was the result of some profound, mystical experience. Not only that, I believed that the only way I could get there was through the transmission of shakti, or divine energy, from an enlightened guru. Clearly for some, this esoteric path of Kundalini yoga has resulted in spiritual awakening. But in my case, it was a way of postponing awakening to some place far off into the future, perhaps lifetimes away. I failed to understand that Hatha yoga, at least as I was practicing it, was *strengthening* my identification with body. I hadn't the slightest idea that awakening—even for a Kundalini yogi—means dropping all identification with body and mind. Little did I know, but all these beliefs would eventually have to be discarded.

In the meantime, I got to develop my *hara* by pumping my belly up and down, and thinking I was on my way to God . . . which I actually was, but not in the way I planned it.

Spiritual Traps
Kripalu Center for Yoga and Health, Lenox, MA, 1987

Allegiance to any spiritual teaching or teacher—any outside authority—is the most treacherous beast in the jungle.
Jed McKenna

I had come to the point in my spiritual journey where I had survived the honeymoon period and considered myself a "professional," full-time seeker. I even had a new name, different clothes, different friends, different priorities. I was in for the long haul, prepared to continue down this path until I was old and grey (except that yogis never get old and grey—they stay young forever, because their bodies are so "pure"). Gurudev often spoke to those of us in his "inner circle," saying, "If I have one dream it is to have all of you close by me when I become older."

"Oh yes," we all swooned. "We'll take care of you."

It was easy to imagine our happy little "family" of close disciples thirty years from now out on the patio in front of Shadowbrook, looking out at the magnificent view as the sun goes down. We'd be sitting on whatever yogis sit on when they get old, with Gurudev, the wise and loving master, sharing his wisdom.

I had developed a kind of tunnel vision. What had launched me on the journey was the promise of true happiness somewhere off in the future. That had morphed into a longing for enlightenment—the bliss of a thousand orgasms. But that longing was a distant memory now. Enlightenment wasn't even a part of the picture. I just plodded down the road day after day, doing what had to be done, having long ago handed over the reins of my spiritual development to my guru. All I had to do was serve my teacher, continue practicing yoga and meditation, and serve others. I took comfort from the Dalai Lama: "If you practice in this way, then after a year or after a decade you will notice at least some improvement in yourself."

This brought me to the next stage—finding my own comfort level within the path. I reached a point where I conveniently found ways of avoiding the routines and rituals I didn't like, such as volunteering for dishwashing (my time is "too important" now). All my old personality stuff began to rear its ugly head—fear of confrontation, wanting to be liked, attachment to comfort. As a program leader, I did endless personal growth work—workshops, intensives, trainings, individual sessions—in an attempt to get free of old personality stuff that held me in identification with ego. I delved into my past, my relationships, my fears, my hurts. I cried, I yelled, I pleaded with God to be free. But all it did was entrench the ego even deeper. On top of that, I now considered myself an aspiring "yogi," and had to protect my image in order to fit into the community. I had to walk slowly, talk softly, never get angry, and always look happy—even when I didn't feel it. I had to adopt a false persona that had nothing to do with who I truly am. How insane!

All the time I thought I was marching down the path to awakening I was walking deeper and deeper into a spiritual trap. Gurudev didn't call me on it, because he had an adoring disciple and good worker-bee. To be honest, he probably did call me (and everyone else) on what these traps were, but it went right over my head. I had reached a plateau where I was frozen into an imitation of what I thought a yogi should look like. All the time I thought I was "destroying my ego," I was reinforcing my sense of personal identity even more. Like just about everyone else, I was playing out a well-rehearsed role, convinced I was advancing down the road to enlightenment.

It's only now that I can see what a truckload of beliefs I swallowed without questioning any of them—everything from the importance of spiritual practice, to the need to be compassionate and serve the guru, to the need to be celibate so that the Kundalini energy could move up my spine. It never occurred to me that these were all just concepts. The most limiting belief of all was the idea that spiritual awakening could only be achieved after years, if not lifetimes, of practice.

This is personified by an old story told that gurus like to tell about enlightenment. The story is about a bird that flies over the peak of the highest mountain in the world carrying a fringed scarf in its beak. Every time it flies over the top of the mountain (once every hundred years) the fringe of the scarf brushes against the top of the mountain. The time it takes to wear down the mountain to nothing is the time it takes to awaken.

My interpretation of the story was that it would take lifetime after lifetime of incarnating in a body (until the mountain was worn down to nothing), before I could hope for enlightenment. What I failed to see is the real point of the story—that awakening happens when it happens. It happens outside of time.

Everything is Yoga
Lac Manitou, Quebec, August 9, 2000

Breathe in. Breathe out. Forget this, and attaining enlightenment will be the least of your problems.
Jewish Buddhism

"C'mon Dad, you can do it," my son Peter says.

It's our yearly family reunion at my sister's cottage in the Laurentians, north of Montreal. The cottage sits on a hill overlooking a pristine lake called Lake Manitou, near where I spent my growing-up years.

"It's been ten years since I've led a yoga class!"

Despite my protests Peter and his girl friend start moving back the furniture in the living room. The cottage is decorated country-style, with antique pine furniture, colorful prints on the wall, and a sloping floor, which adds to its charm. Secretly, I'm thrilled that Peter wants me to lead him in yoga. I've dreamed that he would someday start some kind of spiritual practice and now it's happening.

My sister Beverly comes in, "Oh, a yoga class. Great! I'll get changed."

Linda, who has been lying on the couch reading, says. "Yes, we want you to lead us!" She continues to stay on the couch as a space is cleared in the center of the room.

I'm on the spot. Why did I stop practicing yoga anyway? When I was at Kripalu I breathed yoga, lived yoga, slept yoga, and even ate yoga. Then there came a time when my body just didn't want to do it anymore. My mind wanted to, but my whole being firmly said "NO." So I stopped. Now Peter wants me to lead a class.

"OK," I say. "Let's form a circle." Everyone finds a spot around the big hooked rug. I look at Linda and see her looking back at me with eyes filled with love. I look from my sister Beverly in her sweats, to my son Peter and his girl friend Nicki wearing shorts and a T-shirt, meeting their look of expectation. My heart sings with joy at our being able to come together in this way.

I begin with a centering as we stand in a circle: "Take a moment to close your eyes and notice what's happening in your body. Observe any sensations you may be experiencing, without any need to change them. Now take a deep breath and let it out with a sigh . . . and another one—even louder on the next exhalation. Good! Let out any tension, anything you may be holding on to. Just shake it out."

After ten years it's all coming back! I think. *It's like a duck taking to water.*

"Now let's do some warm ups," I say, shifting into a more active gear. "Raise your arms overhead and swing them down towards the floor in front of you as you bend your knees. Let out a big HAAAA as you do so . . . and again! This time a bigger HAAAA! And again! Yes!" We gradually build up momentum as we stretch out shoulders, necks, and hamstrings.

Wow. This feels great. Why did I stop doing yoga anyway? Maybe I can take up yoga again—without all the rules and structure. Why not do yoga as a child or a cat might do it, from a place of pure spontaneity and joy! That's what true yoga is.

I lead them through a flow of postures that gently stretches the different muscle groups. With each posture I encourage them to go within. "Now, let your arms float gently around behind your back and clasp your fingers," I say, when they are kneeling on the floor. "Bring your shoulder blades together and feel your chest opening wide. Breathe deeply into your chest and notice any minute sensations. Hold it. Hold it. Now release."

Peter, Beverly and Nicki have all done yoga before, and have no trouble following. Linda, with her illness, would be sure to hurt herself if she tried these postures. She's on the couch in absolute bliss, looking at me with eyes of love.

It's no wonder I love yoga so much. It really does help reduce stress and calm the mind. It really does balance the whole nervous system! And it feels so good!

As we end the posture flow I have them lie on their backs for a deep relaxation: "Feel yourself supported by the floor," I say once they're comfortable. "Let go and relax. There's nothing you need do right now. This time is just for you. Scan your body and notice any subtle movement of energy in your arms, your legs, or your torso. Now imagine this energy flowing all around your body to form a protective cocoon. You are safe. You are perfectly safe."

There is a palpable shift in mood as everyone drops in. Stillness fills the room. The sound of birds drifts in. A motorboat can be heard off in the distance. The sweet smell of pine trees fills the air. There are no longer five separate people in the room. There is only peace. I find myself dropping down even deeper. It's difficult to speak.

"Notice the awareness. Let it expand to take in the room, the sky, the hills, and the lake. Remember the name of the lake—Manitou, which means Great Spirit. That spirit, that Source is who you are. It is not your body or your mind. Rest peacefully in that."

We dip into the silence together. After a few minutes, we all come back to being in the room and sitting up in a circle.

"That was great, Dad," Peter says with a big smile.

"Yeah," Nicki adds. "I loved it."

"We should do this more often," Beverly says.

Linda is beaming with pleasure on the couch.

Afterwards, I take the canoe and paddle out to the small island just offshore. As I glide through the silky water a few feet from the shoreline, I hear a loud *SMACK*. Just in front of the canoe a beaver dives beneath the water. I noiselessly drift past the beaver lodge, hoping to see signs of life. Everything is silent, except for the water gently lapping on the shore. The island is uninhabited—at least by humans. Tall white birch trees reach out over the water; dense brush and pines make an almost impenetrable wall around the perimeter. I look down and see old stumps and rocks just beneath the surface. I float through the silence.

My mind drifts off to this afternoon's yoga session. How unexpected to have members of my own family wanting to do a class. I never dreamed it would happen. When I first started practicing yoga twenty years ago, yoga was considered way out there along with witches and weirdoes. Ministers denounced it from the pulpit; yoga practitioners were put on Satan's List. How all that has changed. Yoga has hit the mainstream. Singles do it, seniors do it, pregnant moms do it, kids do it, Christians do it. *Yoga Journal*, which was once a thin little rag, is now as thick (and as slick) as *Vanity Fair*. Yoga props can be found in every store from Walmart to Whole Foods.

Maybe that's why I stopped. It's become too popular!

I continue paddling around the island, aware that each stroke of the paddle is yoga; the position of my body kneeling in the canoe is yoga; my relaxed focus on every movement is yoga. Yoga doesn't just happen on a mat, I say to myself. It's right here, right now, in every moment.

CHAPTER 7

WHEN HEROES FALL

Peter, Peter Jr & Fran Honoring Yogi Desai's Birthday

Gurs, Saints, and Sleazeballs
Barnes and Noble, Charlottesville, Virginia, August 29, 2000

*Some teachers are rascals and coyotes who trick and surprise their students; some
are harsh taskmasters who point out a student's every fault; others can melt us
open with their love and compassion or show us the space and humor in all things.*
                                    Jack Kornfield

Over a period of several years in the nineties, while Linda and I lived in Virginia,
we watched in fascination as a radical new paradigm emerged in spiritual circles
around the world. The epicenter of the explosion was in smelly, polluted Lucknow,
India, where a larger-than-life figure named H.W.L. Poonja (who everyone called
Papaji), brought a revolutionary new message to spiritual seekers: "You already are
that. You need not do any spiritual practice, not even meditation; simply follow
the 'I' thought back to the source and rest in that. Wake up! You are already free."

His message came as a shock to all those seekers who had spent years meditating and doing spiritual practices in the hope they would someday become enlightened. Papaji was teaching the direct path of self-inquiry, which he had learned
from his master Ramana Maharshi. Westerner seekers from all over America and
Europe flocked to India to be with Papaji. Many of them had deep spiritual experiences where they claimed to awaken to the truth of who they are. So many were
said to have woken up being with Papaji, the joke was that all you had to do was
fly over Lucknow to become enlightened (too bad I missed my flight). Encouraged by Papaji, these newly minted teachers returned to the US and Europe (and
Australia) to hang out their shingles and bring the teachings of nonduality to an
eager audience.

Not everyone had to travel to India to spiritually awaken. Eckhart Tolle experienced ultimate understanding in his drab little flat in London. He spent almost
two years sitting quietly on a park bench before someone came up and asked him
a question. Then more people asked questions, and before long he was talking to
small groups. The rest is history. Byron Katie, an American housewife, woke up
spontaneously when a roach crawled over her leg in a half-way house in California.
Satyam Nadeen, a wealthy American who made his fortune selling ecstasy, awakened while serving a 17-year prison term; Suzanne Segal had a profound mystical
experience, in which she saw she was not her body, while standing at a bus stop
in Paris.

Linda and I traveled far and wide to be with these "teachers of one." We spent time with Eckhart Tolle when few people knew of him; we met Byron Katie just after her book *Loving What Is* came out; we flew to Bali to be with an American teacher named Gangaji; we went to intensives in Florida with Satyam Nadeen and Francis Lucille; we drove to Sedona to see Robert Adams; we hosted a retreat for Catherine Ingram in Charlottesville. We even started our own retreat center in New Mexico and had extraordinary teachers come to offer programs there. Man, we were on it.

In between we read the latest books and magazines on enlightenment. In the late nineties there were only a handful of books being published on nonduality, and we devoured them eagerly. One of our favorite pastimes was going to Barnes & Noble to check out the latest publications. After collecting a pile of them, we'd snag a comfortable couch in the back of the store, where there was a cozy reading area tucked among the rows of books.

This is great, I think, as I sink into the comfortable couch. *I can go through all these titles without having to buy any them. Thank you Barnes & Noble.*

Linda settles in beside me and starts flipping through a magazine on her lap.

"They're sleazeballs!" she hisses.

"Sleazeballs?" I reply distractedly, hoping she'll let it go. When Linda gets on her hobbyhorse about dishonest gurus and cults, there's no stopping her.

"Yes, sleazeballs, especially Andrew Cohen, who puts out *this* magazine." she says, slapping the cover of *What Is Enlightenment?*

I glance at the cover, which has the face of a Buddha next to a picture of Freud. The headline reads: *What is Ego? friend or foe . . . ?* The magazine is a thinly disguised promotional tool for Andrew Cohen, a young American teacher, who claims to be leading an enlightenment revolution. Andrew grew up in the Bronx, went to India in the eighties, and discovered Papaji. After several powerful awakening experiences, and years in India, he returned to the US to start a community in the Berkshires.

"If anyone knows about ego, it's him," she whispers. "He's one of the most manipulative, grandiose, narcissistic people I've ever met." Linda is fascinated by teachers who create cults around themselves and abuse their power.

I smile and go back to my pile of books.

A few moments later Linda says, "Look! Here's an interview with your old guru Amrit Desai!"

"Oh my God!" That hooked me.

Linda skims the article, reporting in a hushed voice what she finds: "Andrew and Amrit are complaining about how all their problems are caused by their students, who are still in ego." Her voice rises as she gets more and more incensed. "To think that Amrit, after screwing his female disciples, can say his problems are caused by his students . . . that makes me furious!" She whacks the magazine for emphasis.

A grossly overweight man, who overflows the armchair next to us, looks up at us in disapproval. He's wearing a faded red T-shirt and jeans, and his hair is stringy and greasy. He has a pile of books on the table before him, and like us, probably doesn't plan to buy any of them.

I lean over to look at the picture of Amrit and Andrew. They're sitting on two large, plush chairs, facing each other. "Why can't they put their feet on the ground like everyone else when they talk?" I ask in a low voice, trying not to incite Linda. "Is it a sign of enlightenment to always be sitting cross-legged?"

"Yes, because they're so 'holier than thou.'"

"Look at them," I say. "It's as if they belong to this exclusive club for so-called 'enlightened gurus.' They have their lackeys come and serve them tea and fawn all over them. I remember when Amrit and Yogi Bhajan visited each other. They had their feet massaged by devotees while chatting about their latest achievements. Can you imagine—two Indians who grew up in poverty—having subservient, white Americans on their knees massaging their feet? I think they get some kind of perverse pleasure from it."

"Anyone who appears in this magazine should automatically be disqualified from enlightenment," Linda says.

"Yeah, they love to stroke each other's non-egos," I laugh, delighted at my own wit.

"And they certainly make sure their lowly disciples never get enlightened," Linda adds. "That way they can extract more work from them and be waited on hand and foot. What do they call it . . . selfless service?"

Linda turns a few more pages. "Look at this article by Andrew Cohen. He wants to create a revolutionary army to change the world."

A few years ago we attended one of his satsangs when we lived in Santa Fe. We were astonished to see how he controlled every aspect of the gathering. Only certain kinds of questions could be asked; no one was allowed to challenge what he said; his students were obsequious and looked like they had been cowed into submission. Yet Andrew spoke words of great truth and freedom—an interesting paradox.

"It amazes me," I say. "When Andrew confronts his students and humiliates them, it seems that everything he says is nothing more than a projection of his own ego. He seems to be the only one that can't see it."

"I can't believe that Ken Wilbur admires him. He thinks Andrew's a sage because he gets in everyone's face."

"Yeah, he calls Andrew the 'Rude Boy of God Realization.' He likes Andrew because he's so brutal and uncompromising."

"Or, more accurately . . . abusive," Linda says. She has read *Mother of God*, a book written by Andrew's mother. It paints a picture of Andrew's cruel and obsessive behavior.

"It all seems a little warped to me," I say.

"Look at some of these other teachers!" Linda says, barely able to keep her voice down.

"Shhh . . ." I notice that one of the staff is looking over at us as she sorts books on a table.

Linda ignores me. She's on a roll. "Here's one called Maitreya Ishwara . . . what a joke. All he did was take advantage of his female disciples. Here's another . . . Saniel Bonder. From what I hear, his main interest is in having sex with multiple partners."

"Yet they all claim to be enlightened . . . now that's chutzpah!" Despite my best intentions, I'm getting totally caught up in the story.

"And here's one of your favorites, Ma Jaya." I laugh. "Remember when we saw her in Taos with Yogi Bhajan?" Linda has the magazine open to a full-page ad for Ma Jaya Sati Bhagavati, an American born spiritual teacher known for helping the homeless and people with AIDS. She's also known for seducing Ram Dass many years ago.

"Yeah, I remember. She was shouting at everyone saying, 'I'm going to take you there! I'm going to take you there!' The walls were filled with huge 4 by 6 foot photos of her heroically tending to AIDS victims."

"No, there wasn't any ego there!" Linda laughs. "Yogi Bhajan was even crazier. He railed on about teenagers and drugs for over an hour and there wasn't a single teenager in the room. He didn't make any sense at all."

The fat man lets out a big sigh.

"Keep your voice down Linda. They're going to throw us out!"

"I couldn't care less."

"It's puzzling. All these teachers seem to have some piece of the Truth, but then they claim it for their own egos."

"In no time they're saying, 'Look how *I* awakened.'"

I shake my head in amazement. "How can anyone claim it? No 'one' awakens!"

Linda adds, "Ramana Maharshi would never have said he's enlightened, even though he is one of the greatest sages who has ever lived."

I look at the full-page color ad for Wisdom Master Maticintin, AKA Winged Wolf, whoever she is. It must have cost thousands of dollars to place the ad. "I guess they start to believe their own publicity. They go out and create a huge infrastructure with devotees, ashrams, lectures, books, magazines, donations, websites. Then they have to keep up the identity of being an 'enlightened teacher.' It's such a trap."

"Or, like Andrew, they create a cult," Linda says. "They screw up people's lives in the worst way. Look at Andrew—he rules by fear. His disciples are like whipped dogs."

A page opens to a picture of Ammachi, an extraordinary Indian saint who hugs all those who come up for blessing—often thousands in one evening.

"Well, at least there are some people in the magazine who are pure in heart," I say, "or I hope she is. You never know."

"Remember when she hugged you on your birthday? It was so beautiful."

"Yes, she whispered in my ear, 'ma, ma, ma.' I felt such love from her."

"In truth, we're all enlightened," Linda says. "We just don't realize it."

She tosses the magazine back on the table and goes back to her reading.

The man in the chair lets out a huge sigh of relief.

Seeing the picture of my old guru is a shock. It brings back a flood of old memories.

A Crack in the Golden Egg
Kripalu Center, January 29, 1986

Sacred cows make great hamburgers.
Ray Kroc, Founder of McDonald's

I'm not sure when it all started, but in the late eighties it slowly dawned on me that a major shift was happening at Kripalu. For years Gurudev had remained intently focused on his own spiritual transformation and the transformation of his disciples. His success was our success; his enlightenment was our enlightenment. But lately this had changed. Gurudev seemed to have hit a plateau. He was bored or tired or both. I can't really blame him.

Gurudev had poured his life-energy into the community, transforming it from a rag-tag group of hippie yoga students into a multi-million dollar non-profit organization. He had received just about every prestigious award that could be given, from Maharishi (Great Sage), to Jagadacharya (Great Teacher), Acharya Pravaraha (Supreme teacher), and Doctor of Yoga. He had gone about as far as he could go. Perhaps the thrill had worn off. Who knows? Lately Gurudev seemed more concerned with traveling and building his own house, rather than spending eighteen-hour days overseeing the ashram. He gave seminars in India, Europe, and South America; he received more awards. A book was being written about him by my friend Sukanya, called *In the Presence of a Master*. Visitors began referring to him as an enlightened master and he was happy to go along with it.

For all the disciples and the large extended community of thousands, Gurudev was seen as a pillar of honesty and integrity. Not only did he tirelessly take care of the Kripalu "family," but had a wife and three children who he was very close to. Like everyone else, I saw him as a "master in the art of living," and desperately tried to emulate him in everything I did. He had limitless energy, was always warm and loving, and spoke from a place of great wisdom. Yet, he could also be playful and fun-loving, enjoying life in all its many aspects. No one had any reason to doubt that anything was amiss—at least until that dark, cold winter morning when fifteen other senior residents and I were called to a meeting with Gurudev at 5:00 AM.

After meeting in the main building, we walk up through the snow to the gate house, where Gurudev lives. We squeeze knee to knee on the floor of the tiny room that serves as Gurudev's office during the day and his bedroom at night (his wife and children sleep upstairs). A few minutes later Gurudev enters the room and takes his place at the front. We bow our heads to the floor as someone chants: *Bolo shri sadguru. Bolo shri sadguru.* We all repeat, *Bolo shri, shri Krishnachandra . . . Maharaj Ki Jai.* We sit back up and expectantly wait for news on why we're meeting.

Uma, the President of Kripalu, sits next to Gurudev. An attractive woman in her forties, Uma has been his "right-hand person" for years. Her devotion to Gurudev and tireless dedication to running the Kripalu organization are legendary. She out-works and out-devotes us all. I have enormous respect for her.

She begins by saying, "Gurudev and I feel it's important to bring you together today so that you can hear a first-hand report from us," she says, speaking in a soft, controlled voice. "An incident has come up that has serious implications."

"We wanted you to be the first to hear," Gurudev adds awkwardly. After countless hours of observing him, I have never seen him this uncomfortable.

This is unusual, I think. *It all seems so rehearsed.*

"As you know," Uma continues, "Gurudev and I were just in California, where Gurudev gave a seminar. We met some very important people who invited us to go on their yacht. A former resident named Sita, who all of you know, was also on the yacht. She claims to have seen something happen between Gurudev and me. This is what we wanted to talk to you about."

"We wanted to make sure there was no misunderstanding . . ." Gurudev says.

"What she claims is that she saw Gurudev leaning over me . . . and that there was . . . uhmmm . . . physical contact between us."

The room becomes utterly silent, everyone holding their breath.

"Yes, I was whispering something in her ear, but I wasn't touching her."

"He had something to tell me that he didn't want others to hear," Uma says with a forced smile.

"I just leaned over and that was all. Sita may claim that she saw something else, but it's not true."

Hmmm. If nothing happened, why are they making such a big deal out of this?

Uma continues in a conspiratorial voice, "As you know, Sita has been somewhat disturbed since leaving the ashram. From what we understand she has been sexually promiscuous. I would be cautious about believing anything she says."

"So we wanted you to hear our side of the story before any false rumors start."

Everyone listens with rapt attention. Gurudev has always insisted that the residents—most of them horny young men and women in their twenties—remain celibate. Over the years he has lectured again and again (and again) on how sexual activity drains our vital energies. He teaches that having sex prevents the divine energy from moving up our spine to the crown chakra. If we ever hope to become enlightened, we must remain celibate. He proudly tells us that he isn't having sexual relations with his wife any more.

Rani, one of the senior residents, raises her hand to speak. "Gurudev, I'm so touched that you are telling us what happened. It's just another way in which you show us your love. We know you'd never do anything that would be out of integrity."

"Yes," the others join in. Some have tears in their eyes.

Gurudev brings his hand to his heart and looks at us tenderly. "I love you all so much," he says. The tension breaks. The meeting is over.

As we all leave the room Rani says, "Well, even if something did happen, I still believe he's pure. We must never try to understand the actions of a guru."

I can't believe I'm hearing this, I think to myself. *Something is going on here and no one wants to admit it. But it's all hearsay. What can I possibly do?*

Later in the morning a meeting is held with the other three hundred residents so they can be informed. After going over the same story she told us, Uma asks for a show of hands, "How many of you believe what we've told you is true?" Everyone raises their hands. "How many of you believe Sita's story?" Not one hand goes up.

After a time the incident is forgotten, but an unmistakable and unspoken breach of trust has occurred. Why did no one—including me—ever question it? Looking back, I'm amazed to see how strong the power of denial can become in a community. Over time it can eat away at the truth like a hidden cancer. I, along with everyone else, preferred to live in a world of spiritual ideals than risk destroying the dream of a happy, loving spiritual community that could do no wrong.

Spiritual Candy
Kripalu Center, January 11, 1986

All I really need is love, but a little chocolate now and then doesn't hurt.
Lucy van Spelt, in *Peanuts*, by Charles M. Schultz

Every year thousands of visitors arrived at the Kripalu Center from New York, Boston, and around the world to participate in an array of programs on yoga, health, and personal growth. Many commented on how unique and special Kripalu was from the moment they entered the door. They were touched by the welcoming smiles, and could not help but notice the warm glow that emanated from the residents. When they left, a day, a week, or a month later, they came away feeling healthy, alive, and deeply transformed. This is what drew people to come back again and again. Very few knew what caused the glow. Some thought it was it was the yoga; some thought it was the celibate lifestyle; others were sure that it was the diet and exercise. Only a few knew where it really came from.

Every month or so the eight big doors to the main chapel were closed and the little round windows in the doors were covered over with signs saying, *"Residents only. Do not enter."* What went on behind those closed doors was a secret that most visitors knew nothing about. Ostensibly it was a time when residents had their own personal retreat, to recharge themselves and bond together as a group. That was part of what went on, but there was much, much more.

I vividly remember one of these retreats. As I enter the main chapel, sunlight is flooding. The carpet feels warm and soft under my bare feet . . . it has been walked over by thousands of feet—guests, residents, gurus (cleaned every month, thank goodness), all of them seeking in their own way to open to something greater than themselves. I take my place among the brothers and sit cross-legged on the floor, enjoying the smell of incense in the air. There are about two hundred people in the room, all wearing whites and saris out of respect for Gurudev, instead of their usual slacks and sweaters. I know each and every one of them like family, and like family, I knew most of their idiosyncrasies as well.

The retreat begins with chanting and meditation, led by Rhamba. With the pounding of the drums, and Rambha's powerful voice, everyone is soon up and dancing around. Following a brief meditation, Uma takes her place sitting on the edge of the dais. Next to her Gurudev's chair sits empty, except for the large photograph of him facing out towards the group. She instructs us to break up into dyads (brothers with brothers, sisters with sisters) and respond to a series of questions. We each find a partner and sit opposite each other. Prompted by Uma, one of the partners will ask, "Please tell me about your love for Gurudev," or "What stands in the way between you and Gurudev?" The other person has five minutes to respond, then we switch sides. The idea is to reflect on our love for Gurudev and rekindle our commitment to being good, hard working disciples. Four hours later we are as mushy as melted ghee (clarified butter) and have left our minds at the door.

After being in other retreats, I know something is coming up when Uma has us sit facing the front of the room. "Now I want you to close your eyes and see an image of Gurudev in your mind," she says in a soft and reassuring voice.

We all sit cross-legged, deep in concentration, with eyes closed as instructed.

"Imagine Gurudev standing before you," she continues in a hypnotic voice. "Imagine his hand reaching out to touch your head in blessing."

Tears are streaming down some people's cheeks. One sister starts crying.

"Keep your eyes closed. Feel his love and his energy moving through your entire body, from your head down to your toes."

More people begin sobbing. *Oh no, I've heard this so many times, and it never fails to crack them up. I guess they all just need a good cathartic release.*

"Give it all to the feet of the guru. Just let go. Let the guru take over your life."

I can't resist sneaking a look. What I see astonishes me. Gurudev is quietly stepping onto the stage next to Uma. No one else has noticed him. The picture has been removed from his chair. Uma and Gurudev nod silently to each other. *Oh my God! This has all been staged. It's all part of a show!*

Then I hear Uma's voice.

"When you are ready, you can gradually open your eyes."

There is a stunned gasp as everyone opens their eyes and sees Gurudev standing on the dais before them in his long ochre robe, his eyes closed, his head bowed, and his hands in prayer position. *Wow, it looks like he's magically floated down from heaven!*

Without saying a word, he sits in silence—apparently in deep meditation. Residents scurry around, bringing a harmonium, a microphone, and a small table onto the stage. There is a hush in the room as Gurudev starts to play the harmonium and chant. I hear the familiar sound of his voice chanting *Hare Ram, Hare Ram . . .* mingled with the drone of the harmonium. The sound resonates through the chapel.

I drink in the vibrations of the chanting, my eyes closed, instantly forgetting what I saw a few moments earlier between Uma and Gurudev. It doesn't take much to suck me back in.

With no warning the chant shifts into a long, continuous *Ommm* that rises and falls, shifting from high notes to low notes.

As if on cue, one of the brothers starts sobbing loudly—long, gut-wailing sobs. I recognize right away that it's Dharmendra. He always weeps when Gurudev gives shaktipat, calling forth that mysterious spiritual energy.

The *Ommms* continue. Some residents are standing now, swaying back and forth, arms held high in the air, as if in a trance. There are loud yips coming from the sister's side of the room. I don't even have to look to know that it is Aruni. She lives for these shakti sessions.

The chant changes to: *Oh Divine Mother Shakti, come to me Divine Mother.* Gurudev emits a loud **Huhhh!!!** from deep in his belly, as the shakti blasts through him.

My body jerks involuntarily. It feels wonderful and I want more, but I know after many of these sessions that this is about all that will happen. That's not true for others.

All hell breaks loose. Some are wailing or making strange grunts, others are rocking back and forth, a few are pounding their cushions with their fists. The chanting appears to go on forever. Gurudev has his eyes closed and his energy drawn inwards, but he clearly is in total control, able to stop whenever he wants.

Om Namah Shivayah, Shiva, Shiva, Shiva. Shakti Kundalini.

With three hundred people hooting and yelling and crying, the room is pandemonium.

I sit still as a stone, letting the sound reverberate through me. All the other commotion seems to be happening in some far off place. A sense of peace—almost like a "hum"—descends over me.

Finally I hear Gurudev's words through the chaos: *Hari Om Shanti, Shanti, shanti.* As quickly as it began, the crying stops. There is an audible release of breath as everyone sits down. A few residents are whimpering softly, but eventually that stops too.

Gurudev sits in his chair with eyes closed and in silence. It feels like a palpable sense of peace has taken over the room, as if each person has experienced the ecstasy of merging with God. Their faces are glowing, their bodies soft and relaxed—mine included. We are all sated, overflowing with love for guru and God.

After a few residents come up to share their undying love for Gurudev, the retreat is over. The residents are now fully charged up and ready to go back to serving God and guru for another month—with that knowing smile on their faces.

It would be many years before I understood what really went on in those shakti sessions. According to Indian tradition, shakti is a sacred initiation that activates the Kundalini energy. Once the Kundalini energy is awakened, it can lead to higher states of consciousness and open the way to enlightenment. In my naïveté I believed that if I got a big enough blast of shakti, I would be in bliss and happiness forever. But after experiencing these sessions for ten years, I realized that neither I, nor anyone else in the room, was waking up. In fact, we were becoming more and more dependent on Gurudev for giving us that high.

It finally dawned on me that the shakti given by Gurudev (and many others like him), was not about enlightenment. It was spiritual heroin—the more we got, the more we wanted. We believed that he was the only one with the special power to give it to us. So we came back again and again, begging for more. No doubt Gurudev's intentions were pure in the early days, but over the years I suspect that he intentionally used these sessions as a way to attract (and keep) devotees, and establish his authority as the guru. I often wonder whether the so-called transmission was little more than group hysteria. It certainly had nothing to do with spiritual awakening. No one can give enlightenment to anybody.

The Fall from the Throne
Taos, New Mexico, October 27, 1994

I will always be here for you in your hour of need. The connection to the guru that you have built in your good times will sustain you and give you faith in times of crisis.
Yogi Amrit Desai

It took a few more years before everything blew up. Although I still considered the Kripalu community as my "extended family," it had been five years since I had left the ashram.

Linda and I are having a quiet evening at our home in Taos when the phone rings.

"Have you heard the news?" Ranjana asks over the phone.

"What news?" I ask.

"Rani stood up in front of all the residents and said that she and Gurudev had had sex together. She's kept it a secret for twenty years."

"You've got to be kidding!" I say in shock.

"She describes in minute detail what happened. There's no way she could be making it up. From what she says, it wasn't romantic at all. Actually, it was pretty disgusting."

"What do you mean?" My first thought on hearing the news was, *how nice, two lovers entwined in a glorious union of Shiva and Shakti!* Then I remembered the years of Amrit insisting that the only way to become enlightened was to remain celibate, so that the "scared energy" could move up the spine.

"He just used her to do it, almost like an animal, with no love or tenderness."

"Wow! Has Gurudev admitted any of it?"

"At first he said that it was just one incident. Then he said that it was the guru giving shakti to the disciple and that we shouldn't be bothered by it."

"Everyone must be furious," I say, realizing that most residents had not had sex for years, thinking it would bring them to God. "What a betrayal!"

"Apparently there were others too," Ranjana says excitedly. "They're saying that he and Uma have been at it for the last ten years! The board has asked him to resign."

All the pieces are coming together. Now I know why Uma looked like the cat who swallowed the canary that time I saw her coming out of Gurudev's room in India!

"Remember when Sita said she saw Gurudev and Uma making out on that boat?" Ranjana says. "She's come forward and said that he seduced her as well.

126

What a cover-up. They tried to make Sita out as a liar, when she was telling the truth!

"I always wondered about that." Gurudev and Uma had painted Sita as a promiscuous slut. Well, maybe she was. I had heard tales of her being in an orgy with a famous Hollywood movie star, which only served to incite some wild, inappropriate fantasies.

"And there were others too!"

I start to laugh over the phone, partly out of disbelief, and partly out of seeing the exquisite perfection of all this. From the perspective of where I am now, it reveals how much we suffer get caught up in the story and believe it to be real.

"It's not funny," Ranjana says with annoyance. "The whole community is in chaos. I saw Ananda get up and smash Gurudev's chair to pieces. Everyone is tearing down Gurudev's pictures. It's like a prison riot."

"You're kidding! Smash up his throne? We didn't even dare sit on that chair, it was considered so holy."

My head swims; I can't help but celebrate what's happening. *God couldn't have planned it better. The whole place needed some kind of a shake up. But what a painful lesson for everyone.*

"Gurudev finally agreed to meet with the residents," Ranjana continues. "It was a near mob scene. People were screaming at him. Even when confronted, he still wouldn't cop to it."

What an extraordinary opportunity for Gurudev, I realize while listening to her. *Will he grow and transform from this, or remain stuck in his old beliefs? It's funny. I don't feel any anger towards him; I have nothing but compassion. Am I in denial?*

"What about his wife Mataji and the children?" I ask.

"Mataji is standing by him. I don't know how she does it," Ranjana says.

"And what happens next?"

"The Board has told Gurudev he has to leave. They've planned a series of meetings so that everyone can express their feelings. It looks like all the senior residents are going to leave."

"You mean people like Baladev and Malti, Taponhidi and Jyoti?"

"Yes, and more . . ."

"Wow, I don't believe it!" *It's over. It's all over. Rani will be one of the first to leave. She was seen as one of Gurudev's most loyal disciples. This is the end of Kripalu as I know it. Who would have guessed? After being part of the community for all this time I'm seeing it blow up in front of my eyes . . . guru and all!*

Gurudev is not just a minor figure in my life—like a high school teacher or a coach that I idolized. He has been the primary focus of my world, twenty-four hours a day, three hundred and sixty-five days a year, for fifteen years. I was ready to give up my life for him; I would have put myself between him and an assassin's bullet (at least, that was my fantasy). He was guru, teacher, friend, father, and the greatest inspiration of my life. I had moments where my love for him was so overwhelming that I shed tears of joy. When I was married to Fran, it was as if there were three of us in the relationship—Fran, me, and the guru. Even as Ranjana tells me what he has done, I can't see him as evil. I always imagined that my relationship with him would go on forever. But suddenly, here he is, tumbling off the throne.

The saga continues to play itself out over the next months, with the entire community going though extremes of emotional pain. After years of talking softly and never getting angry, the residents are screaming and yelling at each other. After years of worshipping the ground Gurudev walks on, they are filled with hate towards him. Talk about duality! Most thought they would be taken care of for the rest of their lives. Now they will be forced to go out into the world—a strange, alien planet—and earn a living. Most have never had a bank account, never owned a car, and never paid taxes. Their whole world has suddenly come crashing down around them. What an amazing play of consciousness! This is clearly Gurudev's greatest teaching.

It didn't take long to discover that events like this have happened in just about every spiritual community. With the enormous influx of Indian gurus in the seventies, communities sprang up all across the country. Many of them were short-lived, like comets flashing through the sky. One by one the teachers crashed, usually because they couldn't keep the pickle in the pickle jar (most likely, gherkins). Rumors flared about every well-known teacher, from Yogananda, to Swami Muktananda, Swami Satchidananda, Swami Rama, and countless others. Osho (formerly Bhagwan Shree Rajneesh) became known for his 64 (or was it 67?) Roll Royce's, and seemed to symbolize the excess of the era. As each of them came off their pedestals (or were yanked off), it seemed that the world of the authoritarian guru was crumbling forever.

But was it? My biggest surprise is finding out that nearly every one of these organizations is still flourishing, some even stronger than before! Even Gurudev has created a new community in Florida, identical to the one he started in Pennsylvania, over thirty years ago.

With Gurudev's fall, my experience with gurus is far from over.

In fact, it is just beginning.

Coming Home
King's Arms Tavern, Williamsburg, Virginia, April 24, 1998

Wine comes in at the mouth
And love comes in at the eye;
That's all we shall know for truth
Before we grow old and die.
I lift the glass to my mouth,
I look at you, and I sigh.
William Butler Yeats

"I'm just so happy," Linda says. "Even with this illness, I couldn't be happier. Who would think?"

Linda sits across the table from me, her blond hair tied back in a ponytail, wearing a long velour, burgundy dress. Lit by the soft candlelight, she looks as if she has stepped out of an eighteenth century painting. What better place to be in another era then the King's Arms Tavern in Williamsburg, Virginia. The tavern originally opened in 1772 and now serves meals in several small rooms that are decorated in the old colonial style, with dark mahogany paneling, fireplaces, and bare wooden floors.

"You're so courageous," I say. "Anyone else in your shoes would have killed themselves by now."

"It's not courage. It's just accepting what is. Believe me . . . I'd give anything not to have this pain."

"No, uh, it's more than that. You have the courage to look deep within and discover the happiness that is present even when you're in pain. Only a few rare people can do that."

"It's nothing special really."

I glance around at the other diners in the room, all enjoying the experience of eating the way Thomas Jefferson and his friends did two hundred years ago. I lift up my glass of cool, golden Chardonnay and notice the reflections of the candles glittering on the glass. *How beautiful*, I think, *the only light in the room is provided by candlelight. Why don't more restaurants do this? Think of the energy it would save.*

The server, wearing a white shirt, black leggings, and slipper-like shoes, deftly places a plate of appetizers on the table between us. "These are special relishes they served at the old tavern. They helped disguise the smell of rancid meat."

"Can't wait to try them," I say, glancing warily at the three piles of relish with some dry pinto beans in the middle.

Linda pokes at them with her fork. "It seems like some of the spiritual teachers we've been seeing lately smell like rancid meat, only they cover it up with patchouli."

"That's a good one," I laugh. "You're so right."

For the past few years we've traveled all around the country, getting an insider's view on teachers and spiritual communities. After Gurudev's fall, we founded our own retreat center (a disaster), and continued to immerse ourselves in the "spiritual scene." We were especially drawn to the many young Western teachers who were just beginning to present the radical teachings of nonduality. Along the way we heard story after story of teachers who had abused their power through sex, money, and emotional manipulation.

"I've just finished that book by Peter McWilliams called *Life 101*," Linda says. "I love the subtitle: *What to Do When Your Guru Sues You*. I swear all these gurus are either sociopaths or narcissists."

"It seems that the more outrageous they are, the more students flock to them. I've never figured out why."

"They have this charisma and can give people what appear to be authentic spiritual experiences," Linda says, getting warmed up, "but they're still caught up in ego."

"While telling everyone they have no ego . . ." I

"It's such a paradox—they give the appearance of being loving and wise but they're like spiders that lure a fly into a web, wrap them in a cocoon, and suck all their juices out." The words spill out with intensity.

"Suck their juices out? Wow—what an image!" I look around the room to see if anyone is listening, but everyone is engaged in their own conversations. Thankfully, we have a very private table for two by a window. "But I've seen it happen. Everyone confuses charisma with true spiritual power and before long they're hooked."

"Look at them—Amrit, Andrew, Osho, Werner Erhard, John-Roger, just to name a few. I think they all went to the same spider-training school."

"That reminds me—I was reading an interview with Bikram the other day, you know, the yoga teacher who heats the practice room up to 104 degrees. He said, 'Nobody does Hatha Yoga in America except me! I'm beyond superman. I have balls like atom bombs, two of them, 100 megatons each. Nobody fucks with me.' That's pretty ballsy!"

Linda almost chokes on the pinto beans she's laughing so hard.

"How do people fall for it?" I say.

Linda laughs even harder. "Look who's talking!"

"Yeah, you're right. I was suckered right in even though I had my antenna out for cults every step of the way. Wow, was I ripe for the plucking—growing up in a dysfunctional family, unhappy with Fran, and longing for community."

"You still haven't really dealt with your anger about Gurudev," Linda says, more somberly now.

"Anger? What anger? I still love the guy. He's a beautiful, loving human being. He's not malevolent. I just can't seem to get angry at him."

"Peter, how can you say that after what he's done—using his power to seduce young disciples?"

"Uhhhh . . ." My mind goes numb. I'll do anything not to have to look at this one.

The smoked trout arrives, providing a welcome diversion. Even with all the atmosphere and trimmings, the food still tastes like factory food made by Marriott catering, which it is.

"Recovering from a cult isn't easy," Linda says. "There's so much denial. Everyone wants to make excuses for an abusive guru. I know you must be angry at being taken in."

My mind flashes back to my life before Kripalu, when I was an accomplished author and filmmaker, in the full bloom of my creative expression.

Then it hits me: "Shit, I gave up my whole life and spent ten of my most creative years trying to be humble and selfless and never taking credit for anything. I was told by my guru that the ego was somehow 'dirty' and 'unspiritual'—yet there he was, taking credit for everything himself."

Linda rolls her eyes—she has little respect for Gurudev.

A rush of heat floods into my belly. *Whoa! Where did that come from?* I see an image of Gurudev with his adoring disciples, including me, bowing down before him.

"I'm fucking angry. I gave all my power away to him."

Linda's eyes widen. "You look like a volcano about to explode!"

"The bastard! The bastard!" I say through clenched teeth.

Linda reaches out to take my hand.

"God it feels good to say that. What a relief. That's been in there a long time."

"I'm so proud of you. I know how hard it is for you to express your anger."

The heat in my belly subsides, and I breathe a long sigh of relief. *Whew.*

Suddenly I notice that the noisy babble of conversation has become hushed. For a brief second I have a terrible thought: *They've noticed my outburst and have all turned to look at me!* I'm relieved when I turn to see a woman dressed in colonial garb, who has just entered the room to perform for us. She begins to sing a ballad in a clear, steady voice:

I live not where I love,
I search on and on for my true love.
My love lives far, far from me,
And he shall ner be found . . .

Everyone becomes silent as her plaintive words reach out across the room.

"She's singing about the other side," Linda whispers to me across the table. "It's about coming home."

I nod. Tears come to my eyes in the unbearable beauty of this moment.

We look at each other from a place beyond space and time. All separation falls away. There's no room, no people, no Williamsburg, no us. It is love experiencing love.

Linda sees how moved I am. "If it hadn't been for him, I would never have met you."

"Nor I you," I smile, "We're so lucky. As Ram Dass says, 'There are no accidents.'"

CHAPTER 8

THERE ARE NO PROBLEMS

Fran & Peter Leading a Program at the Kripalu Center

The Way Things Are Stinks
Mt. Ayr Farm, Virginia, May 10, 1999

Duck: "The way things are stinks."
Cow: "The only way you'll find happiness is to accept that the way things are is
the way things are."
From the movie *Babe*

The dogs fly through the screen door, pushing it open with a loud bang as they tear out to greet the intruder. A beat-up old Volvo station wagon is coming down the drive, stirring up a cloud of dust. It's our neighbor Kate. She often drops by for a visit on Mondays, when her little café in the town of Scottsville (pop. 500) is closed. The dogs excitedly run up to welcome her.

"Hi, come on in!" Linda calls from the porch. "We were just going to have some iced tea."

"That'd be nice," Kate says, as she walks down the curving brick sidewalk, with the dogs happily herding her to the house.

Kate gives us each a hug and hands Linda a bouquet of fresh-picked spring flowers.

"We were wondering if you'd want to come back after last time," I say.

"I don't know," Kate jokes. "From what you say, there is no such thing as time. The past is a dream and this is just a dream. So, why would it bother me?"

"Wow! You're really getting it," I laugh.

Kate takes the empty rocker next to mine; Linda is on the porch swing in her long dress, looking like a pioneer woman, as she gently swings back and forth. It is one of those magical Virginia spring mornings, with the sun shining after a few days of rain. Everywhere I look there is dazzling array of color—the shiny dark green leaves of the hundred-year-old holly tree, the silky light green of the mimosas with their pink brushes, the fresh green leaves of the maple tree, bursting with new life. Beyond the grassy yard and the white picket fence, there is a distant view of the Blue Ridge Mountains—a scene right out of a Thomas Kinkaid painting, though much, much better. Top that off with the fragrant smell of honeysuckle, and you're about as close to heaven as you can get.

"Pretty bird, pretty bird," Linda coos, imitating the song of the mockingbird as she swings back and forth.

A moment later comes the reply: *"Pretty bird, pretty bird"* from a nearby tree.

"Mockingbirds can imitate hundreds of songs," Linda tells Kate. "This one can even imitate the ring of our telephone . . . *pretty bird, pretty bird.*"

Sometimes I think Linda is more bird than human. She has an uncanny relationship with birds and animals and can see things that no one else can.

"What a magical morning," I say, taking a sip of iced tea. ". . . a moment of pure happiness." I groan in pleasure as I sniff the freshly picked mint.

We rock back and forth, enjoying the comforting sound of the rockers creaking on the wooden floor.

After a brief silence, Kate can no longer contain herself, and blurts out, "What about all the suffering in the world? Are we just meant to sit here while there is so much suffering going on out there?" There is a brief flash of color in her face, highlighting her strong features. With her long, thick blond hair, blue-green eyes, and full figure in bib overalls and work boots, she looks like an avenging Greek goddess. I can sense a deep well of power in Kate, but she always seems a millisecond away from sabotaging it with anger and resentment.

"I just don't understand it," she says, getting up from her chair and going over to the edge of the porch, where she sits down with her arms clutched around her knees.

Kate seems to have a low threshold for pleasure.

"But where is that suffering right now?" I ask. "Look at the beauty all around us."

Kate looks puzzled. "Yes, this is beautiful, but what about all those children starving to death in Africa?"

"You're right," I say. "We can't shut our hearts to all the pain that's going on in the world. There is, and always has been, terrible suffering in the world—it comes with living in duality."

"There must be something we can do about it—somehow make a difference."

"Maybe we're helping them by sitting here and talking about it?" Linda suggests.

"Maybe we should all join the Peace Corps," I say, trying to defuse the situation and get back to enjoying my iced tea.

"You can't just ignore them," Kate says, a hint of annoyance in her voice.

Here we go, I think, *our happy mood is out the window. Just flow with it. The peace is still there, behind all those anxious thoughts.*

"If we consciously set out to make a difference, we're acting from ego," Linda says. "I'm sure the Crusaders thought they were making a difference when they killed all the heathens, not to mention just about every other war that has been fought."

"For me it's even simpler," I say. "We either act in the moment or we don't—and it really doesn't matter. The entire universe is a projection of the mind. If someone were to walk up right now and ask for food, I would give it to them—or maybe I wouldn't. I'll only know in that moment."

"So you're saying just forget about the starving children."

"No. I'm suggesting you notice that in this moment that suffering exists only in your mind," Linda says.

"We know there are starving children in Africa," I say. "If we were meant to be helping them we'd be in Africa and not sitting here."

"That seems cold-hearted."

"Then why not go inside and write a check to the African Relief Fund right now?" I ask. "Would that relieve their suffering or your suffering?"

"But I'm not suffering. They're the ones who are suffering."

I don't know what to say and remain silent.

Linda walks over to the edge of the porch in her bare feet and gestures towards the lawn and the trees. "Look at this. Everything seems so peaceful, but even as we watch, some bird has a poor dragonfly in its mouth and is flying back to its nest to feed it to its babies. Somewhere else a dragonfly is eating a beautiful Monarch butterfly. And the Monarch is eating a milkweed plant. Everything I love is eating each other! But they don't have a story about it. There are trees dying, yet new life is shooting up from the earth. Billions of life forms are born and millions are dying in each moment. Is that any different from what's happening in Africa?"

"But humans are more important than animals and plant life, aren't they?"

"That's a belief," Linda says. "Are they really more important? Imagine you were up in a spaceship looking down at earth. Would any of these life forms appear to be any more important than any other?"

I can sense Kate resisting. "That sounds so impersonal."

"That's just it," I say. "It *is* impersonal! We think we're so special, but we're not. Our lives mean nothing and they mean everything at the same time—it's a paradox."

A tiger swallowtail flies into view, flitting from one of us to the other, then, just as suddenly, disappears.

Kate seems to be sitting in her own sad little world. Maybe we've gone too far. I want to reach out and hold her.

"I'm so sorry, Kate. There are no easy answers."

Tears well up in her eyes. "It still doesn't solve the problem. I want to help if I can."

"And that's part of the problem," Linda says, going over to sit next to Kate. "We want to help, because we feel that if we can do something, then our life will be worth something. When we get down to it, our life isn't worth any more than those life forms out there in the grass. That's a terrifying thought for us—to think that our lives mean nothing. But it's the truth. If we are willing to accept this fully, and to be in that nothingness, we discover the fullness of it all."

Kate looks unconvinced.

"I don't know," I sigh, searching for something to say. "God, or Source, or whatever you want to call it, created all this. Maybe we need to trust that God, or Source, is taking care of it. We humans so often think we are helping when all we're doing is hurting."

"That's a cop out," says Kate, "What about Mother Theresa? Didn't she make a difference?"

"Yes," replies Linda, "in many ways she did. She brought dying people in off the street and gave them food and love. On the other hand she refused to give them any pain medication and prolonged their suffering. Who's to say if she really helped?"

"No, no, I can't believe that!" Kate says, a flare of anger coming across her face.

"And let's not forget that she was fiercely anti-birth control in a country that is drowning from overpopulation," Linda goes on.

Damn, it feels like we're ganging up on her. That's the last thing I want to do. With all the compassion I can muster, I say, "The real problem is that we want a world where everyone is happy all the time and no one suffers. But that will never happen in this world of opposites. The only way we can really be happy is if we're willing to embrace all of it—the good, the bad, the joy, the suffering. That's when we'll find peace."

Kate nods. Something inside her seems to let go.

Sensing this, Linda says, "Kate, you may want to ask yourself the question, 'who is it that suffers?' If you're willing to go fully into it, you'll discover that 'you' do not suffer."

"You have a choice." I add. "The question is, 'do you really want to be free of suffering?' Some of us—myself included—get very attached to our suffering. It's like a friend. We don't want to be free of suffering, because we can't imagine who we would be without it."

"I've tried to get rid of my suffering," Kate muses, "but with no success. I've tried to eat it away; I've tried to sleep it away; I've tried to cry it away. Nothing has worked. It just pops up again and again."

"You'll never get rid of suffering unless you're willing to go right to the source, which is your own mind." Linda says.

"That sounds scary."

"It is. But what you'll find is that beneath the suffering there is peace and love such as you've never known. When you know that place you can remain open to all the suffering in the world, but it won't touch you in the same way."

"That helps," says Kate, looking at us with her huge green eyes. "Thank you."

"Speaking of suffering, my butt is incredibly sore and I have to pee."

Hands of Light
Easthampton, New York, December 3, 1987

If you detach yourself from identification with the body and remain relaxed in and as Consciousness, you will, this very moment, be happy, at peace, free from bondage.
Ramesh Balsekar

In the years before Gurudev's fall, a general air of complacency settled in at Kripalu. Outside teachers were brought in (something unheard of in the earlier years) to keep the residents stimulated and inspired. It was a Baskin Robbins approach—a new flavor each month. Yoga teachers like Bikram appeared on the scene to promote "Hot Yoga." When the residents complained, he called them sissies: "No more 'I'm too tired,' 'I'm too sick,' 'I'm too weak'!" he shouts. "YOU are a gold Rolls Royce vehicle! You are trying to start it with a Toyota key!" Another swami from India showed up, insisting that the secret to happiness is chewing each bite of food 150 times. A self-important Vedic astrologer overstayed his welcome (in true Indian fashion) and drove everyone nuts. Deepak Chopra, a friend of Gurudev's, came to give talks.

The residents, most of them now in their thirties, were "coming of age," and, like teenagers differentiating from their parents, wanted more independence. No one wanted to be working six and a half days a week anymore; no one wanted to be told what to do. Many of them sought inspiration elsewhere—attending Vipassana retreats, visiting other teachers, and learning new forms of alternative healing.

Behind the happy, caring smiles that guests saw, a hidden epidemic was going on at Kripalu. Some of it was the seven-day-a-week schedule; some of it was a result of what happens when 350 horny young men and women are put together in one building and told not to touch each other (as opposed to Osho's ashram in India, where residents were told the opposite). Many residents developed back problems, chronic fatigue (myself included), and other stress-related illnesses. This was a tough one, because our job was to teach everyone else how to get rid of stress and be healthy. In an attempt to heal ourselves, we flocked to see therapists, chiropractors, acupuncturists, and healers. This coincided with a time when alternative therapies were just coming into vogue—chelation, craniosacral, shiatsu, Reiki, homeopathy, visceral manipulation, applied kinesiology, just to mention a few. Healing was the "in" thing.

Like many other residents, I was suffering the effects of our workaholic lifestyle. I developed chronic fatigue and was exhausted most of the time. Sickness and disease are not an option at Kripalu. Hey, we are a "health" center. No one can get sick (though it's okay to "cleanse"). No one can die (yogis have "ageless bodies and timeless minds," as Deepak Chopra tells us). Those with chronic illnesses were quietly asked to leave, because they could no longer be good worker bees. We were supposed to stay young and healthy forever, like good yogis. Gurudev was our prime example. At sixty, he was slim, energetic, relaxed, and still able to do yoga postures that no one else could.

Some of the residents went off to healing trainings and returned as "healers." They were sought after for their skills and did sessions with the residents. Everybody wanted to be healed. My wife Fran and I were swept along in this wave and became passionate about the idea of becoming healers. A friend came back from a weekend retreat with Barbara Brennan, author of *Hands of Light*, saying, "Barbara is amazing! She has a Master's Degree in Physics and was a research scientist for NASA. She's been doing healing for years! She's just starting a year-long healing course in Easthampton, New York. You have to go!"

On a cold November day Fran and I take the ferry across Long Island Sound and find our way to the old Easthampton Town Hall for the first of ten trainings. We join about fifty others in the charming old meeting room for the first session.

Barbara Brennan looks like some kind of angelic apparition dressed in a long, flowing dress that sparkles like tiny stars. She is stunningly attractive, with salt and pepper blond hair, a warm, open face, and sparkling blue eyes.

After briefly telling us about herself, she introduces her spirit guide Heyoan. "We'll do a short meditation now and invite Heyoan to come forth to this gathering." In no time she goes into what appears to be a deep trance. Without warning, her voice changes in pitch to that of an androgynous male, speaking in archaic English. Still in a trance, she gets up from her chair and goes from person to person around the circle.

She approaches an overweight woman named Grace. "You have come from far away, from a planet in the Pleiades, where you have led many lives," Barbara (or more correctly, Heyoan) says. "You are here to remember what you know and be a healer." Tears of gratitude flow down Grace's cheeks as Barbara touches her face.

With some participants she silently moves her hands over their heads; with others she leans over and whispers into their ear. She speaks to one woman in a strange, raspy voice and the woman starts sobbing uncontrollably.

When she comes to me she says, "You must reclaim your power and be the leader that you are. You are needed on the planet!"

Holy shit, what's going on?

"You have a radiant heart," she says, reaching towards my chest and placing her hand firmly on it. Her breathing becomes loud and rapid: "**Huh, huh, huh.**"

"You must take this light down to your feet, bring it down into the earth." Her hands move down to my feet. My body starts to jerk.

Oh my god, I'm getting shakti!

The air in the room is electric.

"You are a priest, a shepherd, and you feed your flock," she says with intensity. *Oh my God. Does this mean I'm going to be a great teacher?* (Little did I know that years later I would be shepherd to a flock of sheep).

Over the next few days we learn to read auras; we find out how to energetically sense the different chakras; we are given demonstrations on healing energy blocks. We do hands-on work with our fellow students, taking turns as one of us lies on an uncomfortable fold-up picnic table while the other becomes the healer. We practice moving our hands about six inches over their bodies, searching for energy blockages. Before long we can tell whether the chakras are open or closed and how fast they are spinning. Then we lay our hands on areas that are off balance, allowing energy to flow through them. We are taught that this healing energy has its own wisdom . . . all we need do is get out of the way.

I'm lit up by all of this and am flying high. At one point I feel a flood of bliss pouring through me and out my hands as I work on a "patient." Later my partner shares, "It felt like this shield of white light was being placed over my chest." Stunned by the idea that God's healing energy is moving through me in this way, I think, *Yes, yes. This is what I want to do more than anything else . . . be a healer!* My dream is not only to heal others, but to heal myself. Ever since my mother died, I've felt powerless to help others who are sick or in pain—I'm terrified of illness. Now I can reach out and share my love with all who need it.

Every month Fran and I come back to Easthampton for further training. We become friends with Barbara and often visit her house. On one of our visits Fran asks Barbara to look at a lump in her breast that has gotten hard and increased in size. Barbara puts Fran on the table and does a reading. After carefully feeling the lump she says, "No, no, this isn't cancer. It's just a fibrous cyst." Fran is overjoyed to hear the news.

That weekend Barbara and her assistants do a special healing on Fran, performing what they call "spiritual surgery" to clear her body of any disease. With Barbara observing, one of the assistants moves her hands over Fran's abdomen with her eyes closed. "I'm going into the liver now . . . I'm moving across to the spleen. Hmmm . . . everything is normal so far." Barbara gravely nods her head and says, "Good, now clear the adrenals." I feel like I'm watching a group of surgeons operate on a patient. All that's missing are scrubs and masks—and a license to practice medicine.

On our way back to Lenox, we're pumped up and happy to be alive. We spend the night at the Bee and Thistle Inn, an elegant country inn in Old Lyme, Connecticut. After dinner we make love in our canopy bed, which is right over the dining room. In the throes of passion, with the old bed rocking and banging, and both of us moaning like we're in an x-rated movie, we crack up with laughter.

"Imagine the guests downstairs below us," I howl. "They'll think we're the new-lyweds who got married this afternoon."

After more than twenty years of being together, it feels like we've just met.

Before we go to sleep Fran says, "I'm so glad that I don't have cancer, but maybe I should get a biopsy, just in case."

A Hobby for the Healthy
Berkshire Medical Center, Pittsfield, Massachusetts, February 29, 1988

I want to let you in on a little secret. There are no problems. There never were
any problems. There are no problems today, and there never will be any problems.
Problems just mean the world isn't turning out the way you want it to.
Robert Adams

Fran and I are both quite cavalier as we wait for the results of the biopsy. Fran
has had several biopsies in the past and they all were negative. And now we have
Barbara's reassurance that the tumor is benign.

The doctor ushers us into his office with a warm hello and a smile on his face.

"I'm looking forward to getting this over with," Fran mutters under her
breath.

We both sit down as the doctor takes his place behind his desk.

"I have the results of the biopsy," he says. "Unfortunately it's malignant."

"Malignant!" Fran exclaims in total surprise. "Are you sure?"

"Yes, it's definitely cancer and it appears to have metastasized."

I try to remain calm, covering up my shock by taking notes. "Can you tell
how advanced it is?"

"It's a Stage IV tumor, I'm afraid. We'll have to do further tests to see how
much it has spread. It appears to be very aggressive though."

Fran says nothing as she tries to take it in.

"What are the next steps?" I ask, feeling this huge panic well up inside.

"We can do radiation and chemotherapy, but these will primarily be for palliative care." The real meaning of palliative care passes me by completely. It will
be a long time before either of us can accept that she has just been given a death
sentence.

There is no celebration this time when we leave the office. "My God, what am
I going to do?" Fran keeps repeating to herself. Fear wraps itself around us like a
lead blanket. We call a few of our close friends and in no time the whole of Kripalu
knows about it. Everyone does their best to reassure us.

Susan calls to say, "Oh, I have a friend who had breast cancer and she's doing
fine." Our hopes soar.

Someone else calls saying, "I just wanted to tell you how concerned I am. My wife died of breast cancer two years ago."

Our hopes crash.

There is a sinking realization that in one swift moment our whole life has been turned upside down.

"What do you want to do?" I ask Fran as we sit over dinner.

"I want to find every possible way I can to heal this cancer through alternative methods. I'll try allopathic medicine as well—but since the cancer has already spread I'm not going to have my breasts cut off."

"I'll support you in whatever you want," I say.

"I know I don't want to stay here," Fran says, picking at her food. "As much as I love everyone at Kripalu, I would go crazy having them coming around every two minutes trying to heal me."

"Then let's go somewhere else."

Fran lets out a sigh of relief and says, "I feel like I'm being released from the cage of my 'shoulds.' I've spent my entire life trying to be something for someone else. Now I can finally relax and take care of myself."

Fran and I immerse ourselves in learning everything we can about breast cancer. The prognosis is grim and the reality of it begins to strike home. Fran wants to explore alternative healing and calls Barbara for suggestion. The fact that Barbara completely misdiagnosed her 2 ½ inch-sized tumor doesn't seem to bother Fran at all. Barbara recommends someone in Florida named Michael, who is not only a healer and a rabbi, but a 6th degree karate expert. Within days we've extricated ourselves from our busy teaching schedule at Kripalu and are on a plane to Florida.

Behind the horror of knowing that Fran has advanced breast cancer, there is an unexpected sense of aliveness. All the things we once took for granted—dinners out together, seeing our son Peter every few months, teaching at Kripalu, our next vacation—have been tossed out the window. We both know there is no going back. We are starting a new life right in this moment. We know that nothing will ever be the same again, yet at the same time, we realize, nothing ever is the same anyway. As the hours and the days go by, everything we do becomes heightened, whether it's just holding hands or stopping to look up at the stars in the night sky. By looking at death we are discovering how to be alive.

In a tacky suburb outside of Fort Lauderdale we go for our first healing session with Michael. He greets us at the door in black leather shoes and pants, a polyester white shirt and a yamalka. He takes us through his living room, which smells of boiled cabbage, down to his dingy basement. After introducing his healing work, Michael works on various pressure points on Fran's feet, making her yelp with pain. He continues on through her cries, claiming that he is reprogramming the DNA that produced the cancer. From what I can see, it is little more than glorified foot reflexology, done hard enough to create a huge amount of pain. He teaches me his special technique so I can massage Fran's feet twice a day until she heals. Will it work? Fran is optimistic and she likes Michael. I find him arrogant and narcissistic, but who am I to say? I dutifully drive Fran out to his little house in the suburbs every day.

We find a little efficiency apartment on the beach in Fort Lauderdale, where we wake up to the sun flooding through the shutters, the palms clacking in the wind, and ocean breezes filling the room. Here we are in sunny Florida, and for an instant it's easy to believe that nothing has changed. We spend hours walking on the beach, soaking up the healing power of the ocean. Every so often I sneak a glance at Fran, who looks glowing and healthy despite what is happening deep within her body. I try to freeze an image of this healthy person in my mind, knowing it will soon change—forever.

We decide to stay in Florida for more tests. When I complain about how expensive it will be, Fran says, "Look Peter, one day in the hospital at home will cost more than we're spending here. I'm going to stay as long as I can before going back into all that mess." Utterly terrified, she submits herself to a battery of tests, including CAT scans, bone marrow biopsies, and all kinds of blood work. We meet with oncologists and radiologists who impress us with their caring and concern. We have an interview with a surgeon in an Armani suit, Gucci loafers, and a gold Rolex watch, who tries to convince Fran to have a radical mastectomy. Fran leaves disgusted, knowing that a mastectomy won't be of any help at all, since the cancer has spread.

Our crash course on breast cancer continues. We read books with statistics stating that one woman every thirteen minutes dies of breast cancer. We watch a video of a doctor removing a huge tumor from a woman's breast and placing it on a tray.

Welcome to the world of sick bodies.

What a farce—we've been involved with health and healing for years. As "yogis" we preached endlessly on how yoga can make you stay healthy forever. We prided ourselves on being vibrantly healthy ourselves. Now, to our shock, we realize that we know nothing about real illness, nothing about death, nothing about suffering.

It slowly dawns on me that our comfortable world of yoga and healing is little more than a hobby for the healthy . . . and the wealthy.

There are nights when we go out on the deserted beach and walk for hours. Fran wails and cries over the howling wind and crashing waves. "I may be dead before the end of the year," she shouts, "I'm not afraid to die, but I don't want to be burned, cut up, and poisoned!" We both go down on our knees in the sand, my tears joining her tears. *Please, God, don't let her suffer,* I silently plead. All my spiritual ideals about being serene and composed in the face of death go out the window.

Dawn comes.

Another day of Florida sunshine.

As quickly as the wind and waves recede, there is a realization that—behind the story and the melodrama—life is happening, moment by moment. It's no big deal—sickness, health, wind howling, waves crashing, calm seas, sunshine—it's all what is.

Already we're starting to recreate our crazy life at Kripalu, with appointments, phone calls, and a long list of "to do's." Fran finds out that shark oil is being touted as the latest cancer remedy and soon adds it to the huge number of mega-vitamins she is taking. We buy books on healing and devour them—Bernie Siegel, Carl Simonton, Elisabeth Kubler-Ross, and other pioneers in alternative healing. We're reassured when Bernie Siegel says, "For every form of cancer, someone has been healed from it."

"Yes, with God's help I *can* heal myself!" Fran insists passionately. "I want to become a healer and start a healing center in Hawaii."

Healing has become her latest project and she leaps on it with a vengeance.

One evening we have a romantic dinner out at a little Italian restaurant, where we quickly go through a bottle of wine. There are tears and laughter. "I want you to get married again," Fran says, "but promise me you won't marry Kira!" We both laugh. Fran has been jealous of our friend Kira, a strong-willed, lusty woman with a temper just like Fran's.

"But I may go before you. Anything can happen!"

"You can't. You have to stay here for Peter," Fran says. Our son Peter is now in his twenties. Tomorrow he's flying down from Washington to be with us. He has been incredibly supportive over the phone through this difficult time.

"We've been so serious and responsible all our lives," I say. "Let's learn from this and take some time to play."

"All my life I've worked, worked, worked. What does it all mean now?"

"Nothing. Not a damned thing."

"If I have a year to live, I want to move to Hawaii and walk on the beach every day," Fran says, her eyes moistening. "I know I can be healed there."

"Then let's do it," I say, reaching out to take her hand. "We can build a house on our land." The year before we had gone to Kauai looking for land to build a retreat center on, and had bought thirteen acres for $250,000.

Fran squeezes my hand. "This may be the best thing that has ever happened to us."

"Yes, let's live our wildest dreams!"

Our love feels as pure and innocent as the day we met. For years all we did was endlessly talk about our future plans or future trips. Now we have no idea what will happen ten minutes from now, much less tomorrow. We've been dragged kicking and screaming into the present.

CHAPTER 9

THE WORLD OF HEALING

Fran at Ole Nydahl Retreat on Maui

Magical Thinking
Holistic Health Expo, Silver Springs, Maryland, May 3, 1999

At my age, what's to look forward to? If I'm good and I eat real healthy, then I
can get sick and die.
Rodney Dangerfield

A slim bearded man stands on a small platform with his eyes closed and his head tilted down towards his chest. His legs are bent at the knees and his right arm hangs limply at his side, making him look like Michelangelo's famous sculpture of the "Pieta." A man stands behind him supporting his body, and to his right, an overweight woman wearing a long, sequined dress holds his other arm out perpendicular to his body. With a look of intense concentration she moves the man's arm in small circles.

"Oh my God," Linda says. "It looks like some kind of freak show." We've just driven 130 miles to attend the 1999 Holistic Health Expo in Silver Springs, Maryland.

"They're doing magnetic healing," our friend Dona says in a hushed voice, not wanting to disturb the solemnity of the scene. Dona is a therapist and healer from Charlottesville, who has joined us for the day. She makes a striking figure, even among a crowd of very colorful people. She is slim and delicate, with long white hair, and a beautiful face framed by a purple silk scarf thrown around her neck. Dona's face has the kind of universal beauty that makes her look at home anywhere. In Italy she looks Italian; in Costa Rica she looks Costa Rican; in Bali she looks Balinese.

She turns to me with a big smile, "You should try it sometime!"

Dona could be a poster child for the New Age. She always speaks in a soft voice, eats nothing but organic food, and is always trying some new therapy. Recently she paid hundreds of dollars to talk into a telephone hooked up to a computer in Boulder, Colorado. Based on the sound of her voice, the computer printed out detailed graphs analyzing all her internal organs and recommended treatments. For the last year Dona has lived almost exclusively on a diet of nuts and raw food. Her thin body has become almost transparent, her skin soft and luminous.

"Maybe later," I say, shuddering at the thought of making a fool of myself like that guy up on the stage.

The Expo is packed with huge crowds making their way down narrow aisles with booths on either side. I gape in amazement at the scene before me. There are the obvious "professional healers" in their long, flowing gowns and crystal jewelry, New Age hippies with long hair and tie-dye T-shirts, older couples with white hair and curious faces, Sikhs in turbans and white clothing, yogis wearing tights to reveal their toned, taut bodies, fortunetellers in exotic clothing sitting at small tables. There are booths to promote everything from crystals to gemstones to miracle cures. Beyond the babble of voices the delicate sounds of harp music can be heard floating through the air. It has the wonderful flavor of a medieval carnival, except for the plastic booths, loudspeakers, and fluorescent lighting.

We stop at one of the booths, which has a display of healing gemstones. An attractive young woman stands behind the table with a bright light behind her. I squint as I try to make out her face. "I can hardly see you!" I say.

"That's because I'm an angel," she says, smiling and doing a little angel dance. "Yes, you *are* an angel!" I reply with a big smile, really meaning it.

"And so are you," she laughs.

Dona walks up and looks at the gems. "These are interesting," she says. "What are they?"

"They bring in special healing energy from the other planets. You must have a clear aura to receive the energy," the angel replies.

"I'll bet," Linda whispers to me, rolling her eyes.

We walk on, past practitioners giving free massages on their massage chairs, Reiki Masters slowly sweeping their hands over a client's body, yoga teachers demonstrating a half-spinal twist, motivational speakers promoting workshops that promise success and happiness. At another table a group of people with glowing, healthy faces are promoting something called Juice Plus, which apparently can cure everything from cancer to diabetes.

"What a zoo," Linda says, as we struggle to stay together in the crowd.

"Do any of these magic potions actually work?" I ask Dona.

"Oh yes," Dona says. "I have a friend who was cured of cancer by eating raw foods and doing colonics. Her cancer totally disappeared. I wish Linda would try it, but I know she won't."

Ever since Linda found out she has an auto-immune disease, she has been besieged by well-meaning friends who say, "Oh, I had the same thing you did and ate wheat grass. Now I'm healed!" Linda has tried her share of alternative therapies, but none have helped. Their helpful suggestions only make her feel worse.

We find a small juice bar with some chairs. Dona orders a carrot and beet juice mix. I rebelliously order a cappuccino, feeling like I'm committing a mortal sin.

"What do you think of all this Peter?" Dona asks, as she delicately takes a tiny sip of her juice.

"I'm amazed. When Fran had cancer ten years ago, only a handful of people knew about any of this stuff. Now it's a 2.5 billion dollar-a-year industry!"

"Yeah," Linda says with a laugh. "They all promise perfect health and happiness where we never get old, never get sick, and never die. No wonder it's booming."

"I feel they're offering solutions for living a healthier, more balanced life," Dona says in almost a whisper. I have to lean forward and cup my hand over my ear to hear her. "Most people have terrible diets and don't take care of themselves. I think they offer a service, don't you?"

"I'm OK with that," says Linda. "But they equate eating right and pampering our bodies with being spiritual."

"And if we eat badly we're not spiritual," I laugh. "I can't imagine any of these people in McDonald's. New Agers can get very self-righteous at times."

"Do you think so?" asks Dona. "Don't you feel that we need to treat our bodies as a temple as long as we have them?"

"Yes," Linda laughs, ". . . so we can have the best body in the graveyard."

"All this talk about health food is driving me nuts," I groan. "What I wouldn't give for a chocolate brownie . . . and all they have are rice crackers and fresh fruit!"

I turn to watch the river of people flowing by, all with a look of expectation on their faces. It's as if they're searching for something and don't know what it is. Forgetting about my stomach for a moment I say, "All these people really want is happiness. They think they'll be happy if they can find some magic panacea that will keep their bodies young and healthy forever. It's an admirable goal, but doomed to failure."

"Failure?" Dona asks.

"Yes, failure . . . because bodies get old, sickness happens, and death happens. We may postpone it for a little while, but no one gets out of here alive. They're looking for happiness in the wrong place. They desperately want to control something that can't be controlled."

"True happiness has nothing to do with the body," Linda says.

"I love what Ramana Maharshi says," I smile. "'To identify oneself with the body and yet seek happiness is like attempting to cross a river on the back of an alligator.'"

"That's a good one."

"Look!" I say, picking up the program. "Here's a workshop on *How to Bring Happiness and Love into Your Life* at 2:00 PM. Maybe we should go?"

"But you and I have already have that," Linda beams, giving me a hug.

"And here's one called *Raw Juice Fasting, a Purification Retreat,*" says Dona.

"No! No! No!" Linda and I cry out together.

Changing the subject, Linda asks, "Fran tried a lot of alternative therapies, didn't she?"

"Yeah, she tried everything . . . and so did I."

A wave of anger sweeps over me as I think back to all the time and money Fran and I put into trying to find a cure for her cancer. We so wanted to believe that the next therapy would work. When one didn't work, we'd try another, always forgetting that the previous one was meant to "cure" her. We were always looking for the next thing, the next cure, always struggling, always hoping. Fran did what most Americans are conditioned to do-she "battled" her cancer. What would have happened if she had accepted that she had a short time to live and rested in peace? What if she had given up the struggle and surrendered? Ah, no regrets. She did exactly what she needed to do. As I come to this realization, my anger dissolves and there is peace. I can see that the memories are still fresh—all this happened just eight years ago.

A Healer's Paradise
Kauai, April 15, 1988

So we don't own ill health and we don't own health. There is health and there is ill health. Possibly the most powerful healing is when there is no investment to heal, when there is simply present awareness.
Tony Parsons

The Aloha Airline jet slowly circles on its descent into Lihue Airport on the island of Kauai. Sitting on the left side of the aircraft, I see the familiar green mountains dropping precipitously into the sea and waves crashing on the shore. From above, the ocean appears a luscious emerald-green.

"Aloha ladies and gentlemen, welcome to the island of Kauai," the native Hawaiian flight attendant says over the PA system. She pronounces it *Ka-wa-ee* in the Hawaiian manner: "Kauai is called the Garden Island. It is known for its natural beauty, unspoiled beaches and tropical rain forests. It has a population of 52,000 people. The island is oval in shape and thirty miles long at its widest point. Enjoy your stay on the Garden Isle. Mahalo."

Only a few hundred feet from the ground, the plane glides over the huge Westin resort, with its fantasyland of elaborate pools, lagoons, and golf course on the edge of the sea. In the distance I can make out Wai'ale'ale, the cloud-covered mountain in the center of the island. Mount Wai'ale'ale is known as the wettest spot on the earth, with 450 inches of rain per year. Looking toward the north of the island I can see Anahola Mountain, where legend has it that the Star People landed many millennia ago. It is at the foot of this mountain, on a magical spot overlooking the Pacific Ocean, where Fran and I will make our new home.

Tears are flowing down Fran's cheeks as she looks out the window. "I have a feeling I'm coming home," she says. "I need to be here for my healing. I need to walk the beaches and put my feet in the ocean." Does she on some level know she's coming here to die?

We find the rental house we'll be staying in for the next weeks—a small A-frame right on Anahola beach. Our plan is to build a peaceful sanctuary on our land where Fran can live out her days, however long that might be. In just a few weeks we've found an architect (Jack Young—a wonderful, crazy Colorado mountain man with a moustache) and come up with a plan.

Before we start building we invite a Hawaiian priest to bless our land, first in Hawaiian then in English: "May the spirits be appeased; may all those who work here be protected." Next to the small waterfall, Fran and I create an altar of hibiscus flowers, light a candle, then sprinkle rice and flower petals into the stream. We decide to call the farm Aloha Mana, meaning "the power of divine love."

"Someday we'll have beautiful healing gardens here," Fran says to the priest. "On the hill we'll have a house overlooking the ocean. People will come here for healing."

Fran has found her paradise, walking the beach every day, listening to the birds and the ocean, and feeling the soft caress of the breeze on her skin. "Bliss, pure bliss," she sighs. "No responsibilities, enough money, health in this moment, loving each other. What more could I possibly ask for?"

It may be her paradise, but it's not mine. There are mornings when I wake up enveloped in cold waves of fear. I feel like I've been ripped away from everything I love and care about—my son Peter, my friends, my family, my community. My old fear of isolation brings all my core issues to the surface. Here I am, 5,000 miles from home, taking care of Fran, who may be dead within the year. She seems healthy now, but what lies ahead?

From Magic to Magnets
Kauai, 1988 to 1990

Love is the only thing we carry with us when we go, and it makes the end so easy.
Louise May Alcott

Kauai is known as the "healing island" and it doesn't take long for Fran to find all kinds of alternative healers. One of the first ones we meet is a man named Jim. We knock on the door of his condo in Princeville. A few moments later a striking-looking woman with long, straight, black hair opens the door. Her face is extremely pale and her eyes are heavily made up with mascara, making her look like Morticia from the Addams family. "Hi, I'm Jim's wife. Come on in," she says in a soft voice. Fran and I follow her into the darkened condo. We both notice she's wearing shoes. *Shoes? No one wears shoes in a house in Hawaii . . . and it's all dark inside!*

Her husband Jim comes out from the back room, wearing polyester pants and a white shirt with long sleeves. He ushers us into his office, which has all the shades drawn. It looks like a mad scientist's laboratory, with electronic equipment, monitors, pill bottles, and manuals everywhere. "I apologize for the mess," he says. "We just moved here from Florida." He offers us a seat.

"Did you bring your medications?" he asks. Fran dutifully hands him a plastic bag filled with bottles. "Let's start by testing those."

"This is the Vegatest diagnostic system," he announces proudly, bringing forward a computer-sized instrument with German lettering on it. "It's a state of the art system that provides highly sensitive biofeedback. It can tell if the medications you're taking are suited for your body." He places some of Fran's multi-vitamins on a tray and picks up a pencil-like tool connected to the machine. He presses gently onto Fran's fingernail with the tip of the instrument. "This is an acupuncture point I'm pressing on," he says. "It will tell how your body responds to the vitamins."

We all watch the needle, which barely moves.

"The vitamins seem to be OK for you. Let's try one of your medications." Fran hands him a bottle of Tamoxifen, an anti-cancer drug given to patients with breast cancer. He puts it on the tray, then presses on her fingernail. Instantly the machine makes an electronic noise like a screeching Geiger counter as the needle soars up into the red. Jim looks very serious. "As you can see, this medication would cause severe negative side-effects if you were to use it.

"Really?" says Fran incredulously.

"Yes. Each body is unique and despite what doctors tells you, the same medication can't be used for everyone. This instrument will show which medications support your individual body. It can also determine which organs are under stress and the specific toxins that are stored in your body."

Fran's eyes open wide in amazement. The wild swing of the meter seems to be proof of its veracity. "This is amazing—to think I was going to take Tamoxifen!"

As a willing partner on Fran's healing journey, I usually try all the same treatments she does. I tell Jim that I have been experiencing fatigue for several years and have tried everything from a macrobiotic diet to colonics to deal with it. "Hmmm," he says. "I have a hunch. Do you have any old fillings in your mouth?"

"Yes, I've got all kinds of stuff in there."

"Let me show you something." He pulls out another instrument. "This is the Voll machine invented by Dr. Reinhold Voll, a German scientist. It will give me direct bio-feedback on where your energy-drain is." He flicks on different switches and adjusts the dials. "If you'll open your mouth I'll check it out."

He touches different teeth with the probe . The needle on the machine doesn't move. Suddenly there's a loud *BREEEEP!* and the needle leaps up to the high end of the scale. "You see, I just touched the needle to one of your fillings. The reading is up in the 200 area."

"200!"

"Well, 60 is bad and 0 is good. It would suggest that you're allergic to the silver inlays. That's the likely cause of your fatigue."

"You're kidding!"

"If I were you, I would consider having all your fillings replaced. I know of a dentist in Honolulu who can do it."

Three trips to Honolulu and three thousand dollars later, I have five new inlays and no more amalgam fillings. The dentist, a man with big, hammy hands, turns out to be totally inept. I have to go back to another dentist to get the work completely redone for another three thousand dollars. And I'm still exhausted. Is this stuff all New Age quackery?

Fran is convinced that Jim's healing work is helping her. She invites him and his wife to move into the guest wing of our house in exchange for treatments. I'm annoyed at her offering them free space, but if it helps her to heal, I'll do just about anything.

As Fran eagerly embraces each new healing modality, whether it's crystals, magnets, psychics, diets, or acupuncturists, she attracts an astonishing array of people around her. Fran always wanted to have her own healing center, and now she's got it—but not in the way she imagined. The first to join the menagerie is Keani, the nude chiropractor. From what I hear, he once had his own chiropractic clinic on the mainland. When the rat race became too much for him, he set off for Hawaii, bought an old VW van to live in, and gave himself a new name. In exchange for free treatments, Fran gives him permission to park his VW bus under some banana trees. He and his girlfriend Joy spend their days smoking pakololo and hanging out in the little camp they have set up. With his short, stocky frame, black beard, and twinkling eyes, he looks like a modern day Pan. Every few days he puts on a pareo (the rest of the time he goes around nude) and comes up to give us adjustments.

Then there is Nina from Germany, with her clear eyes, radiant skin, and long lustrous light brown hair that goes down to her behind. She cooks us gourmet macrobiotic food every week, which I do my best to enjoy. Then there is Dave, a guy we picked up hitchhiking, who comes by to cook Indian food for us twice a week. He lives outdoors on Secret Beach and seems to have lost some of his shingles somewhere in India. Karuna, a petite Jewish woman with incredibly strong hands, gives us massages every week. Her deep energetic bodywork produces huge cathartic releases for me. Latifa, another healer, gives us acupuncture treatments. Kauai seems to attract people like this by the droves.

One day a plump psychic healer in her sixties shows up at our door. Her name is Margaret. She massages Fran's breasts praying to Lord Jesus to work through her hands and take away her pain. Margaret radiates motherly warmth and love, and is surrendered to whatever life brings her. She lives on a $148 social security check and still will not take any remuneration for her healing. "I'm just doing God's work," she says. Every morning she goes to the hospital and offers free massage to the patients. What a dear.

Lois, another friend, does past-life regressions. She tells us details about our past lives that are so specific that it's hard not to believe her. When she tunes in to my subtle energies she says, "You're fearful of losing your beloved wife. This is an inner challenge for you—a healing in consciousness. You must realize that you are struggling to arrive at a state that you already hold. There is nothing you need to do except trust. Just let go."

Healing into Life and Death
Aloha Mana Farm, Kauai, 1988 to 1990

This is my secret. I don't mind what happens.
J. Krishnamurti

Our experiences with alternative healing are supplemented by trips to the local hospital on Kauai to see Fran's doctor, Neal Sutherland, who becomes a good friend as well. He believes in empowering his patients to take responsibility for their healing, yet is not afraid to be direct when he needs to be. When Fran starts talking about a complete remission, he says, "Fran, you can't keep living in a dream world. You have Stage IV cancer that has spread to your hip bones and your ribs. You now have weeping cysts on your breast. If you don't do chemotherapy, you will soon be in a lot more pain. You may want to think about chemotherapy. It won't cure you, but it will reduce your pain."

Fran continues to desperately search for cures and alternatives. She hears about an experimental treatment for cancer being done at the Mayo Clinic in Rochester, Minnesota. Fortunately, she is able to get money from her trust fund to pay for all her medical expenses. Two days later we're on a plane to Minnesota, where we spend a horrible week of being shunted from doctor to doctor and going through every test imaginable, before being told that her the cancer is too advanced for her to take the treatment. We fly back to Hawaii deeply discouraged.

Someone tells us about another treatment that has been highly successful in Germany. Fran considers flying to Europe, but thank God, decides against it. I tread a fine line between wanting to support her in her search for a cure, and trying to have some objectivity about whether the next panacea will work or not. Healing is now a full time job for both of us. It's a constant roller coaster between blood tests, X-rays, MRI's, and doctors' visits. Nothing can be planned, because one day she's feeling well, and the next she's in pain. Whether I like it or not, I am forced to take life day by day, moment by moment.

Despite all the alternative healing she's doing, the cancer steadily progresses until X-rays show that two ribs have "disappeared" and she has lost much of the bone density in her hip. Her left breast is now covered with tumors that look like hamburger meat. Fran finally opts for chemotherapy, and to her surprise, finds that it's not as terrible as she imagined. Her hair falls out and she's nauseated some of the time, but she doesn't suffer as badly as most do. Week by week we watch the results of the blood tests, going from elation when her CEA level drops, to depression when it goes up. Now it's up to 44.2 and she's limping because of the pain in her hip.

Once a week we attend a healing group led by Neal and his wife Linda at the hospital. Several in the group have AIDS; others have cancer or heart conditions; some have exotic illnesses such as Marfan's syndrome and myelodysplasia. It's a revelation for me to hear the gratitude each person has for the gifts that have come through their illness. Some open their hearts in love for the first time; others learn what it means to be fully alive. We all become good friends—but not for long. One by one just about everyone in the group dies. We attend many memorial services— beautiful celebrations of life held on a beach or a sunlit pier, with everyone barefoot and wearing bright Hawaiian colors. There's a feeling of sadness and celebration in the air, as each person is remembered with love. Death is becoming a familiar friend and much less frightening.

The Chocolate Buddha
Camp Kaenae, Maui, August 29, 1989

We just have to remind ourselves that the source for any happiness is the mind itself.
Lama Ole Nydahl

If I can't escape death, I might as well learn to accept it. Fran and I hear about a week-long Tibetan Phowa retreat to be held on Maui. The Phowa is an ancient Tibetan meditation on conscious dying. Its purpose is to help you prepare for your own death, but it can also be used to help others make their transition from the body. With Fran's cancer having worsened in past months, it seems tailor-made for both of us.

Our teacher is a western Buddhist Lama named Ole Nydahl, who looks like a welterweight boxer, with a strong jaw, a crew cut, and a tough, muscled body. Ole led a rough-and-tumble life growing up on the streets of Copenhagen, before going to Tibet in 1968 where (after a wild ride that had a lot to do with drugs) he studied to become a Tibetan Lama. He likes life on the wild side, whether it's driving over a hundred miles an hour on the autobahn, or having equally fast relationships with other women. He has founded more than two hundred meditation centers around the world and spends his life traveling from city to city, passing on the Buddha's teachings.

The retreat is held at a dilapidated summer camp on the Ke'anae Peninsula, about halfway to Hana. Our meetings take place in a funky old barn, with neon lights buzzing overhead. All the thirty-odd participants are dressed in shorts and colorful shirts. Ole sits at the front of the room, wearing a Marlon Brando T-shirt and running shorts that leave little to the imagination. I've never seen anyone so unselfconscious about their body. He thinks nothing of belching, picking his nose, or scratching his balls while he teaches. Several times during the course, he goes into a shakti-like energy experience, shaking and panting. I can tell that many of the women in the course (including Fran) are taken by Ole's uninhibited male energy.

The purpose of the workshop is to open up the central energy channel in the spine, so that our life-energy can be moved up and out the top of the head at the moment of death. This involves a series of exercises, where we visualize an energy bubble, like a little green ball, moving up the spine. We send it up in five "pushes" while making the sounds *scri, scri, scri, scri, scri* . . . ***HICK!*** Then we imagine it exploding into a mountain of red ruby light above our head. Once this channel opens up, a telltale sign appears on the scalp. It looks like a tiny spot of blood. At first this seems outrageous—a spot of blood on the scalp? I never once questioned the veracity of this bizarre activity. It has been passed down from a long lineage of enlightened Buddhist teachers. What do I know?

After several days most of the participants have "broken through." Of course, Fran was one of the first. Each person has a spot that is clearly visible, like a mark made with a red Pentel pen. By the third day everyone in the course has opened up—except me and two others. It brings back all my old paranoia of being the dumbest person in my class at school. I start to get depressed and begin wallowing in doubt and self-pity. Why are they successful and not me? Maybe I'm just not spiritual enough? Even Don—the fat businessman who had never meditated—had "the sign." Here I am, a professional seeker—and I can't manifest a hole in my head!

The harder I try, the less seems to happen. I feel like I'm struggling to have an orgasm and unable to go over the top. I just can't do it. There are moments when it feels so close—a little tingling in the skull—then nothing happens. Meanwhile, everyone else is talking excitedly about their blissful energy experiences and their love for Buddhism. They all seem to be part of a club of which I could never be a member. I am disgusted with myself.

Finally I just give up. To hell with it. Forget the little green ball! This is hopeless. *So what if I'm the only one in the group who doesn't get it,* I say to myself. *Drop into the heart. That's all that matters. Open into love and compassion for everyone in the room—especially yourself. Just let go. Give up!* Suddenly I'm aware of being in a place of overwhelming peace and stillness. All the aches in my knees and back suddenly disappear. *Maybe I'll let the green ball shoot out my heart instead of my head. I just have a hard skull!*

The session ends and Fran comes up to me.

"Are you open?" she asks.

"My head isn't, but my heart is."

"I was thinking of you during the meditation," she says. "I had this image of a Buddha with a bald head. He had stuff coming out of his head, but it wasn't blood. It was chocolate! As soon as I realized it was chocolate, I knew you had opened up. I know how you love chocolate!"

"Oh, come on," I say. "Nothing happened."

"Let's go see Ole and have him look."

"No way. There's nothing to see."

"Well let me look then." She begins to feel around my scalp.

"See? There's nothing there," I say.

Suddenly she exclaims, "I can see it—a drop of blood!"

We find Ole, who pokes around. I half expect him to say, "Nothing there."

"Ha!" he says. "There it is. A very clear sign. Yes, you did it! You opened up."

What if the Body Doesn't Heal?
Princeville, Kauai, February 20, 1990

The acceptance of sickness as a decision of the mind, for a purpose for which it would use the body, is the basis of healing. And this is so for healing in all forms.
A Course in Miracles

Our new friends Tom and Linda Carpenter invite Fran and I to dinner in their beautiful home overlooking the Hanalei Mountains. The view from their living room is breathtaking—peaks enshrouded in mist and waterfalls cascading down three-hundred foot cliffs. For years they've been leading A Course in Miracles group in their home every week, and have a devoted following. They're two of the kindest, most loving people I've ever met.

Recently Tom had a profound experience while working in his tropical flower gardens. He heard a voice saying, "I am your brother. You and I are one." The voice continued to speak, identifying itself as Master Jesus. Thus began an extraordinary unfolding that brought about a profound inner shift not only for him, but for his wife Linda as well. Out of it came a beautiful book called *Dialogue on Awakening*.

I love being with them. They have that rare capacity to really listen. The conversation eventually turns to healing (or never quite gets off of it). Fran eagerly tells them of all the healing modalities she is trying and how confident she is that she can conquer her cancer.

"You know, Fran," Tom says, as we enjoy the fresh fruit dish Linda has prepared for us, "have you ever thought about what happens if your body *doesn't* heal?"

Fran looks startled. "But I'm sure I can heal."

"Well," says Tom, "That may be so. But it's not so much a question of whether your body heals or not. The invitation here is to see that you already *are* whole. Did you ever consider that who you are is not your body? The body is just an illusion. You are so much more than that."

"It seems pretty real when I'm in pain."

"Yes, I understand that," Tom says patiently. "But by fearfully insisting that the body heal, you're only reinforcing your separateness from God."

"But if my body doesn't heal, then I'll be dead," she says defensively.

"That may be. Your body may disappear but who you are never dies. All I'm saying is that you're under the illusion of being separate, when in truth there is no separation between you, God, and All That Is."

"I don't fully get what you're saying. How can that help me?"

162

"It can give you peace of mind for one thing," Tom says. "Once you stop fighting your illness and just let go, you will see that all is well."

"I don't know . . . it's so hard to let go."

"Maybe it's easier than you think," Linda says with an understanding smile.

Fran shakes her head, disturbed by what she's hearing.

We are still so stuck in our old Kripalu beliefs that we can't hear anything that is being said. It will be a long time before I understand these words of truth. I doubt Fran ever will—at least not in this lifetime.

CHAPTER 10

DO NOT STAND AT
MY GRAVE AND WEEP

Fran

Nobody Gets Out of Here Alive
Nelson County, Virginia, November 10, 2001

Awake, dear friend,
Awake—sleep no more;
The night has faded away,
Awake, dear friend, sleep no more.
Kabir

"I hate the idea of extinction." Jack exclaims loudly, pounding the pillow next to him on the sofa. "When I drop this body I don't like to think that 'Jack' is going to go with it."

Linda and I have just had dinner with our friends Jack and Judy in their stunning mountaintop home in Nelson County, Virginia. We're sitting in their 30-foot tall living room with 185 degree views of the Blue Ridge Mountains, telling stories of our wild and extravagant days of youth, along with much laughter. And now the conversation has turned to one of our favorite topics: death.

"But 'Jack' will not die when this body dies!" I say. "What makes you think that 'Jack' is going to die?"

"Because I've never had an experience of being out of my body. I have nothing to prove that 'Jack' is not going to die when the body dies." Jack is now in his seventies, and with his twinkling eyes and flowing mane of white hair, he is still remarkably handsome.

"Jack, you've always been terrified of dying," Judy says, sitting on the couch next to him with her legs curled up under her. Her strong and intelligent face is framed by her curly jet black hair. Judy is a former songwriter and model—her fingers were used for the famous "let the fingers do the walking" ad in the Yellow Pages. "You've had this fear since you were a little child."

"It's life I care about," Jack says. "I love to get up in the morning and see the sunshine sparkling on a blade of grass. I love to breathe the crisp fall air. I don't want to lose all that."

"But who is it that is aware of the sunshine and the crisp fall air?" I ask, putting down my wine glass. "Is it your body?" *Oh shit, here I go again, trying to "convert" him to nonduality. That's about as nondual as you can get!*

Jack thoughtfully strokes his beard with his thumb and forefinger.

Linda, stretched out on a big, plush chair with her feet up on the ottoman, tries a different approach: "When you were a young boy you had an awareness of being Jack. Now, all this time later, there's not one cell in your body that is the same as when you were that little boy. You have a whole different body, yet the awareness of Jack is the same. Who you are has not changed at all—and it won't when you die."

Jack still looks unconvinced.

Still blindly holding on to my need to convince him, I blunder on: "I know of a person who had a near death experience," I say. "She was in a hospital room and clinically died. She was aware of going out the window and up the outside of the building. Several stories up she noticed a red and blue running shoe on a window ledge, surprised to see a shoe in such an odd place. When she was resuscitated she remembered the shoe. She told the nurse about it, and the nurse didn't believe her. But to please her, the nurse went upstairs to take a look. Sure enough, when she leaned out the window, there was the running shoe. Now, my question is, when the person who was clinically dead saw the shoe, who saw the shoe? It wasn't the eyes in the body lying in the hospital room, was it?"

"I've read all these stories about near-death experiences—hundreds of them—but I think they're all a fantasy," Jack says dismissively.

"But isn't everything else just as much of a fantasy?" Linda asks. "Surely when you go to see all these quack doctors, hoping to find the elixir of youth, that's a fantasy." For years Jack has passionately pursued every possible New Age healing remedy in the hope of prolonging his life. I'll say this for him—at age seventy-five, he's never been in a hospital!

"It's all in what you choose to believe," Judy says. "If you want to hang on to the belief that you become extinct when you die, then that's what will happen."

"You'll have to hang around on that plane for a long, long time," Linda laughs.

"Well, I'm stuck either way," says Jack in frustration. "There's no way out. I don't like that. I just want to go on living *here*."

"From what I've seen, nobody gets out of here alive," I say, leaning forward to grab a piece of chocolate. "A hundred years from now *everyone* living on the planet will be dead—you, me, our children, pets, presidents, saints, beggars—all seven billion of us—dead!

"I hate to see things die."

"The death rate has never changed," enjoins Linda, sitting cross-legged in her chair. "It's one per person."

We all laugh—a slight edge to our laughter—as if we're flirting with something very dangerous.

"Look at this rose," says Jack, picking up a rose from the flower arrangement on the coffee table. "I love the perfume of the rose. I love the velvet softness of its petals. It has its moment of beauty, then it dies. The petals are gone; the perfume is gone. All the petals fall off and rot. They become compost. It's gone forever. I *hate* that!"

"But nothing dies in nature," Linda insists. "And nothing is born."

"The petals rot. They die!" Jack says vehemently, leaning forward in his chair.

Linda sits up too, excited to jump into the fray. "They don't die; they don't disappear. They just take on new form. The petals become compost, and the compost becomes new life. Nothing stays the same in nature."

"They *die*! The rose is not there for me to enjoy anymore," exclaims Jack in a loud voice, almost shouting.

Oh God! They're going to get in a huge argument—I hate confrontation!

"But Jack," Linda says, "you're identifying life as being the form. It's the *awareness* that creates the dream of form. It's all a dream."

"What do you mean by a dream?"

"None of this is real!" she asserts. "There's no rose, there's no you. It's all Awareness."

I know Linda's right . . . but there's no way to explain this in words!

Jack throws up his arms in exasperation. "I say it's all compost. When I die it's over."

"You think birth and coming into this life is a wonderful thing," Linda says. "I can tell you from my own direct experience that birth is one of the most miserable things that happens to us. Compared to what it's like on the Other Side, this earth plane is nothing but suffering. It makes the beauty of a rose seem pale by comparison. On the other side there are colors you can't even imagine. When you die it's like taking off a heavy overcoat. It's a joyful event. There is nothing—I can tell you this—*nothing* to be frightened of."

Ah, now's my chance to cool things down. "I love what Papaji says, 'When I was born, I was crying, and everyone in the room was laughing and happy. When I died, everyone in the room was crying, and I was the only one laughing and happy.'"

"I'm not afraid of death," Judy says. "I've seen a lot of people die. It's only the body that dies. That which animates the body doesn't die." She has worked for Hospice and knows what she's talking about.

"I've had people visit me after their death," Linda says. "My mom came to me several times after she died. Once she came to me while I was driving my car. She was sitting next to me. I actually touched her. 'How can you be in a body?' I asked in disbelief. She just smiled."

"Remember when Fran died?" I ask, turning to Linda. "Four or five people told me that Fran visited them that night—some of them thousands of miles away."

"Tell us about it," asks Judy.

"Well, I told you the story of how Fran and I moved to Kauai after she found out she had breast cancer," I say.

"Yes, that was when we were at your place," Judy says.

"For a time she was doing well with her healing. She had finished her chemotherapy and her cancer was in remission. She even called it a miracle, attributing her newfound health to a visit from Gurudev."

"They interviewed her in the local paper," Linda says. "She was sure Gurudev had healed her. She thought he was god—she didn't know he was having sex with his disciples the whole time."

Ignoring Linda's barb about Gurudev, I continue with the story. "Then Fran and I flew over to the Big Island to spend a few days at the Mauna Lani resort. Fran loved these fancy hotels. I was working out in the weight room when someone came in saying, 'I think something's happened to your wife.' I rushed out and found Fran sitting on the grass next to the beach with people all around her. When I got to her she looked up at me with terror in her eyes, 'I was snorkeling in the water and had a seizure,' she said. 'I thought I was going to drown.'"

"How frightening," Judy says.

"This was when we found out the cancer had spread to her brain. We knew deep down it was the beginning of the end. A month later we flew to Honolulu so that she could have brain surgery."

"What an awful time that was for Peter," Linda says.

Judy and Jack look at me expectantly, waiting for me to continue.

Hawaiian Sunset
Honolulu, Hawaii, August 29, 1990

When we perceive from an undivided consciousness, we will find the sacred in every expression of life. We will find it in our teacup, in the breeze, in the brushing of our teeth, in each and every moment of living and dying.
Adyashanti

"It's so bee . . .bee . . . beautiful," Fran says, looking out at the sun sinking rapidly towards the horizon.

I reach out across the table and take her delicate hand in mine. I'm overwhelmed with love as I take in her fragile beauty. She has on her favorite silk dress, which was hand dyed by an artist from Kauai. It's a rich aquamarine, containing all the colors of the sea. I'm wearing khaki slacks and a button-down shirt, making sure I look like a local. It's odd, but those who live in Hawaii don't like being mistaken for a tourist.

Fran and I, on the surface anyway, appear to be living everyone's dream—having dinner at a romantic beachside restaurant in Honolulu, overlooking the ocean and the setting sun. We're eating outdoors at a restaurant in Diamond Head, which has an ancient hau tree that gives shade to the lanai. The tree has a little plaque saying that Robert Louis Stevenson lounged and wrote books here. All the diners are in a festive mood, lit up by the pink glow of the sun. Waiters scurry around, lighting the tiki torches on the terrace. The soft, gentle sounds of Ola Mana, a popular Hawaiian singing group, drift through the air. In the distance the high-rise hotels of Waikiki sparkle and shimmer, while in front of us an armada of tour boats slowly cruise by as they await the sunset.

"Watch this," I say. "Right about . . . now!"

As if on cue, everyone stops eating and drinking and turns towards the ocean. Only the waiters continue to silently move between the tables, going about their business. In one perfect moment a large catamaran glides in front of the brilliant orange globe of the sun, just before it sinks below the horizon. There is a hushed gasp. With amazing speed, the sun disappears from sight and the sky above turns iridescent orange and green.

A flashbulb goes off as a waiter takes a picture of two young newlyweds. Their faces are pink and happy as they smile for the camera. No doubt they are envisioning a lifetime ahead of them, with a happy home, children, friends, and family. I wish them well. With Fran's cancer, I can't help but think of the more heartbreaking side of falling in love: "The moment two people fall in love there is already sown the seed of tragedy." Whenever we open our hearts in love, we are also opening ourselves to the possibility of pain and loss.

"Wha, wha, what a per, per, perfect sight," Fran says, as she turns to me with a big smile. Her brunette wig almost looks like her real hair. It's a very special night. We've been married for almost twenty-five years and it feels like our first night out. But behind the magic of the moment there is a deep terror welling up inside—knowing that it may be our last.

When Fran found out that she had breast cancer three years ago, it had already metastasized to her bones. That's when we moved to Hawaii. Now the cancer has spread to her brain, creating a large tumor that has affected her speech and paralyzed her right arm. For the past weeks I've been helping her dress, helping her go to the bathroom and helping her eat. She has gone from being strong-willed, assertive and verbal to the innocence and purity of a small child, almost completely helpless and unable to talk. Tomorrow she is scheduled to have brain surgery at the Queen's Medical Center. There is a chance she won't make it through the operation.

"It doesn't get any more beautiful than this, does it?" I say, really meaning it. My heart is filled with love.

"Capital," she says, using a strange new word that has mysteriously shown up in her vocabulary.

"What do you want to eat?" I ask, smiling at her use of the word capital.

She looks down at her menu, her right arm hanging limply by her side. "Mmm . . . mmmaybeee I'll have aaaaa 'sseizure' ssssalad," she says, struggling to get the words out. We both laugh. A few months ago she had terrible seizures; the first one happened when she was swimming in the ocean, scaring her half to death.

"We've had such beautiful times together," I say, tears in my eyes.

"I'mmm nnot ffinished yettttt," she says. "Bbbut, whenn, whenn, I'mm gone yyouu ccan hhave that blond yyou've aalways wwanted."

"No, no, no," I reply, anxiously smoothing out the pink tablecloth with my hand. "We'll get you a blond wig and then I'll have my blond. You're all that's important to me."

By some strange stroke of fate we have come face to face with our own mortality. What we imagined to be permanent is nothing more than that brief flash of light as the sun disappears below the horizon. Yet on some level we know it all to be an illusion. The sun doesn't sink into the ocean; there is no birth and there is no death. It is all a manifestation of consciousness, inviting us to recognize this precious moment. In that moment there is no past and no future. There is only love.

Fighting Reality
Aloha Mana Farms, Kauai, November 3, 1990

When you argue with reality, you lose—but only 100 percent of the time.
Byron Katie

Fran makes it home to Kauai after her brain surgery. For a while it looks like she's going to make it. The radiation to her brain has left her weak and drained, but, like a drowning person coming up for air, she is determined to beat her cancer— even though she knows somewhere deep inside that it is a losing battle.

Day and night she struggles to regain her health. She has to learn every activity she's ever done all over again, from going to the bathroom, to getting dressed, to eating, to washing her hair. Her right arm is still paralyzed and she needs constant help. Yet, there is a sense of wonder when she does even the simplest of tasks. I remember her struggling to rotate her right hand for the physical therapist—her jaw firm, her tongue half-sticking out, her whole body concentrating on this simple movement. Then a big smile as she rolls it over. 'Capital!'"

In a last ditch effort to boost her weakened immune system, Fran impulsively decides to attend a two-week program at the Livingston Medical Center in San Diego. Two days later we're on an airplane, convinced that this (very expensive) therapy will help her regain her strength. Once at the clinic, along with thirty or so other patients and their caregivers, she undergoes massive intravenous vitamin therapy, counseling sessions, psychology classes, and endless rounds of doctor's appointments.

I participate in the program along with her. I learn to give her shots of BCG vaccine; I go to all the classes; I take my own mega-doses of vitamins; and I discover that I have a perfect profile for getting cancer myself. This is a school where the stakes are high—not just pass or fail, but life or death. I can't help but notice that Fran is one of the sicker patients. I do my best to support her, yet I get the impression that the clinic is a very expensive hoax (it was shut down by authorities in 2004).

When we return from San Diego, loaded with thousands of dollars worth of vitamins, something begins to shift inside her. For over forty years Fran has been relentlessly hard driving, determined, and ambitious. She was always looking for the next project, the next challenge. But now, for the first time in her life, everything she cares about—the farm, teaching yoga, leading satsang, or the peace garden project—no longer matters. In a sudden reversal, she informs me that she no longer wants any responsibility, just time to be totally spontaneous with whatever is showing up in the moment. For her, it is time to create—to find 1001 ways to play.

All this throws me for a loop. I am barely adjusting to her being alive, and now I have to adjust to an "all new" Fran who wants to sit back and watch the clouds float by while I take care of her twenty-four hours a day. Without being aware of it, she expects me to clean up after her, keep the house clean, rub her feet, take care of finances, and chauffeur her to appointments every day. At night she wants me to hold her and rock her and sing to her before going to sleep. I don't have any money of my own anymore, because in an all-or-nothing gamble, I put every penny I had into our property, hoping that it would one day support me. As a concession, Fran sets me up with a salary of $150 per month as "farm manager."

Sometimes I feel like I'm a dancing bear.

I keep looking for an end to it, but there is no end. I start to get resentful and frustrated. I fantasize on women with healthy bodies who want to play on the beach all day and make passionate love all night.

To everyone else it looks like Fran is on her way to getting stronger every day. But I see her at night, when she is whimpering and moaning in pain, her body smelling of narcosis from the huge tumors that are breaking through the skin on her breast; I see her when her back is twisted and hunched with muscle spasms that keep her in constant pain; I see her with her belly swollen and scarred, dragging herself out of bed in the morning; I see her when she slurs her words, barely able to talk; I see her bald head and wizened body—and I know, despite all the trials we are going through, that this is the woman I love.

One day she pulls me aside, "I didn't want to tell you this, but something is going on in my body. I've noticed a lump around my collarbone—and it's not just another sore muscle. I don't know how much longer I have to live, but we need to think about how we're going to spend the remaining time we have together."

Something is changing. I sense that Fran is finally beginning to release her tenacious hold on life. She's facing the fact that living in a fantasy world of miracle cures is no longer helping. It only creates more suffering. She's discovering that fighting against her cancer is avoiding the truth of what is going on in her body. It is robbing her of the quality time she could have by relaxing into the inevitability of her death. As Byron Katie says, "When you argue with reality, you lose—but only 100 percent of the time."

On December 16, her birthday, we are at home talking to friends, when suddenly her body starts shaking to its very core. She is having a huge seizure. Margie and Barbara help hold her, and put a facecloth between her teeth so she doesn't bite her tongue. She has one seizure, then another, then a third. It's like being in an earthquake—the earth shaking uncontrollably, then stopping, then shaking again. We all whisper soothing words to her, but nothing can take away the terror in her eyes.

I drive her to the hospital. Once she is in her room, she looks imploringly at me and says, "Honey, I don't want to live any more."

Neal, her doctor, comes in and says, "Frannie, it's time for you to decide whether you want to keep on fighting or not. As long as you keep fighting, you will continue to suffer. There is nothing you need to do—just let go."

"But I'm afraid I'll be in a coma and suffer for weeks. I don't want to die a slow painful death like my mother."

"You're not your mother. You'll go through this as only you can go through it. It is a journey you alone can take."

After Neal leaves, the look of dread on her face softens slightly.

"Is it all right if I let go honey?" she asks me.

"Yes, my love," I respond. "It is."

She begins to drift out as the sedatives take effect and starts snoring.

Out of nowhere she says, "I love you."

"I love you too," I say, leaning down to kiss her.

I kiss her shoulder, noticing the narrow white band left by her bathing suit, knowing there will be no more walks on the beach, no more happy, carefree times together.

Meet the Addams Family
Aloha Mana Farms, Kauai, December 21, 1990

Life is one damned thing after another.
Winston Churchill

Fran stops eating, but try as she might, she is unable to die.

"I want to die," she says sadly, "but I can't."

As she struggles with handing her life over to some greater power, I struggle with my own letting go. What will it be like to be on my own again, after twenty-five years? What will I do? How will I deal with my grief?

I just don't know.

After a week in the hospital Fran's speech has become more impaired as the tumor grows back; she can barely swallow and still is not eating. The heavy medications keep her in a coma-like state.

"I nnnearly kkkicked tthe bbucket last nnight." She says one morning. "It was vvery ffffrightening."

Every day I go to the hospital, staying until midnight, before going home to get some sleep. I cry on my way in; I cry on my way home—cry and drive—as I call it.

People come in droves to see Fran, most of them dear friends wanting to support us, but a few who love the drama of being around someone who is dying. I place a candle and incense on her side table, along with photographs of gurus and saints. Thankfully, the nurses seem to understand. As the word gets out, so many visitors come that I have to put a sign-up sheet on the door. It's like Grand Central, with telephones ringing, people dropping by, and beloved friends coming to sit with Fran through the night.

My son Peter flies out from Washington, DC with his girlfriend Julie. It's her first trip to Hawaii and the first time I have met her. The morning after they arrive, I give Julie a tour of our beautiful home, eager to show her what a normal and loving family we are.

"Peter must have told you about Frisky, our beautiful white cat." I say. "We brought him over from the mainland. He's been part of the family for fifteen years! You'll love him." I look for Frisky, expecting to see him curled up in his usual place. "Where is he?" I ask, walking around the house until I find him in the bedroom. He's standing there, frothing at the mouth, his eyes all distorted. It is like a shrieking apparition out of a Stephen King novel.

"Oh my God, something is wrong with him. I have to get him to the vet!"

I rush Frisky to the vet while Peter drives Julie to the hospital to introduce her to Fran.

After examining Frisky, the vet tells me that he has a brain tumor and there is nothing he can do for him except put him to sleep. He suggests that the sooner I put him out of his misery, the easier it will be for him. I agree to have Frisky euthanized.

This is crazy, I think. *Fran is in the hospital dying of a brain tumor and Frisky, who she loves more than anything, has a brain tumor. It's too much. I'm going to lose it!*

I take Frisky's body and put it in the trunk of the car before going to the hospital. Sobbing, I say to him, "Yes, dear Frisky, I understand why you need to go. You have been such a joy in our lives—and now you need to be on the other side to greet Fran when she arrives. I release you. Go to the light."

Suddenly I start laughing hysterically. This is great. Peter is at the hospital introducing his girlfriend to his dying mother, and here I am with a dead cat in the trunk of my car. What a way to make an impression on a potential daughter-in-law. She must feel like she's just met the Addams family!

Back from the Angels
Aloha Mana Farm, Kauai, December 25, 1990

Kabir is restless, he longs for Thee;
Dear Lord, pray hasten to meet me.
Only on seeing Thee, O Beloved,
Will my lovelorn heart find repose.

Kabir

Christmas comes. Fran is still in the hospital and hasn't eaten or spoken in over a week. Tired and wrung out, about ten of us gather together for Christmas dinner. My son Peter is there, along with all those dear friends who have been supporting Fran day and night—sweet, faithful Bonnie, Michelle, Karuna, Ron, Michael, and Joe. We are like an extended family, sitting around opening gifts—aware of the one person who is absent—when the phone rings. It must be the hospital. I hope nothing's happened.

To my astonishment the voice on the other end is Fran's. "I-I-I've cccome bbb-back ffffrom tthe angels!" she says.

"Oh my God, she's talking again!" I cry out. "It's a miracle!"

We all pile into cars and rush down to the hospital. All ten of us crowd into her room and softly sing Christmas carols. It's as if there is a glow emanating from the room that reaches beyond the door and down the corridor. As we sing "O little town of Bethlehem, how still we see thee lie," Fran sings along with us in a childlike voice, often missing the words, which make it even more endearing. She holds her stuffed cat in her arms and looks at each one of us with a sweetness I have never seen before. Then she opens her presents and acknowledges each of us with a smile and an "OK".

Something has shifted. She's no longer fighting against death; she has dropped into a deep place of acceptance. The fear of death has given way to a place of authentic presence, that pure, unconditional love that we usually cover up all our lives. In this moment Fran is not her body, not her mind; she is a boundless heart, letting her love flow effortlessly out to all of us, showering us in grace.

A few days later Peter prepares to return to his job in Washington, DC, 5,000 miles away. While on the way to the airport, we go by the hospital for a last visit. Peter knows that it is the last time he will see his mother. He sits close to Fran and gently takes her hand. "Is there anything you would like to say to me, mom?"

177

The words come out slowly and with great emphasis. "Yyyou're ttthe gggreatest gggift GGGod hhhas bbbrought into mmmy life," she replies, "YYYou have a gggood hhheart."

"I love you with all my heart," Peter says, tears in his eyes.

Without saying anything Fran looks up at him with an open gaze that is wholly transparent, like clear crystal. Her eyes are those of a child, filled with innocence and love—a purity beyond words. It is time for the final goodbye.

"OK. Go. Eat yyyour dddinner," she says.

Peter leans over and gives her a kiss. He then kisses Fatcat, the stuffed animal he gave to her when she first became ill. It is cradled in Fran's arm. They both know that this is the final goodbye.

She lifts her good arm a few inches off the bed and waves as we silently leave the room.

Tonight Our Souls Are Dancing
Aloha Mana Farm, Kauai, January 21, 1991

Death is nothing at all, I have only slipped away into the next room . . . Why
should I be out of mind because I am out of sight? I am waiting for you, for an
interval, somewhere very near, just around the corner. All is well.
Henry Scott Holland, Canon of St. Paul's Cathedral (1847-1918)

On New Year's Eve day—the day of our wedding anniversary—Christine and Paul help me bring Fran home from the hospital. Neal, her doctor, has told her that he can't keep her there any longer. Terrified that she won't get enough pain medication and will suffer, she has no choice but to leave. We arrange for Hospice to help take care of her.

On the way home we stop at Anahola beach so that she can see the ocean. "Ttttake meee down tttthere," she says. We lift her from the car and lead her down to the water's edge. We hold her upright with her feet in the water, all skin and bones, her head bald from the chemo, the water lapping around her feet. Staring out at the ocean she slowly says, "I nnnever ththought I wwwould see ththis aagain." It is a bittersweet moment.

We get her home and carry her into the bedroom. The bedroom is like a Japanese temple, with a Japanese blue-tiled roof, and a spectacular view of the Pacific Ocean. The redwood ceiling is shaped in the form of a pyramid with a skylight in the top; shoji screens provide a background for the candles, flowers, incense, and photographs of different spiritual teachers. We place Fran in the king-sized bed overlooking the ocean. Friends drop by to see her; the ever so kind Hospice people set us up with medications and everything they can think of to make her comfortable.

Midnight comes. Everyone has left and Fran and I are alone in the house. She lies on her side of the huge bed, the muffled roar of the ocean coming into the room. The room is dark except for the full moon shining in through the skylight. Fran has drifted off, thanks to the pain pills, and her breathing is rapid and shallow. Every so often she utters a low moan. It feels like her life-energy has drawn within. I look over at her ravaged body, which looks like an Auschwitz victim—no hair, cheekbones protruding, mouth half open. Her left hand clasps mine with incredible intensity. I cuddle up close, aware of the unusual smells coming from her body. It is as if she is somewhere far, far away.

I feel like a Tantric yogi, sitting in the graveyard meditating on death.

Tonight our souls are dancing.

How long will this go on? This is the razor's edge. Keep your heart open. Be with it. Be in this moment. This is the most sacred time of times.

Memories come flooding back of anniversaries we've spent together—twenty-five anniversaries in so many extraordinary places, always on New Year's Eve. One of them spent hurtling through the night on a train in China as we danced down the aisle of the dining car with everyone singing, *Oh, how we danced on the night we were wed . . .*; another anniversary where we both jumped fully clothed into the pool at a luxurious resort on Eleuthra Island; a New Year's Eve at our farmhouse in the Canadian backwoods, where our friends arrived on snowmobiles, wearing fancy clothes underneath their bulky snowmobile suits; an anniversary where we both nearly died of double pneumonia in a Norfolk hospital. Such a lifetime together.

"Happy Anniversary, my darling," I whisper into her ear, my tears wetting her cheek. "I want you to know that it's OK to let go. You can let go into the light. Just let go. Know that I'll love you forever. We'll be together again in the blink of an eye."

I go to sleep next to her, listening to the Synchronicity Meditation tapes on my headphones. Behind the strange, ethereal music on the tape, a subliminal message plays over and over again in my ear: *You are peace. You are love. You are all that is.*

During the night her breathing stops for a few seconds. "Is this it?" I ask. Then it begins again, unevenly. Night becomes day . . . and it continues on like this for twenty-one more nights.

Twenty-one more days and twenty-one more nights on the razor's edge.

I am the last person to see the profound transformation that is happening in my own life. There is a relentless stripping away of attachment to form. Looking at Fran's emaciated body, I have no choice but to recognize that she is not this body lying in the bed. In this recognition, my own identification with form is stripped away too. Without even knowing it, a shift happens. From that point on, there is no "me" doing anything. It is strangely exhilarating. Nothing is held back. There is an indescribable knowing that everything is happening with exquisite perfection. I don't have to "do" anything.

Yet the days are filled with nonstop activity—greeting friends who come to say goodbye, calling relatives and friends all over the world to tell them Fran is dying, talking to her doctor and the Hospice workers, taking care of Fran. At night I'm often up ten times, giving her pills, helping her pee, or being with her as she lies in pain, hour after hour.

As time goes on, fewer and fewer friends come to see her. It's not easy confronting death eye-to-eye. However, my love for Fran just goes deeper and deeper. I still see her beauty, as she stares out at me from deep, sunken eyes. She tries desperately to talk, but is only able to manage an "Uh huh, OK, OK." One afternoon

I ask her if I can give her a kiss. She reaches up with her one good hand and silently brings my head down to meet her lips.

Everyone is saying, "Peter, you're going through this with such incredible strength, you're just glowing!" But "I" am not doing anything. There is just the sense of being the witness to all of it—watching Fran go through whatever she needs to go through in order to let go, watching my own heart open up, close down, get irritated, be frightened, be sad, be joyful, watching with compassion as friends grieve. It is all unfolding in present moment awareness. Somehow this "Peter," this body-mind, has tapped into something far greater than the ego.

As the days merge together and I become more and more exhausted, battle fatigue sets in—the kind of numbness that comes from being under intense stress. What a mirror Fran is for my own fears of letting go. There is virtually nothing remaining of the person I spent all those years with. I am forced to see that which does not die, that which was never born. I spend a lot of time alone—eating alone, walking on the beach alone, meditating. There are times when I want desperately to escape the pain, but can't.

The doctor comes by, and to my surprise says, "This could go on for another two weeks."

"Two weeks? Oh God, I hope I can hold on that long."

A Tibetan Lama, named Lama Tharchin Rinpoche, comes by to pray for her. She lies there peacefully as he prays, "Bring the Buddha to your heart. He will protect you and guide you back home."

A new sense of peace comes over Fran, as if something inside has let go and there is not a single thread of attachment to the earth plane. Her clear, brown eyes look out from some vast space. She is completely still.

I keep saying to her, "There's nothing to fear, you are surrounded by love. You're safe, let go, be free. The love is all around you. You are love itself. Let your spirit soar."

I start to feel at peace myself. I find that I'm no longer resisting her pain. I can see the beauty and grace in this awesome dance of life and death.

It no longer matters how long it takes.

Then one morning she just stops breathing. She just stops.

And it is over.

The news spreads quickly and within an hour Bonnie, Ranjana, Michael, Joe, Michelle, and I are gathered around her bed, reciting the words from the Tibetan Phowa, a prayer to be said over the dead: *Let us visualize Fran's consciousness taking the form of a small sphere of light, and flying from her body, like a shooting star, dissolving into the heart of Divine Presence . . .*

As we're chanting I try to close Fran's eyes, but they won't close. Her mouth is still open and her face contorted in pain, reflecting the suffering her body has gone through. I touch her face and feel the coolness of her cheek. Her body is still warm. I sit down and continue chanting with my eyes closed: *May Fran be free from any of the sufferings or turmoil of her death, may she be released into the luminosity and all-pervading space of her own true nature . . .*

Suddenly I look up and see that the expression on her face has changed. There is not only a beatific smile on her face, but her eyes radiate extraordinary peace and joy. "She's free!" I say excitedly. "She's free at last!"

The others look up in surprise. "I don't believe it," Ranjana says. "What a miracle."

I try again to close her eyes, and they close easily. Someone places some flowers in her hand; another places a string around her neck that has been blessed by the Dalai Lama; we dress her in a new white sari. The beautiful sounds of *Om Namaha Shivaya* drift through the room as we softly chant. People come and go throughout the day, touched by what they see. It's so clear that everyone is learning exactly what they need to from this experience. Some need to help, others need to look, and some can't even bear to come into the room.

It's nighttime when the funeral home comes to take away her body. They zip her into a black plastic body bag and wheel her away. There is a finality to this that breaks my heart wide open. It's all I can do to keep from going over the edge.

I have dinner with a few friends, and we break the tension by telling jokes and laughing hysterically. There's no right way to do this, I realize.

By ten everyone is gone and I'm alone in the house. The wind is howling outside, the big bullfrogs are honking in the pond, and I'm alone in the big king-size bed for the first time. The house is ever so still. Then it hits me. She's gone—her body in some refrigerator in a mortuary—yet her spirit is dancing all around me. It's almost more than the mind can comprehend or the heart can bear.

Final Farewell
Anahola Beach, Kauai, January 24, 1991

*For me the moment of death will be a moment of jubilation, not of fear. I cried
when I was born and I shall die laughing.*
Nisargadatta

We gather at Fran's favorite spot on Anahola beach to say goodbye. I'm incredibly nervous. It feels as if I'm going to my own wedding—with a minister presiding, speeches to be made, vows of love, and a reception afterwards. I set up a little altar in the sand with Fran's photo on it along with a candle and flowers. Someone has brought a tape player and the sounds of *Alleluia* are merging with the sound of the waves. It's been raining and the sky is still grey. There are just a few of us, which is fine by me. When people had asked, we said we were going to have a small ceremony on the beach, mainly for family members and a few close friends.

Someone says, "Look!" I turn, and to my astonishment, see a wave of people walking towards us. There must be over fifty of them. Some are in shorts, some in jeans, and others are dressed in brightly colored Hawaiian prints, all walking barefoot down the beach.

There is a festive mood in the air. Even the stray beach dogs come to join in. As each person arrives, I give them a welcoming hug. They place a cascade of flowers around the altar—hibiscus, bougainvillea, lilacs, bird of paradise, and sweet-smelling leis. Everyone is talking and greeting each other when the roar of a big high-wheeler truck drowns out everything. We all watch as it noisily tears down the beach towards us. *Who could this be? What the hell—we're having a funeral here!* A tough looking young Hawaiian guy steps out of the truck. He turns and helps a man with a cane step down from the truck. It is my old friend Leonard, a frail eighty-year-old artist, who managed to get a ride from two locals.

We gather around the altar, sitting on beach towels. I stand up and lead a short prayer: "Take a few moments to be still and to listen to the sound of the ocean. Feel each other's presence as we gather here to celebrate Fran's transition to a place of freedom and light. Become aware of whatever you're feeling in this moment. You all know how much she suffered in the last months. Imagine her now, dancing among us . . . free and radiantly happy. Take that joy into your own hearts and know that is who you are."

Neal's wife Linda, who is both a nurse and a minister, gets up and reads a passage from the Bible; Fran's uncle Leo recites a short Hebrew prayer. My son

Peter stands before the altar, and in a strong voice, reads the Cheyenne Prayer for a Fallen Warrior:

Do not stand at my grave and weep;

I am not there. I do not sleep . . .

I am the soft star that shines at night.

Do not stand at my grave and cry.

I am not there. I did not die.

One by one friends come forward to share stories and testimonials, some joyful, some sad, some hilariously funny. All this time the ocean is lapping at our feet and the sky is a symphony of changing color, from charcoal gray to deep purple.

When the sharing is over, Peter and I get in a small dingy and row out a short distance from the shore. Someone sounds the conch. I hold the jar filled with Fran's ashes up to the heavens, and then tip them into the ocean. While a cloud of ashes blows in the wind, Peter scatters hundreds of flowers on the water. We watch them drift slowly away in the current.

PART II

FINDING IT

Don't look here, there, anywhere. Peace is within you and within the Heart of all beings. So keep quiet, don't look anywhere, don't allow your mind to abide anywhere, and you will see that It is peace, happiness itself. That is the fundamental truth. Every being in the world is happiness itself.
H.W.L. Poonja (Papaji)

CHAPTER 11

OPENING THE LOVE WINDOW

Peter & Linda Lumahai Gardens, Kauai

A Meeting Made in Heaven
Mt. Ayr Farm, Virginia, May 6, 2000

There is some kiss we want with our whole lives
The touch of spirit on the body
Seawater begs the pearl to break free from its shell
And the lily, how passionately it needs some wild darling
Rumi

"Listen!" Linda says, with an intensity that stops me in mid-sentence.

I'm so engrossed in conversation that I have no idea what she is referring to. Neither do Jack or Judy, who make up the foursome around the table. Jack and Judy are former New Yorkers who moved to Virginia fifteen years ago and own a stunning estate on a mountaintop in Nelson County. We met them just recently and they are fast becoming good friends. Tonight we've invited them over for dinner at our farm and are seated outdoors on our brick patio under the sheltering branches of a huge maple tree as dusk creeps softly in.

We listen intently, not knowing exactly what Linda wants us to hear. Moments later a sound drifts out from the darkness of the forest: *Whippoorwill, whippoorwill.*

"It's a whippoorwill!" Linda says excitedly. "They're almost extinct." We breathe in the silence. Once again the distinctive song of this shy little forest bird reaches our ears: *Whippoorwill, whippoorwill.*

We look at each other and smile. Suddenly Judy says, "Oh, look, fireflies!"

In the nearby field the first fireflies rise from the grass, beginning their dance of courtship. We all watch as these extraordinary life forms blink into existence in order to attract a mate.

In one instant we are swimming in the magic of the moment.

"Chardonnay?" I ask, reaching out for the chilled bottle of Kendall Jackson. Jack smiles and nods his head. For a man in his seventies he still looks remarkably young and handsome. I fill his glass and look over to Judy. She holds up her hand and shakes her head.

"Well, where were we?" Jack asks, referring to our conversation before Linda drew our attention to the whippoorwill.

"We were talking about politics, sex, and God," I say, "not necessarily in that order. But I'm famished. Let's have some dinner."

The table is laden with organic vegetables straight from the garden and fresh baked bread. I whisk the ginger-glazed salmon off the grill, cooked to perfection.

We sit for a minute in silence, not because of any prescribed ritual, but because we're all feeling the overwhelming fullness of the moment—the joy of new friendship, the sweet smells of a warm summer night, the colorful feast that lies before us.

What more could I possibly want? I ask myself as I close my eyes and take in a deep breath. *How could I be more happy than this?*

"Well, we told you about how we met," Judy says. "Tell us how you both met." The story of their courtship was breathtaking—a wild, passionate affair, trips to London and Paris, glamorous interludes in some of the most beautiful resorts in the world . . . Jack was a *very* successful businessman.

Linda and I look at each other and smile. "It's quite a story," I say.

"Should we tell?" Linda asks.

"Yes, yes, tell!" Jack says, lifting his wine glass in a toast.

Linda takes a deep breath and drops into that place of precious memory. She closes her eyes for a moment and smiles.

"I had just moved to Hawaii, leaving behind my whole life in Oregon," she begins in a dream-like voice.

"What do you mean, your whole life?" Judy asks, her sharp, intelligent eyes taking in Linda.

"I was a teacher for twenty years and married to my husband Bill for that same time. I designed and built my own farmhouse, where I was sure I would live forever."

"She's amazing," I add in with pride. "She did the carpentry, the brickwork, the painting, all with her own hands . . . and built the whole thing for $40,000!"

Jack and Judy look duly impressed.

"I had a rich and full life with a career, friends, and a beautiful farm. But something inside me started to change. I had this strong pull to move to Hawaii. I ended up leaving Bill, my job, the farm, and even my dog Sarah. I just had to go."

"You left everything?" Judy asks incredulously.

"It wasn't easy, but I had no choice. Sometimes you have to follow your heart."

"And you went to Kauai?"

"Yes, I went on my own. I had just been in a car accident and could barely function. My sister helped me on an airplane and off I went. I landed on Kauai and found a place to live. I was very lonely and kept wondering if I had done the right thing. One day I went to this Shiatsu practitioner named Karen to get some bodywork. While she was working on me I asked her, 'Is there anywhere on the island where I can go for satsang? I love to hear Eastern chanting.' She said, 'Yes, there are these two people, Peter and Fran Mellen, who give satsang every week at their house. You really should go. They have a beautiful property overlooking the ocean.'"

Jack leans back in his chair, wineglass in hand. "So, this is the first time you heard about Peter."

"Yes. And when Karen mentioned Fran, someone else in the room asked, 'How is she? I hear the cancer has gone to her brain.'"

I intercede, "That was the beginning of the end for Fran. We were in San Diego at the time doing this whacko megavitamin treatment."

"When I heard this," Linda says, "my voice said to me, 'Peter is the reason you came to Hawaii. He is the man you are going to marry.'"

"Oh my God," exclaims Judy, her hazel eyes opening wide.

I bark out a laugh, "For all she knew, I could have been an old geezer!"

"Immediately I pushed the thought from my mind," Linda says. "I was having a lot of prophetic dreams at the time. Soon afterwards I dreamt about a young man who I would meet who had curly hair. In the dream I saw that this man would take me to a professor, and that the professor and I would walk up the mountain to God together."

"Peter, was a professor, wasn't he?" Judy asks.

"Yes," Linda says. "And sure enough, a few days later I met Umberto, who was Cuban and had black curly hair. We went out together and every Sunday he'd say, 'Let's go to Peter and Fran's for satsang.' But I didn't want to go. I always came up with an excuse."

"Umberto was an interesting guy," I say. "I liked him."

"Several months went by, and it became clear that Umberto and I could never make it as a couple. I was devastated, because I so wanted it to work. Then I had another dream that left me sitting bolt upright in bed. I was standing in a parking lot in front of another man. I could see that he had straight hair, unlike Umberto, and that he had freckles."

With a smile I point to the freckles all over my arms.

"This man and I were standing in front of a guru . . . a guru with shorts on."

"It turns out that the guru was Amrit Desai," I add. "We even saw him dressed in shorts in the parking lot after we met!"

Linda continues, "When he looked at us, every chakra of both our bodies opened up. It was like sparks flying between us. We were lit up and on fire. We opened into total oneness together. I woke Umberto up and said, 'I've had this incredible dream.' I was very shaken."

"Did he know it was over between you?" Jack says as he brushes back his long white hair with his hand.

"Yes, he knew it wouldn't work. The next Sunday I said to him, 'Let's go to satsang tonight. I feel it's time.' So we drove through the estate where Peter and Fran lived. I was awestruck by the beauty. The driveway curved through beautiful gardens, over a bridge, and up a steep hill to their house. When I walked down the long entryway, smelling the incense in the air, this immense sadness came over me. A voice inside me was saying, 'This is my house. I love it so. I don't want to leave.' I didn't understand where it came from. When we entered the door I found out that Fran had died just a few days ago and that this was her memorial satsang. It was only later that I found out that I had the dream the same night Fran died."

"Fran visited a lot of people the night she died, I say, shaking my head. "Some of them lived thousands of miles away. They told me that Fran had shown up to tell them how much she loved them."

Jack and Judy have stopped eating.

"I went out onto the lanai overlooking the ocean," Linda says. "It was just getting dark and I could hear the gentle roar of the ocean in the distance. Again this terrible sadness came over me. I suddenly realized that I was having Fran's feelings. I started crying. I saw how I had loved this place and hated to leave it. The grief was overwhelming. I still had not seen Peter. Over thirty people showed up for the service. When Peter came out he was dressed in white and looking totally radiant. There was this light emanating from him. It must have come from all that time he spent caring for Fran during her illness. Instead of being in pieces, he was busy comforting everyone else. The moment I saw him, I fell totally in love with him."

"I'm getting goosebumps," Judy exclaims, rubbing her arms.

"It was very moving," I say. "Everyone shared their love for Fran and how she had touched their lives."

"At the end they lifted Peter up and rocked him. I held on to one of his feet, sending this sweet man all the love I had."

"What happened then?"

I laugh a little too raucously, "You don't want to know."

"Peter had to go through his stuff. I knew better than to get involved with him then. The single women of Kauai started to descend on him like vultures even before Fran was buried. It was a free-for-all."

We all laugh.

"I was totally nuts!" I say, laughing and crying at the same time.

"Several months later I came to another satsang. I could see that Peter was still grieving, yet everyone was pretending as if nothing had happened. After satsang I went up to him and gave him a hug, saying, 'I know what it's like to lose the one you love. I so want to comfort you.'"

I reach out and take Linda's hand. "Linda told me that her mother had died of cancer. I sensed that she was the first person who really understood what I was going through, so I said, 'Why don't you come for lunch next week?'"

"So I came to lunch," Linda says with a smile.

" . . . and never left," I laugh.

Jack lets out a huge sigh. "A meeting made in heaven."

Darkness has fallen. I light a candle and we all slip into thoughtful silence, the haunting sounds from the forest reminding us of the mystery of life. *Whippoorwill . . . whippoorwill.*

The Awareness Watching It All
Aloha Mana Farm, Kauai, January 25, 1991

Wake up, my dear friends. There is no suffering at all. It's only a projection of your mind. It's not real. You are dreaming. Wake up from the dream, and all the suffering will end.

H.W.L. Poonja (Papaji)

It is less than a week since Fran's death and my emotions are like waves in a storm-tossed sea. In his book, *A Perfect Storm*, Sebastian Junger describes what happens when a pararescue jumper named John Spillane falls seventy feet from a helicopter into the ocean: "His memory goes from falling to swimming, with nothing in between—he doesn't know who he is, why he is there, or how he got there. He has no history and no future." I feel cut loose just like that pararescue jumper—consciousness at night in the middle of the sea. I am flung into the timeless present in spite of myself, drawing on resources I didn't even know I had.

There is a surprising sense of exhilaration to it all. One moment I'm swept upwards into light-headedness and laughter, the next I'm dashed down into tears and despair. In between there are periods of numbness and fatigue that seem to go on forever. The rapidity with which these feelings change makes me aware that they are just temporary. They wash over me so fast that that I can no longer claim them as "my" emotions. They're just emotions that come and go. They show me that these feelings are not who I am. Who I am is the awareness that is watching it all.

At times I dive into maudlin self pity, fully identifying with the poor Peter who has just lost his wife. I sit alone in the bedroom at night, feeling the immense void left by her absence. My whole being cries out in grief as memories rise up of times we spent together— tender moments with our son Peter cuddling him when he was young, quiet evenings on the couch with our cat Frisky, romantic dinners with the sun setting behind the Bali Hai mountains. Then I catch myself. Every time a memory surfaces, I realize that it is just a story. It exists only as a thought in my mind. What is happening right now? There's no Fran, no cat, no son. I'm sitting alone in a room in the dark listening to the muffled sound of the ocean in the distance. In this moment, everything is fine. Once I notice that these thoughts come and go, just like the feelings, the intensity of the grief subsides. As soon as I grasp on to another memory, the grief wells up again. I see that I have a choice. I can hold on to each thought and be torn up in grief, or I can just let the thoughts come and go. What is deeper than the thoughts doesn't change. I can remember that I am the quiet stillness of the ocean, or I can be tossed around by the waves on the surface. It doesn't really matter.

On the Sunday following Fran's death, I decide to have our usual Sunday evening gathering, and invite Menka to co-lead it with me. Menka is an old and dear friend from the Kripalu Center who arrived on the island the day after Fran's memorial service. It was clear that her arrival at this particular time was no accident. If I was to make a list of all the ways in which Menka and I were compatible (and I did), it would be the perfect union. We shared the same friends, the same teacher, the same background, the same interests, and we both had grown up in Canada. Some were predicting that we would be married within a year.

Is all this being orchestrated by some higher power, I ask myself, *or Fran herself?*

As we wait for everyone to arrive for the gathering, Menka and I stand before the small altar I've set up in the living room, arranging the pictures of Gurudev and Bapuji, along with a photograph of Fran.

"I have always sensed that my being here is a springboard for something else," Menka says, lighting the candles. She looks radiant in her pretty white dress, which sets off her deeply tanned skin and silver-blond hair.

"You're right," I say. I'm dressed in white too, a tradition from the Kripalu days, where we all wore white for satsang. *My God,* I think, *we look as if we're dressed for a wedding . . . and it's not even a week since Fran died!*

We exchange glances, and in a brief moment there is a shift from friendship to something more. *What's happening here? We've been like brother and sister for fifteen years . . . and now this?*

We both catch ourselves.

"It's too soon," Menka says, quickly drawing back. "We mustn't rush this."

"I feel like we're like two characters in a play. We're in the wings watching Act I, knowing that our characters don't show up until Act III."

Menka turns towards me. "I keep wondering—does the universe want to bring us together?"

We tentatively look into each other's eyes. Our hands touch.

"Hello . . . anyone there?" a voice calls out from the kitchen.

"Come on in," I call out. "We're in here."

We both straighten up like we've been caught in the act.

About thirty people show up for the gathering. My son Peter joins us. It's his last night on the island before returning to the mainland. We all sit in silence in a large circle around the living room, with the glass sliders open to the night air. The room is softly lit and the smell of incense and ocean breezes permeates the air. A tray filled with sweet-smelling plumeria flowers and a glowing candle sits in the center of the room.

Menka leads the opening meditation in a calm, soothing voice. "Let your heart open as you feel Fran's presence here with us in the room. I invite you to open to whatever is present for you. If you are grieving, stay with your feelings and allow your heart to soften. Let your inner child come forth to be nurtured and loved. Know that our beloved Frannie has found rest and peace at last."

We then go around the circle, each person sharing from their heart.

Lois speaks first saying, "Peter, I feel that Fran's spirit has become one with yours. It is now time for you to express the power and the beauty of all that you are, to stand on your own and fly." I nod, making a show of how humble I am.

Tears come to Phyllis' eyes as she says, "No one has touched my life as deeply as Fran has. She gave us all so much through the way she consciously faced her own death."

"I've been so touched by your devotion over the past months," Michael says, looking at me with love.

"I remember when we went out on the boat last week," Byron says. "In all the hundreds of times I've been out, I've never seen so many spinner dolphins as that day. It's as if Fran was there celebrating with us."

It comes to my son Peter's turn. "I hear everyone here being really positive and happy," he says as tears well up in his eyes, "but I miss her like crazy."

To my shock, I realize that in trying to be "spiritual" in front of all these people I've covered up my deep feelings of grief. I'm so proud of Peter for being real. The whole room becomes silent.

At Menka's invitation, everyone gets up. "I want both Peters to lie down on the floor and for you to form two circles, one around each Peter."

I lie down on the floor, a little embarrassed by all the attention, while fifteen people gather around me.

"Now gently lift them in the air."

With my eyes closed. I feel fifteen pairs of hands lifting me off the ground. I completely relax into their loving embrace.

"As you rock both Peters back and forth—one who has lost his mother, and the other who has lost his wife—send them your love." Someone puts on a tape and I hear the words from a familiar song: *You're an angel, you're a being of light. You're an angel and I know that I'm right* . . . As everyone sings along, they rock us back and forth.

I wonder what Peter is feeling as he is being rocked. I know he must be in terrible pain. My God, he's only twenty-three and has just loss his mom. He's being so brave. I send him my love from the depth of my being, hoping he will find peace.

Gradually, the gentle rocking soothes me. I feel like a child being held in the arms of the mother.

Little did I know that the person holding on so tightly to my left foot was someone who had never been to one of our gatherings before.

I didn't even know her name.

Only later did I find out that it was Linda.

Babe in a Wood
Kauai, February-March 1991

The search for happiness is one of the chief sources of unhappiness.
Eric Hoffer

Kauai is a tight little island. The number of available men who are not pot-heads, broke, hopelessly degenerate, or marginally insane, is infinitesimally small. It does not take long for the local female populace to spot me as a new catch—not because I look like Robert Redford—but because I appear to have money and own a beautiful house overlooking the ocean. It takes only an hour after Fran's memorial service before I get the first nibble. I'm sitting on the couch, exhausted after the ordeal of the past few weeks, when I feel a pair of hands on my shoulders. I turn around to see Kyra, a healer who has just moved to the island. She is aggressive, East-coast Jewish, with big, frizzy black hair, and a full figure. "You must be so stressed out," she says in a soothing voice. "Just relax and let me take care of you." After giving me a brief shoulder massage, she leans over and gives me a kiss on the cheek. Friends later tell me that they saw her walking around the house, checking out all the rooms, and announcing she was "ready to move in." My son Peter noticed her too and said in astonishment, "Did you see that? She was spraying the place like a tomcat marking its territory!"

It's a time of new beginnings. After three years of watching Fran die it feels like I've done my share of grieving. Through all that time I was at her side every moment, through countless doctor visits, operations, healings, support groups, bedside vigils, and travels all over the country in search of a cure. Unlike many couples where death comes suddenly, we had our chance to say good-bye. We laughed and we cried together; we gave thanks for all the beautiful times we shared; we told each other again and again how much we loved each other . . . and now it is over. A part of me wants to remain faithful and honor our relationship forever. Another part wants to explore being single again.

To be honest, I'm horny as hell.

A few weeks later I cautiously try my hand at dating. I'm as nervous as a virgin teenager trying to get laid for the first time. First there is Barbara, a gorgeous blond yoga teacher from Texas and former swimsuit model. I met her during Fran's illness, and fantasized on touching her perfect, healthy body, especially as Fran began to look more and more like a concentration camp victim. Over the next few weeks I wined and dined Barbara, hoping to get her into bed. But I soon see why she had a reputation for being a tease. After several dates and no more than a kiss on the cheek goodnight, I knew I wasn't going to get anywhere. I decide I can't wait any longer and move on.

With infinite perfection, Sharon appears in my life, I can't even remember how we met. She is Jewish, intelligent, sensual, and unattached. She knows that Fran has just died, and like some mother-earth goddess, is willing to accept the role I am asking her to play—that of initiating me back into my sexuality. With great tenderness she helps me step across the threshold in a ritual celebration of innocence and joy. I talk, she listens, I cry, she holds me. I am filled with yearning, she receives me. We date for a few weeks, but in my emotionally fragile state, I can't come up to the level of intimacy she needs, and we go our separate ways. I will be forever grateful for the gift she gave me.

But, when there is a backlog of desire as deep as mine is, one sexual adventure is not enough.

Like a crazy sex addict I seek out other women and am soon in way over my head. First, there is Sonia, a wild, untamable woman, who also happens to be Jewish, with a full figure and large breasts. Could this have something to do with Fran being Jewish and having big breasts? What a textbook response. We have a wild, passionate fling, which we both know is temporary. But when I accidentally stand her up one night, the shit begins to fly.

When I get home I play back my messages: "You asshole! How can you be such an insensitive son of a bitch? Don't ever call me again!" A few days later I find a note pinned on the door: "I really don't have a whole lot to say to you at this time, nor am I interested in hearing from you . . . and you think you're so spiritual!" Being attacked for not being spiritual gets me where it hurts.

I've been out of the dating scene for twenty-five years and need a few lessons. Even though I thought I was acting with integrity, and made it clear to my dates that I was incapable of a long-term commitment, they obviously wanted something more. When it blew up in my face, I was devastated. Only now can I see how much healing needed to happen. But at the time I felt like a little child of four or five – a babe in the woods- running naked out into the world, arms bravely outstretched, only to find himself utterly alone and terrified.

My heart is heavy.

New beginnings are not easy. In between these crazy forays into relationships, I spend time alone, grieving over Fran. I put on syrupy New Age music and lie in bed alone crying. "Oh Fran, I love you so. I know you're watching over me from the Other Side. Please help me get through this. Show me your presence." I keep hoping she'll show up at the foot of my bed like Patrick Swayze in the movie *Ghost*. But she doesn't. The next morning I have the strongest sensation that Fran has not really "gone" at all—that she is more "present" than ever.

That same day I come across a story about an Indian sage who was dying of cancer. His disciples were gathered around him weeping, begging him not to go. "They say I am dying," says the great sage, "but where could I go? I am here."

My dear friends Tom and Linda invite me to dinner. Of all the people I know, I love being with them most. They live in a beautiful house on a ridge overlooking the Hanalei Valley.

After spending half an hour catching up on recent events, we sit down to dinner.

"Everything that is happening seems to be perfectly orchestrated by God," I say, taking a bite of Linda's delicious food. "I can finally let go of all my fears and relax into the miracle of each moment."

They listen patiently. I've never met anyone who listens like they do.

"I feel I'm letting go more and more and discovering peace within myself."

". . . and freedom?' Tom asks.

"Freedom? No. I haven't made that leap. Freedom is what I always wanted for Fran," I say rambling incoherently. "It's what I want to . . . by the way, what do you mean by freedom?"

"It's who you are," replies Tom.

"Who I am?" I ask, puzzled.

"Yes, who you are."

"And you've just forgotten it," Linda adds, with the smile of an angel.

"Hmmm," I say, totally bewildered. "Perhaps I can learn that freedom from Fran's example. I can be free in a way I never dreamed of . . ."

"You can't learn it from anyone, because you already *are* that freedom," says Tom.

The true meaning of what they are saying barely registers on my radar screen.

My Life Begins with Lunch
Aloha Mana Farm, Kauai, April 20, 1991

With that kiss, I felt as if I could fly through the air with the sheer power of happiness, settle on the clouds, kiss the stars, dance on the moon, and love the whole world.
Gerda Weissmann Klein

It's a glorious spring day in Hawaii, with the sun shining and temperature in the low eighties, making me even more grateful than usual to be living in paradise. Menka and I are sitting on the deck overlooking the brilliant emerald green Pacific Ocean, a few hundred yards away.

"Menka, it's almost 11:30 and Linda is coming for lunch at 12:00. I need to know if we're going to pursue this any further or not."

"Well, I don't know if I'm ready to enter into relationship or not," she says. She is wearing a colorful sundress, her blond hair falling on her bronzed shoulders. It's been three months since Menka and I led the memorial service for Fran. She has been living in our guest wing and we've had many heartfelt talks. She has patiently watched me create disaster after disaster around me until I had my fill; she has been in a relationship of her own. Mentally, we both know we are a perfect match. Emotionally, it's like trying to light a damp fuse.

"We've been talking about this for a month now," I say. "You know that Linda will be here in a few minutes. I can't keep waiting forever."

"But I have to listen to my feelings . . . I'm just not ready yet."

"We have so much in common. I think we could make it work."

Menka looks out towards the ocean, searching for the right words. "No . . . I'm sorry, but I can't."

So this is it, I realize. *We've tried everything and it's not going to work. It's like we were trying to make the whole thing happen in our heads.*

I take her hand and give it a squeeze. "I understand."

Getting up from my chair, I go in to prepare lunch for Linda.

Linda arrives at noon and we go out on the deck where Menka and I had been sitting just a few minutes before. Linda's blond hair is gently blowing in the breeze. She's barefoot and wearing a brightly colored Bali dress that reveals her petite runner's body, tanned by the Hawaiian sun.

Over the next few hours we talk non-stop. I tell her about living in Paris. It turns out she loves Paris. She tells me that she loves to play the piano. I tell her how much I love classical music. I tell her about my rebellious streak. She tells me she is an anti-authoritarian rebel. There's something so easy and effortless about our being together, just like coming home. The time flies by.

"I'm not sure if I should tell you this," she says, looking at me with her thoughtful blue eyes, "but something happened to me that first night I came to your house." She relates her dream and her first experience of walking into the house.

With a shock I remember Fran saying, "Now you can have that blond you've always wanted."

Is this all being arranged from the Other Side?

I reach out and take Linda's hand. It's only then that I notice the scars on her forearm.

"What happened to your arm?"

"I was burned by some boiling oil when I was a teenager. They were third degree burns."

I gently touch the furrowed skin.

It's clear that we both know what it is to feel pain. I sense the vulnerability in her eyes, as if there is some deep sadness that can never be expressed.

After lunch we walk on Anahola Beach, then soak in the hot tub while watching the humpback whales breaching offshore. Afternoon turns into evening as we return to the deck for a glass of wine and a spontaneous dinner that we've thrown together. The sun is setting behind Anahola Mountain sending rays of light shooting up into the clouds.

"I've made quite a mess of things in the few months since Fran died," I say. "I don't want to hurt anyone else. I'm a dangerous person to be in relationship with right now."

"I know. That's why I stayed away."

"Is it that obvious?"

"To me it was."

"I really can't make any kind of commitment right now. It's too soon."

"Don't worry," Linda says, taking my hand. "Just this moment is enough."

"As you know, I'm planning to go back to Massachusetts in a month."

"Thirty days . . . what a gift that would be!"

That was the day Linda entered my life in all her radiant beauty.

The next weeks are giddy with joy as we discover each other and our love for Kauai. The first time we make love my whole body starts to shake uncontrollably in an unbelievable explosion of bliss. It's a meeting in emptiness, where two come together as one—the merging of Shiva and Shakti. My screams rise up over the roar of the ocean.

We step into a magical realm where miracles seem to happen in every moment.

I've never met anyone like her. She's a free-spirited Polynesian goddess who goes barefoot everywhere, wearing nothing but a colorful pareo and a hibiscus flower in her hair. When she walks through the rainforest, birds and butterflies come up to hover near her. She sees things in nature that no one else does. Every so often she reaches out and touches a leaf or a flower, then brings her hands together in prayer position, honoring it with love. She enters into an ecstatic state as she watches a dragonfly hover nearby. I'm in awe of her beauty, but it is her profound embodiment of spirit that touches me the most. She is able to effortlessly slip into that place of divine bliss where the whole universe can appear in a dewdrop.

Fran often makes her presence felt during this time. Her totem animal was the monarch butterfly—we even made an award-winning film called *Monarch* when we were filmmakers. Monarchs are rarely seen on the island, but every day they show up around me, fluttering above my head and landing on my shoulder. It's as if Fran is telling me, "Yes, Peter, yes!" One afternoon a monarch butterfly flies right into the house, not once, but three times, before we finally realize that it's trying to tell us something. On the third time Linda takes it gently in her hands, saying, "Yes, Fran, I understand who you are, I love you." She releases it to the wind. It doesn't come back.

The grief is still there, but a newfound happiness is putting out its delicate and tender roots. I'm still fragile, manic, and totally out of control, but the long process of healing is underway.

CHAPTER 12

AN INVITATION TO AWAKEN

Sri Ramana Maharshi

The Hurricane
Lenox, Massachusetts, September 11, 1992

Dying is easy. Parking is hard.
Art Buchwald

One month after that extraordinary day when Linda came to lunch (and never left), I flew to Massachusetts to set up my new life. Ever since I moved to Kauai to take care of Fran during her illness, I longed to be back in the Berkshires, close to my dear Kripalu friends, my son in Washington DC, and my family in Montreal. I bought thirty acres of raw land near the Kripalu Center, cleared a house site, and started building a huge "Adirondack Lodge," sure it would be the Mellen ancestral home forever. I had only been there a few weeks when Linda flew to the East coast to join me for a visit. Her plan was to go to a Waldorf teacher training in Maine before returning to Kauai in the fall. She never made it.

It didn't take long for us to realize that the love between us had grown into something beyond anything we could have imagined. We were like long lost friends who had found each other again after years apart. We celebrated in ever-deepening self-discovery, as I took her to romantic restaurants in Lenox, concerts at the Tanglewood music festival, and hikes in the Berkshire Mountains. I introduced her to Gurudev and the "Kripalu family," and she bravely endured the close scrutiny of being "Ramakrishna's new lady-friend." This was the first time I'd been back to Kripalu since Fran died, and it was awkward for both of us. But everyone welcomed us with open arms—even Gurudev. Next she met my family, including my son Peter, and my sister Beverly and brother-in-law Bill from Montreal. She came through it all with flying colors, opening her heart to those I love most in the world.

Crazy in love, we set out on a whirlwind tour of Boston, Maine, Vermont, and the Adirondacks, as I showed her all my favorite spots on the East Coast. In between, we flew back to Kauai a number of times to put the house on the market and prepare it for sale. We were inseparable, never spending more than a night apart. On one of our trips, we spent the night in a romantic country inn overlooking Lake Placid in New York. It was a cold March night and the hotel was nearly empty. We ate dinner in the dining room with soft music and wine, looking out at the snow-covered peak of Whiteface Mountain lit by the full moon. Another couple came in, and the man kissed his partner as she sat down. Turning to Linda I say, "Maybe he's proposing to her?" With no premeditation, I add, "Would you like to get married?" She looks at me for what seems like forever, with an incredulous smile on her lips. "Oh yes, my sweet love. Of course yes!"

Far from settling down, our life becomes even more hectic. We finish building the log home; we make additional trips to Kauai; we visit Montreal, Nantucket, Santa Fe, and Taos; we travel to Oregon so that I can meet Linda's friends and see where she grew up. In October we fly from Kauai back to Massachusetts to prepare for our wedding. We're still unpacking and getting over jet lag when the phone rings. It's my son Peter. "Dad, you may want to turn on the television. There's a big hurricane moving towards Hawaii." Linda and I look at each other in alarm. I find the Weather Channel, and there it is—a huge tear-shaped mass slowly making its way towards the Hawaiian Islands. "This is one powerful storm," the announcer says. "We're showing a category Five hurricane with sustained winds up to 175 mph. If it continues on its present course it will pass just south of the island. Now, that's good news for all the folks in Hawaii." We breathe a sigh of relief. But a few minutes later we watch in horror as the trail of dashes that mark the hurricane's path suddenly makes a sharp right-hand turn as it moves due north. Like a long-range missile zeroing in on its target, the storm heads straight for the tiny island of Kauai. The date is September 11, 1992.

The phone rings again. It's Doreen, who has been care-taking our house while we're gone. "Did you hear about the hurricane?"

"Yes, we've been watching the news. It's heading straight for you."

"I know. We're trying to do everything we can to prepare. Jack and Patsy are here. Ron's helping too. We've taped the windows and brought everything indoors. There's not much else we can do."

"Just keep yourself safe. That's all that's important."

"Yeah, we're going to ride it out in the garage. It's built into the hill. We should be protected.

"If anyone else needs shelter, bring them in."

"I have to go now," Doreen says, and rings off.

A wave of helplessness comes over us as we watch the center of the hurricane bearing straight down on the island. Will our friends get through this? What about everyone else on the island? Many live in flimsy houses with tin roofs. Will our house survive? Everything we own is tied up in that property.

With winds clocked as high as 225 mph, Hurricane Iniki smashes into the island, becoming the third most damaging hurricane in US history. It rakes over the island from south to north for six hours before turning around and coming back in the opposite direction. Miraculously, no one is killed, but the island is devastated. The wind damages every home on the island, ripping roofs off houses and moving buildings hundreds of yards from their foundations. It tears up trees, vegetation, beaches, and roads. Scarcely a blade of grass is left standing.

For three long days there is a total news blackout. We have no idea whether Doreen and our friends are alive or dead, or whether our house is a pile of rubble. The phone lines are all down, and we don't hear from Doreen until she gets to an emergency phone five days later. She tells us that they are safe and that our house has only suffered moderate damage (which turns out to be $40,000). Stories start to emerge of friends who were huddled in a closet as their whole house collapsed around them. Our friend Tom Chandler was on the third floor of his condo in Poipu when he saw a Volkswagen fly by his balcony. He hid in his closet asking himself, "Am I staying here just to save all my stuff? That's crazy." Minutes later the glass sliders imploded and he escaped with his life.

The day we hear from Doreen is the day Linda and I get married—5,000 miles away in Lenox, Massachusetts. We are married in our newly completed log home, with thirty of our close family and friends gathered together in a celebration of love. Instead of having a priest or a rabbi, we are married by our dear friend Daniel Bowling, who obtained a special license to perform the ceremony; instead of exchanging rings, we exchange beautiful leis from Hawaii; instead of formal wear, we wear whites and are barefoot; instead of the usual ring bearer, we have our dog Sarah by our side; instead of ballroom dancing, we do Dances of Universal Peace; instead of bland catered food, we have a gourmet vegetarian feast—but we *are* traditional when it comes to wine and champagne.

A month later we return to Kauai. The island is barely recognizable. All the hotels are closed (or demolished) and there is not a tourist in sight. Everyone on the island is going through post-traumatic stress. One in three families have been left homeless and are living in tent cities. Huge piles of garbage— one for mattresses, one for refuse, another for appliances—are stacked up three stories high. The houses that survived are covered with blue tarps to keep out the rain. Many have signs posted out front saying, "Thank You God," "Mahalo Everyone." All the electric lines are down and there is no hope of electricity for months to come. A rainbow of hope shines through all this devastation and loss—it is the Hawaiian spirit of aloha, where people come together in countless ways to help each other.

Linda and I are among the lucky ones—we still have a roof, or at least part of one. However, our once beautiful estate with its Asian-Pacific house and acres of tropical gardens is now a shambles. Prior to the hurricane we rented the house as an upper-end vacation rental. This was our only source of income. Now, no one is coming to the island and we have $40,000 of repairs to take care of. In an act of semi-lunacy, we start to restore a little cottage so that we will have somewhere to live once the tourists start to come back. We do most of the carpentry ourselves. I barely know how to hold a hammer, but Linda quickly demonstrates her remarkable carpentry skills (and her sailor's mouth.)

One of our Hawaiian friends, Kahea, helps us put in a septic tank. I've known Kahea and his family for years. When he's not working for the Water Department repairing broken water mains, he does excavating work, running his backhoe or a huge old bulldozer. In his spare time he's a paniolo—a Hawaiian cowboy, competing in local rodeos. Short and stocky, he has a body used to hard physical work. A few of his front teeth are missing and his rugged face is framed by long sideburns and frizzy black hair.

After a long, hard day of digging trenches, we sit on the lanai having a beer and talking story as the sun sets behind the mountains.

"My grandmother was a kahuna . . . you know, like a healer," Kahea says, pausing to look over at Linda and me before continuing. Many Hawaiians are reluctant To share their culture with 'haoles' or white people, for fear of being misunderstood, but he knows how much we respect Hawaiian tradition. He points to the distinctive mountains that rise almost straight up just a mile away. "Grandma told us that the middle one is called Kalalea, which means being free from care and worry."

"I didn't know its Hawaiian name was Kalalea," Linda says excitedly.

"That's a much nicer name than "Kong," I laugh. From where we're sitting it looks exactly like the profile of a gorilla. No doubt this is why it was included in the famous 1933 film *King Kong*, and later in the 2006 version.

Kahea takes another swig of beer. "The flat mountain next to it is called Hokulea, meaning 'star.' My grandma says that was where the Star People landed thousands of years ago." He turns to Linda with a knowing look, inviting her to understand the deeper significance behind this.

Linda nods her head in astonishment. "I've always felt drawn to that mountain. It's what kept me coming back to Kauai. Every time I left the island I would see it from the airplane and sob, and every time I returned I would see it as we flew in. I always had this huge surge of joy."

Kahea drains his bottle as narrow sunrays shoot into the sky. He has lived in the shadow of this mountain his entire life. "I've hunted wild boar up there. I've been over every inch of it on foot. There used to be a hole in the mountain on the right, but it collapsed in a landslide in the eighties." For Hawaiians like Kahea, the land, or the "aina," is a living thing.

After Kahea leaves, Linda and I sit alone in the semi-darkness, listening to the sounds of the mynahs nesting and the dull roar of the ocean in the distance. Linda takes my hand and says, "Peter, when Kahea told us that legend, I had the strongest feeling that you and I were here together at the foot of this mountain a thousand years ago. We were Hawaiians, living on the land, and we were in love."

"I felt something too."

"I just know that we looked at each other and said, 'Let's meet here again in a thousand years.'"

"And here we are," I say, looking into her eyes with love. "And here we are."

A World Turned Upside Down
Mana Lea Gardens, Maui, March 14, 1993

The words spoken in satsang are vehicles to stop the mind, so that what can be realized is what has never been seen before, never been heard before, never been thought before, and never been realized before.

Gangaji

Over the next weeks Linda and I struggle to renovate the cottage. Because everyone else on the island is rebuilding, the local Ace hardware and lumber yard have been stripped bare of just about everything. Finding a plumber or electrician is near impossible. We finally do find an electrician and give him a large deposit to do the work; he runs off to Honolulu with the money to score drugs. The weather is hot and muggy and the mosquitoes are biting. Before long it feels that our entire days are spent covered in dust and red dirt. Instead of taking time to go to the beach for a swim, we make endless trips to the industrial park in search of plywood, paint, or plumbing supplies. Like everyone else on the island, we are exhausted and desperately need a break.

We decide to fly over to Maui for a mini-vacation. Before leaving, our friend Doreen tells us about a housewife named Gangaji who is holding spiritual gatherings on Maui. That's the last thing I want to do when I get to Maui, which was untouched by the hurricane. I want to spend my time at a fancy hotel, eating, making love, and lying on the beach. Besides, I pride myself in knowing the "who's who" of spiritual teachers in Hawaii and I've never heard of anyone named Gangaji (I'm such a snob).

But when we arrive on the island, and I've had some time to play, I keep getting the message: *go to satsang!*

But I don't want to.

Go to satsang!

We find our way along Kaupakalua Road, a narrow, winding road that takes us through jungle-like scenery to a retreat center with exotic flowers and birds everywhere. It all looks so rich and lush after being in the devastation that is now Kauai. Expecting only a handful of people to show up, I'm surprised to find about two hundred people gathered in the large hall. Linda and I find a place to sit on the floor and glance around. It's the quintessential "Maui scene"—people wearing everything from bright Hawaiian shirts, to Indian whites, tie-dye T-shirts, silk dresses, bathing suits, and fresh-from-the-mainland-neatly-pressed khaki pants and polo shirts. One side of the hall is open to the outside, letting in the sound of a loud, squawking parrot.

To my delight, an old friend from Kripalu comes and sits next to me.

"Niranjan. Great to see you," I say, giving him a hug. "Do you know anything about this person Gangaji?"

"Hey . . . good to see you Ramakrishna . . . yeah, I've seen her before."

"What's her story?"

"She was born in Mississippi . . ."

"Mississippi!"

Niranjan laughs. "That surprised me too. She was a school teacher. She later went to San Francisco and became an acupuncturist."

"How'd she get her name?"

"Her name is Toni Varner. A few years ago she went to India and met Papaji. Do you know about him?"

"Yeah, I've heard of him. He's the Indian teacher everyone is talking about now."

"He gave her the name Gangaji and told her to go out and teach. Now she's giving satsang and retreats around the world."

The room suddenly becomes quiet and we stop talking. I turn to see a large woman in a muumuu bustling in from the back of the room, carrying a meditation cushion, a shawl, a notebook, and a huge carry bag. *Well, that can't be Gangaji.* The woman scatters people aside as she makes her way to the very front of the room, where she opens up a place for herself and plops down. *There's one in every crowd,* I think.

After sitting in silence for a few minutes, I notice a murmur in the audience. I open my eyes and see an exquisitely dressed woman in her forties enter from a side door and walk gracefully towards the dais. She has on a white dress with a blue silk scarf casually draped around her neck. Her hair, much to my surprise, is white. She is stunningly attractive. *I didn't know what to expect, but it wasn't this! She's certainly no housewife—she looks like a movie star!*

I watch carefully as she places a stack of letters on the side table and sits cross-legged on the chair. Beautiful flower arrangements have been set up on either side of her, and there is a blue backdrop behind her chair. It has a large picture of an Indian man on it, who must be her teacher Papaji. She closes her eyes and sits in silence, all without saying a word.

Everyone sits with their eyes closed. There's no instruction on how long the meditation will go on. After a few minutes have passed, I half open my eyes and glance at her. She's absolutely still. The silence in the room is intense—even the parrot has stopped squawking. After fifteen minutes or so there is a slight rustling. When I open my eyes I see her looking quietly around the room, smiling warmly at people she recognizes. The meditation is over. Someone turns on the video camera lights, which brighten up the room with a blast.

"Welcome to satsang," Gangaji says. "Feel free to ask a question, give a report, or say hello. Sometimes, when people are here for the first time, they hold back. That's OK. Check me out and then jump in."

For some strange reason I find myself holding up my hand. She notices me and invites me to speak.

"Gangaji, I can never refuse an invitation to jump in," I say.

"Oh, good, I like that!"

Someone hands me a microphone. My heart is pounding. "I have a question. For years I've longed for a dramatic, earth-shattering mystical experience that will lead to spiritual awakening . . . but it never seems to happen. I feel like a rocket, where the fuse is lit, but all it does is go fizzle, fizzle. I keep waiting for the rocket to explode and shoot into the air, but it doesn't."

"Well, there must be some malfunction," she says. Everyone laughs.

Laughing myself, I turn to look out at all the smiling faces in the room. *This is great,* I think. *I'm entertaining them!*

Turning back to Gangaji, I'm ready to keep my stand-up routine going, "I keep waiting for this great orgasmic union with the universe."

"Yes, you're waiting for some 'thing' in particular."

Gangaji is clearly not buying in to my need for approval from the group, so I tone things down a bit.

"I've read a lot of stories about these earth-shattering Kundalini awakenings. I'm afraid that if that happened to me, I'd never come back."

"Yes, put aside all ideas of what will happen or what should happen. This is a trick of the mind. There is some idea of what it will feel like or look like. In that you are subtly overlooking what is present, which may not be orgasmic at all. It may be much more subtle than that. What you're really speaking about is the source of all experiences."

My mind tries to make sense of what she is saying, but it short-circuits. Not sure where to go next, I say: "I was taught that if you meditate an hour every day, practice yoga, and live a pure life, then this 'something' will eventually happen."

"The practice is noticing what you have been practicing from the first thought in the morning. It is noticing what your twenty-three-hour-a-day practice is. What happens during the time when you're not sitting or doing yoga? It is noticing what you practice, and then dropping it. There is nothing wrong with spiritual practices. They can take you to the gate. But then you must drop everything—every technique, every tool—to discover what needs no practice for the truth of its being."

"What I see is that I'm trying to get to that place of nothingness through 'doing.'"

"That's spiritual practice. You imagine that after years of practice you will get to this gate, where you will pass through and become awakened. But you keep getting to the gate and for some reason you can't get through. That's because the opening to this gate is so narrow that there's no room for *anything* to pass through. No *one*—meaning no individual ego—passes through the gate."

"Hmmm . . ." *Oh, shit, fifteen years of meditation and yoga being flushed down the tube. This is mind-boggling. All my cherished concepts are being blown away.*

"And this gate exists only in your imagination."

"In my imagination?"

"Yes, there is no gate. There's nowhere to get to. You're already there."

"What about the spiritual transmission from the teacher or guru?" I ask. "Don't we need a guru to give us a powerful blast of shakti energy for us awaken?"

"That transmission is what is happening right now," Gangaji replies. "*This* is the living truth. Drop all notions of where you are going, where you've been, or where you are. Then speak to me from there. Then *you* transmit to me."

Energy surges throughout my body, creating involuntary jerks. *And to think that for all these years I thought someone else out there had to give that shakti energy to me!*

"What are you experiencing right now?"

I close my eyes. "It feels like my body is vibrating. There's this huge energy moving through me."

"The source of that energy is within you. Go there. Turn your attention there."

"It's powerful."

"This transmission is the transmission of your own Self."

This is too much. My mind goes blank.

"Let yourself rest," she says, her hands comfortably resting on her lap. "No effort is needed. There's nothing to do. If there's anything to do it's as if this revelation needs something to prop it up. This reveals itself by itself to itself."

Such soothing words! I've done nothing but push myself and it has gotten me nowhere.

Not knowing what to say, I bring my hands together in prayer position and bow my head in respect.

"I'm very happy to see you," she says. "I embrace this perfection."

I look up into her eyes. They seem to burn through me with their intensity. *What just happened? It feels like my world has been turned upside down.*

The Whitest Spot in a White Space
Kilauea, Kauai, March 12, 1993

Ramana Maharshi . . . essentially bypasses all religious and cultural forms,
Eastern and Western. Ramana may be the Einstein of planetary spirituality.
Lex Hixon

Linda and I and our friend Doreen are seated outdoors on the lanai at the Casa di Amici, our favorite restaurant in Kilauea. I love eating under the stars in the warm night air, surrounded by red ginger and huge banana plants dramatically lit by small floodlights. The palm fronds clack gently in the wind, and in the background I can hear the murmur of voices and the soothing sound of someone playing classical guitar.

Doreen has just returned from her second trip to India this year, where she visited her teacher H. W. L. Poonja, or Papaji, in Lucknow. With her full, sensual lips and soft brown eyes, she looks radiant in the candlelight. "I brought back a little gift for both of you," she says, handing us a package. "It's a book on Ramana Maharshi."

As I tear off the wrappings, I'm stunned by the face shining out on the cover of the book. I recognize the photo. It's a faded yellowish photograph of the great sage Sri Ramana Maharshi, who died in 1950. The first thing I notice are his eyes, which appear to look directly into mine. I stare into them for a moment and immediately go into an altered state. Ramana's lips are parted in a half-smile; he has closely trimmed white hair and a beard; his neck and shoulders are bare. I have never seen a photograph that expresses such tenderness and compassion. It reminds me of some of the paintings of Jesus that I used to study as an art historian. I'm deeply moved. I feel as if I've found a missing piece to my life.

"Ramana is one of India's greatest saints," I exclaim in surprise. "I remember that Carl Jung once said that, 'In all of India, he is the whitest spot in a white space.'"

Linda is stunned by what she sees and takes the book from my hands. Thumbing through the pages she says, "How come I've never heard of him?" she says. The book has obviously been printed in India on cheap, shiny paper. There are photographs of Ramana as a young man, scenes of him with the animals he loved so much, and a fold-out picture of Mt. Arunachala. "I thought I'd read about every teacher there is, but for some reason I must have missed him. How could that be?"

212

"Because you're ready now. That's why," Doreen says with a knowing smile.

"I have a little book on Ramana that I bought twenty years ago," I say. "It's still in my library. I've never forgotten him. The problem is, I can never understand a word he's saying."

Our waiter, Steve, appears with a basket of steaming hot garlic bread, placing it gracefully on the table. "Hey, guys."

"Howzit?" I ask. Steve is pure Hawaiian, with smooth olive-colored skin, jet-black hair, and a slim, muscled surfer's body.

"You want to order?"

"Not yet," we reply in unison. Ravenous, we reach into the basket and tear off pieces of bread, the butter dripping down our fingers.

"I remember the story of Ramana's awakening," I say, after taking a bite of the hot, buttery bread. "He was just sixteen, wasn't he?"

"Right," nods Doreen.

"Tell me more," Linda says excitedly. "I love stories about awakening."

I turn to her, trying to recollect the story. "I remember that he was overcome by a violent fear of death. He lay down on the floor of his room and dramatized his own death. He really felt like he was dying. Then he had the realization that when the body dies, he doesn't die."

"He saw that he was not the body," Doreen adds.

"And he never had a teacher?" Linda asks.

"Well, he often said that Mt. Arunachala was his teacher," I say.

"A mountain?"

"Yeah. It's thought to be the most sacred mountain in all of India."

"Where is it?" she asks, wanting to know every detail.

"In South India . . . get this, outside a town called 'Tiruvanamalai.' It took me forever to learn how to pronounce it."

"Ramana went there when he was seventeen," Doreen says. "He never left sight of that mountain for fifty years. He ended up dying there."

"It's an amazing story," I continue. "He cut off his hair, gave away everything he owned—including his clothes—and lived in the cellar of a temple for months."

Doreen picks up where I left off. "Yeah, kids threw rocks at him, but someone showed up to take care of him and feed him a few grains of rice every day. Ramana was so lost in bliss that he was unaware of his body. Insects and rats started chewing on him and he didn't even care."

"You've got to be kidding!" Linda exclaims, her eyes wide.

"No . . . he had the scars all his life."

"And he was only a teenager at the time?"

"Yeah, he went to live in a cave on the mountain, just outside the town. For years he didn't even speak. He didn't take a vow of silence or anything. He just saw no reason to speak. A group of people started to gather around him, recognizing the spiritual energy that emanated from him. Ramana didn't see himself as a teacher or a swami or anyone special."

"I like that," Linda says. "I'm so tired of these self-important gurus."

Steve comes back and we give him our order. We ask for more garlic bread and another carafe of wine.

"I'll never forget visiting Ramana's ashram and climbing Mt. Arunachala," I say.

"You've been there?" Linda asks incredulously. We've only known each other for a few months and there are still parts of my life she knows nothing about.

"I went during my trip to India with Yogi Amrit Desai. We spent a day there. Did you know that there are still holy men living on the mountain? I got to meet some of them."

"Did you see the cave where Ramana lived?" Linda asks.

"Yes. It's about halfway up the mountain at a spot that looks like a little oasis. I didn't know what to expect—it was a small room carved into the rock. I was able to meditate in it alone for awhile. I felt I could have stayed there forever—or at least until dinner. When I came out the sun was going down. It was quite a sight, looking down on the town with its huge Shiva temples, and beyond that the plains, stretching as far as the eye could see. The monkeys were making a terrible racket."

Linda takes all this in, as if recalling some distant memory.

Out of the corner of my eye I see Patrick, the owner of Casa di Amici, walking up to our table. Although I like the restaurant, I find Patrick a little hard to take. He's wearing a loud Hawaiian shirt, which barely covers his protruding belly.

Linda cringes. She doesn't like his energy.

"Is everything OK?"

"Yes, Patrick, we're doing great."

"Enjoy yourselves," he says, heading off to greet the customers at the next table.

Feeling badly that I wasn't more welcoming I ask, "I wonder what Ramana would have done if he was sitting here when Patrick came up?"

"He wouldn't have been here in the first place," Linda quips.

"You got me!" I laugh, feeling guilty about drinking wine and being so self-indulgent when all Ramana owned was a loincloth and a water bowl.

"That's what I love about Ramana," Doreen says. "He would have seen Patrick as being no different from himself. He never saw anyone as separate from Self. When people visited him, it didn't matter whether they were a king, a beggar, a holy man, or an animal. He treated them all the same."

"I still have a little ways to go," I say.

"Don't we all!" Doreen laughs.

"I'm so grateful to you for bringing us this gift."

"And I'm so grateful that you are in our life," Linda adds.

We look from one to the other, drinking each other in, spontaneously reaching out to grasp each other's hand and become silent. The incessant chatter of voices continues all around us, but it feels as if we've dropped into a bubble of peace. For a moment the outside world ceases to exist.

At that moment Steve glides up to the table with steaming plates balanced on his arm. "One polenta, one putanesca, one Caesar," he says, as he deftly places the plates in front of us.

". . . and more garlic bread!"

Silent Teachings That Change the World
Aloha Mana Farm, Kauai, March 23, 1993

*Finally, and most importantly, Ramana would remind us that the pure Self—
and therefore the great liberation—cannot be attained, anymore than you can
attain your feet or acquire your lungs. You are already aware of the sky, you
already hear the sounds around you, you already witness this world.*
                        Ken Wilber

The next day I find the tattered book of Ramana's teachings that I bought so many
years ago. It is still sitting on the shelf, just where I left it. I pull it out and open it
up at random: "If you would deny the ego and scorch it by ignoring it, you would
be free. To be the Self that you really are is the only means to realize the bliss that
is ever yours."

I puzzle over what he means by ignoring the ego. For years I've been trying
to "kill" the ego, but if anything, it just keeps getting stronger. And what does he
mean by "being the Self that you really are?" I try to grasp it with my mind, not
realizing that this is something way beyond what the mind can understand. I read
some more: "Instead of saying there is a mind or an ego and I want to kill it, you
must begin to seek its source and find that it does not exist at all." What? The ego
doesn't exist at all? Mine sure does!

From what I can see, Ramana's method for going to what he calls "the source
of who we are" is by asking the question *Who am I?* That seems easy enough. I
decide to give it a spin: *Who am I? Who am I? Who am I?* Nothing happens. I
try repeating this for an hour or so, expecting some kind of great breakthrough.
But nothing happens. Maybe I have some sort of mental block? Maybe this isn't
for me? *Who am I? Who am I?* At lunch I sit on the deck asking *Who am I?* An
enormous whale breaches as it makes its way up the coastline. *Who is watching the
whale?* I take an outdoor shower, surrounded by an extravagant array of hibiscus,
orchids, palms, and banana trees. The water dances over my skin, making rainbows in the sun. *Who is it that watches all of this?* Lying in bed that night, I look up
through the skylight at the stars and the dark night sky. The question *Who am I?*
drifts in and out of my consciousness. Gradually I let go of expecting an answer.
I let go of expecting some great AH-HA! I swim in the empty space of *Who am
I?* Thoughts come, thoughts go. Seeing happens, hearing happens. There is no
longer anyone asking the question. I rest in the peace of all that is.

The next day I pick up the book that Doreen gave us at the restaurant and look at the photograph of Ramana on the cover. The love and peace that I see in his face overwhelms me. When I first saw this photograph twenty years ago I remember saying, "This is what I want . . . this peace, this indescribable peace." In fact I even tore the picture out of the front of the book and framed it, something I would normally never do. Ramana's look of infinite compassion awakens some distant memory in me, as if he is inviting me to recognize that who I am is love itself. "Turn your vision inward," he says, "and the whole world will be filled with supreme spirit."

I always believed that someone or something out there could give it to me. If I just had a teacher like Paramahansa Yogananda, Swami Muktananada, or Gurudev, they would awaken the love I was unable to find within myself. If I followed their teachings they would take me to God. If I did my practices, purified my body, and lived with other dedicated seekers, I would eventually find the happiness and bliss I longed for.

I was wrong on all counts.

Ramana, I realize, is different from any other teacher I've known. It is immediately clear that his life *is* his teaching. His seemingly ordinary life is totally extraordinary. In his later years, when he had painful arthritis, he followed the same routine day after day. After taking care of personal hygiene before dawn, he would lie back on his couch-like bed in a simple hall, about the size of a small living room. At 5:00 AM the doors would open, and a few devotees would come in and sit on the black stone floor. For the next hour they meditated and chanted the Vedas. Then the hall was cleared, and Ramana would take a short walk and eat the morning meal, clad only in a loincloth. At 8:00 AM he was back in the hall, where he would receive visitors until noon, and then again in the afternoon. He made himself constantly available to all those who came to be in his presence—devotees, wandering sadhus, scholars, and royalty. Westerners, such as Paul Brunton and Somerset Maugham, came all the way from England to sit with him.

During these times he would answer questions or simply sit in silence for hours on end. Often he looked through the newspaper, read letters, or helped clarify a sacred text. During the course of the morning, a mother might bring her child in to be blessed, a monkey might sneak in and grab some fruit, a Westerner might show up and ask questions, a pundit would approach him and ask about the interpretation of a scripture. At times he was serious and considerate; at other times he playfully responded with laughter. Much of the time he remained in silence, gazing off at his beloved Mt. Arunachala, which was visible from the window.

Although Ramana usually spoke when visitors asked questions, he gave his most powerful teaching through silence. It was the awesome force of this silence that had the greatest impact on those who were close to him. Ramana considered silence to be the true teaching. "The truth is beyond words," he once said. "It does not admit of explanation." Many of those who sat in his presence spoke of a spiritual force that emanated from him. For many it led to the direct experience of Self. Yet this was nothing that Ramana did consciously. This mysterious energy flowed effortlessly through him, touching that same knowing in anyone ready to receive it.

Sitting in silence he changed the world.

CHAPTER 13

WISDOM TEACHINGS

H.W.L. Poonja (Papaji)

Happiness Is Who You Are
Aloha Mana Farm, Kauai, March 24, 1993

Feel the happiness and the joy that you really are. Feel it! You can feel it. No matter how many so-called problems you may appear to have, no matter what is going on in your life, good or bad, forget about that. It doesn't matter.
Robert Adams

"Peter, do you know what Ramana said about happiness?" Linda asks, as we soak in the spa after another exhausting day of working on the house. She's been working as hard as I have and still looks relaxed and happy. Her eyes are closed and she seems to be speaking from another world.

"Huh?"

"Ramana . . . he said that happiness is your true nature. You don't have to do anything to become happy. It's who you are."

"Who I am?" I reply, my mind in a fog.

"Yes, who *you* are. Funny, isn't it . . . when you think of all the time we spend searching for happiness, and it's been there all along."

I'm having trouble listening. My mind is racing: *How am I going to get the fridge fixed? I've called the repairman eight times and he still hasn't shown up. Every day one more thing falls apart.*

Warming up to her subject, Linda says, "It's not what we usually think of as happiness. It includes both happiness and unhappiness. It's happiness that doesn't come and go . . . Peter, are you listening?"

"Hmmmm? Whadidya say?"

"Ramana says that it all comes down to the willingness to be still."

"How am I going to 'be still' and get all this stuff done?"

"It doesn't mean you sit around all day doing nothing. You know that. It means resting in the stillness of who you are, without moving. Ramana calls it 'abiding as the Self.' You can do this while you're working, eating, or whatever. The idea is to have a quiet mind."

"How can I do that?" *Empty my mind? My mind is so filled with 'to do' lists I can't even enjoy where I am right now. My God—I'm in the most beautiful spot on earth, sitting naked in a spa overlooking the Pacific Ocean with the one I love, and all I can think of is what needs to get done. There's something wrong here.*

"Try asking the question 'Who am I?'"

220

"I've done that, but it doesn't get me anywhere. Nothing seems to be working."

"Well, ask yourself the question, 'Who is upset'? Trace the 'I' right back to its source. You'll realize that you're not your body or your mind. Who you are is beyond all of that."

"If I'm not my body or my mind, who am I?" I ask.

"That's the whole point. Who *are* you?"

"This is crazy."

"I know. The mind goes ballistic. It's terrified."

"Linda, 'I' am sitting in this spa, feeling very stressed out."

"Yes, that's the "little you." That's who you believe yourself to be. It's the story of Peter, whose wife died, who has to sell this property, who is now stressed out. That's the 'little me.' That's not who you are."

"Then who am I?"

"Look out at the ocean. See that wave coming in? The problem is that you imagine yourself to be that wave, when in fact you're ocean. You're terrified that you'll crash on the beach and be destroyed. But you are ocean, Peter. Who you *are* is ocean!" she says, smiling.

"That's comforting!" I laugh, realizing how caught up I am with being a frothed-up self-important wave.

"Just relax into the recognition of being ocean," Linda says in a soothing voice. "There is nothing you have to 'do'. See if you can just be here with the sweet smell of the plumeria, the song of the cardinal, the sun sparkling on the water. Relax!"

I close my eyes and sink deeply into the hot water. I let out a big sigh. The water envelopes me and I feel myself dissolving into its warmth. A symphony of sounds reaches my ears—the dull crash of the surf, the wind in the ironwood trees, the flutter of a bird's wings as it flies overhead. I sink even more deeply into relaxation, noticing the fragrance of plumeria flowers mixed with the pungent smell of suntan oil. I feel the sensation of Linda's hand on my foot. My eyes open slightly and there is the deep blue of the sky and the billowing clouds. Then there is no thought at all—just spacious presence. It's all so impersonal. Everything is arising in present moment awareness. Ocean is inside me, breeze is inside me, sky is inside me. A phrase I read somewhere comes to mind: "Swallow the Pacific Ocean in a single gulp." This is what Linda's talking about—just this!

"Yes, yes," she says softly, as she notices my smile. "Who are you now?"

Of course, this delicious moment soon fades and I'm back to worrying about how I'll get the fridge fixed. It's hard to imagine being in this place all the time. Who would I be without my worries?

The Fire of Love
Aloha Mana Farm, Kauai, March 31, 1993

The experience of Self is only love—which is seeing only love, hearing only love, feeling only love, tasting only love, and smelling only love, which is bliss.
Ramana Maharshi

Over the next weeks Linda and I devour every book we can find on Ramana. After seeing *The Sage of Arunachala*, a video on Ramana Maharshi's life, Linda says in awe, "I can hardly hold myself together. I'm floating one foot off the ground." She is moved to find that Ramana's life is as pure and simple and radiant as his teachings. Being frugal herself, she is thrilled when she finds out that his only possessions were a loincloth, a towel to wrap around his body, and a walking stick.

Linda also loves the fact that Ramana always insisted on being treated like everyone else, refusing any special privileges. He ate communally in the main dining hall and wouldn't eat anything that couldn't be shared equally with all those present. For years he got up at 3:00 AM to help prepare the food in the ashram kitchen. He never wasted anything. After a few mustard seeds fell on the ground while cooking, Ramana picked them up by hand. When a devotee asked why he did this, he replied, "All these things are created by God. We should not waste even small things." Even when in great pain during the last years of his life (he died from a cancerous tumor on his arm), he still received visitors and never complained.

When Linda learns that Ramana treated animals no differently than humans, she knows she has found a true saint. Ramana fed monkeys and baby squirrels by hand; he sat with a pet deer while it was dying; he cared for a baby sparrow that fell out of its nest. On his walks, wild animals came to up to him without fear. Once, while he was sitting on the hill, a cobra crawled over his legs. Ramana did not even move. He laughed, saying that it felt "cool and soft." The animals seemed to recognize some force in him, just as they did with St. Francis. For years, Lakshmi, the ashram cow, came to him precisely at noon and bowed down before him. Lakshmi lived on the ashram grounds for twenty-two years. On the day she died, Ramana placed his hand on her head and gave her a special initiation. He considered her to be fully liberated.

Linda is very skeptical of gurus. She was living in Oregon when the Indian guru, Osho, had a large ashram community there, and stories of his rampant abuse of power emerged. In one infamous case, Osho's right-hand person, Ma Ananda

Sheela, poisoned the food in a town called The Dalles so they could win a local election. Linda knows of countless gurus involved in sex scandals with their disciples; she has a fascination with cults and the dynamics of brainwashing. But Ramana is different. Linda comes to embrace Ramana as her true teacher and her one great love. She has a series of vivid dreams where her sense of identity crumbles.

"Ramana sets me on fire," she says one afternoon, as we're sitting on our lanai overlooking the ocean. "After all the unusual spiritual experiences I've had, this comes the closest to the truth."

"I agree. Ramana has opened my heart too. He goes straight to the truth, without any of the usual dos and don'ts of yoga or Buddhism. It's so simple."

"Yeah, and it's a ruthless path where you must be willing to die to the ego. He cuts the bonds to your every thought, to every belief that you ever held or cherished. If you don't believe it, just wait! You must be willing to be swallowed by the tiger. Ramana is the tiger, and once he has you in his mouth, it's all over."

"I love it. He can take me anytime." I cry out, holding my arms up in surrender.

"You'd better be careful what you wish for. This path can be ruthless. Remember when Da Free John said, 'Dead gurus don't kick ass?' He didn't know what he was talking about."

"You sure had your ass kicked in those dreams."

Linda jokes, "What's closer to the truth is, dead gurus don't take your pocketbook— that's what most gurus do."

"Especially Da Free John, or Adi Da, or whatever he calls himself now."

"Peter, do you realize that Ramana is just as available now as when he was alive? Isn't that extraordinary?"

"Yeah, I remember the story of when he was on his deathbed. All his devotees gathered around him pleading, 'Please don't leave us.' Ramana said, 'They say that I am dying but I am not going away. Where could I go? I am here.'"

Shaking her head in amazement, Linda says, "Where else could he go? He's right here, right now. I can feel his presence so strongly."

We both laugh, our hearts on fire.

Something is different about Linda. There's a new sense of inner peace and calm. Even though our external life is in chaos, she is happy. There has been a shift, and I don't even think she sees the change.

I am That
Aloha Mana Farm, Kauai, April 15, 1993

A quiet mind is all you need. All else will happen rightly, once your mind is quiet.
Nisargadatta

As so often happens, the opening of one door leads to the opening of another. I search in the bookcase and pull out another book that has traveled around the world with me. The book jacket is worn—not from use—but from being packed and unpacked so many times. Every so often I read a few lines and put it back on the shelf. I can still barely understand a word of it, but somehow I know it is one of those seminal books not to be given away. It is called *I Am That*, and is a translation of a series of talks given by an Indian sage named Sri Nisargadatta Maharaj, who died in 1981. When it came out in the seventies, it became an underground sensation.

Nisargadatta, which means "one who dwells in the natural state," was the most unlikely of sages. He grew up in a small village outside of Bombay in the poorest of families (now, that's *really* poor). In his mid-twenties he married and moved to the tenements of Bombay, where he opened a small shop selling *bidis*, a kind of hand-made cigarette, along with other household goods. He and his family lived in a small room over the shop. When he was thirty-four he met a guru who initiated him and gave him an unusual spiritual practice: "You are not what you take yourself to be," he said. "Find out what you are. Watch the sense *I am*, find your real self."

Three years later Nisargadatta realized his true nature. He continued to operate his *bidi* shop and look after his family. It was only later in his life that a few seekers began to discover him. Over time a steady stream of Indians and foreigners ventured into the seediest and most polluted part of the city to seek out his little shop. They climbed the rickety stairs to his room on the top floor where they sat and asked questions. Some were in for a surprise.

After watching a video of one of his talks, I can see why. Instead of a blissed-out saint, they are greeted by a little old man with no teeth, disheveled hair, and dark piercing eyes. He has a fierce intensity about him. When he talks in Hindi, he gesticulates wildly, pacing the floor with a bidi in one hand, while ranting and raving at his visitors. Over all the hubbub, a translator shouts out the translation in English.

Often he'd quiz his visitors on arrival, asking them why they had come. If he wasn't satisfied with their answer, he threw them out and told them not to come back. For those who could see beyond the appearances, there was an extraordinary sense of joy and presence that radiated from him. As Jeanne Dunn, an American devotee, once remarked, "He was whatever was needed: kind, gentle, patient, abrupt, abrasive, impatient. Moods passed over him like a summer breeze, barely touching him."

His message was simple: you already *are* free! You never have been bound! There is nothing you have to do or change to realize that freedom. All you need do is understand that this body and this mind are merely a play of the elements. When you recognize that you exist as pure awareness, you will find great happiness and freedom. Even when he was dying a painful death from throat cancer (yes, even sages smoke and die from lung cancer), he would say, "In my world there are no problems."

As I sit down to read one of the talks in *I Am That*, the words leap out at me like hand grenades going off.

Questioner: Why has God made me as I am?

Maharaj (his devotees refer to him as Maharaj): *Which God are you talking about? What is God? Is he not the very light by which you ask the question? 'I am' itself is God. The seeking itself is God. In seeking you discover that you are neither body nor mind, but the love of the self in you for the self in all. The Two are one. The consciousness in you and the consciousness in me, apparently two, are really one. Seek unity and that is love.*

To be honest, I have to read his answer several times before I can make any sense of it, but the underlying message is clear: All there is is consciousness; there is nothing *but* consciousness. Even the one asking the question about God is God. Maharaj starts with the premise that the one thing we know with certainty is that we exist. The certainty that "I exist" is undeniable. What we then do is superimpose the objective world of appearances—in other words, the entire universe—on the *I am*, and mistakenly believe it to be real. If we can turn our attention around and focus on the *I am*, we will access that which is *prior* to it . . . in other words pure consciousness, our natural state of being.

Described in this way it sounds very mental, but what he's referring to has nothing to do with intellectual understanding; it can only be known through direct experience. I saw that I had to somehow get my mind out of the way if I was to get the true meaning of his words. Maharaj says, "The feeling *I am* is consciousness. Hold on to that." It's a puzzle to be solved and the way to solve it is to meditate on it. He doesn't mean to sit on a pillow and meditate on it, because there is no "method" that can bring about this understanding. It means to continuously hold on to what you *are* and not what you know. This takes a certain fearlessness, a willingness to drop all concepts until there is the realization that whatever exists is not separate from the self.

Time to put the tattered book back on the shelf. I can only handle this in small doses.

Wake Up and Roar
Aloha Mana Farm, April 19, 1993

You are like fish in the river saying, "I am so thirsty. Where is the water?"
H.W.L. Poonja (Papaji)

Linda and I are sitting on our lanai, enjoying a perfect morning in a place made of perfect mornings. The ocean is exceptionally calm, and in the distance I can see a lone fisherman out on the reef casting his net—a throwback to ancient Hawaii which touches something elemental in me. The sun is lighting the morning dew in the ironwood trees, creating sparkling pearls of light. A red cardinal flies by on his way to peck at the rear view mirrors of the car. He's so like us humans, attacking his own image in the mirror, thinking it's the enemy. The smell of fresh ground Hawaiian coffee, mixed with salt air and scent of pine, is making me dizzy with pleasure. I've just started drinking coffee again after twelve years of abstinence, so it hits me extra hard. Linda, wearing running shorts and a T-shirt, is holding her mug in both hands, looking out at the ocean for whales, her blond hair lit by the sun. It doesn't get much better than this.

The quiet tranquility is interrupted by the sound of gravel flying as a car roars up the steep hill to the house.

"It's Doreen!" I say, recognizing the sound of her old Jeep Wagoneer. Doreen has just returned from yet another trip to India, where she went to see her teacher Papaji.

A few moments later she appears on the lanai, looking resplendent in a bright summer dress and her sunglasses perched on the top of her head. She looks stunning for someone who has just spent twenty-two hours on an airplane.

"You're back!" I say, giving her a hug. "We missed you."

"What a trip," she says, sitting back on a comfortable chaise.

"You must be exhausted!" I exclaim.

"It wasn't bad at all . . . look at these shawls I brought back. Aren't they beautiful?" She unveils four or five pashmina shawls she found in New Delhi—delicate earth green, light coral, and rich cream. "Doreen has exquisite taste and loves rich fabrics.

"They're so soft," Linda says, caressing them with her hand.

"And I brought this for both of you to look at," she says, handing us a manuscript. "It's a book by Papaji called *Wake Up and Roar*. You're the first to see it. It isn't published yet."

"I love the title," I say, taking the hefty manuscript.

"Papaji says that we're all pretending to be sheep, when we're really lions," Doreen says. "He says it's time for us to wake up and roar like a lion—to accept our own divinity—to recognize that we are That."

Linda starts flipping through the manuscript. "Oh my God," she says. "You won't believe this . . . listen to what Papaji says: 'There is a river of thought waves. Everyone is being washed downstream. Everyone is clinging to these thoughts and being washed away. Just give rise to the single thought, *I want to be free.*' That's exactly what my dream was about! Last night I dreamt that we were all being swept down this river towards God!"

We look at each other with disbelief. "I'm really high," I say. "And I don't think it's just the coffee. Tell us more about Papaji."

Doreen pulls out a packet of photographs and passes them around. We look at the first few photographs—pictures of busy streets filled with scooters, donkeys, carts, trucks, people.

"That's Lucknow, where Papaji lives. It's one of the most polluted cities in the world."

Linda winces, "I could never go there. With my chemical sensitivity, they'd have to carry me out in a coffin."

We turn to the next photograph. It shows Doreen and her friend Radha standing on either side of a large man with a huge smile on his face. They both are wearing bright-colored silk saris. They look ravishing. Papaji is sitting on a chair, dressed Indian style, with an immaculate long white kurta. His head is shaved and his eyes are gleaming with incredible intensity. He is obviously having a great time.

"Papaji made us get up and sing in front of him," Doreen says. "He loved it."

"He also seems to like beautiful women," I add with a smile.

"Oh yes, he likes women, and makes no excuses about it. He's so much larger than life," Doreen continues. "There are times when he does nothing but laugh for a whole hour. At other times he becomes so moved that he starts to cry. I've also seen him get angry and banish people from the room."

A few days later I sit down with the manuscript, thumbing through the well-marked pages. There are sections with big stars on them, other passages marked "excellent." I start to read these first: "You don't need anything. Eternity is here. Happiness is here. You walk out chasing after desires and they are never fulfilled."

A few pages later he says, "The present moment is freedom. Look into the present moment. Freedom itself. You are always looking into the past moments. This instant is the present moment. Look into it. Then you will see your face."

He makes it all sound so easy.

For fifteen years I obediently followed my teacher Gurudev with loyalty and devotion, trusting that if I stuck with him through thick and thin, I would eventually get there. Now I read: "You must go alone. All alone. No one can do it for you. This way is not a beaten track where you can be led by someone else. You don't need any help and there is no track."

What about all those years I spent doing meditation? The next sentence floors me: "Meditation is little more than concentration. It may calm the mind for some time, but it will not destroy it. The mind must be destroyed. Any effort or trying just takes you further away . . . Freedom doesn't require any effort or method."

I think about all the years I tried to purify my body, doing everything from fasting, to colonics, to macrobiotic diets, to pouring water up my nose, to "cleaning" the insides of my presumably dirty body. According to Papaji this is all nonsense: "You are that emptiness itself. Where can dust alight?"

What have I been doing all this time? Was it all for nothing?

A short time later Doreen brings over a video with an unusual title: *Call Off the Search*. It's a compilation of interviews with Papaji. On the video I get a clearer picture of what Papaji looks like, with his piercing brown eyes, and powerful, commanding presence. He completely blows my image of an enlightened teacher. Papaji laughs a lot—he laughs uproariously like a gleeful child; he weeps openly when he talks about his beloved teacher Ramana Maharshi. He gets angry at those who stubbornly turn from the truth. One scene shows him mischievously eating chocolate with a grin on his face, "I shouldn't be doing this," he says to the camera. "I'm diabetic!" There is a scene of him squeezed in a room with other devotees, watching a cricket match on television, rather than giving satsang that day. His beautiful Dutch 'friend' Mira appears in some of the scenes—no one seems the least concerned that Papaji has a wife and an extended family of about eighty.

The video makes me want to get on an airplane for India, yet something holds me back. Then I remember him saying, "Don't look here, there, anywhere. Just be still."

I take him at his word.

Take It All
Aloha Mana Farms, Kauai, October 6, 1993

You are not ready to accept the fact that you have to give up. A complete and total surrender. It is a state of hopelessness which says that there is no way out. Any movement in any direction, on any dimension, at any level, is taking you away from yourself.
U.G. Krishnamurti

It seems that spiritual openings are always accompanied by some kind of chaotic upheaval on the physical plane—often referred to as a test of faith—just to make sure we have gotten the message. In my case, I blithely talked about surrender over the years, but never grasped what it meant. It was one of those spiritual buzz words. Now I have to ask myself, am I willing to go *all* the way—to give up completely and accept my divine helplessness? There's no half way with this one. Like most people, I want to have my cake and eat it—to have my comforts *as well as* be surrendered to what is. Unfortunately, it doesn't work that way. If I'm serious about spiritual awakening, I need to be willing to accept *everything* that shows up—the good, the bad, the ugly, the pleasurable, the painful—and even death. This is not a path for the faint of heart.

After opening to the teachings of Ramana Maharshi, Nisargadatta, and Papaji, my life takes some interesting turns. Disaster after disaster strikes around me. Perhaps it is a coincidence, perhaps not. First there is a flash flood that sends a wave of water six feet deep down the nearby Anahola River, killing a neighbor. Our creek floods over, wiping out acres of farmland, two small houses, and a bridge. I spend all night in the drenching rain, dragging equipment up to higher ground, watching floodwaters tear out the driveway, and destroying organic gardens that took years of hard work to create.

Then Hurricane Iniki rips through the island in September 1992, sending property values plummeting and destroying most of the island. The hurricane batters my finances and I have no choice but to put the property up for sale. This is more than selling a house—it is the end of a precious dream. Fran and I built this place from scratch and poured our hearts into it. She died here and her ashes are scattered on the land. I'm not only letting go of one of the most beautiful homes on the island, but letting go of Fran as well. I've poured every penny I have into the property—now I have no job, no income, and have gone through almost all my savings.

With Linda's help, I arrange a huge estate sale, selling off all the possessions that Fran and I had accumulated over twenty-five years. Her memory is still fresh; it has been two years since she died. Hundreds of people come to the sale, picking through memory-filled belongings like a horde of locusts. I watch as an excited buyer grabs a quilt that Fran's mother had made; someone else carries off a Hawaiian print that had been given to us by someone we love; a red "sold" sign is placed on furniture that traveled with Fran and I from Europe to Canada to Massachusetts to Hawaii. Every time I feel a tug to hold on to something, I hear the words: *Let go. Let God.*

"How can you sell all of this?" a friend asks in amazement. "Isn't it difficult to leave everything you love behind? It's all so beautiful!"

"It is," I respond. "It's always hard to let go, but at the same time I feel like I'm being set free; it's like taking off a huge burden. I no longer have to take care of all this stuff!"

After everyone has left, the house is bare of furniture—beds, sofas, chairs, antiques, paintings, books, linens, all gone. It looks like a Zen monastery. I stand on the deck for the last time, overlooking the ocean. The moon breaks through the clouds and white slivers of moonlight dance on the waves. I can hear Fran saying, "Don't you know that you'll always be looked after? There is no need to worry. I will always be with you."

The house sits empty for months. No one wants to buy property after the hurricane. Linda and I struggle to keep everything from falling apart. The salt spray from the ocean wreaks havoc on the big sliders in the living room; the fridge breaks; the spa stops working. It is a full time job keeping up on the repairs.

One night I am alone in the house high up on the hill when a violent thunderstorm comes rolling in. Thunderstorms are very rare on the islands and this one is formidable. Torrential rain pours down in blinding sheets, as can only happen in the tropics. Gusts of wind blow rainwater through the glass sliders onto the oak floor. I struggle to mop it up before it ruins the wood. Bright, jagged bolts of lightning light up the dark night.

I'm standing barefoot in the water when a sudden flash and simultaneous *CRAAACK* jolts right through me. My hair and skin tingle. I'm stunned to be alive.

"Take me! Take me if you want!" I yell out at the top of my lungs, raising my arms up to the sky. "You can have it, God. Take it all!"

Linda is down in the cottage watching the storm. She sees the lightning directly hit the house and has no idea if I've been electrocuted or not. Later she tells me that she screamed out in agony, "Take him, if that's what you're going to do! I give up. I give up!"

The storm passes over. I didn't fry and I didn't die. I realize that a part of me still hasn't let go, still hasn't fully surrendered. I light some Nag Champa incense and go through each room of the house offering a prayer: "May whoever lives in this house find great happiness and love here," I say, passing my hand over the incense to send it's sweet smell throughout the room. "May Fran's spirit and my spirit be set free. I release you. I release you." As I stand over the spot where Fran left her body, I look out to the horizon. A long, pulsating flash illuminates the entire night sky. Two days later I receive an offer on the property.

CHAPTER 14

NOTHING TO CHANGE, NOTHING TO FIX

Gangaji

Sex, Wine, and Chocolate
Church Street Café, Lenox, Massachusetts, June 14, 1991

You can live to be a hundred if you give up all the things that make you want to
live to be a hundred.
Woody Allen

Thirty days after meeting Linda, I left Kauai and returned to the loving arms of the Kripalu community in Lenox, Massachusetts. Ever since my sudden departure three years ago, when Fran found out she had breast cancer, I longed to be back with my "Kripalu family." Coming home was like being nurtured by mother's milk. I imagined that I would be part of the community forever and that we would all grow old together. Who wouldn't want to spend the golden years with spiritual friends you loved with all your heart, and who shared the same vision of a spiritual path that would eventually lead to enlightenment?

A month after my return, Linda flew from Kauai to the East Coast on her way to a Waldorf teacher training in Maine. She stopped off in Lenox for a visit. We spent a thrilling afternoon getting to know each other again, with both of us realizing that we are falling deeply in love. That night I took her to dinner at my favorite restaurant, the Church Street Café. I've eaten here dozens of times before and know the owners well. Jim, the host, escorts Linda and me to a cozy table in the back room. As we walk between the tables, diners turn to look at us. Once we're seated (and I've taken a moment to appreciate the starched white tablecloth, the neatly folded white napkins, and the tiny arrangement of spring flowers on our table), I say to Linda, "Did you see that? Everyone seems to be looking at us!"

Linda smiles, "Yes, of course they are . . . they're drawn by the irresistible perfume of love." I look at her in awe. She looks stunningly beautiful—her blue eyes sparkling, her blond hair back in a pony tail, and her body tanned by the Hawaiian sun. Her colorful, flowered dress and fresh, healthy skin make a dramatic contrast to the dark, drab clothes and pale faces of the New Yorkers and New Englanders at the other tables. Glowing after an afternoon of love-making, we each order a glass of wine and some French bread, eager to make up for weeks spent apart.

Linda tells me stories of her own spiritual journey, which is so different from mine. "I was at a retreat with Ram Dass," she says, dipping her bread in olive oil, "and had this experience that sent me out into the universe."

"Out into the universe?"

"Yes, I was in a Tai Chi class where the teacher, whose name was David, recited a poem. Something inside me just opened up. I saw that *everything* is joy, that *everything* is absolute perfection, love, and beauty. When I tried to eat lunch I became so lost in the beauty of the light reflected on the tines of the fork that I couldn't get the fork in my mouth. The man across the table at dinner looked at me and said, 'What are you on? Whatever it is, I want it.' People had to take care of me because I could barely function. It lasted for days . . . I didn't ever want to come back."

"I'm so jealous. I've never had anything like that happen to me. A friend of mine had an experience like that. He said it was like having a thousand orgasms all at once. Imagine . . . a thousand orgasms! God, I was willing to die if that's what it took to become enlightened."

"So you went off and lived in an ashram . . ."

"Yeah, ten years trying to find God—doing yoga every day, meditating, fasting, eating vegetarian food, praying. I even tried celibacy—can you believe it? At the end of it I realized that I wasn't any closer to God than when I started."

Linda rolls her eyes. "I get so tired of all those self-righteous yogis who think you can get to God by eating the right foods and cleansing your colon. That has nothing to do with enlightenment."

"Well, try telling them that. I know one resident, who is so holier-than-thou that he boasts about not putting raisins in his oatmeal. He thinks this will make him even more pure."

Struck by an unexpected thought, Linda muses, "Wouldn't it be funny if it was just the opposite?"

"Opposite?"

"Yeah, what if, when we got to the Pearly Gates, we were told that the only way we could pass through was if we had fully celebrated life in the body? If you hadn't fully enjoyed sex, wine, and chocolate you'd be turned away."

"That's great, I like that!" I laugh. "All the purists would have to go right back and start all over again!"

"Wouldn't they be shocked!"

"Asceticism was never my thing," I say, taking a cool sip of chardonnay. "I love what W.C. Fields said: 'I like to cook with wine. Sometimes I even add it to the food.'"

Linda laughs her delightful, infectious laugh.

We order our dinner—I choose the lemon-glazed wild Scottish salmon with herbed breadcrumbs, greens, and roasted red potatoes. Linda has the pan roasted honey and spice- glazed duck breast, with rice and barley pilaf, and summer fruit chutney. And of course, we order two more glasses of wine.

Carried away by this celebration of the senses, I add, "Oh God, you must try their chocolate mocha torte. It's sensational . . . but you must be tired after your trip."

"No, no. I can't get enough of you. We've only known each other for a few months—and yet it all seems so easy."

"It's like we've been together forever," I say, reaching out to take her hand. I can feel the rough scars beneath my fingertips. *I can see why I'm so attracted to her . . . here's someone who has been through pain, suffered the loss of loved ones, and understands life.*

"Thank God we worked out most of our stuff the first time around," she says. "Weren't you married to Fran for twenty years?"

At the mention of Fran I look down at the tablecloth, brushing off the crumbs with my hand. "Uhhhh . . . it was twenty-five. Fran and I used to come here for dinner at least once a week. There are a lot of memories."

Linda looks at me with compassion. "I was ready to move into a nunnery in Thailand before meeting you. I had given up on finding someone I could be totally vulnerable with."

"Somehow I can't quite see you in a nunnery," I smile.

"Then I had the dream where you and I walked up the mountain to God together."

"Yeah—I remember you telling me about that dream . . . all our chakras opened up and we merged into each other."

Reluctantly I drain the last sip of wine. I can scarcely believe that Linda, who I met just a month ago, is sitting opposite me here in Lenox, 5,000 miles from Hawaii. How did I find this beautiful being, who is both a mystic and wildly sensual at the same time?

Our eyes lock together and we disappear into another world. Suddenly a huge jolt of energy blasts through my body, jerking me off the seat like I've just been electrocuted. Shocked, I turn around to see if anyone is watching. "Do you think anyone saw that?"

"No one ever sees it," Linda laughs. "It's so beyond people's ordinary percep-tions that they miss it entirely."

"What is it with the two of us?"

"You and I are willing to celebrate all the sensory delights of being in a body and at the same time we have this deep longing for God."

"That's why I prefer sex, wine, and chocolate to yoga these days. It's a high spiritual calling—when we make love, we're two separate beings that merge into one; when we drink wine, our sense of separate identity melts away; when we eat chocolate, we raise our endorphins and open to love. It's so simple."

Linda smiles as she caresses my leg with her bare foot. All I can think of is getting back to the house, remembering the rumpled sheets and the intoxicating scent of love. I feel like a horny twenty-year old, even though I've just turned fifty-two.

Somehow I get the feeling that I'm not the same obedient, pious Kripalu resident that I was when I left here three years ago. But come to think of it, I liked sex, wine, and chocolate even then. Some things never change.

You Won't Find God Here
Kripalu Center, Lenox, Massachusetts, June 18, 1991

The only thing worse than an 'egoic me' is an 'egoic us'.
Eckhart Tolle

Linda arrived in Lenox at the perfect time of year, just as the fireflies were blinking into life in the fields around Tanglewood, the summer home of the Boston Symphony (if it was winter, she wouldn't have lasted a week). I proudly introduce her to my friends and the guru himself. To my delight, they like one another. Linda falls in love with the Berkshires and we both fall more deeply in love with each other. We go to breakfasts at the Red Lion Inn, have more dinners at the Church Street Café, and attend concerts at Tanglewood. I am in heaven. It feels like I am picking up where I left off before moving to Hawaii.

Before long I am being asked to lead programs, organize events, and be on different committees. But it's as if a magnet is pushing me in the opposite direction. I turn down request after request—even when one friend goes down on her knees, pleading for me to help. No matter how much my mind says "yes," my body clearly and definitively says "no." Part of the reason is that there has been a dramatic shift at Kripalu over the past three years. Gurudev, who has tirelessly led and inspired the residents since the community was founded, no longer seems inspired himself. When he gives a satsang, it is mainly to cajole the residents to work harder. Most of his energy is going into traveling and building a lavish new home for himself. He spends a lot of time on the road, giving seminars in South America, the Caribbean, and Europe. Who can blame him—after twenty years of nonstop dedication, he deserves a little break. But when he hits a plateau in his own spiritual evolution, the delicate flame that keeps the high ideals renewed and alive begins to waver.

In a perfect reflection of Gurudev's life, the residents begin pulling back too. They become more interested in having creature comforts than living the life of a renunciate; they begin to look outside the walls of Kripalu for inspiration, going to other gurus and programs; they no longer want to burn themselves out working seven days a week for a measly $30 per month; they want their own independence and not to be told what to do by the guru. All of that comes at a price.

Soon after my return, plans are launched for Gurudev's sixtieth birthday celebration. A new book is in the works, called *In the Presence of a Master*. Gurudev receives more adulation and awards, and starts to believe his own publicity. Guests refer to him as an "enlightened master" and he is quite happy to go along with it. For the first time ever he begins talking about "transforming the world through Kripalu Yoga." All my alarm bells about gurus and cults go off (with a little help from Linda).

I begin to question the entire premise that my spiritual life is based on—honoring the guru, serving the community, practicing yoga and meditation . . . and *perhaps* someday becoming enlightened. I have this fantasy of one day "waking up," along with the other senior residents at Kripalu (of course the junior residents would need to stay unenlightened so they could look after us). We would live happily ever after, sitting cross-legged on our rocking chairs overlooking the lake, with Gurudev presiding over this big, happy family. But the someday never comes. After years of taking retreat after retreat, enlightenment intensive after enlightenment intensive, no one in our community has come close to spiritual awakening. Why doesn't anyone ever graduate?

I share my concern with Linda one warm summer morning as we walk down the curving, half-mile drive to the main gate of the Kripalu Center. "It's crazy," I say, "but some of the residents have been here for twenty years, and they're no closer to realization now than they were then. Why is that?"

"It's obvious," Linda says, walking barefoot beside me. "The quickest way to get thrown out of a spiritual community is to wake up. It happens everywhere. I just read Daniel Quinn's book *Ishmael.* He had an authentic awakening experience while he was a Trappist novice at Gethsemane—and guessed who kicked him out?"

"Who?"

"Thomas Merton!"

"I had no idea . . ."

Two residents, Dinabandhu and Ila, jog by in the opposite direction, doing their pre-lunch run. I wave as they go by. "Those two are amazing," I whisper to Linda. "They virtually run the whole place. Dinabandhu was my coordinator for years."

She's not impressed.

Apart from one or two lone walkers, the drive is almost deserted. Most of the five hundred or so guests are in programs in the huge four-acre building that houses the Kripalu Cener. There are usually six or more programs going on at same time, such as "Deepening Your Love," for those wanting to learn about relationships, "The Raw Juice Program," for those interested in losing weight, and "Yoga Teacher Training," for future yoga teachers. Others are there for the "Rest & Relaxation" program, which I helped to create. The guests are looked after by a staff of 365 residents, who work six and a half days a week to take care of them.

"I always thought the whole idea of spiritual community was to provide an environment where people can become enlightened," I say. "Isn't that why there are places like Kripalu? And what about Buddhist monasteries . . . aren't they about waking up?"

"Hah! Communities depend on keeping their members seekers rather than finders. If everyone woke up there would be no community. Where would Gurudev be without all his worker bees?"

"Hmmm, I never saw it that way before."

I take her hand as we walk past the well-tended flower gardens and towering old maple trees. The grounds resemble a lavish country estate, which it once was. We come to a grassy field with a stunning panoramic view of Lake Mahkeenac and the Berkshire Mountains. This marks the spot where the original "Shadowbrook" once stood—an enormous "Berkshire Cottage" that was built in 1893, and later purchased by the American financier Andrew Carnegie. After his death it became a Jesuit seminary, before it tragically burned down in 1956. Now all that remains is a green lawn—a testament to the temporariness of all things. Linda and I pause to look out over the lake.

"Don't you need an enlightened teacher to guide you?" I ask.

"No," says Linda with a laugh. "It's just the opposite. This is one journey you have to make alone. No community, no teacher, no teachings, and no practices are going to take you there. They can open the door, but you must go through it alone."

"Yeah, I see what you mean. Christ woke up alone in the desert; the Buddha woke up under the Bodhi tree; Ramana woke up alone in his bedroom. I guess it depends upon how much you want awakening. Most seekers enjoy the seeking. They don't want it to end."

"Because waking up means losing everything—your Buddhism, your yogic beliefs, your individual ego—everything you think you are."

Two young sisters walk by in the opposite direction. As they pass, one of them turns to us and says in a snippy voice, "You shouldn't be holding hands in public. We practice celibacy between men and women here."

I smile and ignore them.

"Screw them," Linda mutters, putting her arm around my waist. "No one is going to tell me that we can't touch each other, especially when those two have their hands all over each other."

I laugh. "So, this is the new Kripalu—rules and regulations with self-important young recruits to enforce them. That would never have happened when Fran and I were here. It's amazing how quickly a spiritual organization can forget what's true and replace it with empty rules. No wonder I'm pulling away from Kripalu. The only thing that interests me is awakening to the truth of who I am."

"Well, you're not going to find it here."

Personal Growth 101
Stockbridge, Massachusetts, August 2, 1991

You are not a black hole that needs to be filled; you are a light that needs to be shined. The days of self-improvement are gone, and the era of self-affirmation is upon us. It is time to quit improving yourself and start living.
Alan Cohen

Now that I'm back at Massachusetts, it doesn't take long to find out that the latest buzz word going around the community is "self-empowerment." Friends come up to me saying much the same story: "For years I've given away my power to the guru and to everyone else. Now I need to find out who *I* am and reclaim *my* own power." They've all just come out of a self-improvement seminar at Kripalu and word is out about an advanced program to be held next weekend.

I get sucked in along with everyone else and sign up for the seminar. Although skeptical, Linda agrees to join me. On the day of the program we take our seats in neatly lined-up rows of chairs, watched over by neatly dressed hall monitors, who take their job very seriously. When everyone quiets down, the seminar leader, dressed in a short, trim, business-like suit, walks on stage. She introduces herself as Barbara, and proceeds to set out the rules, somehow making it seem like they are rules we've all agreed upon before coming here: no changing seats, no bathroom breaks or you're out of the program. One man frets about his seat and is unceremoniously banned from the room. We're all aghast. She has us exactly where she wants us.

Three hours into the program, things begin to heat up. "Your relationships stink," she tells the seventy participants, and, with an air of disgust, adds, "Your lives are empty and meaningless."

Everyone sits in silence, afraid to open their mouths.

I can't just sit here and listen to her saying my relationships stink.

Without thinking, I raise my hand. *Why am I doing this? Oh shit, I'm walking into a trap.* She looks at me with a slightly annoyed expression. Glancing at my nametag she says, "Yes, 'Peter.' What do *you* have to tell the group?"

I stand up and say, "Well, my relationships are great. My wife died seven months ago and I have found someone I love very much. Her name is Linda and she's here with me today. We have a wonderful relationship based on deep love and trust. I also have a deeply meaningful relationship with my son . . ."

"So you think your relationships are perfect?" she snaps.

"Not perfect . . ."

With a look of disdain, she asks the other participants, "How many of you think that 'Peter' here has a 'wonderful' relationship with Linda and his son . . . not to mention his wife, who died seven months ago?" she says, pointing at me.

I turn around and see about three raised hands. One of them is Linda's.

"Now, how many of you think he has lousy relationships?" she asks.

I look around and see a sea of raised hands.

"You see, Peter," she says with a knowing smile, "not everyone thinks your relationships are perfect. They're not joyful at all. They stink."

"From what I've seen so far, you're not the one to talk about joyful relationships," I say, furious at being manipulated.

"I'll tell you, Peter. There's a story of a Sufi master who comes up to a man who has been poisoned. He's coughing and dying. The Sufi master whacks the man, who coughs up the poison. The poison here is that your life is empty and meaningless. It doesn't matter what you say. Your relationships stink, your life stinks . . . just like that poison."

Oh shit, there's no way to win this one. It's a set-up! I silently take my seat feeling hurt and embarrassed.

Welcome to Personal Growth 101.

As Barbara flips through the pages of the loose-leaf binder on the podium in front of her, it's clear that she is working from a well-crafted script that produces very predictable results. It's a form of pressure and release. First, she takes away everyone's comfort and security, then wears down their resistance, then chips away at their identity piece by piece. Just when everything seems hopeless, she amps up the pressure even more. At this point, the group is ripe for a breakthrough— a simple, brilliant formula that changes how we view the world. All it takes is for one or two in the group to "get it," then everyone "pops" as the pressure is released. Before long even the shyest ones are standing up to make heartfelt testimonials. Just when it seems that it will never end, the program is over. Everyone is euphoric at having survived the ordeal.

After the training I come away high as a kite, eager to put into practice everything I've learned. Along with the other participants (who are now bosom buddies after this shared experience) I enthusiastically try out the power phrases and success formulas. I attend follow-up seminars and hear moving testimonials of how people's lives have been transformed by the program. I'm told that if I really want to "get it" I must take the advanced training, which only costs $1,000. Soon my new "friends" are calling to make sure that I sign up. How can I say no?

A month later I take the next training and come away all pumped up once again. Not surprisingly, in a few weeks the excitement has worn off. Some of the insights continue to be helpful, but it's not long before my old habits have returned and I'm just as miserable as I was before spending all that money. Maybe the next self-improvement program will have the answer? Everyone is talking about this new program called Nexus. I'm a sucker for punishment.

It takes a while before I realize that the purpose of all these self-help programs is to create a new and better ego. I'm basically being told that if I adopt *their* belief system, I will be self-empowered, fulfilled, and happy. Clearly there's something wrong with me and I have to fix it. But all I'm doing is grafting someone else's beliefs onto my own messed up, insecure little ego. It's bound to fail. The basic problem is that the "little me," or the ego, is exactly what is creating the problem in the first place! The human ego will *never* be happy. It will always want more. As someone once said, "It's like trying to rearrange the furniture on the deck of the Titanic as it goes down."

The whole point is for me to discover a deeper dimension beyond the ego where I *already am* whole and complete. When I awaken to my true nature it no longer matters what the ego does. The Self with a big "S" doesn't need any "self-help." Who I truly am needs no fixing or self-improvement. Think of all the money I'll save!

It dawns on me that as long as I stay attached to my story, it doesn't matter how much work I do on myself. There will always be more "stuff" that comes to the surface. It's like tossing a bucket down to the bottom of a well, then trying to empty the well by pulling up bucketful after bucketful of water. No matter how many buckets I pull up, there will always be more to drag up to the surface—and on and on and on.

Making a Difference
Boston, Massachusetts, October 10, 1994

*If you want to awaken all of humanity, then awaken all of yourself. Truly, the
greatest gift you have to give is that of your own self-transformation.*
Hua Hu Ching

A few months later I find myself at yet another seminar, in some anonymous
ballroom of an anonymous hotel on the outskirts of Boston. It's the last day of
the program, and after a mind-blowing weekend, we're gathered together for the
grand finale. Suddenly all the lights go off, plunging us into darkness. On the
stage, the seminar leader lights a candle, then lights the candle of the person next
to him, who in turn lights the candle of the person next to him. In less than five
minutes, every candle in the room is lit. The shift from total darkness to a room
glowing in candlelight is astonishing. The leader takes the microphone , "If just
one person shared his light and love with two others, and each one of them shared
his light with two more—and this progression continued daily—in just 33 days
every heart in our family of humanity would be touched."

What a powerful statement on how our actions can impact the world.

I come away from the training eager to "make a difference." Shall I fly to Cal-
cutta and help the poor? No, someone else has already done that. Shall I teach yoga
in prisons? No, too scary. Shall I give away all my money to the starving in Ethio-
pia? No, I need a new car. I open up the magazine section of the Sunday newspaper. My God, look at all those people "making a difference!" I get exhausted just
thinking about it.

I think of the times I've consciously set out to *make* a difference. Every time
"I" tried to make a difference it was a disaster, whether it was trying to start a
retreat center or trying to "heal" people. What suffering I created for myself (and
for them)! Then I remember different friends who have told me how I make a difference in their lives. My dear, sweet neighbor Virginia shares with tears in her
eyes how important my visits are for her, saying that her whole life has changed
as a result of our time together. My son Peter tells me about something I said in
a phone conversation two years ago and how profoundly it impacted him. I don't
even remember saying it. We never know the ways we touch the world.

I realize that making a difference doesn't necessarily mean taking on some
huge, herculean undertaking. We don't have to be a Gandhi, a Mother Theresa,
or a Nelson Mandela. We make a difference just by being who we are. I love the

story of Mark Bittner, a homeless street musician in San Francisco, who adopted a flock of wild parrots. Without any thought of "making a difference" he became the "St. Francis of Assisi of parrots"—taking care of and feeding these beautiful birds, which most people saw as pests. A filmmaker made a documentary called *The Wild Parrots of Telegraph Hill*, which touched people all around the world. Mark didn't sit down one day and say, "I'm going out there and make a difference." He *couldn't help* doing what he did; he simply followed his heart and did the next thing.

For most of us, making a difference means one "little me" going out helping another "little me." We do it because it feels good; it makes us feel as if we're doing something worthwhile; it gives us a sense of purpose. Nothing wrong with that. But the real question to ask is, "Is there anyone out there to make a difference to?" If we are all one spirit, not separate from God, how can there be an "us" to help "them"? From the perspective of Pure Awareness, there is no "one" out there to make a difference to. As Adyashanti says, "Selflessness arises out of the realization that you are the world and much more as well. All arises within you and is an expression of *you*."

Using the Trance to Come Out of the Trance
Santa Fe, New Mexico, October 25, 1993

Once the subtle structures of mind activity are realized, you can stop making waves,
and the mind can surrender and come to rest.
Eli Jaxon-Bear

I thought I was finished with workshops and seminars, but in fact I was just beginning. After meeting Gangaji on Maui, I discovered that her husband Eli Jaxon-Bear was leading a training in Santa Fe on "Self-Realization and the Ennea-gram." In his book, *Healing the Heart of Suffering*, he asks, "Why is it that so few people are truly happy? If our true nature is happiness and bliss, why has it been so rare for people to realize this about themselves and to live their lives in gratitude and love?" From what I heard, his training offers an answer to this puzzle. That was enough for me.

Linda and I arrive late for the workshop (as usual), after getting lost in Santa Fe's narrow streets (and spending too much time having a cappuccino at a colorful local cafe). We enter the small living room where the workshop is being held and see Eli sitting cross-legged on the floor in front of a kiva fireplace. Next to him there is a small photograph of Ramana Maharshi. There are about ten other people in the room, some on couches, others on the floor. We quickly find a seat.

"Welcome," Eli says. "Why don't we first go around the room and introduce ourselves?" With his twinkling eyes, broad smile, close-cropped hair, and rounded belly, he looks like a Laughing Buddha.

An attractive young woman raises her hand and starts to speak: "My name is Andréa. I met Eli in Boulder when he was teaching there. I was very impressed and wanted to take his course," she says with a strong French accent.

"I'm not sure why I'm here," says a shy looking young man. "I've been attend-ing satsang with Robert Adams in LA, where I heard about Eli. So here I am."

An interesting man with a shaved head says, "My name is Barry. I'm in love with Gangaji, and since Gangaji is married to Eli, I imagine he must have some-thing important to say. I have no idea why I'm here."

Everyone laughs.

I hear a woman in the front start to cry. She looks at Eli with tears streaming down her face. "Eli, you are my teacher. I don't care what this training is about, I just need to be with you."

"And here you are," he says with a big smile.

246

Between sobs she says, "Eli, I have chronic fatigue and am worried that I won't have the energy to get through the training. I feel so weak right now that I think I'm going to faint."

"Well, faint then!" Eli says, laughing, giving her permission to faint if she needs to. It's clear that he's not buying into her plea for attention.

When it's my turn I say, "I'm at a place in my life now where everything is opening up. I've just moved to Santa Fe, I have plenty of money in the bank, and I'm ready for whatever comes next. I guess anything is possible since I create my own reality."

Eli looks at me. "You may want to think about what you mean when you say that you 'create your own reality.' It's arrogant to think that you are creating anything. Everything is a creation of consciousness. *You* don't do anything."

Me and my big mouth! I see what he means. From the bigger perspective it is arrogant to think that "my" little ego creates this reality. How embarrassing.

Linda volunteers next, "I feel so blessed to be in a room where Ramana Maharshi is honored. I feel his presence so strongly here." Eli stares at her intently. There is a long moment of silence . . . the room is filled with it. To my astonishment, tears start appearing at the corner of Eli's eyes. I turn to Linda and she is crying too. Eli looks at Ramana's picture, bringing his hands together in prayer position and bows his head.

Now why didn't I say that? I'm such an idiot. The whole mood of the room has shifted. Everyone has dropped down into their heart!

"Well, a little about me," Eli says, "In the 60's I was a civil rights activist, and like many others, experimented widely with hallucinogens (everyone laughs). My search for freedom led me into Tibetan Buddhism, and for a time I ran a Dharma Center for Kalu Rinpoche in California. From there I went to Japan to explore Zen Buddhism. Still I was not satisfied. Along the way I studied shamanism with a medicine pipe holder of the Arapaho, or the Blue Sky People. I was also initiated into a Sufi clan on the coast of Morocco. But I desired something more. After marrying Gangaji I was teaching at Esalen and spending most of my time traveling around the world leading workshops. I had everything in the material world I wanted, but I still was not fully awake."

Eli takes a sip of water. "So, in 1990 I went to India searching for a teacher who would be a living transmission of the truth. By pure grace I was led to Papaji, a disciple of Ramana Maharshi. I spent several weeks with him and experienced the silence that is beyond the mind. When I returned to America, he gave me a mission: to bring the no-mind teachings into the world of therapy. My job is to help you awaken from the trance. There is no other purpose to life other than to wake up from this trance and discover the truth of who you are."

My heart soars. *Yes! This is what I want for my life!*

247

Eli continues, "You see, you are living in a trance—the trance of 'me and my story.' What we'll be learning here is how to use the trance to come out of the trance."

I'm flying high—yet again. As the weeklong training begins, Eli first teaches us the basics of hypnotherapy, then we study Neuro-Linguistic Programming (NLP). In between we do practice sessions with each other, where we apply what we've just learned.

In one of the sessions my partner Andrea leads me into an age regression back to my earliest memories. Since I have almost complete amnesia about my childhood, I'm curious to see what will happen. Andrea begins with an induction. "Just take some deep breaths and relax your mind," she says in a soft, soothing voice. "Feel yourself become calmer and calmer. Once you are fully relaxed, see yourself enveloped in a soft, protective cloud. Imagine yourself being lifted up in this cloud," she says, "rising up higher and higher, until you are floating in space. Now let yourself travel back in time to your childhood, surrounded by this protective cloud."

I find myself regressing back in time, like a movie running backwards, to seeing myself in my twenties, to myself as a teenager, then a little boy. Images flash to mind, as in a reverse time warp, some clear, some fuzzy. I have the sensation of being painfully hungry. From somewhere far away a distant memory surfaces of my tummy hurting. I'm crying and screaming. No one will come and feed me. I feel rage and terror at the same time. I realize this is not just a matter of being hungry—I'll literally *die* if I don't get fed. I feel totally helpless.

"Just stay with the feeling of being helpless," Andrea says.

As if in a dream-state, I mumble, "Yeah . . . I was always fed on a strict schedule. No matter how hard I cried, no one picked me up or fed me."

"So you felt alone and helpless . . ."

"Yes, yes. I never felt I could get enough."

"Within the trance, have the adult Peter come and pick up the little Peter in the crib."

Like watching a movie, I can see myself walking into the bedroom where the baby Peter lies in a crib, frightened and crying. I take him in my arms and hold him. Tears come to my eyes. I tell him that he is loved and he stops crying.

A profound healing takes place.

It happens in an instant.

Creating Your Own Reality
Santa Fe, New Mexico, October 26, 1993

It's all happening precisely as it is supposed to be happening. It could not be happening any other way. There is nothing whatsoever you could do differently.
Wayne Liquorman

After the workshop, Linda and I drive down Guadalupe Street to Santa Fe's Old Town. The city is breathtakingly beautiful at this time of day, with its softly rounded adobe buildings lit by the late afternoon sun. The New Mexican sky has taken on that deep cerulean blue that disappears into infinity. I'm intoxicated with pleasure. But it doesn't last for long. I'm still beating up on myself about the workshop.

"I feel so stupid," I say.

"Why's that?"

"For telling Eli that I 'create my own reality.'"

"No one even noticed," Linda says.

"I'm still not sure what Eli means when he says it's arrogant to 'create your own reality.' I used to teach workshops on creating your own reality. People loved them."

Turning the corner onto Water Street, I search for a parking place and can't find one. "Watch this," I say, visualizing a parking space opening up. Sure enough, a car starts to pull out half-way down the block. "See? That's creating your own reality!"

"Sure, Peter."

"I would always quote the famous Reverend Ike when I taught those workshops. He could get a crowd worked up in no time: 'You wanna new Cadillac?' he'd ask. 'Then you gotta *feel* that car as if you're already sitting in it; you gotta *feel* the steering wheel in your hand; you gotta *smell* that new car smell; you gotta know that you *deserve* that car. God doesn't want you to be poor. God wants you to be happy.'"

"Yeah," Linda says. "I've heard all that magical New Age stuff about manifesting money so many times. I had friends who had money magnets all over the place. They put all their energy into magic, rather than going out and getting a job. They were always broke—and probably still are."

"But there is some truth to it," I say, getting out of the car. "It's all based on the idea that 'as you think, so shall you be.'"

"Well, did it work for Fran?" Linda asks, as we walk down the street, lined with colorful shops selling paintings, oriental carpets, sheepskin rugs, Native American Indian drums. "She used to torture herself because she thought she had somehow created her own illness by not thinking the right thoughts."

"I know. She read Louise Hay, who believes that any disease can be reversed by simply reversing the mental patterns that created the illness. You know the idea—if you've got breast cancer it's because you weren't nurturing yourself. All you have to do is go back to nurturing yourself, repeat positive affirmations, and you'll be healed."

"That makes me so mad," Linda says. "It suggests that Fran was not only thinking the wrong thoughts, but she must somehow be 'less spiritual,' because a spiritual person would only think right thoughts. That's a pretty heavy trip to lay on anyone—and it all goes back to the belief that I create my own reality."

We stop to look in a store window filled with huge crystals, medicine wheels, Tarot cards, healing books, posters by Gilbert Williams of the astral plane, and copies of the *Celestine Prophecy*.

"All that New Age stuff is so seductive," I say. "It gives people a sense that they can manipulate the world and have some control over it. But you can't."

"It all comes from a fear of death," Linda says. "It's a desperate attempt to stay in control of our lives. The New Age healers are more terrified of death than anyone I know."

"I guess some people find it comforting to think they have control over their destiny."

"Yeah, if you prefer an illusion based on fantasy and false hope."

We turn onto a narrow side street paved with cobblestones. "The strange thing," Linda muses, "is that on one level we *do* create our own reality. As Source manifests through us, it creates the universe, literally and figuratively. Therefore the 'Self that I am' is none other than God manifesting the universe. The implications of this are huge."

"That blows my mind."

"Source or awareness is not only manifesting through us, we *are* Source."

"So that's why it's arrogant to think that I create my own reality!" I say excitedly. "I think that the 'little me' or the ego is the one doing it. My ego wants to take credit for it by saying '*I* create *my* own reality.' That *is* arrogant!"

"It's even bigger than anything we can conceive of," Linda says, looking up at the sky, which has turned an even deeper blue as darkness comes. "On the one hand we're just dust motes floating in empty space, on the other we are the great source that is nothing but love and creates itself over and over."

It's too much for my mind to take in. Suddenly I remember how hungry I am. My stomach wins out over talking about God as I lead Linda off in the direction of the Blue Corn Café, just around the next corner. Of course, that's God too.

CHAPTER 15

FOLLY OF THE EGO

Ramana Retreat Center, Tajique, New Mexico

Land of Enchantment
Taos, New Mexico, May, 1993

If you don't know where you're going, you'll end up somewhere else.
Yogi Berra

When Eli's workshop ended, Linda and I returned to our new home on a mountainside outside of Taos, New Mexico. We had moved to New Mexico in 1993, after an exceptionally brutal Massachusetts winter. "A person could die out there," Linda said upon experiencing her first winter in the Northeast. After living in Hawaii, I found that I couldn't handle the grey, frozen winters either. So we put our log home on the market and sold it within six weeks. We had visited Santa Fe earlier, and, like a kid in a candy store, I fell madly in love with what the New Mexican tourist bureau calls the "Land of Enchantment." I am gaga over the beauty of Santa Fe, with its adobe buildings, trimmed in bright blue and turquoise; I swoon over the colorful displays of red chili peppers and Indian rugs; I am knocked out by the historic beauty of the downtown area, with its plaza and old churches; I am in heaven walking the narrow streets and breathing in the dizzying aroma of mesquite burning in the air. And the restaurants . . . ah, the restaurants: The Coyote Café, Geromino's, Pasqual's, The Blue Corn Café—the list goes on and on. I celebrate being in a place where Hispanics, Native American Indians, locals, and tourists all managed to get on together (for the most part). It's hard to believe I am still in the United States.

But nothing compares to seeing the New Mexican landscape for the first time. Driving Highway 68 from Santa Fe to Taos, there is a special moment where, after winding along the Rio Grande gorge for twenty miles, the road crests a hill and a vast expanse of desert comes into view, stretching out as far as the eye can see. On the right, the snow-capped Sangre de Cristo Mountains rise straight up out of the desert like sentinels. I pull off the road to take it all in (like everyone else who sees this view for the first time), reveling in the soft greens and pastels of the desert. Nestled at the foot of the mountains is the vibrant little town of Taos—a Mecca for artists, writers, actors, musicians, eccentrics, hippies, healers, skiers, and nature lovers.

I prefer the more sophisticated Santa Fe, but Taos is Linda's town. She especially likes the lack of pretention—the Walmart parking lot filled with dirty, mud-splashed pick-ups (including, from time to time, one belonging to Julia Roberts). Spiritually, she is lit up by the natural beauty of the mountains and desert, but she also is drawn to a small temple devoted to the Hindu god Hanuman, hidden away in the middle of the town. The temple contains a large murti (statue) of a blissful, flying Hanuman, known as the "Monkey God" in the Ramayana—revered for his courage and loyalty. Linda and I often meditate in the tiny temple and attend the yearly Bhandara , where Ram Dass, Krishna Das, and other pilgrims come from afar to pay their respects to their teacher Neem Karoli Baba and chant the Hanuman Chalisa.

We end up buying a small hippie house high above the town at 8200 feet. The lower level has slanting greenhouse windows which enclose a workshop area that the previous owner used for weaving. Only later did we find out that the owner had weaved Linda's precious mohair shawl—a rich tapestry of purples and pinks—in that same room. On the upper level there is a tiny bedroom, bathroom, and kitchen, and a four-sided living room with a traditional white kiva fireplace. I finally get to have my traditional ceiling of vigas and latillas—natural round beams of timber that support the slender sticks that make up the ceiling.

Sitting in our hot tub, with steam rising all around us, we watch storms march across the desert. Once, close to sunset, an enormous grey-black storm cloud appears in the sky, and slowly makes its way north, with dark rain falling from underneath it, all set against a brilliant pink and orange sky. In the distance we can see the long, deep cut made by the Rio Grande Gorge, which plunges almost 800 feet straight down to the river. To our left is Taos Mountain, which is considered sacred to the Taos Indians. Near its summit is the famous Blue Lake, where young men are still initiated into the tribe at puberty. Far below we can make out the Pueblo, which lies a few miles outside of Taos. At night it's easy to tell which is Indian land and which is the land of the white people—in the midst of all the glittering lights, there is a large area of complete darkness—the Pueblo. How reassuring to see that the relentless spread of Western civilization has not taken over everything.

Linda and I are in awe of the Taos Indians. We often come across them in the post office talking in their native *tewa*, and are spellbound by the sounds of their ancient language. There are some two thousand Taos Indians living on the pueblo, a reservation of 90,000 acres. About one hundred and fifty of them live in a four-story adobe building that is one of the oldest inhabited structures in the world, dating back 900 years. It has no electricity or running water, but has a small creek that runs by it. We attend the Deer Dance and the Corn Dance; we take horseback lessons from Stormstar, an Indian who runs a stable on the pueblo; we ride with him over Indian land where no white person is allowed; we hear legends of his forefathers and quickly learn that life on the Pueblo is not all peaches and cream. Both of us are fascinated to hear that they still hold secret ceremonies in an underground kiva, where according to one story, they are able to move large stones with the power of their minds. The Pueblo Indians seem grounded in the earth in a way no white man is.

Many unexplained events happen on the mountainside. There is a tale of a white man falling off a cliff in 1930, screaming on his way down. The Indians claim they can still hear the man's screams when they go near the cliff. One night we hear the sound of drumming as we drift off to sleep. At first we think that it's some hippies down the road, but then we realize that it's the ritual drumming of the Indians floating up through the cold night air. We've been told that in their ceremonies they will often "shape shift," taking on the form of different animals.

Later that night we wake up to find two large coyotes staring in at us through the sliding glass doors of our bedroom. To get there they would somehow have to avoid alerting our two dogs, climb a narrow stairway, and walk thirty feet along a deck to our bedroom. We look at the coyotes . . . and we look again, saying to each other, "Did you see that?" Suddenly they are gone. Are they real? Is it just our imagination?

The Taos Terror
Taos, New Mexico, April 11, 1994

When everything is taken away until you get down to the last bit of you, the essence of you, until all is snuffed out, there you find God. This is something terrific.
Thomas Merton

In late December a huge snowstorm dumps four feet of snow on the mountain. The roads are impassable and we are surrounded in whiteness with nowhere to go (and we thought Massachusetts was bad). It happens at a time when I am taking Flagel for an intestinal bug I picked up in Bali. All my props have been taken away from me—no chance of soothing my anxiety with food or wine, no friends I can distract myself with, no trips to town for some diversion. Even Linda is unavailable. She is lying in bed coughing and feverish.

One night I spiral into depression. Linda and I are in the bedroom, with the lights off, except for Linda's reading light, and the moonlight shining in through the sliding-glass doors. All that day I have been feeling uncertain about the direction my life is taking. *What am I doing here?* I ask myself. I get out of bed and lie on the floor. Waves of terror sweep over me. I curl up into a fetal position, wrapped in misery.

"Are you OK?" Linda asks.

"I'm terrified," I say in a faint voice. "All this fear is coming up from nowhere."

"What's the fear?"

"It's the fear of being helpless. I'm afraid I won't be able to do anything. I feel worthless, as if everyone is judging me."

"Who's judging you?"

"Everyone . . ."

Sensing how upset I am, Linda pulls herself out of her own discomfort and is totally there for me. Even in my misery I'm grateful for her love.

"Why don't you go even deeper into this paralysis?" Linda suggests. "Let yourself feel totally worthless . . . and see what happens."

"Oh shit . . . I don't want to go there." I close me eyes and a numbing paralysis creeps over me like a cold glove. "What an awful feeling. I'm useless. No one likes me. I hate myself." *Oh my god,* my inner voice says. *You're just wallowing in self-pity!*

"What else?"

"I feel so alone. It terrifies me." I force myself to relax into the terror. It is icy and indifferent.

"What's beneath the terror?" Linda asks, as if speaking from some far off place.

A wave of desolation comes over me, so black it feels as if it's going to engulf me. "This horrible despair," I say, tears coming to my eyes.

"Tell me about it." Linda asks, sniffling from her cold.

"I feel like I'm going to die . . . that I'll be annihilated."

"Just be with that for a time . . ."

I breathe deeply and sink into the hopelessness. Suddenly an image comes up of floating in the darkness of outer space. There is a memory of having been here before. As a twelve-year-old boy, I went into this same black, empty universe the instant I heard my mother had died. I have been running from this emptiness my entire life. But now it doesn't seem so terrifying. I stay with the sensation of floating in space and start to feel very peaceful.

From far off, I hear Linda's voice, "You won't believe this, but I was just reading Ram Dass' book *Grist for the Mill*. He has a guided meditation that would really help you right now. Shall I read it?"

"Yeah," groan. I'm not crazy about visualizations, but I'll try anything at this point.

"Ram Dass says, 'Bring your attention to the middle of your chest and imagine a golden mist floating above it. Let the mist take the form of a tiny being, right in the middle of your heart. Notice there is a light within it. See the light pouring out from it. Feel its compassion and its love. Let yourself be filled up with its love.'"

I imagine a being of light close to my heart and drop down even more—how I don't know. I sense I'm falling through a black hole. To my astonishment I open into a place of total love—a profound, unmistakable knowing that I *am* that being of love and always have been.

Tears of despair become tears of joy. I begin to laugh—a wild hysterical belly laugh—that has me rolling on the floor. I laugh and laugh until I can't laugh any more. The laughter is followed by a deep calm such as I have never known.

The Taos Terror is gone.

Silent Explosion
Breitenbush Hot Springs, Oregon, September 26, 1994

What I have to say to you cannot be said. What you have to hear cannot be said. It cannot be found in continuing discussion. It can be found in the silence of your being.
Gangaji

A man wearing shorts and a tank top stands in front of the main hall doing yoga stretches before lunch. The same person was doing stretches the day the retreat began, looking like he was showing off for the crowd. Now he no longer seems to care whether anyone notices him or not. Several others are stretched out in the grass, seemingly lost in their own private worlds. One or two retreatants are in the smoking tent enjoying a cigarette. A small group of women are sitting at a picnic table on the porch laughing hysterically. Since they can't talk, they laugh, until someone politely asks them to be quiet. Strange things happen after one hundred people spend eight days in silence together (and have six more to go).

Linda and I are at a silent retreat with Gangaji at Breitenbush Hot Springs in Oregon. Everyone (except, perhaps, for the women at the table) seems to have dipped into the magic of simply being still—something few of us get to experience in our lives. I've spent days sleeping, sitting in satsang, soaking in hot springs, and eating healthy vegetarian food. Linda and I are staying in a tent and sharing a communal bathroom. For two brief weeks I'm in a place where there is literally nothing to "do," nowhere to go, nobody I have to talk to. I've gone through the hell of seeing all my "stuff" come up, and the bliss of having my mind be quiet; I've struggled with distractions and let go into peace; I've felt the discomfort of feeling alone and the joy of shared community.

I imagine that many others in the group are going through a similar experience. As the days go on, there has been a perceptible shift in the group energy. We came here as one hundred "separate" individuals with busy agendas, and are now discovering that there is no separation to be found anywhere. For a brief moment in time, we have voluntarily forsaken the usual mental noise and emotional turbulence of our lives to become a single unified presence.

When I first arrived, my mind was like a pinball machine in an arcade, *WHAANG, BING, WHARRUP, BING, BING, BING!* Then, suddenly, it felt as if someone had pulled the plug. Silence, blessed silence—precious moments where there is no thought at all. What a relief! My mind still jumps to distractions, just out of habit, and I still fill up my day with different activities—anything to escape from just being still. I notice my mind obsessively grasping on to things, mostly of no importance whatsoever. Then back to silence. Coming back to silence becomes more natural and effortless as I realize it is just the mind doing its own thing.

Linda is in heaven. She comes alive in these woods, which are so much a part of her. She grew up in Oregon and came here with her parents as a young child, and later on as an adult, when she lived in nearby Salem. In the morning we take a walk along the Spotted Owl trail, which goes through old growth forest to spots where we can see Mt. Jefferson and Mt. Hood. Linda walks barefoot like a Native American Indian, touching each leaf and branch, as if greeting a long lost friend. She caresses the soft moss by the creek and steps into the cool clear water, bringing her palms together in prayer position, honoring the trees, the sky, the earth, the water.

As I slow down more and more from my usual frenetic activity, a deep sense of peace begins to emerge. My body comes alive as I soak naked in the warm meadow pool, where the hot water spontaneously bubbles up from deep in the earth. I sit in the funky steam room, fed by the steaming hot water, until I can't stand it anymore, then dip myself in the cold tub. The healthy food and lack of any coffee or wine has cleaned out my system. My daily hikes with Linda have cleared my mind, and the hours spent in meditation have cleared my heart.

It's almost dark when Linda and I walk over to the main hall to attend the evening gathering with Gangaji. Unlike most spiritual retreats there is no required schedule, which is both refreshing and challenging, because there is no easy escape into routines. Gangaji begins with a silent meditation, then reads letters she has received from participants. At her retreats people are allowed to ask questions at satsang. Someone raises their hand and asks Gangaji about Ramana Maharshi. She answers, "Ramana basically gave one teaching. It was simply to 'be still.' Retreat from every object, every subject, every emotion, every conclusion—just for an instant at least. Yes. That's right. Who would have suspected? Here, all along, just being still."

In silence Linda and I find our way along the path back to our tent. The September air is filled with the fragrance of cedar and wood smoke. A gentle rain has started and we can barely make out the path through the towering cedars and Douglas firs. The forest is filled with the sound of chirping crickets and the wind in the trees. All our senses are alert as we feel our way through the dark. We find the tent and go through the intricate ritual of preparing for bed, while making sure that our clothes stay dry. Once inside, all we can hear is the sound of the rain softly falling on the roof of the tent. Silently we slip into the same sleeping bag, sensing the delicious warmth of each other's bodies. No words are exchanged as we gently kiss, feeling the fire rise up from within. No words are needed as we caress and explore each other. It is all so familiar, and all so fresh, and all so new at the same time. No words are spoken as we enter into the vast silence together. We are witnesses to all of it, letting go fully into the miracle of the moment, letting go into a vast explosion of silence that seems to last forever. Silently, we wish this joy and this love on the whole world as we fall asleep in each other's arms.

Cold Turkey
Santa Fe, New Mexico, November 4, 1994

Here in the world
Some crave pleasure,
Some seek freedom.
But it is hard to find
A man who wants neither.
Ashtavakra Gita

In most of the retreats with Gangaji I'm content to watch the show, awed by her ability to bring forth the most profound realization from those who ask her questions. Her responses are often hilariously funny (there is no one who laughs quite so delightfully as she does), sometimes ruthless and real (there is no one who remains as true to the truth as she does), and at other times heart-opening and blissful (there is no one who can express such unabashed devotion as she does).

One day, feeling a bit reckless, I put up my hand. There are over three hundred people in the room. Gangaji calls upon me and someone passes a microphone over. "Gangaji," I say with great seriousness, "from what you say, spiritual practices will never lead to awakening. What if we were to make sex, wine, and chocolate a path to God?" I can hear titters of laughter from the audience. "What if we all found out that once we got to the pearly gates, that only those who had celebrated all the joys and pleasures of being in a body, got through?"

Gangaji smiles and looks at me. She knows my question is half playful, half serious. I have no idea how she will respond.

"There is this idea that if I give up pleasures," she says, "I will give up joy. But in seeking these pleasures you are grasping for joy. These pleasures are very short lived; pleasures must be followed by pain. This is the nature of the dichotomy of the mind-body. If you reach for pleasure, there is pain in there somewhere, either in the loss of this pleasure or in the fear of the loss of it."

"Hmm," I say. *This is not what I expected!*

"Nothing can be held on to," she continues. "In that realization, there is great joy. There is no longer any need to hold on to or grasp anything. Then you discover that the joy you were reaching for is your very Self, needing nothing, finding joy everywhere, seeing with joy eyes, hearing with joy ears."

"So, how do I let go of this reaching for pleasure?" I ask.

"Because of the deep conditioning of these pleasures, cold turkey is the fastest, quickest, most radical surgery."

"Cold turkey!" I say with a gasp. "Oh, no!" Everyone laughs.

"This is your choice then. Continue to go for sex wine and chocolate. Then tell me. Otherwise be intelligent. There's nothing wrong with sex, wine and chocolate. But is it giving you what you are searching for? If it is . . . wonderful! If not, then tell the truth."

She's not telling me not to do it, as Gurudev would have. She's saying watch what happens and see if this is what you really want. Wow.

"See how you reach for alleviation of pain by seeking out pleasure."

I smile, feeling self-conscious. *She has my number; she sees right through me. I'm not really interested in awakening; I just want to have a good time.*

"Realize what has never been touched by pain *or* pleasure," she says, looking at me very intently. "This is discovered in quiet. Then see. Tell the truth—ruthlessly."

Afterwards I realize that every spiritual practice, whether is it sex, wine, and chocolate, or sitting on a cushion, is about telling the truth. All too often spiritual practices become a way of escaping the truth and "feeling good." Rather than waking you up, they put you to sleep. Rather than helping you find the happiness you are searching for, they become a way of postponing what is already present. These simple misconceptions can mean a lifetime of searching down the wrong road. What I came to understand is that sex, wine, and chocolate are no more or less spiritual than celibacy, tea, or tofu. It's all the same—an invitation to awaken.

Come to the Silence
The Ramana Retreat Center, Tajique, New Mexico, January, 1995

All trouble in the world is due to the fact that a man cannot sit still in a room.
Blaise Pascal

After selling the property in Hawaii and the log home in Massachusetts, I have enough money not to have to work. If I had any sense at all, I could have lived a life of peaceful, still, awareness. But, filled with spiritual idealism, an inability to sit still, and a desperate need for recognition, I come up with the idea of starting a retreat center.

"We've been given such gifts," I say to Linda one morning while sitting by a creek outside of Crestone, Colorado, where we've been attending another retreat with Gangaji. "Wouldn't it be great if we could share our good fortune with others? I've wanted to run a retreat center for years. Fran and I talked about it all the time—even before we went to Kripalu."

"Well, it would be nice to have a place where anyone who wanted to could come and be in silence," Linda responds cautiously. "We could even name it after Ramana. He, more than anyone I know, points to the silence that already exists within each one of us."

"That sounds great!" I say excitedly. "We could buy a large property and hold silent retreats. That two-week retreat with Gangaji really changed my life. I'd love to be able to offer that to others."

Who could ever question my sincere desire to share what I have with seekers who are looking for a place where they can be silent? And, by naming it after Ramana, surely I can keep my own ego from getting involved. I simply want to be a humble servant of God and come from my heart. What a perfect way to practice "right livelihood" and make a difference in the world!

Oh, how sneaky the ego is. I might as well have hung out a sign saying, "Kick me God!"

Linda and I travel from one end of the country to the other in search of land—from Asheville, South Carolina to Ashland, Oregon, from Middlebury, Vermont to Vancouver Island, BC. It is a heady experience, flying around the country looking for the perfect spot. Realtor's eyes light up when they see us coming; friends in different parts of the country welcome us with open arms; Gangaji and other spiritual teachers give us encouragement. Everyone is duly impressed with our utopian ideals and our mission. Over the next months we view some extraordinary properties, but there is always something that doesn't quite work—zoning problems, accessibility, cost, buildings in disrepair, or no buildings at all. After a year of looking, I still haven't found anything. Disappointed, I give up the search. That's it—the message is clear: stay home and be content. But do I listen?

A few days later, on our way to the airport, we look at a property in the mountains east of Albuquerque. I can't believe my eyes. The property consists of 100 pristine acres surrounded by the vast wilderness of the Cibola National Forest. There are flowering meadows, clear streams, towering ponderosas, and ancient juniper trees, some of them over 600 years old. Besides a working windmill, there are some impressive buildings—a huge three-story lodge, an exquisite one-room adobe chapel, and several guest cottages. It began as a Franciscan monastery, then became a silent retreat center run by an eccentric Episcopalian minister. After being abandoned for years, two women, Sonia and Jade, bought it (and unsuccessfully) tried to start a lesbian community. They tell us about the 225 species of wildflowers on the property, the varieties of wildlife and birds. They even mention seeing a huge UFO from the second floor of the lodge. I can understand why. We are in the middle of nowhere and not far from Roswell, New Mexico. UFO's or no UFO's, we buy it on sight for $700,000, and before we know it, there are people lining up to become part of our fledgling community. It seems too good to be true.

It all starts well. Within a few months we have our non-profit status, a board of directors, a full-time staff of seven, and accommodations for thirty-five guests. We offer gourmet vegetarian meals and a variety of accommodations, from luxury rooms with private bath to inexpensive dorm rooms. Unlike many retreat centers, we have few rules, rituals, or requirements. People can read, walk in the woods, or just be still. Yet for those who want it, there is daily yoga and meditation.

We hold several work retreats, where some remarkable angels show up to help. We renovate the adobe chapel and cottages, repair the plumbing, and prepare for guests. Our grand opening is on Memorial Day, 1995, when Gangaji and more than a hundred friends come for a special opening ceremony. Over the next weeks we hold retreats that are attended by people from as far away as Hawaii, Oregon, and Illinois. One retreat is led by an extraordinary Indian doctor and meditation teacher from Bombay, named Bhagwan—an extraordinary man who embodies the silence he teaches about. Another is led by Ganeshan, the grandnephew of Ramana Maharshi. He grew up in Ramana's ashram and used to sit on Ramana's lap. He is filled with devotional stories about Ramana and his teachings.

Inspired by their visits, we decide to do silent retreats of our own, agreeing to take turns doing two-day retreats in St. Bruno's Hermitage. The Hermitage hut is one of those surprising little "extras" that came with the property. About a five-minute walk from the main lodge, it sits at the top a thirty-foot cliff over-looking a stream and acres of forest. The building is a tiny hand-made cabin with a hand-carved sign over the door, "St. Bruno's Hermitage," made in the days when it was a Franciscan monastery. It contains a rough-hewn bed, a small wood stove, and a rustic table and chair—no running water, no electricity, no phones, no clocks, no TV, no toilet—except for a quaint little outhouse out back.

The Five Star Hermit
Tajique, New Mexico, June 23, 1995

The thing I like about meditation is that it makes doing nothing respectable.
Strange de Jim

Linda is the first to volunteer to do a retreat in the hermit hut. There is nothing she loves more than being alone in nature. She recently did a week-long retreat at the Lama Foundation near Taos and loved it. We set up an arrangement where meals will be brought up for her and placed in a cooler about one hundred feet from the hut. If Linda has any special needs, she can leave a note in the cooler. All visitors and staff are asked to keep a respectful distance when the "hermit" is in residence.

I keep on with my busy (and very important) life as "The Director" while Linda retreats. Two days later I excitedly wait for her to come back down the hill. Late in the afternoon she walks down to the lodge, greeting me with a big hug and a kiss. "That was so wonderful," she says, looking radiant and refreshed after being silence for two days.

Hugging her tight, I say, "I've missed you so much . . . tell me what happened?"

"This morning I walked uphill along the small stream, trying to find its source. There were birds singing and the happy sound of water bubbling and gurgling over the rocks. It was so beautiful in the morning light. Eventually I came to a place where the stream disappeared, and only patches of mud and ice were visible."

"Oh, I know that spot."

"I just stood there. The vast silence rang down like a giant bell jar dropping over me. My eardrums strained to hear—but there was no sound. Suddenly there were no birds, no wind, no sound of any kind, no matter how hard I listened. The only thing I could hear was my heartbeat. All thoughts died away and there was just peace."

"Oh Linda," I say. "What a gift you have. All it takes is a moment for you to drop into that inner stillness."

When it comes time for my retreat, it's clear that it will be a little different from Linda's. I gather my stuff and carry it up to the hut with the help of Linda and Bodil, a beautiful Danish woman who is on our staff.

"I'm not even sure if you can last two days," Linda quips. "How are you going to survive without your gourmet meals?"

"And your wine," Bodil adds with a laugh.

As we get to the cliff edge Linda whispers, "Look, there's a lynx!" Just over the edge we see what looks like a huge oversized cat with pointy ears. It has white fur on its chest and its coat is a mix of grey and tan with black spots all over it.

"What a beautiful creature—what power!" Bodil says in awe.

The lynx makes a loud snarl, revealing its huge teeth, which have been carefully designed by nature to stab deeply into its prey.

We all quietly back off so we won't disturb it.

"Hmmm," I say, a little nervously. "I think this is an auspicious beginning to the retreat."

Once I get set up, Linda and Bodil disappear down the trail, leaving me alone with myself—and the lynx. I sit out in front of the hut on the rickety Adirondack chair, looking out at the serene valley bounded on both sides with tall pines. Night is falling and it's getting colder by the minute. I fix myself an *aperitif* of roasted almonds and Perrier with lime and settle in to watch the sunset. I realize that it's been years since I've actually "watched" a sunset, and not just glanced at it for a few moments before going on to do something else. Gradually I become aware of the sounds all around me—the whoosh, whoosh of bird's wings as they fly overhead to their nests, the wind rustling through the Ponderosa pines.

I remember a Zen saying, "Enlightenment is eating when you're hungry and sleeping when you're tired." Well, I'm hungry, so I eat. For my first meal I've come prepared—not gruel and water—but fresh sushi from Wild Oats in Santa Fe. I delight in every morsel, tasting it like never before. For dessert (I always have to have my sugar) I eat half a brownie, saving the other half for tomorrow. There's no reason for a modern-day hermit to suffer.

As darkness descends, the cool New Mexican night air (and the possibility of a lynx looking for its dinner) has me retreating into the hut. The cozy interior is still warm from the sun. I light the kerosene lamp and its glow suffuses the cabin. Then I create a little ritual by lighting the candle in front Ramana's picture, asking for his blessing on the retreat. Sleep comes easily on the hard, narrow bed, snug in my sleeping bag.

I wake up in the morning feeling the warm sun pouring through the window and onto my bed. I lie there and watch a fly walk across the screen. My mind goes through a list of all the things that I want to do today, but then I catch myself. This is retreat. I heat up some water on the stove and prepare a cup of French vanilla coffee. Sitting at the little table, sipping my coffee, I watch the day sparkle into life—insects buzzing, birds singing, and the sun melting the light cover of snow—drip, drip, drip. I fix myself a bagel with strawberry jam.

266

I find myself thinking of all the people around the globe who are on some kind of silent retreat right now—Buddhist monks in Thailand, nuns in Nova Scotia, Carthusian monks in a monastery high in the French Alps, sadhus living in caves in India, solitary individuals off in some remote cabin in the wilderness. All these souls are holding the space of silence, while the rest of us rush about, our minds churning, our desires driving us to do the next thing, our world in turmoil. No wonder we humans are at war with ourselves. The words of Ramana take on new meaning: "You are the Self now and can never be anything else. Throw your troubles to the wind. Turn within and find peace."

Later that morning, after a short walk, some writing, and a nap, I hear the gong signaling that someone has put my lunch in the cooler down the hill. What a sweet sound! It's the first time I've ever been dependent on someone else (who I don't know), to prepare my food and bring it to me. Sitting in the cooler is a beautifully laid out plate with fresh greens, cheese and fruit, as well as a red napkin and a "love note." A deep, uncaused sense of joy wells up within me—and it's not just the good food. I take my lunch back to my lair and eat outdoors in the old, funky chair. The salad literally bursts in my mouth, brimming with aliveness.

After lunch, I go back to the cooler and leave a note: "Please bring my laptop when you come back up." At the bottom I add, "And a cold Corona as well." With a chuckle, I can imagine the purists and "serious retreatants" rolling their eyes. "This is no retreat," they would huff. "This is a joke!" But who makes up the rules? Why does everyone believe you have to suffer to in order to awaken? Spiritual awakening has nothing to do with rules, asceticism, or rituals. *Awakening is right here, right now!* I think as I put the note in the cooler.

The day stretches out as if it has no beginning and no end. The wind has picked up and is roaring through the pines with angry ferocity. I sip my tea. I listen to the sounds. Time slows down until I'm aware of each in-breath and each out-breath. All is peace opening up to infinity. An urge arises to move. One moment I'm sitting and the next I am walking. There's not the usual debate about if I should go or where I should go. I hike up into the Cibola National Forest where I walk for miles down primitive roads without seeing a person or a car. There are bears and coyote in the woods, but they never bother me. I walk by gnarled junipers that date back hundreds of years; I walk through areas scarred by forest fires; I find myself in a meadow filled with bright reddish-orange Indian paintbrush flowers dancing against soft green grasses. I marvel at the ordinariness of it all and the miracle of it all.

The late afternoon entertainment is a thunderstorm in full Dolby sound. As the black clouds move in, the landscape takes on an eerie luminosity. Then it becomes dark and ominous. The rain falls in blinding sheets—thunder and lightning hit with ground-shaking force. I sit in my hermitage watching it all. I have a perfect front row seat as the storm unleashes its fury. Is all this real? Is it a dream?

The storm passes, leaving everything alive with the pungent smell of a rain-soaked forest. The hours go by and darkness falls. I finally look at my watch and see that it's nine o'clock. I realize that I haven't heard the sound of the dinner gong. *Have they forgotten me? Maybe they're going to starve me after my request for a laptop and beer!* I go down the path and there is the cooler. Sitting on top of it is the laptop. *Oh my God—it's soaked!*

I bring the computer and the food back up to the hut. Anxiously I dry off the laptop and boot it up. It still works! God is good. Now for my meal. Tonight's menu, eaten by candlelight, is Ziti a la Putanesca, tomato salad with pine nuts, and crisp garlic wafers (and my remaining half brownie). No Corona, but just as well. Ah, the life of an ascetic!

In the morning I light the wood stove to take off the chill. The delicious smell of wood smoke and the crackle of the fire is a meal in itself. I start to notice things around me that I haven't seen before—that all the posts in the hut have been painstakingly pieced together without nails, that there are new wildflowers in bloom right outside my window. I've only been on retreat for thirty-six hours, but it feels like I've stepped outside of the circle of time. I don't want the retreat to end. Silence has become my friend. That silence is who I am.

The Fall of Icarus
Ramana Retreat Center, Tajique, New Mexico, July 25, 1995

*Mamma always said life was like a box of chocolates. You never know what
you're gonna get.*
Winston Groom, *Forrest Gump*

The retreat center continues to flourish. As summer approaches we are all riding
high; we have repaired the buildings, built tent platforms alongside the creek for
more affordable housing, and upgraded the kitchen. Many are so excited about our
vision that they want to be part of an ongoing community, especially now that we
have our 501 C3 nonprofit status. We envision a small group of "land stewards"
who invest in the property and build their own homes. Our master plan calls for
an ecologically based, sustainable community, with straw bale houses, solar and
wind power, and organic gardens. Everyone loves the idea. In July we are voted
'Best Spiritual Retreat Center in New Mexico' by *Crosswinds Magazine*. Gangaji
agrees to become our spiritual director, and there is talk of her holding regular
retreats at the center. We send out mailings and newsletters and wait for the
people to sign up, happy in the knowledge that "if you build it, they will come."

I am in a constant whirlwind (the very opposite of a quiet mind), playing the
role of director, head of marketing, chief fund-raiser, program leader, staff director, construction supervisor, and more often than not, toilet cleaner. Inspired by
our vision, talented and committed people offer their skills in carpentry, plumbing, electrical, cooking, and management. Everyone volunteers their services in
exchange for food and lodging. We're on a roll.

For me, it is the realization of a twenty-year dream. I wanted to run a retreat
center long before going to Kripalu, and now it's happening. I am serving God
with all my heart and soul. I am sharing the blessings of my resources with others. I am stretched to my fullest capacity and beyond. I am hanging out with wise
spiritual teachers. I am in demand. I am the decision-maker. I am the star! What
I don't see is that I am flying headlong into disaster.

Like Icarus, the higher you fly, the further the fall. And fall I did.

Oh, did I fall.

It began with a terrible drought, 90 days without rain—parched soil, creeks
drying up, and the constant threat of fire in the tinder-dry forest. Like a wildfire
racing down the mountainside, things start to go wrong. Even though the initial
response to the center has been wildly enthusiastic, no one is showing up at the

door. With no money coming in, feeding and housing the volunteer staff becomes more and more of a liability. With nothing to do, they become frustrated and bored and start sniping at each other. Always wanting to be the "nice guy," I find it difficult to set limits and give firm direction. The summer wears on and there are no guests; the money continues to gush out at $18,000 per month—all of it from Linda and my savings. We send out more mailings and drop our rates in half. Still no one comes. Then Phil, the most supportive member of our team, leaves to join his girl friend in Arizona.

It all begins to implode.

Linda and I thought our retreat center would attract mature spiritual seekers who knew how to take care of themselves and make a contribution. Many of them did, but we also get needy and neurotic people showing up at our door, looking for a free ride (and a mommy and daddy to take care of them). It's not long before word gets out to their friends and they start turning up in droves, wanting to live in a beautiful retreat center in the woods and enjoy three gourmet vegetarian meals a day. They have no money so they agree to work in exchange for room and board. But in no time they are complaining that they can't do much—if any— work, because of health problems. The retreat center starts to resemble a home for the needy. One of our volunteers, who has named herself Grace, carries around a portable air filter on her shoulder all day to ward off allergies; a young guy with a Mohawk plays drums in the meditation hall; Nina spends her time baking cookies that no one wants or needs. When Linda and I refuse to play mommy and daddy for them, they write letters to Gangaji, complaining that we are not taking care of them.

Linda's health begins to deteriorate, marking the beginning of an autoimmune illness that rapidly becomes more and more debilitating. I'm stressed out and barely functional. Then there are the finances. We find out that everything we invested in the property could be lost because of a simple mistake made by our accountant. Meanwhile, we are committed to making decisions by consensus (a choice I made out of spiritual idealism and sheer stupidity). People who have been there a week, and don't have a penny in the center, expect the same decision-making power as Linda and I. They criticize our mission statement; they want to keep our dogs out of the lodge; they want a television set in the meditation hall; they complain that we gave them some "non-organic" food; they become upset because we're feeding the hummingbirds sugar water. When I turn down their requests (or say yes to some and no to others), it all comes back at me.

A strong leader would be able to sail through this, but I have to face the fact that I can't lead my way out of a paper bag. I'm just too nice. When I hear that the founders of just about every retreat center in America get kicked out by reformers, losing their entire investment, I realize I'm in a no-win situation. Rather than wait for that inevitable moment, I decide to end it before it ends me. "Oh Jesus,"

I write in my journal, "it's all falling apart. The retreat center is crumbling. My dream is shattered."

I tell the staff that we have no choice but to close down. They are shocked and confused. I'm no longer the sweet, altruistic, Peter who wants nothing more than to share his love for Ramana Maharshi and the truth; I'm just another a**hole landlord tossing everyone out on the street. Anyone who has donated money to the Center now wants it returned. They send off angry letters to Gangaji, who writes back with wisdom, "Honor THAT WHICH IS OF TRUE, LASTING IMPOR-TANCE. All the rest (high and low) obviously comes and goes. What is TRUE remains."

The closing of the center is the death of a cherished dream, and I go through worse grief than I've ever known. Friends come up to me and say in hushed tones, "I'm so sorry to hear you're closed." Others call and are dismayed at the news. "We were just about to make a reservation to come and stay!" Some still wander onto the property wanting to see the center. A group of Germans show up. "Das center ist geschlossen?" they ask, reacting in surprise. I smile and say, "Yes, what a relief." I thought that running a silent retreat center would help me to enter into the silence and lead towards enlightenment. How slippery the ego can be! I obviously needed to be knocked over the head by a 2 X 4 to get the lesson.

Within a few horrendous weeks I have said goodbye to our last staff member and our last visitor, closed the doors, locked the gate, and whooped with sheer joy at having it all over.

Then I got royally drunk.

CHAPTER 16

CHASING THE CARROT OF ENLIGHTENMENT

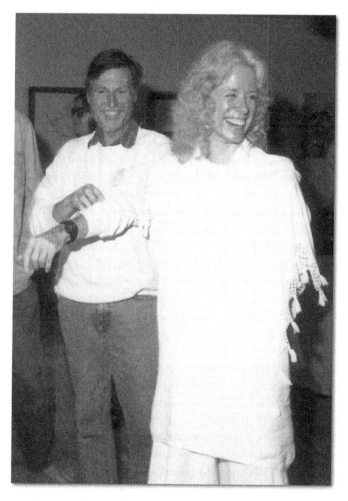

Peter & Gangaji at the Ramana Retreat Center

Paradise Found
Charlottesville, Virginia, May 6, 1996

*I suggest that you never settle for less than awakening to the Truth that you are.
Here, at this critical and marvelous time, we stand at the edge of the cliff. The
light of this time demands a ripening of the human spirit.*
ShantiMayi

After living in the drought and dryness of New Mexico for so long, Linda and
I hunger for moist soil, rich vegetation, and water—lots of water. As we drive
east across the country, we imagine finding a peaceful farm in Vermont with rolling farmland, winding country roads, white board fences, and bubbling streams.
When we finally arrive in Charlottesville, Virginia, we realize we've found what
we're looking for. The surrounding area, with the Blue Ridge Mountains to
the West, its rolling farmland, white board fences, winding country roads, and
water—lots of water—is some of the most beautiful countryside I've seen. It's
everything we dreamed we would find in Vermont. We just got the state wrong.

Charlottesville has been called "the Santa Fe of the East." It is the home of
Thomas Jefferson and the University of Virginia; it has sophisticated restaurants,
great bookstores, and every resource we could ever need. After living in the wilds
of Tajique, New Mexico, I feel like I've landed in paradise. The residents, I find,
are gentle and a gracious—an interesting blend of North and South. Unlike Santa
Fe, which has an almost jaded spiritual community, there is a freshness and an
innocence here, with numerous and diverse groups co-existing together.

It also helps that my son Peter lives in Washington, DC, just over a hundred
miles away. Linda and I rent a house in town and settle in to our new life. Freshly
certified as a Clinical Hypnotherapist, I open an office on the fourth floor of an old
building on Main Street and start taking on clients. I love what I'm doing. My
practice transforms me as much as it does them. With each client, I lead them into
a deeply relaxed state, then travel with them into unexplored realms where they
experience revelation upon revelation. As we both enter into a place of deep peace
that is beyond the mind, change happens effortlessly. After doing this for countless hours I more naturally slip into presence, seeing that it is always there, always
available. The knowing of it becomes tangible and real.

After the insanity of community living and the retreat center, Linda and I begin
to enjoy a more normal life. We hold gatherings in our home, travel to be with a
variety of spiritual teachers, and gradually absorb the nondual wisdom teachings on
a deeper level. It is a time to let this understanding steep like a big pot of tea.

A Flowering of Human Consciousness
Mt. Ayr Farm, Virginia, March 15, 2000

Buddha, Jesus and others were rare flowers, the first few flowers. And now we are about to experience a collective flowering of human consciousness. It's a completely new dimension in consciousness arising.
Eckhart Tolle

Over the next few years Linda and I travel all over the map to be with leading-edge spiritual teachers who are bringing forward a radical new paradigm to the world—Eckhart Tolle, Byron Katie, Satyam Nadeen, Gangaji, Robert Adams, Tony Parsons, Adyashanti, and many more. Our meetings might be as brief as a single evening, to several days sharing our house with Catherine Ingram, to a weeklong retreat with Francis Lucille, or an Inner Directions conference in La Jolla with a whole smorgasbord of teachers.

I found that each teacher I met had his or her own unique expression of the truth, but the message was essentially the same: awakening is possible for anyone who sincerely desires it; there is nothing you have to "do" in order to awaken—you already *are* what you're seeking. All it takes is a shift in everyday perception to realize this ultimate understanding. You don't have to do twenty years of spiritual practice, you don't have to purify your body, you don't have to become a Buddhist or become celibate (thank God), you don't have to perform endless rituals (unless you want to). The happiness you are seeking is right here, right now—it is your own true nature.

What is so unusual about these teachers (even the ones with the weird names) is that they are all westerners. They represent a new breed, unlike the gurus of the seventies, with their thrones, their Rolls Royces, and their adoring disciples, these "Teachers of One" are young, wise, unpretentious, and more often than not, female. They are very human, very fallible, and very dedicated to sharing this message of freedom. Like the itinerant sages of old, they travel the world giving talks to anyone willing to listen. They are more spiritual friends than gurus; they sit on a simple chair instead of a gilded throne; they honor everyone on their spiritual journey, and they're usually the first ones to laugh at themselves. Their sole job is to point us inwards, inviting us to recognize the truth of who we are.

According to Eckhart Tolle and others, their appearance points to a "quickening" that is happening in the world. There is talk of a major shift in human consciousness unlike any that has happened before. Isaac Shapiro, one of these teachers, says, "We are now at a point where the stage is set for a mass awakening. We must change for survival." As the world seemingly heads towards self-oblivion, more and more people seem to be waking up—not just a rarified cadre of Buddhist monks and Indian ascetics—but ordinary Americans, Europeans, young, old, rich, poor, white, black, and (believe it or not) women. For centuries the Buddhists claimed that only men could become enlightened.

As I met with first one, then another, I saw that each of them had some piece of the puzzle that I needed to discover. Sometimes it took years to see what that piece was, sometimes just a few hours. As I heard the same truth spoken in so many rich and diverse ways, all my preconceptions about what it means to awaken are popped like so many balloons.

I am getting close—so damned close that I can smell it.

Happiness Is Your Real Nature
Sedona, Arizona, September 9, 1995

Everyone here is Absolute Reality, Pure Awareness. This is your real nature.
Right now, not some time in the future. Not when you get enlightened. Not
when you search for the answers. But right this minute. This is what you are.
Why will you not accept it?
Robert Adams

When Linda and I owned the retreat center, we drove 400 miles across the desert
to see Robert Adams in Sedona, Arizona. Friends insisted that we see him, saying,
"He's one of the few 'true teachers' alive today." There was even talk of him wanting to come and live at our retreat center, which, of course, stroked my ego no end.
We arrived in Sedona the night before his talk and spent the next day wandering
around the New Age bookstores and cafés of Sedona. Every time I'd see an older
man, I'd whisper to Linda, "I wonder if that's Robert Adams?" Once, when a dis-
tinguished gray-haired man with glasses smiled at us, Linda nudged my arm and
said, "Look, I'm sure that must be him!"

That evening we sat quietly at the front of the room waiting for Robert
Adams to come and take the empty seat in front of us. There were twenty-five
of us in a spacious living room, with huge windows overlooking the red hills of
Sedona. After twenty minutes of sitting in silence, I heard a slight disturbance.
I opened my eyes and saw a man making his way to the front of the room. *This
can't be him! He looks like a Hell's Angel!* He is wearing a black knit hat, an old
gray windbreaker, sweat pants, and gray leather boots. I thought you had to wear
holy-looking long robes and be barefoot to be enlightened! He sits down, peering
out at the group from behind his aviator sunglasses. I notice he has a heavy gray
beard and no front teeth. So much for my preconceptions about what enlightened
beings should look like.

We know that Robert has Parkinson's disease and can't speak very clearly, so
we're prepared when he begins speaking in a raspy voice that is barely decipher-
able. "It's good to be with you. I welcome you with all my heart." Despite the slur-
ring I can vaguely make out what he's saying. "Why are you here? You're looking
for something. You want to be happy. You're looking to change your life. You're
looking for something outside yourself. And as long as you do that, you'll never
find it. Truth, Reality, lies within you." He signals someone to put a chanting tape

into a small tape player and everyone listens to the squawky music. That's it for the talking.

My mind starts to ask all kinds of questions. *Who is this person I've driven 400 miles to see? Is his physical appearance just a smoke screen?* The music is followed by a short meditation. Blessedly, my hyperactive mind becomes still. To my surprise, when I come out of the meditation, Robert appears out of focus, almost as if he has dematerialized. "Are you happy?" I hear him say. "Are you really happy? You have no problems. You are all perfect just as you are. Stop thinking. Happiness is your real nature. You are happiness. Happiness is another word for you."

Robert is not your conventional spiritual teacher. He grew up in the Bronx, where as a young boy, he often woke up seeing a strange figure with white hair and a white beard at the foot of his bed, talking in a foreign language. At the age of fourteen he had a dramatic awakening experience in the middle of a math test. Soon after he came across a book with a photograph of Ramana Maharshi in it. He instantly recognized that this was the man at the foot of his bed. When he was sixteen he left home for California, where he met Yogananda, the author of *Autobiography of a Yogi*. Yogananda encouraged him to go to India, in search of his true teacher. Two years later, at age eighteen, Robert set off alone for India—a remarkable step in itself. He spent the next three years at Ramana Maharshi's ashram, until Ramana's death in 1950. He then wandered around India and the world for the next 30 years, before settling in America. He found interesting ways to support himself, such as managing an apartment building, without ever taking on a full-time job. Wherever he landed people would seek him out, eager to hear the truth. Once the group became too large, he would move on to a new place, not at all interested in attracting large numbers of seekers.

Robert asks if there are any questions. No one replies. "Cowards!" he mutters. It is obviously an "in" joke, because everyone laughs. He has someone read a section from a book about Ramana. Then, as suddenly as it began, the talk is over. People from the group come up to him to whisper greetings or hold his hand. I go up to him and say a few words about the Ramana Retreat Center, (imagining that I will receive all kinds of praise and recognition). All he says is, "How long are you here?" We clasp each other's hands and I look into his eyes.

At first I don't feel anything. I begin to wonder if all these people may be wrong. Perhaps he is just an old Hell's Angel who happened to wander in by mistake. But as I leave at the end of the evening, my mind is totally empty. It's as if someone has sucked it clean with a vacuum cleaner. All I'm aware of is this deep, unwavering silence and peace. "That's no ordinary nice old man," I say to Linda as we drive down the hill.

We plan to return for several more satsangs with Robert, but the next morning Linda wakes up with acute appendicitis and I have to rush her to the hospital. If you want to make God laugh, make plans.

Surfing the Silence
Inner Directions Conference, La Jolla, California, March 29, 2001

The leap from self to Awareness is difficult to make, however. It signifies the mystical union experienced by saints and described by poets, in which the separate self is left behind and dissolved into God, going home to what we really are.
Ram Dass

Linda and I went to numerous retreats led by Ram Dass, at Breitenbush Hot Springs and the Omega Institute. We always came away filled with inspiration and gratitude. In 1997 Ram Dass had a stroke that left him partially paralyzed. A year later we flew out to see him at an Inner Directions conference in La Jolla. It was the first time he appeared in public since the stroke. As he rolled onto the stage in his wheelchair, all four hundred people in the audience spontaneously rose to their feet and gave him a standing ovation. It was a heartfelt expression of love, because Ram Dass had profoundly touched the lives of every person in that room. For many he was the one who opened the door to a whole new world of spirituality.

Back in the early 1960's Ram Dass was a brilliant young professor at Harvard named Richard Alpert. Together with Timothy Leary he created a national stir when he and Leary were fired from their jobs at Harvard for experimenting with LSD. In 1967 he set off for India to meet holy men. When he returned several years later, he was no longer Richard Alpert, but Baba Ram Dass—Ram Dass meaning "servant of God." What an unforgettable image he made, sitting cross-legged before an audience of gray-suited businessmen, with his long flowing beard, traditional Indian clothing, and mala beads around his neck. He was the quintessential image of the Woodstock generation.

Over the next twenty-five years Ram Dass traveled the world, giving retreats and talks, bringing his message of love and service to thousands of people. His first book, *Be Here Now*, became a bible for many spiritual seekers during the 1970's and 80's. It was followed by many more books: *Grist for the Mill, The Journey of Awakening,* and *How Can I Help?* Spirituality was all so new, all so exciting—it was not yet big business. For me his retreats were like immersing myself in a warm bath with four hundred other people. Ram Dass regaled us with his tales of India and its saints. We laughed at his jokes, cried at his heart-opening stories, and shared in the ecstasy as we sang sacred Indian chants in Sanskrit. Through Ram Dass I discovered the depth and beauty of eastern spiritual teachings. He was wise enough not to take on disciples, wise enough not to say he was enlightened, and wise enough to let us laugh with him at his own human frailties.

As he rolled onto the stage in his wheelchair, many were thinking, "This is the end of an era." Ram Dass looks his familiar self—the bald head, the white mustache, the long strands of white hair down to his shoulders (wherever hair will still grow), the twinkling eyes, and the infectious smile. There is a delightful hint of mischievousness in his face—as if he is ready to laugh at himself and the craziness of the world, which he usually does.

We all wait patiently while a microphone is attached to his sweater.

The room falls silent.

"My primary method is *guru krippa*," he says with painful slowness. Where there was once a glib and facile flow of words, each word now comes forth with great effort. "It means 'grace of the guru.' My teacher had a funny attitude about grace. He used to say that suffering brings one close to God. Then I had this stroke. So—grace of the stroke."

As we struggle to adjust to his laborious speaking, we begin to hear what is behind the words. The message he has to share with us is somehow even more profound than when the words rolled off the tip of his tongue: "This illness gives me a ready-made excuse to be in silence. See what grace this stroke has been? So, I say to people like you, 'Come on in and surf the silence.' When you surf the silence inside, you come to the silent essence—which is God. Ah, to have a sickness that takes you to silence . . . ha, ha, ha. I don't want you to get jealous!"

As the audience laughs along with him, many have tears in their eyes. There was a sense of relief to see that it's still the same old Ram Dass, with his wit and playful sense of humor. But there's something new, an even greater sense of peace and spaciousness. Ram Dass is, as ever, leading the way for us all. Long ago he introduced us to an inner world of meditation and sacred chants. Then he showed us how to share our love in the world through selfless service. Now he is showing us how to enter the process of aging, sickness, and death with dignity, humor, and love in our hearts.

From Onions to Pearls
Inner Directions Conference, La Jolla, CA, March 30, 2001

How will you be after you're awakened? Exactly the same way you were before.
Your bills still don't get paid, you still don't get to meet your soul mate, you still
get stopped in traffic for tickets.
Satyam Nadeen

At the same Inner Directions conference where we heard Ram Dass, Linda and I attend a session given by Satyam Nadeen, an American spiritual teacher who looks like a benign version of Bob Hope. Nadeen is the author of *From Onions to Pearls* and *From Seekers to Finders*. His down-to-earth perspective on spiritual awakening and his irreverent sense of humor soon has us rolling the aisles.

He tells us the remarkable story of his life. In 1988, at the age of fifty-four, Nadeen (then Michael Clegg) found himself in a county jail in Florida, "The only white boy in a cell full of young, violent, black gangbangers." The room had no windows, no ventilation, and no air conditioning. The temperature seldom went below a sweltering 100 degrees. He was held in this hellhole for two years while awaiting sentencing. Every week there was a rape, a suicide, or a murder attempt. From there he went to a federal prison for three years, locked up with 1600 angry, violent men.

In his previous life, he had been a high living, jet-setting entrepreneur, with houses in Costa Rica and the US, an airplane, a yacht, a wife and a young daughter. He experimented with every fad and spiritual practice imaginable, from EST to Osho, to yoga and meditation, colonics, macrobiotics, channeling, and 40-day fasts. He was one of the first to take the drug Ecstasy, and after experiencing the power it had to open the heart to love, he set out on a mission to bring Ecstasy to the world. That was before it became illegal. The DEA didn't approve, and set out to make an example of him by arresting him and taking away all his possessions. They threatened to put his daughter in an orphanage. He was given a seven-and-a-half-year sentence in federal prison.

If nothing else, being in prison gave him a lot of time to read. One day he picked up a book by Ramesh Balsekar, called *Consciousness Speaks,* and had a profound awakening. "It was as if I had been sleepwalking my whole life and thinking I was an entity separate from God and all the others, when suddenly I just woke up and remembered that I am the Source of it all." Two weeks after his release from prison in 1996, Nadeen was invited to talk to a group of people in

Santa Fe. This began a new life as a spiritual teacher, traveling around the world to give retreats. A year later he published *From Onions to Pearls*, which soon became an underground bestseller.

Linda and I traveled to Florida for a weekend intensive with him. As we sat in a stuffy, airless hotel conference room with thirty other people, I kept thinking what it must be like to be stuck in a room this size for two years with thirty "gangbangers." Even one day—with very conscious men and women—is almost too much for me. And we had air conditioning!

Nadeen's approach to the intensive is to have each one of us tell the story of our own spiritual journey, and to share how the longing for God has manifested in our life. As the stories unfold, a beautiful and simple process of entrainment takes place. It becomes clear that we are all the same "One" talking, and that there is no difference between us. Nadeen himself is unpretentious and affirming, inviting us to embrace life as it is and to drop all concepts about enlightenment. "Everyone," he says, "by the very fact of being alive and conscious, is already that—pure enlightenment."

"But don't we need to have a mystical experience of God in order to awaken?" I ask, still stuck in the belief that it has to be some great cosmic orgasm. This is the same question I ask every teacher—it takes me a long time to get it.

"Awakening isn't the result of some big experience," he says, sitting relaxed in his Holiday Inn chair, wearing a sport shirt and slacks. "It's an effortless shift that happens over time. Source, or God, is waiting for the mango to get ripe enough to fall off the tree by itself. When that mango is ripe it falls off—not a day too soon or a day too late. You're in the chute. I predict that within a year you'll have made the shift."

"I feel stuck. I'm sick of all the searching. Nothing seems to have any meaning anymore."

"That's the dark night of the soul," Nadeen says. "That's the half-way point on the journey. It's a subtle process when all of the efforting you've done your whole life as the doer crumbles, along with your identity of who you thought you were as the doer."

"Yeah, that's it," I say, happy to have an explanation for my malaise.

"When you let go of who you thought you were, then you relax into this incredible, delicious space of just being ordinary. The driving force of being special that pushed you all your life into fixing and making better is gone."

My mind goes tilt. *Being ordinary? My God, I've fought my whole life to be special. All I do is strive to be better. Someone is giving me permission just to be who I am!*

After the retreat is over, it feels like the journey is finally getting a lot simpler. It is more about "undoing" than about "doing." I begin to see how all the concepts I've accumulated about enlightenment, spiritual practices, yoga, and meditation have been more of a hindrance than a help. What a novel idea—relax in my own being!

This Is It
The Omega Institute, Rheinbeck, NY, May 31, 1998

You already are free. You already are at peace. You already are what you are seeking. And you are not who you think you are. So stop. And see for yourself.
Gangaji

I have no idea how many retreats I went on with Gangaji. They were always different and I never ceased to be amazed by her awesome ability to express the inexpressible. During her retreats she invites participants with questions to come up and sit next to her on what is referred to as the "hot seat." Taking the hot seat is always a risk. Anything can—and usually does—happen. It's not like getting up in a workshop or a classroom, where you can hide behind intellectual concepts. Gangaji is above all a teacher of truth, and like the Archangel Gabriel she wields the sword of truth relentlessly, revealing any lies you are hiding behind. "I do not take this lightly," she says. "You must be willing to be true to the Truth." I've seen those who have come up and been honored for their wisdom, and others who have metaphorically had their heads cut off.

This retreat I'm determined to take the hot seat—even if it means making an ass of myself. More than anything I want to be FREE. I want to make the final cut—now! Today is the first day of a seven-day silent retreat. I should have known better than to get up and share on the first day. Everyone is still shell-shocked at being thrown into seven days of silence, where the only opportunity to speak is to get up and share in front of the group with Gangaji during one of the morning gatherings. I can tell that Gangaji is in a serious, no-nonsense frame of mind. If I had any sense at all, I would have waited until the sixth day, when everyone is flying high at the end of the retreat and the room is a mushy puddle of love. If I got up to share then, all I would need to do is sit there and smile like a grinning idiot. But I want to share now. Heart pounding, I raise my hand.

My reptilian brain is screaming *Danger! Danger!* as I make my way to the stage at the front of the room. I do my best to appear relaxed and at ease as I sit down next to Gangaji in front of three hundred people—an array of video cameras and lights pointed in my direction and a microphone a few inches from my mouth. There is an underlying sense of terror beneath my casual, laid-back appearance.

"Finally!" I exclaim, once I sit down. "I've had my hand raised for the last four retreats, but you never call on me!"

Everyone laughs, including Gangaji.

So far, so good.

"Well, today is a good day to die," I say, "and I need your help."

With these few words I have unwittingly set myself up for disaster. First, I am saying that I am ready to be crucified—to have my ego slain. She will show no mercy. By adding the words "I need your help" I am suggesting that she can somehow do it for me. In that one sentence I have given away all sense of who I am and projected onto her the role of omnipotent teacher. It is an old pattern of mine that kicks in like a Pavlovian response. I have shifted into the role of respectful and loving devotee. In my mind, every word she utters is the absolute truth—and I know nothing. I am overtaken by a crippling desire for her approval. With my every gesture and my every word, I reek of neediness.

I stumble on. "I see how terrified I am of falling into that place of Pure Awareness. I've stupefied myself and sedated myself to keep from falling in. I feel like I'm hanging on to this rope where there are only a few strands left before it breaks . . . and I let go into an endless free fall. I know that there's no 'me' and no rope—but I can't let go."

Gangaji looks at me directly and says, "Don't 'know' that there's no you and no rope. If you know it intellectually, or even have a past experience of it, what you're clinging to is a belief—but it's like clinging to a piece of cardboard."

"Hmmm."

I'm beginning to lose it. This is not going the way I expected. My mind is starting to freeze and go numb. I start to implode. *She knows the truth and I don't.* Rather than reveal what's *really* going on inside, I blunder onwards, pretending to understand everything she says.

"So, in this experience of hanging by a rope," Gangaji continues, "What is it that is feared? If the worst were to come true, and the rope was to break, what might happen?"

"Sitting right here, it feels like I would fall into ecstasy, into pure . . ."

"Good," she interrupts. "Many people think that fears are about pain and suffering, but the fears about bliss are equally powerful—because either way *you* are annihilated. In my usual way I invite you to experience what you fear, so that you can see what the reality of it is. Are you willing to experience this ecstasy that you fear so much?"

Nothing I've rehearsed is going to work anymore. This is the moment I am terrified of. She is asking me to go into my worst fear in front of three hundred people. It feels like stepping off a cliff . . . oh shit.

She stops talking and stares steadfastly into my eyes. I gaze into her eyes, and my body suddenly jerks with the energy passing between us. Time stops, even though I'm aware somewhere of sitting in front of all these people. We hold our gaze for what seems like an eternity. The room is deadly silent.

The words come tumbling out of my mouth. "This is it?"

In that instant all my preconceived notions about spiritual awakening crumble into dust. Awakening is not about fireworks and lightening. With the next breath comes the startling revelation, "Wow. This *is* it!"

Gangaji smiles. After a moment of silence she says, "Then there is the capacity to see what is deeper than the ecstasy. Who is experiencing the fear, who is experiencing the ecstasy, who is dying?"

"No one," I say. "There's no one there."

"What is there? What is that 'no one there'? Now the opportunity is to directly experience what is true, to be able to say 'I don't know anything.' When you don't need to know anything, there is a knowledge that is pure, free of past and future. It is fresh. It is alive. This is meeting yourself. I wish you that."

She smiles and takes my hand. I begin to feel a glimmer of safety, as if I've just been pulled back from a yawning abyss. "Thank you Gangaji. I'm so grateful for all that you've given me over these years." I'm barely able to take in the beautiful affirmation she has so freely offered.

Then, without realizing it, I spring from that empty presence straight back into total ego-identification, like a taut rubber band going *thwack*. This would have been the perfect moment to get up and return to my seat. But I want more. I *need* more.

This is my undoing.

"By the way," I say, making an impulsive decision to tell her a story I had rehearsed beforehand, "I have a belated report. Do you remember when I asked about the idea of sex, wine, and chocolate being a path to God?"

"Yes, I remember that. It was in Maui, when we first met."

"You said to try it out and to report back on whether it works or not. Well, after five years, I'm happy to report that the chocolate is beginning to lose some of its appeal."

Everyone laughs uproariously.

"Well, that's the best of the three, anyway!"

More laughter. *I'm entertaining everyone! Gangaji likes me! Aren't I great!*

"I realize I may not get up here for another four years . . ." More laughter.

This is going even better than I imagined! I take a sip from the water glass on the table between us as if I'm settling in for a long stay. *Oh no! I just drank from her water glass. No one has EVER done that. What a sacrilege! Aaaargh!*

Suddenly I notice that Gangaji is not buying into any of it. Satsang is not about indulging the ego. She totally ignores me and picks up her stack of letters, ready to move on. Then she turns to the group and says, "I can't get him down! Everyone loves being up here." To me she says, "Just bask in it."

The audience remains silent, disapproving. Now that she's turned her attention from me, as far as they are concerned, I don't exist. Their entire attention is on Gangaji. If she ignores me, they will ignore me too. I'm about to ask, 'Is there any mail for me?' when my sense of propriety snaps back in. I sheepishly step down from the stage and return to my seat.

The next few days are a self-induced hell. As I pass people in silence I imagine them thinking, "There goes that jerk who made such an ass of himself in front of Gangaji." Of course, this rampant paranoia exists only in my imagination. None of them could care less. But it puts me face to face with my desperate need for approval. The word usually reserved for this kind of experience is "ego-burn." And I still have another six days ahead of me with no escape from my own worst enemy!

I have plenty of time to think about that moment of revelation when I realized that "This is it." How could "This be it" when a minute later I am so totally identified with my ego? How could I "lose" it? The spiritual journey is seldom neat and tidy, where there is a single moment of revelation, and the ego drops away once and for all like an old sack of potatoes. We would all like it to be that way, but most of us stumble along blindfolded through the maze, going from insight to insight, until eventually we realize that there is nothing to be "lost," because it was there all along.

The retreat ended and it wasn't until several years later that the full significance of "This is it" struck home. I was walking down the long driveway at the farm to get the morning paper. The early morning sun was peeking over the tops of the trees, lighting up the dewdrops in golden, sparkling light. The beauty of the scene overwhelmed me. I took a sharp in-breath. *This is it!* The knowing came to me, not as a thought, not as a feeling, but as something beyond the mind. It dropped in with a KERCHUNK. There was no holding on to it, because the "it" was that instant of recognition. As soon as I tried to grab it, it was gone. I thought to myself, "How could every moment be a *This is it?*

For the next weeks, I find myself going about my daily activities, with *This is it* popping into mind at the most unexpected moments—opening the door of the fridge . . . *This is it*, brushing my teeth . . . *This is it*, turning on the computer . . . *This is it*. Instead of thinking about every action, I'm totally in the moment with whatever is happening. There's no past and no future. I don't question what I'm doing before I do it, and I seldom think about what I did after I've done it. Is *This* it?

Could it be this simple?

CHAPTER 17

THE END OF THE ROAD

Eckhart Tolle

The Ground of Being
Nelson County, Virginia, May 27, 2001

The essential basis of self-realization is the total rejection of the individual as an independent entity.
Ramesh Balsekar

"All this nonduality stuff is bullshit," Jack says, taking a sip of red wine.

"Bullshit?" I say excitedly. "I love it!"

"You talk about how you aren't your thoughts, you aren't your feelings, you aren't this body. But I love my thoughts. I love my feelings!"

Linda and I are back with our friends, Jack and Judy, in their spectacular mountaintop home, having one of our never-ending discussions about spirituality as we sit around the table after dinner. Jack served his mouth-watering orange-roasted chicken with mushrooms, figs, onions, potatoes, and carrots; Judy made a fresh organic salad; Linda and I brought a decadent chocolate mousse for dessert. Our friendship with Jack and Judy continues to deepen. We've watched them go from ardent Sai Baba devotees to embracing (or trying to embrace) the radical teachings of nonduality.

"But who is it that has thoughts and feelings?" Linda asks, squirming in her seat with discomfort. Linda hates sitting in straight-backed dining room chairs because her entire body starts to ache after an hour.

"That's just more word games," Jack says. "I'm Jack and I'm happy to be Jack."

"Jack, you have to live in the paradox," Judy says, her intelligent hazel eyes radiating a sense of playfulness.

"That's just more bullshit," Jack says, waving his hand dismissively. "You keep saying you are One, but that means you are nothing but an automaton. I don't want to be an automaton. It's boring."

Letting out a sigh, I say, "Like it or not Jack, you're nothing but bi-pedal feeding tube when you get down to it." I take another sip of wine. God, it tastes awful. Jack, who can afford $100 bottles, always buys the cheapest wine he can find. I think he actually prefers it.

"I know what you're talking about," Judy interjects. "We're all puppets and we don't have any choice in what we do."

"That's crazy. We always have a choice," Jack insists.

"Yes, Jack," I say, desperately trying to communicate what I know to be true from my own experience. "We make choices, but they are only *apparent* choices. It's all happening in Consciousness. You still want to identify yourself as a wave, when you are the vastness of the ocean."

Jack shakes his head. *Damn, I can see that he's not getting it and doesn't want to get it. Why do I care so much? Why can't I just let him have his own viewpoint? Perhaps because I still don't really get all this myself. At times it feels like I'm parroting back all the books I've just read.*

"Well, I'm 'choosing' to lie on the floor," Linda says, getting up from the table and lying down on the thick plush carpet. All three of us know how hard it is for her to sit up with the pain she is in, and there is scarcely a break in the conversation.

"Jack, you can be so stubborn at times," Judy says.

"I don't want to be the drop in the ocean," Jack says, brushing his fingers through his white hair. "I don't want Jack to disappear forever."

"Even if being 'ocean' means you can be at peace?" I ask.

"I'd rather be a wave named Jack and take my chances," Jack replies, "even if it means crashing on the shore."

"I'd rather be peace," Judy says. "Sometimes I can feel it, but then it goes away. I get it about 98 percent of the time."

"Wait a minute," Linda says, lying on the floor, her blond hair and long purple velour dress standing out against the deep orange of the carpet. "How can you say 'I' have peace and that 'I' lose it? You can't lose the peace. You can't lose any of it. You *are* it!"

"What do you mean?" Judy asks.

"Think of it this way," Linda says, raising her arms straight up and bringing her wrists together to form a V with her hands. "Think of this as the bottom of a pond. The bottom of the pond supports all the life within it—from the fish to the algae to the frogs and the insects. No matter how stirred up the water may be, or who is being eaten, the bottom of the pond is always at peace. Without the bottom, there would be no pond. It's that which gives life as well as an integral part of the life of the pond itself. Someone may throw a stone into the pond, but the bottom remains untouched."

"But what happens when a developer comes along and builds a parking lot over it?" Jack asks. We all laugh uproariously.

"The earth's still there," Linda continues. "In the same way, who we are remains untouched by all the apparent events taking place around us. Just as the bottom of the pond cannot be destroyed, that peace within us is ever present. It is the ground of being."

Getting tired of all the talk, I look out the huge windows as the sun slips quietly behind the Blue Ridge Mountains and the sky turns a deep cobalt blue, with faint wisps of orange streaked across it. A red-tailed hawk flies by, lit by the last rays of sunshine.

"And it's all happening right now," I say, more to myself then to them. "Just look out the window. This is all there is, just *This!* It's totally, fully, vibrantly alive. It includes the mountains, the sky, all four of us, the carpet, the food, the table, the air. It includes peace and it includes chaos."

"And Jack?" Jack asks.

"And Jack," I add. "You can't escape being the bottom of that pond even if you want to. It's who you are."

Passionate Presence
Mount Ayr Farm, Virginia, November 3, 1999

But the truth is much more simple and ordinary. You are no longer looking
for some peak experience like a junkie out for a high. You are at ease in just being
and it is glorious enough.
Catherine Ingram

At a Ram Dass retreat at Breitenbush, Oregon, Linda and I meet a teacher named Catherine Ingram, the author of *Passionate Presence*, and are drawn by her warmth, wisdom, and complete lack of pretention. "It would be fun to invite her to come to Charlottesville and give a talk," I suggest to Linda. She agrees. Catherine happily accepts, and makes plans to stay with us for four days. With the help of a few friends, we arrange a space, rent the chairs, and get the word out to friends.

To our surprise, over seventy people show up for the evening session and it's an unqualified success. Once it's over, we wrap up and drive the twenty miles back to the farm. Over some ice cream and hot chocolate sauce, Catherine, Linda, and I recap the evening. We're a little high and giddy after all the excitement.

"Did you notice that person asking all those questions about spiritual practices?" I ask, savoring the delicious contrast of hot fudge and cold ice cream.

"Oh him!" replies Catherine. "He seemed a little strange."

"Yeah, he sees himself as the 'best meditator' in Charlottesville," Linda laughs. "He went out with a friend of ours and drove her crazy. He was so busy meditating all the time that he couldn't be in relationship."

Catherine gives one of her delightful laughs, "Ah, one of those!"

"He was so shocked when you said that spiritual practices wouldn't bring about spiritual awakening."

Catherine should know. She was a Buddhist meditator for years and cofounder of the highly regarded Insight Meditation Society in Barre, Massachusetts. It wasn't until she went to India and met Papaji that she found what she describes as "awakened awareness."

"Some people become so identified with their practices," Catherine says. "It can be the one thing that holds them back. You can't avoid your true nature even if you wanted to."

After being with teachers who demand all kinds of special treatment—from first-class travel, to 600-count pillowcases, to specially cooked food—I am happy to see how relaxed and laid-back Catherine is. If we drink coffee in the morning, she has coffee; if we eat lunch out, she'll try the meatloaf special; if we have a glass of wine with dinner she'll join us. We spend most of our time laughing, telling stories, eating, playing, and gossiping (there's nothing quite so much fun as spiritual gossip). "This is like one long pajama party," she jokes.

I watch more of my concepts about spiritual teachers go down the drain. Our time together cuts the last threads of any beliefs I have about what it means to be awake *right now*. I realize Catherine would be just as happy if we had been strict vegetarians, spent all our time in silence, and only drank tea. What I saw was her willingness to be in the moment with *whatever* was showing up, without any concepts or rules. It is clear that she lives from that place of what she calls "passionate presence." Because she is so at ease in just being, I find myself comfortable with who I am. It is all so effortless. Through her actions she reveals what it is to live in the fullness of love. This is Catherine's greatest gift—just being herself.

A Heavenly Buffet
Inner Directions Conference, La Jolla, California, March 3, 2001

You're sitting in paradise, believing that it's somewhere else.
Tony Parsons

In 2001 Linda and I fly to California to attend the Inner Directions conference held in La Jolla. This is an annual event that brings together nondual spiritual teachers from America, England, and Europe. Each presenter has a morning or afternoon session to do their thing—usually a short talk followed by questions from the audience. Between presentations Krishna Das comes onstage and chants, Coleman Bark reads poems by Rumi, and Rabbi Rami Shapiro entertain us with his jokes. It is the academy awards of the spiritual world—except that no one gets a golden statue. As Ram Dass says, "I used to go to India to make this happen." It is pure joy to be with others who share the same love of truth, celebrating five hundred hearts laughing as one. Where else can you meet so many different teachers in one place, from Eckhart Tolle, to Byron Katie, Adyashanti, and so many others? It is like sampling from a heavenly buffet.

More than any other teacher, I wanted to hear Tony Parsons, who has written a book called *The Open Secret* (his other book, *As It Is* had not yet been published). I wasn't disappointed. Tony soon has the audience entranced with his self-deprecating sense of humor and his easy-going manner. "Liberation isn't one fixed space," he says. "It embraces everything, from anger, to sadness, to thought. But what arises is what 'I am,' which is awareness. So go on hearing the message that you are helpless. Go on feeling that longing—just let it be there."

Unlike so many other teachers he doesn't promise a perfect life in la-la land. He's inviting us to give up. "Just give up," he says, "and there is the Beloved. The Beloved is always there. It is perfect loving. There is no way that anyone in this room can avoid 'what is.' You are the divine expression."

My heart sings with his words, yet I know his message is not for everyone. During the question period a man asks what kind of "practice" he can do in order to get there. Tony has just spent his entire talk saying there is nowhere to get to, but this fellow obviously had trouble getting it. "They have ears, but cannot hear," Tony answers with a smile. The man walks out of the room in disgust. Tony responds to another question with a lightness that has the audience howling with laughter. "We have a picture of how an awakened being should be—serving others, always gentle and kind, speaking softly, and moving slowly. Well, that's bullshit!" More laughter. When asked why he goes around teaching, he disarmingly replies (along with a wink), "It's because of the money."

After his presentation we have a friendly talk. It's like meeting with an old friend. He responds warmly and enthusiastically to the idea of a book entitled *Ultimate Happiness*. Tony is the furthest thing from a self-important guru one could ever imagine. He is almost offhandedly "normal" in the way he talks, dresses, and enjoys life. Born in London, England, he lived a very conventional life—even working as a car salesman—until one day he was walking across a park and became aware that, with each footstep, it was totally new. "Then the next footstep was there and then it wasn't," he recounts. "This was stunning, you know. Right at this moment, this was the first time this had happened. And it will never be like that again. Isn't that *amazing*!" Even Tony's experience of awakening seems unusually "normal."

But there is nothing "normal" about his message. Tony is ruthless in insisting that there is "no one" there; it is all just Consciousness manifesting. When people ask, "What about the suffering in the world?" he replies, "Suffering happens, but no 'one' suffers." He is also clear that this understanding is available to everyone, and that everything—*everything*—that happens is an invitation to awakening, whether it's going out for "fish and chips" or sitting in satsang. For him we are all dreamed characters in a divine play: "You've already joined the club. You're already in the drama. All that needs to be discovered is that there isn't anyone there, there is just the drama happening. It's as close as that. Simply drop the idea that there's anyone in the drama."

Tony has a way of presenting his radical nondual message with deceptive charm and an irrepressible sense of humor. Like going before a wise old Aikido master, I find myself unexpectedly flipped upside down on the mat before I even know what's happening—and quite enjoy being flipped. He leaves my ego with no place to stand and does so while keeping me laughing the whole time. I love his earthy zest for living and his refusal to get caught up in the idea that he is more special than anyone else. He is one of the few teachers who is willing to speak out about what he considers to be the phoniness of many of those who claim to be enlightened.

Yet he always comes back to the deepest truth: "Everything is divine," he says. "Everything comes from awareness. Everything is the Beloved. Wherever your awareness rests, it rests on the Beloved. There isn't anywhere where the Beloved is not."

The Power of Now
Inner Directions Conference, La Jolla, California, March 3, 2001

When you surrender to what is and so become fully present, the past ceases to have
any power. The realm of Being, which had been obscured by the mind, then opens
up. A great stillness arises within you, an unfathomable sense of peace.
Eckhart Tolle

The other teacher I am curious to see is Eckhart Tolle, who had recently self-published a little book called *The Power of Now*. This was long before he appeared on Oprah and sold millions of copies the world over. I wait, along with an auditorium full of people, for him to appear. An uncomfortable looking chair sits alone in the middle of the huge stage with some exotic flowers on either side. Suddenly there is an expectant hush as the lights dim, and a short, slightly hunched man walks out wearing loafers, dark trousers, an open-necked shirt, and a European style vest. He looks more like a philosophy professor about to give a lecture on Hegel then a spiritual teacher. He sits on the chair and looks around the room with a neutral expression. No big smiles or high fives to those he recognizes in the audience.

The room becomes quiet and he begins talking as if in mid-sentence: "No expectancy . . . not waiting for anything to happen . . . being completely present here," he says in a slow, measured voice. "We're not here to learn more knowledge. We're really here to relinquish concepts and ideas—ultimately to relinquish thought. What is stillness other than the state of consciousness that is free of noise?"

Everyone listens attentively. The clarity and directness of his words reveal a deeper strength that is not apparent in his fragile form. "For most of us," he says, "our world revolves around the 'little me'—our sense of personal identity. If there's a 'little me' sitting here in the audience, there may be one or two thinking, 'he may be talking about everyone else, but *I'm* OK.'" His delightful sense of humor begins to show, as he punctuates his remarks with his delicate hands in little chipmunk-like gestures. He takes short little in-breaths when he laughs, as if he is surprised at what he has just said. He probably is. The audience is enchanted and hanging on every word. I find him so endearing. I want to take him home with me.

When Eckhart speaks, it's as if he's having a private conversation with himself. He's not trying to impress anyone, nor does he really seem to care whether anyone gets what he has to say. The words just come from his mouth in a kind of free-form association, one thing leading to the next. There's no sense of being preached to or being told what to do. There's an openness and a spaciousness between the words that allows a gentle inner shift to happen for the listener. It reveals the silence behind the words. What's happening here is all the more remarkable, I realize, because he doesn't use any of the eastern terms that most teachers sprinkle throughout their talks. What a relief—no dharma, no karma, no satsang, no sadhana, no gurus, no lineage—he's speaking in real English!

After the talk I'm standing outside the men's room when he happens to walk by. Our eyes meet and I reach out my hand. He takes my hand in his and we just look in each other's eyes from a place beyond time. After what seems like minutes, I smile and say, "Thank you." He nods his head and gives a slight smile, as if he's surprised to find himself standing in the hallway. We go our different ways. Nothing more needs to be said.

Acceptance of What Is
Mt. Ayr Farm, VA, November 30, 2000

The experience of awakening or enlightenment is a transcendent event. It is one in which there is a shift completely from the personal to the impersonal.
Wayne Liquorman

There are many ways of going deeper into the nondual teachings without flying all over the country or going to India. Every week Linda and I hold a gathering at our house with ten or so friends where we get together to meditate, share our spiritual journey, and talk about different teachers. Today the flavor of the month is Wayne Liquorman, a somewhat daunting teacher who never hesitates to tell the truth as he sees it. We slip in a video of a talk he gave in Berkeley, California, before a small group of people.

The video begins with an intense bearded young man raising his hand and saying, "Hi Wayne. My name is Bernie. I've had those experiences of letting go too."

"Uh-hmm," Wayne responds. He is slouched back in his chair—a big, imposing man with a nearly bald head and a dark beard.

Doing his best to impress everyone, Bernie keeps on talking, "I've had experiences of a very deep nature . . ."

"Uh-hmm."

"I'd be interested to know if these experiences are what you're speaking about."

"Uh-hmm." Wayne sits there stroking his beard, clearly disinterested.

"Why doesn't someone shut Bernie up?" Linda interjects.

We all laugh, having been in workshops with other "Bernies."

Wayne continues to stroke his beard, repeating "Uh-hmm, Uh-hmm." as he watches Bernie patter on and on. When Bernie finally stops, Wayne begins to talk, totally ignoring everything Bernie has said: "The model I use is the pendulum."

As Wayne talks, he holds his elbow high and lets his forearm dangle down like a pendulum. "In any life there is a swing between these two poles," he says, swinging his arm back and forth. "That's the nature of life. If one's identification as an individual doer is at the far end of this pendulum where my hand is, as it swings, so swings you." Everyone in the video laughs; we laugh too.

"That's me!" exclaims Sarah, who is watching Wayne for the first time.

Wayne continues, "If you're feeling intense suffering or you're feeling intense joy, you're probably at the bottom of the pendulum. There is a very clear sense of 'this is happening to me' as you swing from one extreme to the other."

"Just like the people yelling at each other on *The Jerry Springer Show*," I throw in. "You can't get much lower on the pendulum than that!"

"Once there is a sense of dis-identification—even at the intellectual level—what happens is that we move up the pendulum," Wayne says. "Even though the swing continues, the movement, from the perspective of the individual, is much smaller. There is always movement up and down though . . . it's a *greased* pendulum!"

"That's my life!" Jim laughs over the sound of Wayne talking. "All I seem to do is work my way up to the top, then slide back down again."

Wayne continues: "You can get right to the top of the pendulum, where you see that none of your actions have any sense of personal doership. But, as long as there is identification with the pendulum, there is still a sense that they are happening to 'me'. There is still a 'me' to whom these things are happening. The final step is in the movement from the pendulum to the fulcrum. That is a transcendent movement. It literally has nothing to do with the pendulum. The pendulum goes on swinging. The locus of the identification has shifted irrevocably from the pendulum."

"I don't buy this," I say over Wayne's voice. "I still believe there can be awakening at the top of the pendulum. It's not an on/off switch."

"Well, it makes sense in terms of physics," Stan says. "I wrote about that in my book." Stan is a physics professor emeritus at the University of Virginia and has just published a book called *A Course in Consciousness*.

Wayne stops talking for a moment. His eyebrows curl up and a strange smile comes over his face.

"He looks just like the devil!" Cynthia blurts out.

"Oh my God, I was just thinking the same thing!" says Sarah.

Wayne provokes an interesting response in people. He is a large, gruff man with a black beard and a boisterous belly laugh. With a patch over one eye he'd play well as a pirate. His spiritual training was, to say the least, unconventional. He spent nineteen years as an alcoholic and coke addict before waking up one morning and realizing that it was time to stop. He happened to attend a gathering with Ramesh Balsekar one evening and "fell hopelessly in love with the guy." He arranged Ramesh's American tours and edited his first book, *Consciousness Speaks*. He then went on to write his own books, including *NO WAY for the Spiritual "Advanced"* under the pseudonym of Ram Tzu and *Acceptance of What Is*.

In the video Wayne picks up a copy of his book and reads something he's written: "Ultimately, all attempts at discussing Truth leave you sounding like a fortune cookie."

Suddenly I realize that the whole time we've been watching the video, our dog Luke has been going from person to person around the room, looking up at each one with his big brown eyes until they give him a pet on the head. Everyone responds differently. Sarah warmly hugs him, Jim gives him a perfunctory pet, and Stan recoils. No matter what the response, Luke remains perfectly serious, going from one person to the next and looking into their eyes from a place of total presence.

I smile.

All the time we've been watching a so-called spiritual teacher presenting a message of "Truth" on videotape, the true teacher—in the form of a dog—has been giving his blessing to everyone here. And no one even notices.

Eternity Now
Treasure Island, Florida, February 29, 2000

We are hardwired for happiness. Its absence is the driver of all action. The search for happiness cannot occur without unhappiness, or suffering. It is this desire to complete ourselves, to make ourselves whole and complete, this notion that we are incomplete as we are, that motivates us to "do."
Francis Lucille

Linda and I wake up to sunshine and quiet. The palm trees are rustling in the wind outside the window of our condo on Treasure Island in Florida. The air is warm and moist. A small tugboat is making its way up the coastal waterway. Less than twenty-four hours ago we were back in Virginia in snow and ice. Did we somehow recreate the molecules that constitute reality overnight? If everything is an emanation of the mind, perhaps I'm really somewhere else and am projecting this whole scene with my mind?

I've signed up for a weeklong retreat with Francis Lucille, a French-born spiritual teacher. But why? I've attended so many retreats over the past few years. How many more do I have to go to before I get it? Who knows? Maybe this will be the last? The first session is being held in a large rectangular room with floor to ceiling glass windows overlooking the Gulf of Mexico. Participants are chatting in small groups. Most of them seem to know each other. Francis is busy setting up his own sound system with the help of his wife Laura. Unlike most teachers, he doesn't have a whole crew of volunteers doing his work for him. I find a place by the window and sit quietly with my eyes closed. My mind calms down. I'm relieved that I don't need to chat or make conversation.

I open my eyes and see Francis unceremoniously take his place at the front of the room and sit cross-legged on the floor. No dramatic entry with devotees holding doors open for him, no flowers around him, no pictures, no books—just a glass of water by his side. It's all very Zen. Francis is a slim, handsome dark-haired man in his forties, clean cut and healthy. There is a simple elegance about him that carries over into the way he dresses—a white polo shirt and khaki trousers.

He begins talking in his distinctive French accent. "When you make enlightenment an object," he says, "you will never find it. You are placing it off in the future somewhere, when it is right here."

Born in France, Francis was a pilot in the French Air Force, then a physicist and a diplomat for the French Government. I'm amused to think that he was a student in Paris at the same time I was—in the sixties. After a profound spiritual awakening, he gave up his career and moved to Middletown, California. He has been teaching all over Europe and the US for the last ten years.

"Your thoughts are not real," he says. "Your feelings are not real. All you need to do is accept the possibility that you are not a 'thing.' The truth is completely impersonal."

There is a long pause. He seems to search in some far off place for the right words. "The mind has to understand that enlightenment is totally beyond its reach. When this is understood, the mind becomes naturally quiet, because it has no place to go. This spontaneous and effortless stillness of the mind is pure welcoming. In this openness lies the opportunity to be knowingly that which we are."

I look around at the other participants. They are focused on him with rapt attention. I can tell by the blank expressions on some of their faces that they are hearing Francis for the first time. Francis is cerebral, and not for everyone. Others have been attending these same retreats for years. They nod knowingly as Francis talks. *How often do they need to hear these words before they get it?* I think. *A hundred times—a thousand?* A light goes on. *They don't want to get it! They want this search to go on forever. They'll be hearing these same words years from now, and still nodding their heads.*

Someone raises their hand and asks, "Does life have any purpose?"

There is a peal of laughter as the veteran retreat-goers turn to look at each other, as if to say, "Such a naïve question—do you remember when we used to ask questions like that?" Francis is unfazed. He ignores the tittering and honors the questioner with respect.

"Real life has no purpose," he says in his deliberate, slow manner of speaking. "Real life is pure joy, pure freedom. Now, if by life you mean this existence between birth and death, it could be said that its purpose is to know the truth."

As I sit there, it suddenly occurs to me that I don't need to hear this anymore. Maybe I've heard it for the hundredth time, maybe the thousandth. Maybe I'm bored with it all—whatever. It doesn't matter, I realize. I'm done. FINITO. FINISHED. It's time to say ENOUGH! The answer is not going to be found in this retreat or the next one. It won't come when the next teacher looks into my eyes and gives me a hit of shakti. It won't come when the next teacher says, "Peter, you're finally enlightened, you have my blessing—now go out and teach." Nor will it come when I do all kinds of austerities and spiritual practices that supposedly will bring me to awakening. These are just other ways of putting off what is right here, right now.

After the session I share this new understanding with Linda as we walk along the boardwalk back to our condo.

"I'm finally ready to call off the search," I say, squinting in the bright sunlight. "I'm finished with retreats." My bare feet are deliciously warm from walking on the sun-heated wooden planks of the boardwalk. I glance over at the wide stretch of beach and the Gulf of Mexico beyond. The wind is whipping the water into whitecaps and it looks muddy brown. A huge dredging machine pounds in pilings offshore: CLONK, CLONK, CLONK.

"Well, at least you can be in the retreat," Linda says. "I can't even go into the room because of that toxic paint! But I'm just as happy to have my own retreat, watching the lizards and the birds."

"I like Francis. He doesn't seem to have any of the usual stuff around money, sex, or power." Over the years Linda and I have developed fine levels of distinction about spiritual teachers. Anything slightly off key leaps out like a flashing red light.

"I was thinking the same thing," says Linda. "He lives what he teaches. But what bothers me is that he talks about how we'll have perfect health and a transparent body if we let go of the body-mind identification. He promises that we'll all go to happy la-la land if we awaken. Ramana Maharshi would never say that. Bodies get sick and die. That's what they're supposed to do."

I let out a big sigh. "I'm *finally* getting that there's no such thing as the perfect teacher who has all the answers"

"They're all human, sometimes more human than we'd like."

"I've learned something from each one, but *they* can't do it for me."

"Only you can."

The boardwalk rises up over a dry creek bed, forming a small bridge. On either side there are low sand dunes covered with shrubs.

I'm so much in my head that I forgot where I am! Suddenly I start to notice all the life, all the smells, all the beauty that is around me. "Mmmm . . . Take a deep breath—salt air!"

Linda smiles and closes her eyes, breathing in. We lean on the railing, silent for a few moments. In that silence the world comes alive—butterflies struggling in the wind, seagulls flying overhead, the sand shifting at our feet, a vole darting through the underbrush.

"All this has been here all along," Linda says softly. "We just couldn't see it."

"*This* is why I came here," I say, putting my arm around her and looking into her eyes. "For this . . . *This*! The love is everywhere."

We hold each other tight, merging our bodies together. I nestle my face in her sun-drenched hair, smelling its sweet scent, the scent of the ocean, of life itself.

The sense of presence is so close that I can reach out and touch it. This is the Beloved—a vast impersonal awareness. There is only the Beloved seeing the Beloved. My seeing is all "seeing"; I AM that seeing. My hearing is all "hearing"; I AM that hearing. It is effortless. It is ever-present. It is who I am. I don't have to go anywhere, do anything, or be with anyone to realize this. It's right here, right now.

Where is there to go after this taste? I stick it out to the end of the retreat, but I can't get into all the camaraderie of being with other seekers who are on "the search" together. It's time to go home to Virginia and just be quiet. The words of an old Chinese proverb came to mind: "Teachers open the door, but you must enter yourself."

PART III

LIVING IT

When I see I am nothing that is wisdom and when I see that I am everything that is love. And between those two my life moves.
Nisargadatta

CHAPTER 18

COMING HOME

Peter and Lambs

The Shiny Red Mower
Charlottesville, Virginia, April 1, 2002

You don't want to look. If you look, you lose control of the life that you are so
precariously holding together.
Anthony de Mello

In March 2000, after the last retreat with Francis Lucille in Florida, I stopped running around the country in search of the newest and hottest spiritual teacher, and began a seven-year period of staying mostly on the farm. I spend my time writing, hanging out with Linda and friends, and tending to my sheep and goats.

Life is occupied with simple things, like bush-hogging the fields with the tractor, clearing trails, or taking care of the Mellen menagerie of a dozen sheep, three goats, two cows, and one chicken. When I drive to the nearby town of Scottsville for supplies (population 564), I'm just another guy in dirty old jeans and work boots buying feed for his animals. Nobody at the co-op or the hardware store knows anything about me, or seems to care (though they probably know a lot more than they let on). After being an apparent "somebody" for many years as an author, professor, filmmaker, workshop leader, and "very important" director of a retreat center, I suddenly am "nobody."

It reminds me of the old joke about the rabbi who thought he was somebody:

One day a rabbi, in a frenzy of religious passion, rushes in before the ark, falls to his knees, and starts beating his breast, crying, "I'm nobody! I'm nobody!"

The cantor of the synagogue, impressed by this example of spiritual humility, joins the rabbis on his knees. "I'm nobody! I'm nobody!"

The custodian, watching from the corner, can't restrain himself either. He joins the other two on his knees, calling out, "I'm nobody! I'm nobody!"

At which point the rabbi, nudging the cantor with his elbow, points at the custodian and says, "Look who thinks he's a nobody!"

At first I feel invisible and unseen—like I've disappeared off the edge of the planet. It awakens a primal fear in me—the fear of annihilation. The little child in me is crying out, "Look at me, look at me—if you don't notice me, I'll die!" On a conscious level I know that this "somebody" called Peter will never find happiness until he is OK with being a "nobody" (and that there might even be a day when being "nobody" is too much). As Ram Dass once said, "The game is not about becoming somebody, it's about becoming nobody." But try to reassure the frightened little boy inside who thinks he may die. When the egoic "little me" begins to crumble, as it is now, all the parts I've managed to keep buried for a lifetime come flying to the surface.

This time, when the scared little child shows up, I know that I've got a big one on the line and that I need some outside help. It is one of those deep existential fears that goes to the very core—it is the primal fear of emptiness that I've been running from all my life.

It all comes out during one of our therapy sessions with Kerry. Linda and I have been seeing her for a few months, trying to work out our issues around money. We meet in her fourth floor office located in an old brick building in Charlottesville. Kerry is one of the warmest, kindest people I have met, and possesses a wisdom beyond her years. She's petite, with dark curly hair, sparkling eyes and a soft, gentle voice.

She listens intently as Linda starts to tell her why she's upset: "You said you weren't going to buy anything more, and now you want a $1000 mower!"

"But what are we going to do?" I plead. "I can't cut all those acres of grass with a hand mower!" (I neglect to mention that I've been researching ride-on mowers for months, and have found a bright, shiny red one that has a built-in cup holder and a 42 inch deck. I have to have it.)

"You already have a tractor to do that!"

"No, it's too big for the lawn. The only alternative is to pay someone to do it, and that will be expensive. We need the mower. I'm trying to *save* us money!"

Linda looks furious.

"Linda, what are you feeling now?" Kerry interjects.

"I feel powerless. He does this all the time . . . he bulldozes over me until he gets what he wants. It's like getting scammed over and over again."

"Is that true Peter?"

"Yes," I sigh, knowing I've been caught red-handed. "I'm good at it. I just keep on until she gives in. It's like Chinese water torture."

"How do you imagine Linda must feel when you do this?"

"Awful . . . Linda's right. My spending is an addiction. I do need to slow it down." The minute the words come out of my mouth, a sense of panic wells up in me—like a heroin addict being told his supply will be cut off. Kerry notices the change in my expression.

"What just happened?" she asks.

"I'm terrified—I feel this anxiety right in the pit of my stomach."

"Why don't you close your eyes and go into that feeling."

As soon as I shut my eyes I feel a huge amount of tension in my belly. An image surfaces of me as a small child. I'm in a dark, black hole, struggling to crawl up the sides, desperately trying to get a handhold on the dirt walls. But they keep crumbling. I look back down. I have never been so terrified in my life. "I feel something coming after me," I say. "All I can see is an angry face and big fists."

"Just stay with that," Kerry says gently.

"This black shape keeps coming towards me. I can't escape." Tears well up in my eyes. "God, it's terrifying. I feel so helpless."

"Keep going."

"I'm struggling to get away, but I can't. I'm exhausted. I can't do it anymore. I'm lying at the bottom of the pit."

Once again the image of an angry face appears in my mind. It's my father. "Oh shit, he's going to hit me. I can't do anything about it. There's no one there to help me. I'm stuck. I can't move."

"Just be with the helplessness."

A total sense of despair washes over me. Everything goes numb.

After a long pause, Kerry says, "Yes, that's what it felt like. You *were* totally helpless. No one could help you. It wasn't your fault. There was nothing you could do."

I feel weighed down by this immovable mass.

"I can't get out," I groan. "Now I can see my father. He's huge and strong. I hate him. I'm going to smash the shit out of him."

With my eyes still closed, I can hear Kerry and Linda cheering me on, "Yes, you're a ninja, and you can do anything!"

"The bastard, I'm bashing and bashing him until he gets smaller and smaller—'til he's nothing more than a little pebble—I'm grinding him into the dirt. Arrgghh!"

I'm surprised to hear both Kerry and Linda clapping. It seems as if they're off in some other world.

I open my eyes. Everything is bright and shining.

"Wow," I laugh. "That feels good!"

Two weeks later, after I stop pressuring Linda (and she finally sees the wisdom of having our own mower), I am happily riding over our lawn on my shiny new red machine, with a nice, cool soda sitting in my cup holder, and the smell of fresh cut grass filling my nostrils. Life is good!

A Dark and Stormy Night
Mt. Ayr Farm, Virginia, March 19, 2002

We have forgotten what rocks, plants, and animals still know. We have forgotten how to be—to be still, to be ourselves, to be where life is: Here and Now.
Eckhart Tolle

Living on the farm has a profound effect on me. For the first time ever, I feel that I'm a participant in the natural world, rather than an observer. Both as a kid and as an adult, I felt that nature was there for my enjoyment, whether it was skiing, swimming, camping, sailing, or hiking. I spent countless hours in nature, but never got my hands dirty. So, I couldn't quite believe it when I found myself burying a stillborn lamb, chopping the head off a chicken, or sitting in poop and urine, pulling a bull calf out from a cow. I quickly discover that nature is not a Budweiser commercial, with twenty-year-olds frolicking in a pristine country lake, nor is it a glistening package of hamburger meat, neatly enclosed in Saran Wrap.

The animals become my teacher, showing me that birth and life coexist with death and destruction. Yet behind these apparent opposites, everything is in perfect balance. The more I'm with my sheep and goats, the more I notice how they respond directly to whatever is happening in the moment, whether it's trying to run when I need to give them an injection, or nearly knocking me down when I have feed for them. Unlike us, they don't make up a story about their lives. There is an innocent purity in their relationship with spirit, and, if we are willing, they are always ready to share that connection with us.

I remember the first time I experienced this.

It was a dark and stormy night in March—one worthy of Snoopy's eloquent prose—with rain and sleet alternately whipping against the farmhouse. March is lambing season, when the ewes need to be checked every few hours, especially when it's cold. If a newborn lamb doesn't receive its mother's milk in the first hour, it will die of hypothermia. Part of being a shepherd is getting up two or three times a night to check on the animals. At midnight, I climb out of my warm bed, and bundle up in long underwear, my dirty old ski jacket, hat, and rubber boots. Stepping out into the night, the wind and rain lashes my face as I walk over to the pasture, my flashlight beam cutting through the dark. I scan back and forth across the field, lighting up first one sheep, then another. Some are standing, others are lying down. *How do they do this?* I ask myself. *They actually seem to enjoy being out in the rain and cold!*

I recognize each sheep as the beam picks them out of the darkness—Curly the ram, Millie with her baby lamb, and the twins Abigail and Alice. Finally I see Emma standing quietly behind some bushes, looking out at me, her eyes caught in the glare of the flashlight. She's the ewe that I'm looking for. Earlier in the day I noticed that she was setting herself apart from the flock, a sure sign that she is about to have lambs. Then I see a white shape on the ground next to her.

I walk up to her, reassuring her with my voice, "Hi my dear sweet Emma, don't worry, I'm here to help you." There on the ground, partly in the mud, is a baby lamb. *Is it alive? It must only be a few minutes old!* I notice that it's still covered in fluid and is cold to the touch. I gently pick it up and walk back to the shelter of the barn holding it inside my parka to keep it warm. I can feel the pounding of its little heart. The mama follows me, bleating in distress at having her lamb taken from her.

Once I have the ewe and her lamb in the stall, I gather my lambing bucket, filled with towels and other emergency items. I sit down on the straw next to the mama, who is licking her baby. Even though the lamb is only a few minutes old, it is struggling to get up. What a miracle to see this tiny creature trying to move its long legs for the very first time. It gets partway up, falls down, then tries again, and is soon staggering around like a drunken sailor. I turn my attention to Emma and strip her teats to get the milk flowing. After a few tries the warm milk squirts onto my hand. This fresh colostrum means life or death to the lamb. I guide the lamb to the teat and its little tail starts wiggling as it takes its first suck.

Then I notice a huge sack coming out of Emma's vulva. *She must be having twins!* First the front hooves appear, along with the head, and it seems as if the lamb is going to dive headfirst onto the ground. Encased in its amniotic sack, it slips gently down onto the straw. I watch in amazement as the lamb does a little shake and takes its first breath. Her mother turns and starts to lick her baby rapidly. She knows exactly what to do.

Then I notice something else coming out from her vagina, and it doesn't look like a lamb. *Oh no! Maybe she has a prolapsed uterus. This can be serious!* I desperately start looking through my trusty *Storey's Guide to Raising Sheep* (which I keep in the lambing bucket), hoping to get an answer. The book says, "In some cases the uterus can prolapse, which requires immediate medical attention." I look at the ewe, then back at the book, wondering what to do. *Oh no, I have no idea what's happening and there's no one around to help.* Then, to my amazement, I realize she's giving birth to a third lamb! I put on my latex gloves and gently help the lamb slide out. The mama is still busy licking the other two.

Once on the ground it lies there, not breathing. Tentatively, I reach out and give it a little nudge. Nothing happens. I use my finger to clear away the amniotic sack from around its mouth. I give it another nudge and still nothing happens. Emma notices that the lamb is not breathing. She turns to look at me with her big brown eyes, with a look that says, "You and I are in this together." She licks the lamb vigorously while I clear away the fluid. She paws at it with her hoof, hitting it so hard that I fear for its life. Suddenly my mind drops away and there is no "me" doing anything. Actions are happening from some deep inner knowing as the momma and I attempt to bring the still form to life. Finally the lamb gives a big shake and starts breathing.

I sit with the soft light illuminating the momma and the three lambs. They have all found their mother's teats and their little tails are wagging fiercely. The barn is warm; I can hear the sound of the rain spattering on the metal roof. I take in the wonderful smell of straw, sheep dung, wool, old wood, and the new life around me. It is a moment out of time. It could be now; it could be two thousand years ago. *It's no accident that Christ was born in a stable.* I think. *There's no place more holy than this.*

When I step out of the barn into the darkness, the rain has stopped and it's past two AM. The sheep have gathered under the shed, drawn by all the excitement of the birthing. I sit on the ground next to them, where I can make out their bulky shapes a few feet away from me. Some are chewing their cud, others are breathing gently. I close my eyes and notice the magical sound of tiny peepers coming from the pond. I can taste the coming of spring in the night air.

With my eyes shut, I hear the sound of breathing close by. I smile, knowing that it must be Isabel, my favorite ewe, because she always comes up to greet me. She comes closer and closer, until she's breathing right into my ear. I feel the rapid whoosh, whoosh, of her breath against my ear. Her breath is soft and sweet-smelling. It's as if she's saying, "Come, come with me. Experience what I experience. Just for one second—*let go*. Let go of your mind and *be*."

Suddenly a jolt of energy hits, and a huge sound wells up inside me, coming from somewhere deep down in my belly: ***Huhhhhh!!!*** The sound startles the sheep and they all jump up, wondering what happened. I start to laugh hysterically as they look curiously at me. They must be thinking, "This guys is nuts—or he's finally got it!"

This is what I've been searching for all this time. It's closer than my own breath.

Shift Happens
Albemarle County, Virginia, September 26, 2000

*When you're no longer thinking ahead, each footstep isn't just a means to an end
but a unique event in itself.*
Robert Persig, *Zen and the Art of Motorcycle Maintenance*

It's a beautiful fall afternoon with the sun sinking fast towards the mountains. I'm
riding my bicycle along a deserted country road with my dogs Sky and Luke running beside me. Our shadows chase us along the roadside, gracefully flowing over
bushes and grass as we go by. I can hear the sound of the dog's paws rhythmically
going *brrummp, brrummp, brrummp* as they hit the dirt road, echoing the sound of
their breath. Their joy in running is palpable. This is what they live for. I'm feeling the same freedom—just wind, running, breathing, seeing. *This is it,* I think.
This is all there is. For a moment there is no thinking . . . just dogs, man, bicycle,
fall day.

Suddenly it's as if I am somewhere above and behind Peter, watching him
bicycle down the road. I'm aware of him bicycling, but I'm not the guy with the
jeans and khaki shirt riding on the bicycle. I have nothing to do with this person
called Peter. It doesn't make any difference what Peter does. It doesn't matter
if he's worrying about tomorrow or what happened yesterday; it doesn't matter
whether he's happy or sad; it doesn't matter whether he crashes his bicycle or rides
it down to the bottom of the hill. Then my mind jumps back in, and I hear the
sound of the dogs panting as they run along beside me. *Well that was interesting,*
I think. *Maybe this is what it means to awaken!* As the thought passes through my
mind, I look down at the front wheel of the bicycle, watching it turn. The treads
on the wheel go from being blurred, to momentarily appearing as treads, then
blurred again. The bike flies down the road, as if floating on air.

The next day, with Sky and Luke as my constant companions, I take the trail
down to my meditation spot by the creek. After a quarter of a mile, the trail
connects to a path that parallels the creek bed. The path, a former roadway from
colonial times, is little wider than a car. It is covered with soft grass and fall leaves.
With the afternoon sun lighting it, I feel as if I've suddenly been transported to
another plane. On both sides there are wild azaleas, mountain laurel, and wild rho-
dodendron. Huge oak and maple trees tower overhead. The leaves rustle underfoot
as I walk down the path with the dogs leading the way. The smell is intoxicating—the fecund smell of decaying leaves, the crisp scent of fall air. Someone once

told me that Thomas Jefferson used to ride on horseback down this same road on his way to Scottsville. I can easily believe it.

I find my spot by the creek and take my usual place on a flat rock overlooking the small waterfall, which has a drop of about two feet. The mesmerizing sound of water splashing over rocks instantly calms me. I relax and stare at the water, until there is a sudden shift of perception, and the water suddenly appears to flow upwards, rather than downwards. I smile inwardly, thinking, *Wow . . . that's what awakening is—a subtle change in perception!* I turn my eyes towards the forest and it vibrates with life. It's as if I'm seeing it for the first time—eyes report sunshine, nose reports the smell of fall air, ears report the sound of water. I take a deep breath into my belly. *Wow,* I think, *these are not "my" eyes, "my" nose, or "my" ears; they are awareness seeing itself as awareness.* It's completely impersonal.

No one is ever going to understand this, but in truth it's more real than my two hands. Obviously you had to be there . . . but many of us have had experiences like this while watching a sunset or looking out at the ocean, even if only for a few seconds.

What shocks me is that the senses, which I assume to be "my" senses, have nothing to do with this person called "Peter." They are the means through which awareness experiences the phenomenal world. With just a tiny shift in perception, I am no longer "Peter," but the awareness watching it all. It's like seeing the waterfall flow upwards. *Wow, I've got it!* I think, laughing out loud. *It's so simple!* But the instant I think, "I've got it," it's gone. Oh well.

A psychiatrist might say that I'm dissociating and that it's time to increase my anti-depressants. Others will say, "His cheese has slipped off his cracker." Who knows? I've always said you have to be crazy to want this.

Does this mean "Peter" is finally enlightened? Oh, I wish. Unfortunately (or fortunately) this "Peter" will never become enlightened. Someday he may arrive at a place where he no longer identifies himself as Peter, or he may not. It really doesn't matter. The "little me" has nothing to do with it. Everything *is* that time-less awareness—including the part of me that thinks I am this individual personality.

I'm startled out of my reverie as the dogs start barking wildly and chasing after a squirrel. "Boys," I cry out. "Come back here!" A few minutes later, they are standing next to me, wagging their stubby tails and looking up at me. It seems like they have a smile on their faces, saying, "Oh, you finally got it!"

I give each of them a pet, my heart overflowing with love—not just for them—but for the life all around me. For a brief moment I'm seeing with new eyes—no separation between me, the dogs, forest, water, air, sunshine. It's all so simple. Then my thinking mind sneaks back in—worries about Linda, who is having a bad day, concern about my upcoming operation, and the promise I made to visit our neighbor Virginia today. I take another deep breath, realizing that the deep peace I was experiencing a moment ago has been replaced by obsessive think-ing. *Let go of the thoughts,* I say to myself. *Let go of this thought; let go of that thought; they are not even real.*

It reminds me of a popular old Zen story about two monks who are walking down a path and come to a creek, probably very similar to the one where I am sitting now. They see a pretty young woman in a silk kimono struggling to cross the rushing water. The first monk approaches her and lifts her in his arms, carry-ing her to the other side. After she expresses her appreciation to the monk who carried her, the two monks continue down the path. Hours go by in silence with each of them walking side by side. The second monk appears irritated and fuming. Finally he blurts out in an accusatory tone, "You shouldn't have picked her up. We monks don't go near females, especially pretty ones. Why did you do that?"

The first monk says, "I left the girl back there at the creek. Why are you still carrying her?"

Hmmm, I think. *I'm just like the second monk—sitting here worrying about what I have to do an hour from now. Wouldn't it be a delight to have a mind free of obsessive thoughts so I could be continually present to what is happening right now?* I sigh and start walking back up the path.

Sit Happens
Mt. Ayr Farm, Virginia, October, 2000

I have noticed that these days I happen to get up around 5 AM, and after the usual morning ablutions, I find myself sitting in my rocking chair. The rocking begins but stops automatically, frankly I do not know when! Then the meditation happens . . .
Ramesh Balsekar

As I spend time with the animals and slip into the silence with them, I notice that my formal meditation practice falls away on its own. In retrospect, it feels like I have been clinging on to spiritual practices like a drowning man clinging to a life preserver. For years I pushed myself to practice every day, because I was sure that if I were to stop, I'd be right back where I started. What a horrible thought—twenty years of meditation down the tubes! I still remember all those fierce admonitions from teachers. "If you stop now, all those years will be wasted. Meditation practices are cumulative. Stop now and you'll never become enlightened!" But now I see that this is just another belief—who says that practices will make you enlightened anyway? In many ways they are a way of *postponing* awakening—a continual denial of what is here *right now*! It makes me think of the Jewish Buddhist joke: Be here now. Be someplace else later. Is that so complicated?

So I stopped meditating. It didn't matter whether I meditated or not—meditation happened. I would find myself sitting comfortably on the couch in the morning and naturally slip into meditation. There was no effort, no looking at the clock, no trying to "do" anything. Even my cat Obi noticed the difference. Every morning, when I sat on the couch, my coffee mug on the table in front of me, Obi would curl up on my lap and purr—a deep, vibrating purr that instantly took me into stillness. Then I got it: *That's what meditation is all about. It's purring!* Obi isn't trying to get anywhere with his purring; he's just purring. What a teacher he is.

I begin to see *everything* as meditation. It doesn't matter whether I'm washing the car, having dinner with friends, making love, or asleep. Meditation becomes a twenty-four-hour-a-day event, and it is clearly not a willful practice. It is surrendering into the "not knowing" again and again, moment by moment, thought by thought. Adyashanti—a Zen meditator for fifteen years—puts it very clearly: "Meditation is nothing more than dwelling in your own natural state."

Previously, I used all kinds of techniques to try and control my mind—breath, mantra, visualization. Now I allow *everything* to come to the surface—restlessness,

317

thoughts about sex, thoughts about work, having to pee—without censoring anything. I drop into a place of *allowing*, letting go of any attempt to control my experience. If I watch closely enough, thoughts and sensations pass through and are replaced by more thoughts and sensations. All I need do is embrace them and let them go. I give up on the idea of "stilling" my mind, because I see that the minute I get off the pillow, there it is again. The mind has no problem with thoughts. Let them come, let them go.

By relaxing and not forcing anything, I go deeper and deeper.

Just sitting.

Just breathing . . . breath in . . . breath out.

The aromatic smell of rich coffee reaches my nose—Whole Foods Blend #12984.

What is it with Buddhists and tea? Why are they always talking about tea—the cup half full, the tea spilling over, drinking a cup of tea, I stop the war? The whole Buddhist religion would fall apart without tea.

Let it be. Knees hurt.

And what is it with those scary looking Zen guys in their black robes and shaved heads sitting in front of a wall for days on end . . . why can't they lighten up a little?

A smile—who is having this thought? Who is it that is chasing enlightenment?

There's nothing but this moment, right now.

With no effort, some thirty minutes later, the meditation ends. I pick up my mug and head to the kitchen for another half cup of coffee.

There is a delightful story about a Zen student who goes to a monastery, hoping to enroll as a monk. After the obligatory twenty-four wait outside the monastery door, the Zen Master allows him in saying, "You can stay, but you must keep silence for twelve years." The young student agrees.

After twelve long years of practice, the student comes before the Master.

"What have you got to say?" the Master asks.

"The bed is too hard," says the student.

"You must do another twelve years," says the Master.

After still another twelve years of austerities, the student comes before the Master and is given the chance to speak.

"The food is terrible," he says.

"Go back for another twelve years," says the Master.

Still twelve years later he comes and bows before his teacher.

"I quit," he says.

The Master answers, "Good, you've been doing nothing but complaining anyway."

I'm not sure what all this has to do about just sitting, but I like the story.

Swimming in Love
Mt. Ayr Farm, Virginia, November 25, 2000

You are awareness itself,
Never changing.
Wherever you go,
Be happy.
For see!
The Self is in all beings,
And all beings are in the Self.
Ashtavakra Gita, c. 800 CE

"So, what does it mean to be awakened?" my son Peter asks Linda, leaning forward in his chair, not wanting to dirty it with his mud-spattered shirt. He and I have just come back from an afternoon of mountain biking and we're muddy and sweaty. At thirty-three, Peter has a strong and handsome face, made all the more interesting by the barely visible scars from a recent bicycle accident that broke almost every bone in his face. Unlike me, he is big-shouldered and muscular. He has an authority and presence about him that commands respect.

Linda looks over at Peter, "What does it mean to be awakened? Hmmm . . . awakening is all things at once, in all places, at all times, with no question, no problem, and no possibility that it will ever disappear. It is love swimming in love, watching itself swim in itself."

Linda looks frail lying in the huge bed, covered by the eiderdown. The late afternoon sun is pouring through the three arched windows onto the wall behind her, creating a triptych. It lights up the headboard, which is made of one-hundred-year-old shutters, that have the greenish patina of aged copper. Propped up by the pillows, she reminds me of an early Renaissance painting, with her hands folded over her chest and her blond hair unfurled on the rust colored pillowcase. A new flare has just started—her skin is crawling, her joints are aching, and her temperature is up. Living with a chronic illness is not fun. It's like getting the flu over, and over, and over again.

Peter carefully repeats what she has just said, struggling to grasp its meaning. "It's swimming in love, watching itself swim in itself."

"You are the awareness of itself, expressing itself through itself," she says.

Peter repeats: "I am the awareness of itself, expressing itself, through itself . . ."

"Yes!"

"I get it!" Peter exclaims triumphantly.

"Then what's the problem?" Linda says with a smile.

I listen to all this a bit dumbfounded . . . awestruck by their interchange. Linda is clearly channeling this from somewhere beyond herself. Peter is staying right there with her, fully present to what is happening. I feel that I am witnessing an extraordinary moment in time.

"The problem," Peter says, "to the extent that there is a problem, is still the question, 'what does it mean to be awakened?'"

Linda closes her eyes for a moment and says, "It means love expressing itself through itself. That's it. The human mind cannot experience that. It's like a camera. It's designed to take pictures of everything but itself. The one thing it can never see is itself."

"OK."

"The joke is, it's made by love, expressing itself as itself, aware of itself, in everything. The miracle in all this, the unexplainable part, is that it knows itself, and has known this all along! The second the camera breaks, the second you throw the camera on the rock, it sees itself—which is impossible—because the lens is broken."

I listen to her voice; it's so clear and strong. I know she's in pain and feeling terrible. How does she do it? That's just it . . . it's not her doing it!

"So, there are awakened people who live in this awareness?" Peter asks, determined to get an answer to his question.

"No matter how much you try to get my muddled mind to answer that, you won't diminish love being aware of itself, as itself, seeing itself . . . in this room right here, right now! That's all there is. Everything else is mind stuff, including your question." Linda laughs.

"I see what you mean," he says, smiling.

"Can't you see? It's playing a game with us. It put us into the hard drive, hooked us up, and it's having us do this thing. Do you see the joke of it?"

"I do!" Peter laughs.

Whew. I so want Peter to get it. He has such an extraordinary mind. It's his greatest strength and his greatest weakness. If he can just short-circuit it for one second he will go right through the veil. He's so close.

"Source is playing a trick on itself. What you're doing is looking for love when you actually are love," Linda says. "And the moment you question it, you're even further away. That's part of the game. That's part of the way love expresses itself."

"Right," Peter says, "The question I keep coming back to is whether it's possible for a human being to live as love being aware of itself as love."

"Sure it's possible; it's our natural state." Linda says. "We all could do it if we just let go of our minds. That's why it's easy for goats and hummingbirds and dolphins to live in this awareness. Their minds don't get in the way. It's easier for humans to have this awareness when they leave the body."

"We'll all find that out when we die," I say jokingly. Neither of them seems to hear me. This is obviously a dialogue between Peter and Linda and I'm just there as a witness.

"So, consciousness is not limited to a physical body?" Peter asks, beginning to relax more in his chair as the mud dries on his shirt.

"It doesn't even need a body," Linda says.

"Right," Peter says.

Wow. He's already caught on to the fact that he's not limited by a human body!

"Is that what people call the soul?" says Peter.

"I hate to put a word to it. That's like putting a little box around it called 'soul.'"

"It's unlimited, then." Peter says.

"It's all love, expressing itself as love, experiencing itself as love. 'Soul' is tricky, even 'human' is tricky. There's just love."

"So, ultimately, love is all there is," Peter says.

"Part of the game is that you get to choose the hard drive, you get to choose the movie. You also see that you're choosing the movie –you don't see it—but the one who is dreaming you sees it. You are the one who is dreaming you!"

I hear what she's saying . . . this is more than the mind can understand . . . and that's the whole point!

"How come some people are supposedly awakened and others are not?" Peter asks, relentlessly pursuing his original question. "Is awakening a state that happens to some of us?"

"No! No! It's not a state," Linda replies fervently.

"But I've heard you say that Ramana Maharshi was awakened."

"All I can say is that Ramana was aware of love that is aware of itself. He had absolutely no personal agenda; there was nobody to teach, nobody to change, and no one to awaken. He was the last one to say he was anything. People used to come to him when he was living on the mountain and ask, 'Where is the swami?' He would say, 'I don't know. There's no swami here.' No one was more special to him than anyone else. It was all Self."

"Is awakening like some binary switch that gets turned on and stays permanently on, or does it go on and off?"

"Why is this so important to you?"

"There's a lot wrapped up in being awakened or enlightened. There are all kinds of spiritual teachers out there who claim to be awakened."

He's so savvy. That's my question too. What about all those teachers who are setting up Web sites, writing books, giving retreats, and collecting devotees? They may not say they're awakened, but they sure make sure everyone knows that they are. How will Linda respond?

"You're right. That's just an ego trip. It's more of 'me and my story.' It's them saying, 'I have an awakened ego, I have something to teach you.' There's no such thing as an awakened ego. You can be certain that anyone who claims to be awakened is still in ego."

"Well, you've finally answered my question . . . by showing it can't be answered."

"Yes, you're the only one who can answer it," Linda says. She looks over at Peter with a deep expression of love in her eyes.

Peter looks silently into her eyes, then reaches out to touch her hand.

"I'm tired now," she says.

We get up quietly and leave.

CHAPTER 19

PARKING IS HARD, DYING IS EASY

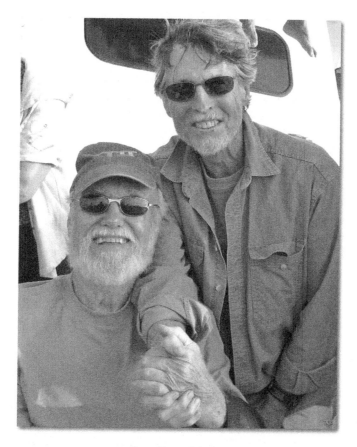

Ram Dass & Peter

Fierce Grace
Canoe Lake, Algonquin Park, Ontario, Canada, August 19, 2002

*The stroke caused me to lose faith, and it was a cold, cold place. I suddenly
realized it was fierce grace—fierce grace was what I called it—because it was the
grace that turned my life around.*
Ram Dass

Six years ago, Linda was diagnosed with a rare auto-immune illness called Behcet's
Disease, which is very similar to Lupus. She went from being a runner with a box-
ful of trophies to barely being able to walk. Her day-to-day flirtation with pain is
a white heat dharma bell that keeps her constantly focused on what it means to be
in a body. Most days she can do little else except lie on her back and read. A good
day is when she can go for a short walk or drive in to town with me. Because she
has multiple chemical sensitivities as well, it's almost impossible for us to travel
without her getting even sicker. Any exposure to exhaust, petrochemicals, avgas,
or formaldehyde (which is in just about everything) triggers severe reactions. So
we buy a used Roadtrek camper van, which allows us to take trips even when
Linda is not feeling well. We jokingly refer to it as the "port-a-corpse" because
when she is ill, she can lie in the king size bed in the back while I drive. It also
means we can bring our two dogs, who serve as co-pilot and navigator. The interior is like the cabin of a luxury yacht, with white walls and ceiling, French blue
upholstery, and oak cabinets. Its highly efficient design includes a fridge, a stove,
an air-conditioner, a heater, a "head," an indoor shower, and a bed that converts
into a dining area.

To celebrate our newfound freedom, we make a trip to Canada, visiting friends
and family along the way. Our final destination is Algonquin Park, a vast wilderness area in Northern Ontario with maple hills, rocky ridges, and thousands of
lakes. After a thousand miles of travel and a week on the road, we pull in to one of
the many campgrounds in the park and sign in. After driving by a colorful assort-
ment of other vacationers, we find our camping spot (#28) overlooking a pristine
lake. While Linda feeds the dogs, I hook up to the power outlet, unroll the awning
on the van, bring out our lawn (a 12 x 14 green indoor/outdoor carpet), folding
chairs, a table, and some wine—an instant "home away from home."

Linda and I relax and enjoy the magical setting—the sound of water lapping
on the shore, the scent of pine trees and fresh, clean water. Wood smoke from a
nearby campsite stirs my appetite. A family walks by and our dog Sky goes ber-

serk barking at them. Two young campers in a red canoe glide silently by, laden down with gear. I pull out my portable grill and make some hamburgers, which taste like they've come from a five-star restaurant. For dessert we have a home-made apple pie we picked up at a bakery in a little town along the highway.

For me it's like coming home. I spent many weeks here while researching a book that I wrote on a group of Canadian artists. The book was called *The Group of Seven*, and ended up becoming a best seller in Canada, selling over 40,000 copies. It's about a group of artists who went out into the wilderness and painted the rugged beauty of the landscape in pure, vibrant colors. One of the artists I write about in the book—a tall, dark, handsome man named Tom Thomson—camped and painted on this very lake around the time of World War I. At the age of forty, he mysteriously drowned in a canoe accident. Some thought he was murdered. Now I'm back with Linda and our two dogs in the relative comfort of our motorhome.

Darkness creeps in, and despite the fact that it's August, the air becomes crisp and cool. We retreat to the comfort of our motorhome, and lie on the bed looking out at the star-spangled sky through the three rooftop windows. I cuddle up to Linda while the two dogs settle in on the floor.

"I'm so happy you brought me here," Linda says.

"It's been my dream to share this with you. I love this place; it's my home." I was born and brought up in woods like these. They awaken a profound sense of place inside me.

"Listen!" Linda says suddenly. A pair of loons call to each other across the lake. One of them, surprisingly close by, makes its haunting call: *Ooooo, ooooo,ooooo.* A few moments later its mate responds with the same eerie wail: *Ooooo, ooooo,ooooo.*

"What a beautiful sound," Linda says before drifting off to sleep.

Around 2:30 we both wake up to a far off sound that becomes more and more distinct.

"Peter, it's wolves!" Linda says excitedly as she sits up in bed. Both the dogs perk up their ears.

One wolf howls in the night. *Aaaa . . . oooo, aaaa . . . oooo!* We listen in awe as the calls echo back and forth through the mountains. Soon, another howls back, then another. We look at each other in the dark in stunned amazement.

The next morning Linda shakes her head in wonder, "I've never heard such beautiful sounds in my life—first the loons, then the wolves."

"That was amazing," I say. "It brings out my Canadian blood."

Then I hear Linda groan.

"How are you doing?" I ask, already suspecting the worst.

"Not so good," she says. "I had groin pains last night."

We both know what this means—the beginning of another flare. Every ten days or so Linda gets a "flare." It's like having the flu over and over again, with aching joints, fever, chills, and debilitating fatigue. Because the disease attacks the mucous membranes, she usually has painful mouth sores, nose sores, vaginal sores, and terrible nausea. This has been going on for years and shows no sign of letting up.

"Right now it feels like my skin is on fire."

"Oh Lin, I'm so sorry."

"It's what is," she says with resignation.

"Well, you could do some visualization or take a homeopathic remedy," I say jokingly. One of the ways we make these flares a little more bearable is by having a little fun at the expense of the New Age healers.

"Sure," she laughs. Linda is very knowledgeable about her illness, and has superb doctors that monitor it. She has explored every allopathic and alternative treatment available. Yet friends constantly bombard her with the latest remedy that they are sure will heal her.

"Or you could transcend the pain-body by realizing you are not the body," I say in the same jocular tone. Transcending the "pain-body" is one of the latest buzz words.

"I'd like to put thumbscrews to people who talk about how easy it is to transcend pain," she says with a grimace. "Anyone who says that has obviously never experienced real pain."

"I get so frustrated when people say that you're creating your illness through your thoughts."

"Yeah, it's cruel—even though they mean well. This illness has nothing to do with 'wrong thinking,' otherwise why would little children suffer from cancer and other diseases—not to mention animals?"

Chronic illness and pain are one of the last taboos—affecting millions of people, yet no one wants to talk about it. Even Oprah and Dr. Phil avoid these topics. It's all the more challenging for Linda because she was once so healthy.

"I remember taking five-mile hikes up Mt. Jefferson in Oregon," she says. "I had more energy than I knew what to do with. Now I can't even get out of bed without feeling like I'm going to throw up." Linda was an unstoppable ball of energy, building her own house, teaching elementary school, taking care of her farm, and winning 5K races on the weekends.

"I don't know how you do it," I say.

"Yet, there is so much happiness underneath all this sickness—even in the face of the pain."

"That's the miracle, that's the grace."

This is ultimate happiness, I think, *a happiness beyond the mind, beyond the body—a happiness that doesn't come and go, even amidst physical pain.*

How extraordinary are the ways in which grace manifests. If Linda didn't have this illness, we wouldn't be here in Algonquin Park enjoying the comfort of our little motorhome; if she didn't have this illness, we wouldn't be sharing in the howl of wolves and the cry of the loons; if she didn't have this illness, I wouldn't be writing this right now.

Linda spends the entire day lying flat on her back, too sick to get up. Disappointed at not being able to take her out in a canoe and show her the land that is so dear to my heart, I take the dogs on a walk. Unlike me, they have no expectations of paddling around the lake. They excitedly explore their new surroundings with wild exuberance. To them it's all a new adventure. What teachers they are.

That evening we watch a video on Ram Dass called *Fierce Grace* (and yes, our little motorhome has a small TV and video player). In his inimitable way, Ram Dass tells of his recovery from a serious stroke. The video shows him going to a speech therapist, doing physical therapy, being wheeled around in a wheelchair, talking to groups of people, and working on a book called *Still Here*. It is a moving testimony to one person's faith and courage.

"The stroke," he says, "brought me into intimate contact with pain, and I found pain to be a worthy adversary for my spiritual practices. Working with constant pain pushed my spiritual practices to their limit."

This is when the spiritual rubber hits the road, I think. He's letting us know that at some point, we too will face the challenges of aging, of illness, and of death. And how we respond in those moments is the real practice—knowing that behind all the pain, all is well. It's all grace.

Linda is walking this same path of fierce grace.

I am blessed to be walking it with her.

When Life Hands You a Zinger
Mt. Ayr Farm, Virginia, August 29, 2002

In my world there are no problems.
Nisargadatta

The phone rings.

I've just come in from an exhausting day loading hay bales in the sweltering August heat. My body is so stiff and sore I can barely make it over to the phone.

"Hello, this is Peter."

"Hi Mr. Mellen, this is Dr. Steers from UVA." Dr. Steers is head of the urology department at UVA Hospital. Like many surgeons, he can be unbelievably arrogant at times, but he knows his stuff.

"Dr. Steers, how are you?" I ask, walking over to stand behind the couch where Linda is reading. She looks up at me in curiosity when she hears his name.

"We got the results of the biopsy back and unfortunately they were positive. You do have prostate cancer, I'm afraid." *Oh boy. I half expected this. What the hell am I going to do now?*

"Can you tell how advanced it is?" Immediately I see the expression on Linda's face turning to one of alarm. I turn my gaze away so that I can concentrate on the call.

"Well, the biopsy shows cancer in each of the four tissue cores of the left prostate. The Gleason scale was four plus three, which means a score of seven. The highest is a ten." I try to register the numbers, but my mind numbs out. I can't make sense of numbers even at the best of times. I see Linda's face transform from alarm to sadness.

"Is that aggressive?" I ask.

"With a PSA of 6.2, it's right on the edge."

What does he mean by on the edge—that *the cancer has metastasized and I have a year to live?* I start pacing back and forth behind the couch, oblivious to my sore body. "What are my options?"

"At your age I would consider radiation or surgery. There's a new robotic prostatectomy that looks very promising."

"If you had these scores, would you do the surgery?"

"Everyone asks me that. This is something you'll have to look into and decide for yourself." *Damn, he's not going to tell me and he knows exactly what treatment would be most effective.*

After hanging up the phone, I'm still in shock, "Well, that's interesting news," I say more to myself than to Linda. "I have prostate cancer."

Linda walks over and holds me tight. "I think we both knew the test would be positive."

My cool response reminds me of a favorite scene from a television show called *Scrubs*. Dr. Cox, a cocky young doctor, comes into a hospital room and stands before his patient—a distinguished-looking businessman who is sitting up in bed in a hospital gown. With his carefully brushed grey hair, he looks like he's ready to conduct a board meeting. His neatly dressed wife stands by his side.

"I'm sorry to tell you that you have prostate cancer," Dr. Cox says. The man's face remains expressionless. His wife drops her head a few inches and looks sad.

The businessman turns and notices the expression on his wife's face. In an annoyed tone he says, "Catherine, please leave the room."

He then says to Dr. Cox, "I apologize for that emotional outburst. She just can't control herself."

Wide-eyed, Dr. Cox says, "Gee, are you WASPS?"

This was not the first time I've been told that I had cancer. A year ago I was diagnosed with melanoma, an aggressive and often deadly cancer. I had surgery and barely thought about it afterward. Somehow this is a little different. For one thing, my father died of prostate cancer.

As the news sinks in, I'm surprised to see that my reaction is one of excitement. I feel vibrantly alive, like I've just won the lottery. Perhaps I'll get to go home! For me, death has always seemed like the last great adventure. Suddenly, the old question, "What would you do if you had a year to live?" is not just hypothetical. *Okay, what would I do—buy $15 bottles of wine, instead of $10 bottles? Fly to France and stay in beautiful country inns? Live every hedonistic dream I've ever had?* To my surprise I realize that there's almost nothing in my life that I'd change. I would play more, be more spontaneous, cuddle Linda, take the dogs on walks, have naps, and relax and enjoy the sunsets. But I'm already doing that. I don't need to go anywhere or do anything—just be. What a blessing.

I remember when Timothy Leary learned that he was dying of cancer. He called his old friend Ram Dass, "I've got great news! I have terminal cancer!" Then he posted a sign outside his house inviting all his friends to "The Mother of All Parties." Leary opened up an exuberant new vision of what dying can be. "Instead of treating the last act in your life in terms of fear, weakness, and helplessness," he wrote, "think of it as a triumphant graduation."

Linda is loving and concerned. That night we end up lying on the living room carpet cuddling the dogs. "Just one lifetime won't be enough for us," she says, "There wouldn't be enough time for us to love each other."

I look into her shining blue eyes. "I'm so grateful that you're in my life. I'm even grateful to have this cancer appear in my life. Everything is happening exactly as it should."

"You can't leave without me. How come you get to have a good disease and all I get is chronic pain that goes on forever?"

"Well, you do have a good chance of lymphoma. Your mom died of it. So there's still hope for you," I laugh.

"You're so precious to me. You promised me you'd wait until the next cycle of the cicadas in 2013 before you go."

"I'll wait, my love. I'll wait."

On the practical side I do my research and eventually make the decision to have surgery. On the spiritual side I move on with living my life. Every day I spend time in the woods, stunned by the beauty around me; I hold Linda close every night, appreciating how lucky we are to have each other; I meet friends for lunch, touched by their concern and caring. I feel like my eyes have been opened. There is nothing but love everywhere I look.

Yes, there are times when this "unnamed anxiety" comes up from nowhere and wallops me from behind. Thoughts about the operation flash to mind. I wonder what it will be like to have my belly sliced open from my navel to my pubic bone and have my prostate removed. However, I find that when I don't dwell on the thoughts or make up a story about them, they are gone in a flash.

Perhaps I'm in some kind of la-la land, but I've squarely faced every aspect of having this disease. I could be dissociating, but I'm right here experiencing whatever comes up, both the good and the bad. The only thing that's different is that I'm a little more obsessive than usual—wanting to keep things neat and "in control." But so what? It doesn't change the ground of being, which is peace itself. Let the obsession be there.

Several months later I'm ready to fly to St. Louis for the surgery. Well-meaning friends reassure me: "Oh, my father had that operation and he's fine." Some of my New Age friends are uncomfortable with my choice for surgery. "Why don't you go see John of God in Brazil?" they ask, or "Have you tried saw palmetto?" I smile. When my first wife Fran had metastasized breast cancer, she tried just about every alternative healing method known to man, but none of it worked. Now that I have a full-blown cancerous tumor, I'm not going to put my faith in saw palmetto. Surgery is the gold standard for ridding the body of prostate cancer, but it is also one of the most delicate, intricate, and difficult surgeries in the book. A lot can go wrong. At this point I have no way of knowing whether the cancer has spread to the lymph nodes, whether I'll end up incontinent, or be impotent for the rest of my life. Not to mention all that messy post-operative stuff of catheters, diapers, and physical pain.

It's not exactly a walk in the park.

Halfway to the Moon
St. Louis, Missouri, Barnes-Jewish Hospital, October 24, 2002

I'm just killing time 'til time kills me
Jed McKenna

The day of the surgery Linda and I show up at the hospital at 5:00 AM, where they prep me for the operation. I hand over all the familiar things that make up my everyday identity—my clothes, my watch, my glasses, my wallet. I'm dressed in blue scrubs with a robe and special pressure stockings on my legs. Even my hair is covered by a sanitized cap. The only thing left to identify me as "Peter" is the plastic name band around my wrist. *This is neat,* I think. *There's nothing left of "me" and it feels great. I feel more fully who I am than ever before. Everyone should try this!*

Like a death row inmate walking the green mile, I walk down the long fluorescent-lit underground corridor towards surgery, with Linda on one side, and the orderly on the other. He comes to a big door and stops.

"This is as far as you can go, ma'am," he says to Linda.

Linda and I look at each other knowingly.

"I'll be fine," I say, holding her tight. "I love you."

"I love you too—more than you'll ever know," she whispers in my ear.

I turn to follow the orderly through the ominous double doors.

"You look so handsome in your scrubs," Linda calls after me. "You should've been a doctor!" I look back and wave as the doors swing shut.

In half an hour, Dr. Catalona, one of the most skilled surgeons in the world, will slice through layers of skin, fat, and muscle, probing far down into my abdomen to reveal a small walnut-sized organ. He will carefully cut out the prostate, plus the seminal vesicles, plus anything else that may be malignant, while doing his best to spare the nerves. Then he will join the urethra to the bladder and sew me up again. How fascinating! I wish I could watch.

The orderly leads me to one of the dozen or so gurneys standing side by side in a brightly lit windowless room and helps me onto it. An army of people come up to me, one after the other, checking my name, putting an IV into my arm, rechecking my name and what I'm there for, telling me about the procedure, then rechecking my name again—just to make sure they have the right person and don't cut my leg off by mistake. I'm surprised to find that there is no fear, just curiosity. Everyone is scurrying around in their blue scrubs, like actors preparing for a theatrical event. Some have wacky hats on, some are goofing off, others are serious. I'm cheerful and smiling, enjoying the whole show.

A short, stocky Asian man comes up and stands next to the gurney. I notice that everyone defers to him and that he has a gimpy leg. He's obviously my anesthesiologist. "My name is Dr. Hue," he says politely. "I will be in charge of your anesthesia today. I will be giving you something that will make you sleep, hmmm?" He looks down at me with twinkling eyes and an engaging smile. "You may hear things, and you may even talk while you sleep, but you won't remember anything you say. You understand?" He smiles again and places his hand on my wrist. "I will be putting a tube down your throat . . . yes? Some people say they have a sore throat afterwards. Not always so."

Something more is going on here while he's talking, something far beyond the words—and we both know it. He's like a Tibetan priest performing a sacred ritual. We smile and laugh together.

They start wheeling me off towards the operating room. I haven't gone ten feet when I'm out . . . just gone . . . halfway to the moon. The next thing I remember is waking up in the recovery room. What a shock to come slamming back into the body. I'm aware of a nurse sitting beside me filling out forms. At first I revel in the pleasant sensation of being stoned until I hear a woman on the gurney next to me crying out in pain. I send her a prayer as I drift in and out of my short-lived euphoria. From a distance I can feel someone putting an oxygen tube up my nose. "You're doing fine," a nurse says. "We just have to give you some more blood before we can let you go." I feel sublimely happy that it's all over. "And," she adds, "you did talk when you were out . . . and quite coherently." How did I do this without my conscious mind being in control?

As the anesthetic wears off, I have a chance to directly explore the realm of physical pain. From the dreamlike high of waking up in the recovery room, to the gradual ebbing of this cocoon-like shield that keeps the pain at bay, I watch the ever-shifting sensations in my body. First there is the dry mouth, so dry I can't talk. Like an angel, Linda appears at my side and feeds me little pieces of ice, which help. Then there is the nausea induced by the anesthetic, causing dry heaves that make my stomach feel like it is being ripped wide open. The pain level shoots up to a ten and beyond.

An hour later, (even though my body feels like it has been run over by a truck), the nurses want me to get out of bed and walk. *Get out of bed and walk? I can't possibly do that! How will I be able to stand up without ripping all the stitches out?* But nurses do what nurses do, and the pain is quite tolerable (I've always been very stoic) as I walk up and down the hallway with Linda at my side, carrying my urine bag and pushing my cart with the IV pole.

Back in bed I start to feel this urgent, desperate sensation of having to pee, even though I have a catheter in. I'm able to handle it for a while, but it doesn't stop. It goes on for hours and hours, without letting up. Nothing seems to help. I remember the Nazis used to torture people by not allowing them to pee. I ask for stronger pain medication, but my plea falls on deaf ears. Anything stronger than an aspirin is frowned upon in this Midwestern hospital. I experiment with self-hypnosis techniques that I used when I was a practicing hypnotherapist, but they only help for a few minutes at most. I try a Buddhist meditation on embracing the pain. Whoever made up these damn "pain meditations" has obviously never been in severe pain! There is nothing left to do but watch it come and go, like ocean waves washing up and washing out.

What I discover is that the pain brings me fully into unconditional awareness. There is no escape from it. It's just *there*. Knowing there is no way of fighting it, I do my best to relax into it . . . not always succeeding. Instead of making a story about it, I accept the pain as much as I can. I notice that every attempt to resist it makes me contract around it even more. I try to distract myself, but the brutal intensity of it keeps bringing me back to the "now" again and again. I give up and let the pain be there. It just is. It's what's happening right in this moment—nothing else. My mind goes quiet as I sit with eyes closed, focusing on my breath. Nothing changes. The pain doesn't let go, even for an instant. *Shit, this hurts,* I think, *but I can live with it—at least for now, and now is all there is.*

Underneath I'm aware of a peacefulness that doesn't come and go. Perhaps this is what they refer to as "practicing presence."

In the midst of all this, a stream of doctors, nurses, and hospital staff flow in and out of the room. Linda is there, sweetly tending to my every need. I drink in her love. Even with the pain and discomfort, even with the floating in and out of awareness, there is nothing but love, nothing but gratitude. It's as if it is all taking place in a dream, and I am the witness, watching myself in the dream.

Third Time's the Charm
Mt. Ayr Farm, Virginia, April 16, 2003

Health is merely the slowest possible rate at which one can die.
Anonymous

"Aieeee!" I cry out from the bathroom. "That hurts."

I hear Linda call out, "Are you OK?"

"Yeah, yeah, I'll be OK. Owwww . . . that burns!"

I've just injected a half inch long hypodermic needle into the side of my penis—voluntarily. As I press the plunger, the clear fluid burns as it goes in. It's called Caverject—some brilliant marketing person's wordplay on cave, erection, ejaculation . . . who knows? Welcome to the world of ED—erectile dysfunction— a bizarre compendium of vacuum pumps, injections, implants, Viagra, and other hard-to-believe claims made in magazines. It's been three months since my prostate surgery. When they removed my prostrate, the surgeon damaged some of the nerves in the process. This means I'm unable to have an erection, possibly for the rest of my life—a very common side effect. But at least they removed all the cancer. At least they think they did.

Now that I'm feeling better, I long to have the kind of intimacy that Linda and I shared for so many years. I miss our love-making. Even though we still cuddle, and get deep satisfaction from it, it's not the same thing. I've tried injections twice before, and both times I was able to get an erection. The only problem was that it wouldn't come down (just like those rapidly voiced warnings on the TV commercials). Both times I went to the hospital emergency room, and (thank God) it subsided before seeing the doctor. "Third time's a charm," I think, with naïve optimism.

"I hope this works," I say, walking naked into the bedroom. My desire for pleasure outweighs all common sense. I find Linda kneeling on the bed in her negligee. The bedside lamp is covered with a red scarf for effect. Every little bit helps.

"It's working, it's working!" I say excitedly, like a teenage kid having his first hard on, as I see "little Petey" standing up to attention.

"Oh, Peter, I love you. You're so brave to try this."

As we make love I revel in our shared intimacy. But almost immediately my penis starts to burn like it's on fire. I refuse to stop, even though the burning becomes even more intense.

When I finally reach an orgasm, it's so painful I scream out in pain.

Afterwards I lie there panting.

"Oh my darling," Linda says, cuddling up to me. "I'm so happy."

"I am too, but the damn thing won't go down."

Half an hour goes by. I lie on my back under the sheet with this tent pole sticking up in front of me.

"I think I'm going to have to go to the hospital," I groan.

"The last time we drove all the way there and it went down the moment you got in the emergency room."

"I remember. What fun." I must be crazy to have tried this again.

Another half hour goes by. "I can't stand it anymore," I say, struggling to pull on my jeans. I can't zip them up because of the protrusion.

"Let me come with you," Linda says. It's 10:30 at night.

"No you stay here. You've had a hard day." Linda has just started a new flare. "You're sure?"

"I'm good. I'll probably get half way there and turn around again."

The twenty-mile drive in the dark to the UVA hospital in Charlottesville seems interminable. I drive with one hand and try to comfort my poor throbbing member with the other.

Even though the waiting room is almost deserted, the bored-looking receptionist says, "Take a seat and we'll get to you as soon as we can." I wait and wait, unable to sit down because of the pain. No one goes in or out. A half hour goes by. Finally I can't stand it any longer and go up to her, "Look, you've got to get me in there! You just have to. This pain is a 'ten'!"

The receptionist sighs, and in a disinterested voice calls the treatment area. At long last I'm ushered into the back. A male nurse gets me settled. "That must hurt," he says with a sympathetic smile.

"You'd better believe it," I laugh.

Soon the room starts filling up with nurses and technicians. Two women doctors come in and check me over. "I'm Dr. Green and this is Dr. Sandburg. We're from urology and we'll be taking care of you. We're going to have to put you out and then draw blood from the penis." In the meantime, about ten people have gathered around the bed. It's standing room only. Even the head of urology pokes his head in. *What's he doing here at this hour?*

"Hey, Dr. Steers," I say. "This is quite a show."

"Well, we only get one of these situations every few years. It's very educational."

"Fine by me," I laugh. "Just get it done!"

Dr. Green pulls out a syringe with an enormous needle. "Does this hurt?" she asks, gently touching my penis. *Aieeee!* I scream involuntarily.

Then they knock me out—thank God. Afterwards they tell me that they took out about a half-pint of blood.

Over the next nine months I gradually accept the fact that Linda and I will never make love like we used to. I have to accept that my happiness doesn't depend on sex.

In September Linda and I drive to Washington, DC, for my son Peter's wedding. We're staying in our favorite hotel, the Westin Embassy Row. As the bellman takes us up to our room he says, "You're very lucky. They've given you one of the best suites in the hotel. Michael Douglas and Catherine Zeta Jones stayed in it just last week."

"Wow, really?" I say.

That night, exactly one year to the day from my surgery, and on my son's wedding night, I spontaneously have an erection, with no help of any kind.

From that point onwards "little Petey" bravely rose to the occasion all on his own every time he was asked.

Miracles still do happen.

Dancing Between Life and Death
Maui, February 26, 2006

When you're secure in the Soul, what's to fear? There is no fear of death, of anything your incarnation can bring.
Ram Dass

Several years later I find myself with Ram Dass once again while on a visit to Hawaii. Ram Dass now lives on Maui, declaring that he's here "for the duration." Every month he holds a satsang, where seventy or more people show up. In Maui, an event like this is more of a costume party—musicians from the Hare Krishna group sit cross-legged on the floor, looking like they just stepped off a plane from India; women in their colorful "divine goddess" robes flit from friend to friend giving Maui hugs; men in sadhu outfits—turbans, dhotis, and mala beads—look appropriately spiritual for the occasion; young earth mothers nurse their babies in public; men with Rasta dreadlocks tucked under their caps, sit on the floor, swaying back and forth with their eyes closed; a few pale tourists in neatly pressed pants and Hawaii shirts look awkward and a little out of place.

After a rousing Indian chant led by the Hare Krishna's, Ram Dass tells us he has just gotten out of the hospital and is having a reaction to antibiotics. "To be honest, I feel lousy today," he says, "but here I am." Over the next half hour people ask questions about psychedelics and drugs and whether marijuana can help bring about enlightenment. Ram Dass goes along with it all, relating his old story of giving his guru Neem Karoli Baba enough LSD to kill an elephant, only to have him smile and say, "Good medicine." I must have heard the story ten times. Then a young woman asks, "I was raised as a flower child and my parents took drugs all the time. I'm wondering whether I should take them or not?"

"No," Ram Days says with surprising force. "For you I would say no—definitely no!"

I can't stand it anymore. When Ram Dass finishes answering her question, I raise my hand. "Ram Dass, I'd like to talk about something more fun . . . like death."

Ram Dass gives me one of his mischievous smiles. "Ah, death."

Everyone laughs.

"Two days before coming to Maui I had a mini-stroke," I say. "I was driving at the time and ended up bashing into a truck in front of me. I had no idea where I was and was seeing double."

"A stroke . . ." Ram Dass nods his head. His stroke happened over seven years ago. He is now in a wheelchair, his right arm and hand useless.

"Now I'm enjoying the delightful play of not knowing whether I could keel over right now, five minutes from now, or a year from now." Ram Dass smiles. I continue on, "Could you tell me what you've learned from being on that edge of not knowing whether you might drop the physical body in any moment?"

He ponders my question a moment, looking up towards the ceiling as he searches for words. "You're talking about being at home with your own death—and that also means being at home with your life. The two go together."

"Yes, I feel that," I say. "I make sure to put on clean underwear every day, just in case I'm in another accident." Ram Dass laughs and everyone else howls.

"Be grateful for life, be grateful for death," he says. "Live between the two—life and death, life and death."

"I do feel that gratitude," I say. "I'm grateful at the end of each day that I'm still here; I'm grateful when I actually wake up every morning."

"Yes, and grateful for each moment—grateful for life. You're grateful here and now, for this . . ." He raises his good arm and sweeps the room.

A beautiful, sweet recognition of love passes between us—an empty space opening up between the chatter of words. This is what it is all about.

CHAPTER 20

LIVING IN LOVE

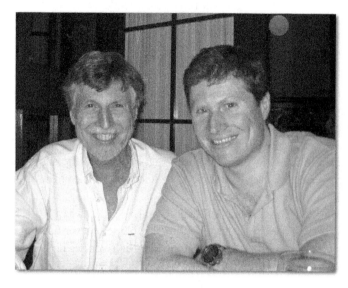

Peter & Peter Jr

The River with A Thousand Voices
The Hatton Ferry, Virginia, July 30, 2000

Above all he learned how to listen, to listen with a still heart, with a waiting, open soul, without passion, without desire, without judgment, without opinions.
Herman Hesse, *Siddhartha*

"This is heaven," Linda says in a dreamy voice.

We're sitting on the riverbank next to the Hatton Ferry Crossing, a twenty minute drive from our farm, watching the majestic James River flow by on its way to the Atlantic Ocean. Upstream a lone fisherman stands knee deep in the rapids, his rod rhythmically snaking back and forth. Giant sycamores hang out over the river's banks, with pieces of debris high in their branches, the result of floods that sweep through every few years, bringing water levels up thirty feet or more. Because no houses can ever be built on the flood plain, the entire scene looks the same as it would have centuries ago.

"I can't ask anything more of heaven than this," Linda says.

I sit in silence, mesmerized by the broad expanse of river flowing by. Minutes pass. "It's amazing . . . from here, it seems like the river has no beginning and no end."

"The river is talking," Linda muses. "It's singing its song—a song that supports all life. It doesn't try to do anything. It just is."

A blue heron lifts off gracefully into the sky in the distance. Red-winged crane flies and water bugs dance at our feet. Our two dogs are lying quietly by our sides, watching all of it with relaxed alertness.

Moved by the exquisite beauty of the moment, I put my arm around Linda's shoulder and lean close to kiss her blond hair, warmed by the sun. "I'm so happy you're in my life," I say softly into her ear. "Your love for nature has taught me so much. Without you I would never have experienced this joy." She turns to lovingly kiss my cheek.

Nearby, the ferryman prepares to cast off and take his next load across the river—a car and a few passengers. The Hatton Ferry is one of the last pole ferries in the United States, and has been in operation for over a hundred years. I watch as the ferryman uses his long pole to push the ferry away from the bank. A taut cable connected to the ferry spans the river. As the water pushes up against the side of the barge, it propels it across—an ingenious way of man and nature working together. With surprising speed, it moves towards the opposite side. The landing is nothing more than a small opening in the woods where a dirt road comes down to the shore.

As I watch this age-old ritual in quiet awe, I think of Vasudeva, the wise ferryman described in Herman Hesse's *Siddhartha*, a novel depicting the spiritual journey of an Indian boy named Siddhartha, who later becomes Gautama, The Buddha. The young prince Siddhartha meets Vasudeva while wandering the country and feels compelled to stay by the river with him. Vasudeva, who was a very simple man, says to Siddhartha, "The river knows everything; one can learn everything from it."

Siddhartha lives with the ferryman for several years, doing the everyday tasks of looking after the boat, gathering firewood, picking fruit, and working in the rice fields. Days and months go by as he learns from the river. Siddhartha sits on its bank for hours at a time, listening to its message. As Herman Hesse writes, "He learned that the river is everywhere at the same time, at the source and at the mouth, at the waterfall, at the ferry, at the current, in the ocean and in the mountains, everywhere, and that the present only exists for it, not the shadow of the past nor the shadow of the future."

Like the river was for Siddhartha, the animals and the farm are for me. Every day I feed my sheep and take care of them. Inevitably some of them get sick and die. As I tearfully watch them surrender into death, I learn about acceptance; as I help with the birth of their lambs, I participate in the miracle of life; as I sit out in the field with them at night, I learn about the simple joy of being. Over the years I witness the warp and rhythm of the changing seasons. In winter I split firewood to keep warm; in spring I sow seeds for crops; in summer I cut the hay and harvest it; in fall I bring in feed for the animals and prepare to start all over. Months go by in blessed peace. A deep sense of happiness starts to emerge spontaneously from within.

Dog Darshan
Brown Toyota, Chrysler, Subaru, Charlottesville, VA, December 20, 2000

To meet everything and everyone through stillness instead of mental
noise is the greatest
gift you can offer to the universe.
Eckhart Tolle

Once I stop looking for anything, life becomes one surprise after another. Even mundane, everyday events are a reminder of what is truly important—and it's never what I expect. What a surprise to watch it all unfold.

The other day my old Subaru was having problems, and I made an appointment to bring it in to the dealership by 8:30 am. As usual, I end up running late, tearing into the service area at 9:20. *Damn, I'm late for my appointment and I've got ten other errands. How am I going to get everything done?* A woman service rep with an oval name tag saying "Cathy" greets me. "Just leave the keys in the car and it will be ready in about an hour," she says with a smile.

In a nervous frenzy, I grab my book and head towards the waiting room. I've taken a few steps before I remember that the dogs are in the back of the car. *Oh my God, what am I going to do with them? They can't stay in the car while it's being worked on!*

I go back to the car and pick up their leashes. Holding the door open, I say, "OK boys, out you come." They look at me quizzically, then hop out, ready for anything.

It's bitterly cold out, so I take them into the showroom. I watch them perk up in excitement, noses twitching as they take in the unfamiliar smells. They're also picking up on my excitement . . . I'm a sucker for auto showrooms, with that new car smell and the cars looking like colorful, gleaming sculptures on the shiny marble floor. Luke is wagging his short little stub of a tail like crazy, trying to get my attention. Sky is pacing about like a wolf on a prowl.

Oh dear, what will I do if they pee on the marble floor?

"Peter," a voice says. "What are you doing here?" I turn around to see Larry, a respected healer and Tai Chi teacher in Charlottesville, dressed in black pants and a shirt and tie.

"Larry! I guess I should ask you the same question."

The dogs rush up to him and he pulls back in alarm to avoid touching them. "Luke . . . Sky!" I say firmly. "Easy!"

342

"I work here," He says, eying the dogs warily.

"Great! Now I know where to come if I ever need to buy a new car." *Things must have gotten pretty bad for him to become a car salesman! I wonder if I could do that?*

As we're talking, a cheerful looking young woman comes up, wearing a heavy winter coat. "Larry, what are you doing here?"

"Peter just asked the same question."

The dogs start wagging their tails with this new arrival. She reaches down and pets them all over. "Oh, such cute dogs," she exclaims. "They're Australian Shepherds, aren't they?"

"Yes," I smile. "This is Sky. The other one, who's a bit of a thug, is named Luke."

She gives the dogs another pet and turns back to Larry. "What about your healing work?"

"Well," he says, holding his body poised and erect, "someone has to bring light and healing into places like this!"

Right, I think.

After a brief conversation we each go our different ways. I head for the waiting area and sit in one of the blue plastic chairs with metal legs. The smell of stale coffee and motor oil permeates the area. The dogs soon settle down beside me. To my right is the door to the service bay, and before long a stream of people start passing by—mechanics, service managers, salespeople, and clients. When they see the dogs, a smile appears on their faces.

"What kind of dogs are these . . .?" one person asks.

"Are they friendly . . .?" a man in blue coveralls asks.

Over the next half hour at least six more people stop to talk.

"Oh, what pretty coloring. Are they blue merles?"

"I once owned an Aussie. They're the best dogs ever . . ."

"Look at his eyes! He has one blue eye and one gray eye. Is that normal?"

I respond to each person with the usual banter about Aussies having different colored eyes and being so intelligent, loyal, etc. It doesn't take long for me to realize that something deeper is happening here.

I notice that the dogs greet each person as if they are the most important being on the planet, with no preconceptions whatsoever. If they sense that the person wants to pet them, they go up to them for a pet. If they feel the person is not interested, they keep their distance. Everyone walks away with a smile, feeling a bit more love in their lives.

A homeless person comes through the door, probably trying to get warm. He has a weatherworn face, and is wearing dirty jeans and a grubby old black parka, with a huge knitted cap on his head. *Please don't stop,* I pray, trying to remain invisible.

Sure enough, he stops right in front of me. "Beautiful dogs," he says.

"Thanks."

"They from 'round here?"

Pointing at Luke, I say, "This one is from Virginia. The other is from Colorado." I'm very aware of my educated Northeastern accent. I'm sure he is too.

"Real nice," he says, giving Sky a pet. "Real nice."

Then I notice the dogs are responding to him exactly as they do to everyone else. They don't make the same distinctions as I do about appearances.

I feel my heart softening and something starts to shift inside. I look into the man's eyes and suddenly see myself. He looks at me and suddenly there is a twinkle in his eyes.

"Well, y'all have a great day now . . . like your dogs!"

For a while no one comes by and I start reading again. It dawns on me that all I have been doing is sitting here with two dogs. At least ten people have walked by and somehow been changed by the experience. The dogs aren't trying to do anything or be anything; they aren't trying to change anyone or fix anyone. They accept each person as they are. They give healing just through their very presence. I finally get it. *These dogs are embodying love. They aren't making a story about it—they're just being!*

An older man comes by and notices Sky. "Do you mind if I pet him?" he asks.

"Go ahead, he's friendly."

He kneels down on one knee beside Sky. "I had a dog like this," he says, his voice trembling a little. "He died a year ago. I really miss him." As he gently pets Sky, I see that his eyes are tearing up. Sky sits there, very serious, still as can be. He's fully aware of what is happening in this exchange. The man caresses Sky's head while Sky looks into some far off place. *This is true compassion,* I think, *and it's between a man and a dog!*

The man silently stands up, nods his thanks, and walks away.

A moment later the perky service rep pokes her head through the door saying, "Mr. Mellen, your car is ready."

I don't want to leave.

Living in the Paradox
Starbucks, Washington, DC, April 8, 2006

Man, if you gotta ask, you'll never know.
Louis (Satchmo) Armstrong

Running a little late, I come around the corner and see my son Peter standing outside of the Starbucks on Massachusetts Avenue NW. "There you are!" I call out excitedly. I've just driven from our farm to DC, and have arranged to meet him for coffee. Peter is now forty and lives close by in Bethesda with his wife Val, and Elisabeth and Will (my two beautiful grandchildren).

"Hey Dad," he says, turning off his cell phone and coming over to give me a big hug.

"So glad you could make it." I'm always surprised to see how big he is—taller than me and about thirty pounds heavier, from working out. It's a cool fall day and we're wearing jeans, sweaters, and running shoes.

"You're looking great!" I say, following him in through the door. Suddenly I get an instant high as I breathe in the aroma of coffee, frothed milk, and chocolate. Peter goes up to the counter. In a glistening curved display case, an array of croissants, cupcakes and other sugar-laden pastries tempt my better wisdom.

"What can I get for you sir?" the cashier asks.

"Iced decaf venti skim latte non fat," Peter says with surprising speed and authority.

The cashier barks out the order to the coffee brewer next to him, who mans levers and spouts that make hissing sounds.

"Iced decaf venti skim latte non fat!" the brewer shouts back.

"I love the way they do that," I say with admiration.

"Yeah, it's a very efficient drug delivery system," Peter says.

"And you sir?" the cashier asks with a smile.

"Uh . . . a uh . . . cappuccino please." I say, trying not to look like an addict waiting for my next fix.

"Size?"

I glance up at the bewildering array of drinks on the board behind him, aware that four people are now waiting in line behind me. "Small . . . I mean tall . . . I mean grande"

". . . and will that be whole milk, lowfat, nonfat, or soy?"

"Uh . . . nonfat."

"One cappuccino nonfat grande!" he shouts.

Once we get our "drugs" (including a chocolate croissant to split between us), we find a table. The place is full, with some customers at their laptops, others sitting in twos, and a few reading *The Washington Post*.

I take a sip of my cappuccino, and get a buzz as the coffee, foam, cinnamon, and sugar hits my olfactory senses.

"Wow, this is all so unreal," I say, shaking my head and looking out at the swarm of activity going on around me. Living on a farm, and seeing nothing more than my sheep most of the time, it is major sensory overload.

"You're always saying this is unreal," Peter says, raising an eyebrow. "But what do you mean by unreal?"

I swallow more coffee, hoping the caffeine will jolt my mind into remembering the famous quote on nonduality by Shankara, a wise sage who lived a thousand years ago in India. *Ahhh . . . now I remember: Brahman or God is real. The universe is unreal. Brahman is the universe. How am I ever going to explain this?*

"What the Indian sages say is that God alone is real. The world as we know it—meaning Starbucks and all that is going on around us—is unreal. It's an illusion, a dream. But here's the kicker . . . who we are as the individual self is none other than God or the universe."

"Sounds like a Zen koan," Peter says. "Tell me more."

How amazing, he really wants to talk about it! He has such a deep hunger for truth. I'm so proud of him.

"Well, what I just said is the central teaching of Advaita, or nonduality. It literally means 'not two.'"

"I still don't get what all this means. Can you explain it in layman's terms?"

Damn, I knew he was going to ask that. This is so frustrating, because it can't be explained in words.

"Okay," I say. "Do you agree that we live in a world of opposites—pain and pleasure, love and hate, happy and sad, good and evil?"

"Yeah . . ."

"Well, that's the world of duality. Nonduality refers to that which is beyond opposites. It's that place where there is no separation between you, me, God, the coffee, the table, the people in this room. All there is is consciousness."

"What do you mean by consciousness? It seems so vague."

"Actually, that's the big joke. It is utterly simple. It's just this—sitting here right now in Starbucks, holding this cup of coffee, looking at you as my heart bursts with love. It is the awareness that is seeing it through these eyes, these senses. You don't have to look any further. *This* is it!"

"That still doesn't help me much."

"Think of it as a shift in perception. Do you remember when you used to look at those *Magic Eye* puzzles and the flower turned into a sailboat? Although you couldn't initially see it, the sailboat was there all along."

Peter laughs. "I never could do those things." His eyes turn towards the door. Mine do too. A striking woman with long blond hair has just walked in, wearing jeans (very tight), a black turtle neck, and uggs.

"Whoa," I smile.

"Now *that's* real!" Peter winks.

"At last we agree upon something!" I laugh. "But she's an illusion too!"

"Well, you can have your illusion. I'll take the real thing," Peter chuckles. "Dad, so far this sounds like some dry, abstract philosophy. I want to know what it means for *you*!"

Squirming uncomfortably, I pray for inspiration. This is the moment when he always puts me on the spot. I freeze up.

"Uhm, uhm," I say, fidgeting with my cup and stalling for time.

"C'mon Dad, you can do it," Peter smiles, his dimples showing.

After a long pause, I say, "OK, OK. The way I experience it is that I have glimpses—and at this point they're just glimpses—that this individual 'Peter' is not real. I'm not real in the sense of not being this individual ego with a history, wants, and preferences. My ego is really nothing more than a bundle of thoughts. It doesn't even exist. In the same way, you're not real, the people here in Starbucks aren't real, the tables aren't real."

"I still say it's too easy," he laughs. "It's not built on solid scientific data."

"What about quantum physics?" I ask. "You know as well as I do that this table is nothing more than electrons dancing in space—and there is more space than there is matter!"

"You're right. But we all have to live in the three-dimensional world."

"That's the challenge—to be in the world, but not of it."

"Living in the paradox . . . holding both 'realities' simultaneously," Peter says, his face lighting up in recognition.

"You've got it!" I say, hitting the table excitedly. *God he's good. How does he know this stuff?*

"And how will that make me happy?"

"Because all our unhappiness comes from identifying with the ego—by believing this apparent world is 'real.' You've seen the Jerry Springer Show. Look at how the contestants really *believe* in their stories and their dramas. They think they're 'real' . . . and what suffering they go through!"

"So you're saying that if I don't identify with my ego—or my story—I'll be happier."

"Yeah . . . no story, no worry."

We both laugh.

"Let the happiness begin!" I say, swirling down the last bit of foam.

"Well, I'm happy," Peter laughs. "I have a 60 inch plasma TV and yours is only 42!"

Paradise is Right Here
Charlottesville, Virginia, May 10, 2005
*Give all your wonderful experiences away to others, as gifts, keeping nothing,
not even a memory, for yourself . . . Instant enlightenment is to give your
happiness away to others.*
David Deida

Ram Dass once said, "If you want to know whether you're enlightened or not, go visit your family for a week. They'll let you know very quickly." (Ram Dass could have added, "You'll know that you're enlightened when you realize that you *don't* have to visit your family for a week"). Family visits are a test I've tried again and again and always fail. I feel like Peanuts kicking the football for the umpteenth time and having Lucy pull it away at the last moment.

I have another litmus test for enlightenment, and that is to visit the local Walmart. Just like my family visits, I inevitably end up judging everyone and dying to get out of there. Of course, I've yet to see a spiritual teacher master this test—have you ever seen a guru shopping in Walmart? Anyway, I decide to give it another try.

After ten minutes looking for a parking space, I know things are not boding well. I find a spot at the outer edge of the parking lot. As I walk purposefully down the endless row of cars, I fall in behind a family of three walking along at a snail's pace. Grandma has a kerchief around her permed hair and a cigarette dangling from her lips; her daughter looks as if she is in her twenties. She's hugely overweight and is wearing tight stretch pants. Walking next to her is her six-year-old son, hitting her on the leg, yelling, "I want that video game! You promised! Gimme!" She ignores him, pretending not to listen. He keeps yelling. I repeat a mantra of forgiveness under my breath for all the nasty thoughts I'm having. I'm already in a bad mood and I haven't made it to the front door.

The electronic door slides open and a blast of cold air hits my face as I step inside. People are lined up at the return counter to my left, and shopping carts are stacked a hundred deep on my right. I give a friendly smile to the Walmart greeter, knowing that someday this could be my job. I grab a cart and head down the main aisle, past women's clothing, groceries, and stationery, before turning left into a maze of side aisles. I walk down them, pushing my empty cart in front of me, overwhelmed by the profusion of choices (just why do we need fifteen brands of laundry soap?). I finally reach the automotive section at the back of the store and find my prize—black vinyl floor mats for my car, reeking of formaldehyde (cost: $9.88). Of course, I can't stop there. Since I've gotten this far, there must be something else I need to get. I find a value pack of 24 toilet paper rolls, a ten-pound box of Tide laundry detergent, and some plastic storage boxes, none of which I really need. It doesn't take long for the formaldehyde-laced products to trigger my chemical sensitivity. I start feeling dizzy and irritable. Soon I'm so disoriented I can't tell the direction of the exit.

As I wander down the shoe aisle (Men's Workhorse Steel Toe Boots: $49.89) looking lost, I hear a deep voice behind me saying, "Can I help you?" I turn to see a salesperson in his blue and red Walmart vest. He is a large man with a warm smile and kind eyes.

"Can you tell me where the exit is?"

He chuckles, "You lost?"

"Just confused," I laugh.

"It's a big place," he says, clearly sensing I don't quite fit in here.

"Yeah."

Behind our innocent exchange of words something else is happening. For no apparent reason, a profound sense of recognition passes between us, as if he knows—and I know—that we are both one and the same. My God, we really *are* brothers!

"It's over there," he says, pointing towards the far corner of the store.

"Thanks."

"You have a great day," he says with a wink.

"You too," I smile.

We both wave to each other as we turn and walk away.

I make my way to the cash register, my cart now full.

Standing in front of me in the checkout line is the family I saw in the parking lot. The boy seems happy now, immersed in his video game. Grandma is keeping a close eye on the clerk as she scans each item. The mother is staring off into space—enjoying a brief lull in her dreary life of cooking, looking after kids, and surviving from one day to the next. Suddenly my heart fills with compassion for her. Such a difficult life—she is doing the very best she can.

Perhaps sensing my looking at her, she turns around. I give her a warm, knowing smile. She smiles back. All sense of separation falls away. In this moment there is nothing but grace, beauty, and love.

Even in Walmart, paradise is right here.

The Spiritual Hedonist
Mt. Ayr Farm, Virginia, November 18, 2003

*Breathe in. Breathe out. Forget this and attaining enlightenment will be
the least of your problems.*
Jewish Buddhism

It's a cold November day, with the sun about to sink behind Virginia's magnificent Blue Ridge Mountains. I'm sitting in the study of the farmhouse, looking out at the sheep grazing in the pasture. The last rays of sunshine highlight their coats as they nibble on what's left of the summer grass. I move my head back and forth an inch or so, enjoying how the rippled panes of old glass distort the sheep, making them thin, then fat, then thin again. *God,* I think, *how I love those animals. I used to be such a city-boy, and here I am, a gentleman farmer in my sixties! How did I ever get here?* In a last blaze of glory, the sun blasts the huge oaks in a dazzling array of gold, green, and red just before it drops behind the mountains. Breathing out a deep sigh of satisfaction, I turn back to my desk, knowing that the barn is full of hay for the winter and the animals have been fed.

I reach for my wine glass, which sits next to the computer. Thus begins my evening ritual. I hold up the glass, admiring the rich, ruby red color before taking a sip. The first taste explodes in my mouth. *Mmmm. I must buy this Cabernet again— it only cost fourteen dollars. When I have a year to live, I'll go up to twenty-dollars a bottle. Maybe I should start now?*

I put the glass down. Next to it is a blue-rimmed white ramekin filled with pistachio nuts. Mindfully, I pick up a nut, split open its shell, and pop the nut in my mouth, enjoying the salty flavor after the sweetness of the wine.

Then I start writing:

To think that for twenty years I believed that enlightenment was some great cosmic orgasm that could only happen after years of spiritual practice and purification. I remember how I used to try and purify my body, as if there was something "dirty" that had to be "cleansed." I cleaned out my nostrils with a dumb little cup; I drank foul tasting Kombucha tea; I tried to be celibate; I stood on my head; I meditated three times a day. What a crock. At least the celibacy part didn't last. I far prefer the path I'm on now—a path of sex, wine and chocolate.

I take another sip of wine and feel the warm glow of pleasure as it slides smoothly down my throat. Wondering what to write next, I look around at the hundreds of books on the bookshelves of my study, including three big art books that have my name on them. They are standing up and facing out towards me for inspiration—but I never look at them. I can scarcely believe that one of them was a best-seller in Canada, bringing me fame and fortune at the tender age of thirty.

I get sidetracked into another memory: *God, what a cocky young ass I was. I thought I had the world by the balls, recklessly pursuing every pleasure I could find. But it was never enough. Underneath there was so much anger and self-loathing. My marriage was falling apart and I was miserable.*

I pick up another pistachio, enjoying the process of opening the shell and finding the nut. I wash it down with a little more wine. My dog Sky, a blue merle Australian shepherd, lets out a long sigh. He is lying across one of my feet, and I can feel his warm body through my sock. Our other Aussie, Luke, is lying in the doorway, his head on his paws, watching every move I make.

My fingers move to the keyboard: *What led me to stumble into a yoga class that day and find a sense of peace I had never known? I fell head over heels in love with yoga. Everyone thought I was crazy when I moved to the United States and joined a tiny yoga ashram. What a time that was . . . riding the wave of success as the community grew into the largest residential yoga center in the world. It was like living in a big house with three hundred of my best friends! I really thought I had found the happiness I was looking for.*

My typing is interrupted by Linda calling from the great room: "We're going to need more firewood!" I can hear the clang of metal as she stokes the fire in the old wood cook stove. She's a master at it, getting the fire to just the right level so the oven will heat evenly. I can already smell the mouth-watering aroma of roasting chicken wafting into the study.

"I'll get it," I call back. "Just let me finish what I'm writing."

"Not too long," Linda says. "The fire is getting low." I know exactly how far I can stretch the time by the tone of her voice.

I put my feet up on the desk and look out the window. It's completely dark now and the temperature has dropped to freezing. I go back to writing: *Then my neat, self-contained little spiritual world was turned upside down when I was given a book on Ramana Maharshi. What a shock to find that true happiness is not somewhere off in the future. It's right here, right now, sipping my wine, eating pistachio nuts, and writing this. Who would have guessed?*

Linda appears in the doorway to the study. "Dinner is ready," she says to our two Aussies. Their ears perk up and they stare at Linda with fierce intensity. Luke wags his stubby tail, understanding every word she says. Linda comes around behind my chair and slips her arms around my shoulders, kissing my neck and nibbling my ear. "Soon it will be time for your dinner too, big boy," she purrs, imitating a Hollywood vamp.

"Hey, not now," I cry in feigned distress. Linda has been feeling better lately.

"Why not?" she whispers provocatively. "I mean right now—on that warm sheepskin in front of the fire?"

"No," I moan. "I'm writing!" Sky suddenly starts barking, and Luke joins in. Are they hungry or are they picking up on our energy . . . or both?

We both start laughing.

"Quiet boys!" I shout. They both settle down. Linda kisses me on the lips and I return the kiss. "I'm so happy you're feeling good today," I say, looking into her eyes. "It's as if you're coming back to life." Linda has recently upped her prednisone, which helps her with her auto-immune illness.

"You shouldn't talk, my love," Linda says. "You've just gotten over surgery for melanoma."

"I'm doing fine,' I insist. "That was nothing, especially after the surgery for my prostate cancer."

"Let's celebrate. Dinner's almost ready."

"Okay, I'll get the wood."

I slip on my old parka and step outside. The dogs rush out past me, barking loudly as they clear the area of any potential intruders. I take a deep breath of the cold, crisp air—it is scented with the intoxicating smell of wood smoke. As I walk to the woodshed I glance up at the stars, which are just beginning to glitter in the cobalt blue sky. From a distance I can hear the *baaas* of the baby lambs as they call for their mothers. They're safely out in the pasture, having found a place to curl up for the night. I fill the wheelbarrow with firewood—wood that comes from oak trees that I cut down and split myself. The dogs dance around in circles next to me, eager to play. "C'mon boys, how can I get this wood in if you keep banging into me? Move it!"

The woodstove has heated the great room up to eighty degrees, just the way Linda likes it. She pulls the chicken from the oven. I can't resist sneaking a bite. "Oh my God," I say groaning in pleasure. "The skin is crispy and brown. This is perfection!"

We sit at the old pine trestle table and light some candles. An abundance of food sits in front of us—the chicken, which is still in the blue enamel baking pot it was cooked in, along with baked russet potatoes, fresh organic vegetables, and a bottle of red wine. I'm dressed in baggy brown cords, which smell of lanolin from the sheep, and an old, torn sweater. Linda is wearing her long burgundy velour dress and heavy woolen socks. With her blond hair and blue eyes, she looks like a Swedish homesteader, which is not far from the truth. Her great grandparents emigrated from Sweden and rode the Oregon Trail out West.

"There's nothing like food cooked in a woodstove," Linda says, chewing on a thigh, her fingers covered in juices. She once had her own farm in Oregon and grew everything she ate. She tosses a few scraps to the dogs, who are sitting at attention, their eyes never leaving her.

"What did we do to deserve this?" I ask, washing down the delicious food with a swallow of wine. "I can't imagine experiencing more joy than I'm feeling in this moment."

"It's a miracle," Linda sighs. "You've had cancer twice; I have this chronic illness; you just found out your sister has leukemia. Yet we're still happy."

"And let's not forget—they cancelled our health insurance today. I'm so pissed off."

"This happiness includes being pissed off too," she smiles.

"You're right" I say looking into her eyes in the candlelight. "It doesn't depend upon what's happening outside of us . . . though if I have ice cream with warm chocolate on it for dessert, then I'll be *truly* happy."

"Do it . . . life is short!"

An hour later we are in bed making love, when both dogs start yelping. "Oh no," I cry. "Not again!" Every time I get close to an orgasm they start howling, which presents some very interesting challenges in concentration.

Linda laughs a deep belly laugh. "They must be smelling our pheromones!" Meanwhile the barking goes from a series of sharp barks to long wolf howls: *aaaa . . . oooo, aaaa . . . oooo, aaaa . . . oooo.* Linda and I are now laughing so hard we've temporarily stopped our lovemaking. From a distance we can hear a return wolf howl from the dog belonging to our nearest neighbor, who lives half a mile away. He wants in on the act too.

Fortunately human hearing is not as acute as that of animals. If our neighbors had been able to hear us that dark November evening, they would have heard wolf howls emanating out into the night, followed by the sound of hysterical laughter, and eventually loud cries of pleasure. Half an hour later, all these sounds would become enfolded in silence and peace, except for the lonely cry of the owl coming from deep in the woods.

EPILOGUE

I am the soft-footed wind which walks on in ecstasy.
I am the ever-gliding form, which goes on as time.
I descend as waterfalls on the mountain slopes, reviving the faded plants.
I make the roses burst into laughter.
Swami Ram Tirtha

It has been five years since Linda and I sold our 130-acre farm and moved to Maui. We lived on this beautiful Virginia estate for ten years. Why would we leave our family, our friends, our animals to move 5,000 miles away? The answer was simple: every time we left the cold Virginia winter and arrived in the warmth and tropical splendor of the Hawaiian Islands, Linda's health improved dramatically.

"You have to move here," our dear friend Ranjana told us. "Linda's health is the most important thing. She gets sick when you go back east; she gets well when she comes here. It's a no-brainer."

So we moved.

We bought two acres of land in Haiku with a distant view of the ocean, and built our dream home. This was the thirteenth or fourteenth home we had built or renovated, and as far as I'm concerned it was going to be my last. Over the next few years the raw, red dirt of the construction site was transformed into a lush jungle of heliconia, red ginger, banana trees, orange trees, palm trees, night-blooming jasmine, and flowering plants. Big toads showed up from nowhere to inhabit the pond that we created off the lanai. We put ten little guppies into the pond to eat the mosquitoes and they soon multiplied into a swarm of tiny fish. We had found our paradise. We called it Maluhia—place of spiritual retreat.

Linda and I settled into our routines. I spent mornings working on the book and afternoons taking the dogs to the beach or up to the forest for a hike; Linda read her usual five books a week, began writing, and watched her favorite shows on TV. On weekends we saw our friends, or went to the odd event, such as a Krishna Das concert at the Studio Maui. We had each other, our beautiful home, the glorious Hawaiian weather, and a loving community of friends. Who could imagine a more idyllic life?

But even in paradise, shit happens.

After the first year, Linda's health worsened. Her flares became more frequent. It was like getting the flu three times a month. No sooner had she gotten over the aches, chills, joint pain, and fever from one flare, than another one would hit. Behcets Disease can be very nasty. Then her illness started to manifest in still more ugly ways—painful sores that appeared all over her legs, stomach ulcers, vaginal sores, nose sores, and mouth sores.

By 2009 she was spending most of her days lying on the couch, unable to get up except to move around the house. There were usually three or four days a month when she felt good, and had enough energy to go out. We'd go to the beach or take a walk—activities that most people take for granted—but for us were banner days. It was hard to watch this former runner and vibrantly healthy woman now confined to a couch. Yet Linda dropped into a deep place of acceptance around her illness. "I'm so happy," she'd say, "even with all this pain."

After years of being beaten down by this day-to-day struggle, Linda often said, "I don't want to stay in this body. I want to go home." It was as if she was living with one foot in this world and one foot in the next. Death was something she longed for, not just to be free of physical pain, but because she knew from her own profound experiences that when she got to the other side she would be free. "You have no idea what awaits you," she told our friends—even when they were reluctant to hear it. "The other side is pure joy, far greater joy than anything you can imagine. I know . . . I've had experiences of crossing over. My mother was there waiting for me. So was my dog Sarah. There is such love . . . there is nothing but love. It is so immense."

Linda died unexpectedly on September 10, 2010, after accidentally taking too many pain pills.

She finally gets to be what the great Indian mystic Ram Tirtha describes as, "The soft-footed wind which walks on in ecstasy, the ever-gliding form, which goes on as time."

A few weeks after her death I took a long hike in the Makawao Forest with my two dogs, enjoying the sweet smell of the eucalyptus trees, the soft air, and the distant view of the ocean. After a difficult morning of deeply feeling her loss, I was relaxed and at peace. Suddenly I stopped dead in my tracks, hit by a stunning realization. A few hours earlier I had been weeping uncontrollably, crying my heart out, wailing, sobbing, and soaking up a dozen Kleenexes. I felt like I was being torn to shreds—her physical form gone forever and an enormous chasm separating us. This is the story I told myself, and I realized, *this is suffering*.

And now, walking in the woods with the dogs, I am totally joyous. My mind is quiet and free of thoughts. All there is is pure awareness, and in that place Linda is right here with me. How could she not be? When Ramana Maharshi lay on his deathbed, his devotees where bereft. "They say that I am dying," he said, "but I am not going away. Where could I go? I am here." It's as if she is seeing through my eyes, hearing through my ears, smelling through my nose. There is no separation between us, because the true essence of who "Linda" is (and who all of us are), is Spirit, Source, or God.

Earlier on, I was totally identified with the story of her being dead, grieving that I would never see her again—which on one level is true. But it is also a "story" created by my thoughts. Do I want to stay in that story and go on suffering, or do I choose to bring my attention to this moment right here, right now, and experience the beauty all around me? *Breath in, breath out,* I say to myself. *This is all there is. Just This.*

There's nothing wrong with having a "story" about Linda dying; in fact I celebrate letting the grief come up and move through. I only have a problem if I cling on to the story or indulge in it. That's when it becomes unnecessary suffering. I have a choice—I can continue to feel abandoned and alone, or I can relax into unconditional awareness, knowing that this "Linda" is right here. All that keeps me from this joy is my thoughts. As Byron Katie so wisely says, "I am the cause of my own suffering—but only all of it."

Wow. After the terrible trauma of abandonment when my mother died when I was twelve, and then my first wife Fran dying of cancer twenty years ago—and now once again experiencing loss—I'm finally seeing that the end of the physical body does not mean annihilation and separation. In fact, Linda is more present to me now then she was during the many days she was in terrible pain. And so is my mother, Fran . . . and everyone else I have ever loved.

What stopped me in the forest is the stunning recognition that I have been given an incredible gift. I know that the core issue I came into this life to work on is my terror of abandonment—and until this very moment, it had eluded me.

This is Linda's gift. What a gift.

ACKNOWLEDGMENTS

Thanks to Jasmyne Boswell, who is not only a dear friend, but my writing coach and editor. It was in her writing groups that I first read my work, received feedback, and learned how to support others in their writing. To Jasmyne, and all those other extraordinary writers in the classes—Shannon, Sharyn, Pamela, Gail, Kranto, Maribeth, Wayne, Helen, and more—my unbounded thanks.

My gratitude also to several remarkable editors—Peter Guzzardi, Sara Jenkins, Linda Sivertson, Rebecca Serle—for their early support of this project when I was blindly groping in the dark. And to Pamela Dyson, mahalo for a superb job on the final edit.

To my dear, dear friends Judy Scher, Christine Warren, and Dona Matera, untold thanks for reading the manuscript at various stages and encouraging me on the journey. And to my beloved Ron and Ranjana, you have supported me in countless ways.

The perennial philosophy that permeates this book is the result of years on the spiritual path. I humbly offer thanks to all those wise teachers who have helped point me towards myself. My journey into yoga began after meeting a remarkable yogi who dramatically changed my life: Yogi Amrit Desai. He and his teacher Swami Kripalu (Bapuji), showed me the importance of a path with heart. Years later two American teachers, Gangaji and Eli Jaxon-Bear, introduced me to the teachings of the great Indian sage Ramana Maharshi—who is in my heart at every moment. To these, and many more teachers along the way (including my sheep, my goats, and my dogs), I offer heartfelt thanks.

And to my son Peter, thanks for your unfailing patience as I bombarded you with yet another idea for a title or a proposal. With your incredibly sharp mind (trained by the Jesuits at Georgetown University), you kept encouraging me to be more rigorous in my thinking. And immense gratitude for your practical help and business skills. This book is my gift to you.

There is always one person without whom a book would not get written, and in this case it is Linda, whose presence is felt on every page. "You need to go deeper," she would often say. "I want to hear more. I know you have it in you." I wish she were here to see this book finally come into print.

As this chapter of my life comes to a close, I am surprised and overjoyed to have found the love of my life, my partner and wife-to-be Susan Lulow (who I met on my first Match.com date). Who would have believed? Susan has showered me with her beauty, compassion, and wisdom. Thanks to her, I'm beginning my next book: *Ultimate Happiness: A Practical Guide for Everyday Living*!

A NOTE ON THE AUTHOR

Peter Mellen is the author of three previous books on art, including one that was a best-seller in Canada and another that was Book of the Year in 1979. A third book on Jean Clouet, a sixteenth century French artist, was published by Phaidon Press in London and Flammarion Press in Paris. He was also a nationally known authority on Canadian art and an award-winning documentary filmmaker. During the 1980's he was on staff at the Kripalu Center of Yoga and Health in Lenox, Massachusetts, where he taught programs in yoga, health and personal growth. In 1996 he founded the Ramana Retreat Center in New Mexico, which was voted best retreat center of the year by the New Mexican. He now lives in Maui.